THE OPTIONAL PROTOCOL TO THE UN CONVENTION AGAINST TORTURE

The Optional Protocol to the UN Convention Against Torture

RACHEL MURRAY
ELINA STEINERTE
MALCOLM EVANS
ANTENOR HALLO DE WOLF

OXFORD
UNIVERSITY PRESS

OXFORD
UNIVERSITY PRESS

Great Clarendon Street, Oxford OX2 6DP

Oxford University Press is a department of the University of Oxford.
It furthers the University's objective of excellence in research, scholarship,
and education by publishing worldwide in

Oxford New York

Auckland Cape Town Dar es Salaam Hong Kong Karachi
Kuala Lumpur Madrid Melbourne Mexico City Nairobi
New Delhi Shanghai Taipei Toronto

With offices in

Argentina Austria Brazil Chile Czech Republic France Greece
Guatemala Hungary Italy Japan Poland Portugal Singapore
South Korea Switzerland Thailand Turkey Ukraine Vietnam

Published in the United States
by Oxford University Press Inc., New York

First published 2011

British Library Cataloguing in Publication Data
Data available

Library of Congress Cataloging in Publication Data
Data available

Typeset by SPI Publisher Services, Pondicherry, India
Printed in Great Britain
on acid-free paper by
CPI Antony Rowe, Chippenham, Wiltshire

ISBN 978–0–19–960219–3

1 3 5 7 9 10 8 6 4 2

Foreword

This book by Bristol University's OPCAT team is a welcome contribution to our understanding of a unique advance in the field of protection against torture and other cruel, inhuman, or degrading treatment or punishment. The authors are well placed to examine how OPCAT has built on existing international human rights law concerning prevention of torture, whilst marking a historic departure in UN human rights treaties: the first treaty instrument with a primary focus on implementation and work in the field rather than the traditional emphasis on monitoring through a reporting system. OPCAT's central concept involves a system of visits at the international and national level for the prevention of torture and other forms of ill-treatment. This concept is analysed in detail, with attention to each of the component parts of the OPCAT system:

- the Subcommittee on Prevention of Torture (SPT), as a new generation of UN treaty body focused on preventive operational work;
- the National Preventive Mechanisms (NPMs), arguably the most important new feature, as independent mechanisms that States Parties are obliged to develop and maintain at national level to carry out regular visits to all places of deprivation of liberty; and
- the various international bodies already carrying out similar work at the universal or regional level.

In its sequence of chapters, the book considers OPCAT within the context of international law relating to torture and other forms of ill-treatment and examines the key issues as they have emerged over time: during the drafting stages, the eventual adoption of OPCAT, and through the first years after its entry into force. It is important that these developments are viewed from a variety of perspectives; the team brings research to bear on the complex challenges posed by OPCAT, demonstrating the range of ideas about how torture and other ill-treatment may be prevented in practice and exploring the variety of models that might be developed in future.

As the SPT and the emerging NPMs have struggled to fulfil the different but equally important elements of their mandates as set out in OPCAT—to carry out visits regularly, to cooperate and to engage directly with their counterparts at other levels—they have faced serious challenges deriving not only from the difficult work of torture prevention but also from the contexts in which they must operate. OPCAT provides for considerable powers to be accorded to the visiting bodies, both in relation to the visits themselves and their wider preventive role in improving the system of safeguards within each state through recommendations for legislative and policy improvements. In addition, the SPT has faced obstacles in the form of deficiencies in the support provided by the UN, especially as regards the mandated work with NPMs. Similarly, the NPMs have been confronted with numerous challenges including a frequent lack of ring-fenced resources to take on their preventive role, deficiencies in their legal mandate, and limitations on their independence.

As the enlarged SPT and developing NPMs continue to demonstrate commitment to the preventive mandate, they will benefit, as in the past, from the significant support of the key organizations forming the OPCAT Contact Group, including Bristol University's OPCAT team. The group has provided much needed support to the SPT in its creative and determined search for opportunities to work directly with NPMs, including in regional meetings across the world organized by the APT, Bristol University, the Council of Europe NPM Project, Penal Reform International, and the OSCE.

The book's contribution of an academic perspective on the issues at stake provides an opportunity at this crucial stage in OPCAT's development to step back and consider both its origins and its future possibilities. It also reminds us of the imperative to maintain an open, but constructively critical, stance towards the variety of models emerging in the many different settings in which the vision of OPCAT will be translated over time into a working reality.

Dr Silvia Casale
Former Chairperson of the Subcommittee on Prevention of Torture (SPT)
And former Chairperson of the European Committee on the Prevention of Torture (CPT)

Preface

This book arises out of research funded by the Arts and Humanities Research Council (AHRC) of the UK to examine OPCAT and the role of its National Preventive Mechanisms (NPMs) in particular. The three-year study enabled us to interview some 150 individuals, from international and regional treaty bodies, national governments, NHRIs, national NGOs, and civil society organizations of nearly thirty countries. We have covered all regions of the world and selected countries that have ratified OPCAT and already had established or were in the process of establishing their NPMs. We visited countries that had only signed OPCAT and were preparing for ratification and also those that had decided not to ratify the instrument at all. We of course interviewed the SPT members and spoke with the staff of the Office of the High Commissioner for Human Rights (OHCHR) and interviewed representatives of international civil society. The project team hosted a range of high profile seminars in the UK, in Bristol, Cape Town, Prague, and elsewhere, bringing together key policy stakeholders to discuss implementation of OPCAT. In September 2006 we established the OPCAT Contact Group, a gathering of civil society organizations that all work on aspects of OPCAT's monitoring and implementation. The OPCAT Contact Group has gained standing before the SPT and has participated in all but one sessions of the treaty body, providing assistance and support to the SPT. It now comprises Amnesty International (AI), Association for the Prevention of Torture (APT), International Federation of Action by Christians for the Abolition of Torture (FIACAT), Human Rights Implementation Centre (HRIC), International Disability Alliance (IDA), Mental Disability Advocacy Centre (MDAC), World Organisation against Torture (OMCT), Penal Reform International (PRI), Rehabilitation and Research Centre for Torture Victims (RCT), and World Network of Users and Survivors of Psychiatry (WNUSP). Throughout the course of the project we also participated in numerous events surrounding the implementation of OPCAT, provided expert advice to various States on the aspects of its implementation, and produced a number of policy papers and other academic articles.

As a result, our research findings are driven very much by what those we spoke to were saying was relevant in the actual application and implementation of OPCAT in States and by the SPT. This book reflects those findings and therefore does not purport to provide a comprehensive analysis or description of OPCAT. It takes as its starting point the background to the drafting of OPCAT and discussions that took place prior to its adoption and is then structured around the observations we have picked up, from visits to States, participation in the UN SPT sessions, hosting of events, and other activities. These observations may not have been what we initially thought would be the focus of OPCAT on the ground but they do reflect the reality faced by those at the national, regional, and international levels as they go about implementing OPCAT.

OPCAT had not entered into force when this project was conceived. It entered into force in June 2006 just as this project commenced, and so in some ways this has been a common, and at times shared, journey. Our understandings and perceptions have of course evolved as the practice under OPCAT has evolved, and to that extent we are examining a constantly 'moving target', with all the challenges that that brings. However challenging this has been, it pales in comparison to the challenge which the SPT now faces: as this book is completed it is preparing to meet for the first time as an expanded body of twenty-five members—making it, remarkably, the largest of the UN human rights treaty bodies. It is hoped that the publication of this book at this time will provide a timely opportunity to reflect on the experience of the 'old' SPT in a fashion which can help inform the thinking of the 'new' as OPCAT steps into its next phase of development.

As authors of the book, we have therefore gained a unique insight into how OPCAT is operating in its first years and we hope to be able to reflect that here. Elina Steinerte was also a member of the Independent Monitoring Board in HMP Bristol for part of the time that she worked on the research. In addition, during the course of the research and writing of this book one of our team, Professor Malcolm Evans, became a member of the SPT, with effect from November 2009. As a result, it is important to stress that in writing this book the authors have relied solely on information concerning the work of the SPT which is in the public domain, or which is the product of their research interviews. The positions taken and opinions expressed reflect those of the research team and do not represent the views of the SPT, except to the extent that they are a reflection of those public materials. As regards views expressed in this book regarding the composition and work of the SPT itself, Professor Evans, as a member of the SPT, does not associate himself with them, in either a positive or negative fashion, these having been determined by the other members of the research team in order to preserve the independence of the research and its findings and to respect the independence of the members of the Subcommittee.

Rachel Murray
Elina Steinerte
Malcolm Evans
Antenor Hallo de Wolf
Bristol, February 2011

Acknowledgements

First and foremost we must thank the Arts and Humanities Research Council UK (AHRC) which funded the initial three-year project from which this book stems. Its support has not only enabled us to undertake this research but also provided us with a solid platform upon which to continue to examine and be involved in the monitoring of the implementation of OPCAT.

We would also like to thank the current and previous members of the Subcommittee on Prevention of Torture (SPT) not only for their openness and willingness to engage with us during the lifetime of the project but also beyond. Similarly, the Office of the High Commissioner for Human Rights (OHCHR) staff supporting the SPT, those in the National Institutions Unit, and others who have shared with us documents and their opinions and facilitated our participation in sessions and other events.

The Association for the Prevention of Torture (APT), an NGO synonymous with OPCAT, has provided invaluable support for our work and through the hosting of most of the OPCAT Contact Group meetings enabled us and others to work closely together and acquire information that would otherwise be difficult to come by.

We would also like to acknowledge all the members of the OPCAT Contact Group (Amnesty International (AI), Association for the Prevention of Torture (APT), International Federation of Action by Christians for the Abolition of Torture (FIACAT), Human Rights Implementation Centre (HRIC), International Disability Alliance (IDA), Mental Disability Advocacy Centre (MDAC), World Organisation against Torture (OMCT), Penal Reform International (PRI), Rehabilitation and Research Centre for Torture Victims (RCT), and World Network of Users and Survivors of Psychiatry (WNUSP)), a group of civil society organizations that we brought together when OPCAT came into force and which since then has played a central role in monitoring OPCAT at the UN, regional, and national levels.

During the course of the research we spoke to many individuals, including members of UN committees, staff at the OHCHR, members and staff of regional human rights bodies, government representatives, members of designated and potential NPMs, and other civil society organizations. Their comments have formed the core of this research and we would like to thank them for their willingness to engage with us.

Table of Contents

Table of Cases xv
Table of Treaties xvii
List of Abbreviations xix

1. The Origins and Background of OPCAT 1

A. Introduction 1
B. The Origins of the Optional Protocol 6
C. The European Convention for the Prevention of Torture 10
1. Drafting the ECPT 10
2. The work of the CPT and some implications for the drafting of OPCAT 18

2. Drafting OPCAT—Towards Deadlock: 1991–2000 22

A. The Return to the UN and its Consequences 22
B. The Principal Points of Agreement Prior to the 2001 Session and Their Place in the Final Text 27
C. The Principal Points in Dispute Prior to the 2001 Session 31
1. The visiting programme 32
2. Restrictions on access to persons in, or to places of, detention 35
3. The aftermath of a visit or mission 36
4. Reservations 37
D. An Assessment of the Overall Situation 38

3. The Text of OPCAT 39

A. The 2001 Session: New Ideas and New Controversies 40
1. The Mexican Draft 40
2. The EU proposals 43
B. The Chair's Compromise Text: The Optional Protocol and What It Requires of States 45
1. The Subcommittee and its visiting mandate 48
2. The National Preventive Mechanisms 53
3. Conclusion 57
C. The 'What' and the 'With What' Questions 57
1. The 'Concept of prevention' 58
2. Standards 63

4. The Scope of OPCAT 68

A. 'Deprived of liberty' 69
B. Public and Private: '. . . either by virtue of an order given by a public authority or at its instigation or with its consent or acquiescence', Article 4(1) 70

C. '. . . are or may be deprived'/'installations and facilities' 73
D. 'any place/all places of detention' 73
1. Prisons, police, and pre-trial facilities 73
2. Refugee, asylum, and immigration centres 74
3. Military detention facilities 75
4. Mental health institutions 75
5. Care homes, foster homes, older persons, and other places 76
E. '. . . under its jurisdiction or control' 77
1. Nationally 78
2. Extra-territoriality 79
F. Article 14(2) Objection to a Visit by the SPT 81
G. Some Core Issues 82
1. Different approaches and requirements 82
2. Expertise 83
3. Coordination 85
4. Consistency in standards 87
H. Conclusion 89

5. The Role of the Subcommittee on Prevention of Torture (SPT) 90

A. The Membership of the SPT 92
B. The Interpretation of Its Own Mandate and Rules of Procedure 95
C. Pillar I: Visits to States Parties 97
1. Selection of the countries: criteria, types of visits, and frequency 97
2. Content of the visit: choosing places of deprivation of liberty to be visited 102
3. Preventive approach and visits 103
4. Outcomes of a visit: the ongoing dialogue and follow-up 105
D. Pillar II: work with the NPMs 108
1. SPT as adviser to the NPMs 111
E. Pillar III: Cooperation with Other UN and International and Regional Bodies 112
F. Challenges Noted by the SPT 112
G. Conclusion 113

6. The Role of NPMs 115

A. Introduction 115
B. Visiting Powers and Mandate 117
C. Independence 119
1. Factors within the control of the State 120
2. Factors within the control of the NPM itself 124
D. Accountability and the Relationship with the SPT 128
E. NPMs Should Ensure States Comply with the UNCAT and Other Relevant Legal Standards 132
F. As a Forerunner to SPT Visits; Continuation of CPT Nationally; as a Small SPT on the Ground 133
G. Have Expertise 134
H. Large Expectations and Role Not Always Clear 136

I. Additional Factors for an Effective NPM 136
J. Conclusion 137

7. OPCAT within the Broader UN and Regional Systems 139

A. OPCAT and the Convention Against Torture 139
B. Engagement with Other UN Bodies 143
C. Engagement with Regional and Other Bodies 146
D. Some Common Issues 155
1. Confidentiality 155
2. Standards/norms 156
3. The need for consistency in engagement with NPMs 157
E. Conclusion: The Need for Systematic and Strategic Engagement 159

8. Regional Trends towards Ratification and Implementation of OPCAT 162

A. Reasons For and Against Ratification 162
B. The Added Value of Being Parties to OPCAT 168
C. Trends in the Choices for NPMs 170
D. Some Concluding Thoughts 172

9. Conclusion: Emerging Trends and the Future of OPCAT 174

A. Expansion of Membership of OPCAT 175
B. Expertise on OPCAT 176
C. A 'System' of Prevention Through Visits 177
D. Budget and Financial Resources 178
E. Standards and Accommodating Regional Differences 179
F. Influence and Lessons for Other Treaties 180
G. Conclusion 183

Appendices

Appendix I: Optional Protocol to the Convention against Torture and Other Cruel, Inhuman or Degrading Treatment or Punishment 184
Appendix II: Rules of Procedure of the Subcommittee on Prevention of Torture and Other Cruel, Inhuman or Degrading Treatment or Punishment 195
Appendix III: Guidelines of the Subcommittee on Prevention of Torture and Other Cruel, Inhuman or Degrading Treatment or Punishment in relation to Visits to States Parties 205
Appendix IV: Preliminary Guidelines for the Ongoing Development of National Preventive Mechanisms 212
Appendix V: Guidelines on National Preventive Mechanisms 214
Appendix VI: The approach of the Subcommittee on Prevention of Torture to the concept of prevention of torture and other cruel, inhuman or degrading treatment or punishment under the

Optional Protocol to the Convention against Torture and Other Cruel, Inhuman or Degrading Treatment or Punishment 218
Appendix VII: Members of the Subcommittee on Prevention of Torture (SPT) as at January 2011 222
Appendix VIII: Chronology of States Visited by the SPT 223

Bibliography 224
Index 237

Table of Cases

African Commission on Human and People's Rights *Curtis Francis Doebbler v Sudan*, Communication 236/2000 (2002) 72

EUROPEAN COURT OF HUMAN RIGHTS

A v UK, European Court of Human Rights, No 25599/94, 23 September 1998 72
Amuur v France, Appl no 19776/92, European Court of Human Rights, 25 June 1996 74
Bankovic and others v Belgium and 16 Other Contracting States, Appl No 52207/99, European Court of Human Rights, 12 December 2001 . . . . . 77, 80
Cyprus v Turkey, Appl No 25781/94, European Court of Human Rights, 10 May 2001 80
Gafgen v Germany [GC] No 22987/05 Judgment of 1 June 2010 59
Ilascu and others v Moldova, and Russia [GC] No 48787/99, ECHR 2004-VII 77
Loizidou v Turkey (Preliminary Objections), European Court of Human Rights, 23 March 1995, Series A, vol 310 80
Ocalan v Turkey, Appl No 46221/99, European Court of Human Rights, 12 March 2003 . . . 73, 80
Orhan v Turkey, Appl No 25656/94, 18 June 2002 73
Plattform "Ärzte für das Leben" v Austria (1991) 13 EHRR 204 71
Refah Partisi (The Welfare Party) and others v Turkey [GC] (2003) 37 EHRR 1 71
Storck v Germany (2005) 43 EHRR 96 72
Tyrer v UK, Series A, No 26, 25 April 1978 72
von Hannover v Germany (2005) 40 EHRR 1 71
X and Y v The Netherlands (1986) 8 EHRR 235 71

UN HUMAN RIGHTS COMMITTEE

Alzery v Sweden, Communication No 1416/2005, CCPR/C/88/D/1416/2005, 10 November 2006 81
Celepli v Sweden, Communication No 456/91, CCPR/C/51/D/456/1991, 26 July 1994 77
GRB v Sweden, Communication No 83/1997, 15 May 1998 71
Higginson v Jamaica, Communication No 792/1998, CC PR/C/74/D/792/1998, 28 March 2002 72
Karker v France, Communication No 833/98, CCPR/C/70/D/833/1998, 26 October 2000 77
Nqalula Mpandanjila et al v Zaire, Communication No 138/1983, UN Doc Supp No 40 (A/41/40) at 121 (1986) 77
Osbourne v Jamaica, Communication No 759/1997, CCPR/C/68/D/759/1997 (2000) 72
Pryce v Jamaica, Communication No 793/1998, CCPR/C/80/D/793/190 (2004) 72
Vjatseslav Borzov v Estonia, Communication No 1136/2002, CCPR/C/81/D/1136/2002, 26 July 2004 Zealand, 754/97, 7 IHRR 44 (2000) 81
Vuolanne v Finland, Communication No 265/87, 7 April 1989 75

UN COMMITTEE AGAINST TORTURE

Dzemajl and others v Yugoslavia, CAT/C/29/D/161/2000, UN Committee Against Torture (CAT), 2 December 2002 71

INTER-AMERICAN COMMISSION AND COURT OF HUMAN RIGHTS

Ceasar v Trinidad and Tobago, Inter-Am Court of Human Right (SERC) No 123 (2005), 11 March 2005 72
Coard v United States, Case 10.951, Inter-Am CHR, Report No 109/99 80

INTERNATIONAL COURT OF JUSTICE

Application of the Convention on the Prevention and Punishment of the Crime of Genocide (Bosnia and Herzegovina v Serbia and Montenegro), Merits, 26 February 2007, ICJ Reports 2007 77
Legal Consequences of the Construction of a Wall in the Occupied Palestinian Territory, Advisory Opinion ICJ Reports 2004. 80
Questions Relating to the Obligation to Prosecute or Extradite (Belgium v Senegal), Provisional Measures, Order of 28 May 2009, ICJ Reports 2009 4

CASE LAW FROM DOMESTIC JURISDICTIONS

A and ors v Secretary of State for the Home Department [2005] UKHL 71 59
Al-Skeini and others v Secretary of State for Defence, Al-Skeini and others v Secretary of State for Defence (Consolidated Appeals) [2007] UKHL 26. . . . . 77, 79
Amnesty International v Canada (Attorney General), 2008 FC 336 (CanLII), 3 December 2008 . . . . 79, 80, 81
R *(Al-Jedda) v Secretary of State for Defence* [2008] 1 AC 332
R *(Al-Saadoon and Mufdhi) v Secretary of State for Defence* [2009] EWCA Civ 7 77
R *(Binyam Mohamed) v Secretary of State for Foreign and Commonwealth Affairs* [2010] EWCA Civ 65 59

Table of Treaties

Council of Europe Convention for the Protection of Human Rights and Fundamental Freedoms, ETS No 5, 213 UNTS 222, 1950 . . . . . . 1, 179, 180
International Covenant on Civil and Political Rights, GA Res 2200A (XXI), 993 UNTS 171, adopted 16 December 1966 . . . . 1, 77, 143, 179
Vienna Convention on the Law of Treaties, 1155 UNTS, adopted 23 May 1969 . . . . 70, 78
Hague Convention for the Suppression of Unlawful Seizure of Aircraft (860 UNTS 105), 1970 2
Montreal Convention for the Suppression of Unlawful Acts against the Safety of Civil Aviation (974 UNTS 177), 1971 2
New York Convention on the Prevention and Punishment of Crimes against Internationally Protected Persons (1035 UNTS 167), 1973 2
New York International Convention against the Taking of Hostages Convention (1316 UNTS 205), 1979 2
Convention against Torture and Other Cruel, Inhuman or Degrading Treatment of Punishment, GA Res A/RES/39/46, adopted 10 December 1984 (1465 UNTS 85) 2–7, 22–38, 41, 42, 44, 59, 60, 61, 71–72, 77, 78, 79, 100, 132–133, 139–142, 179, 182, 218
African Charter on Human and Peoples' Rights, CAB/LEG/67/3, rev. 5, 21 ILM 58 (1982), adopted 27 June 1981 149
European Convention for the Prevention of Torture and Inhuman or Degrading Treatment or Punishment, CETS No. 126, adopted 26 June 1987 . . . . 10–21, 29, 34, 50, 65, 66, 78, 98, 100, 133–134, 146–148, 156, 164, 168
International Convention for the Suppression of Terrorist Bombings (2149 UNTS 256) 1997 2
European Charter on Regional or Minority Languages (CETS No 148, in force March 1998)
International Convention for the Suppression of the Financing of Terrorism (2178 UNTS 197), 1999 2
Optional Protocol to the Convention Against Torture and Other Cruel, Inhuman or Degrading Treatment or Punishment, A/RES/57/199, adopted on 18 December 2003
Arab Charter on Human Rights, 12 IHRR 893, adopted 22 May 2004 166
International Convention for the Suppression of Acts of Nuclear Terrorism (2445 UNTS 89), 2005 2
Convention on the Rights of Persons with Disabilities, A/61/611, adopted 13 December 2006 . . . . 29, 158, 180–182

Abbreviations

ACHPR	African Charter on Human and Peoples' Rights
AI	Amnesty International
APF	Asia Pacific Forum
APT	Association for the Prevention of Torture
ASEAN	Association of South East Asian Nations
CAT	UN Committee Against Torture
CEDAW	UN Convention on the Elimination of All Forms of Discrimination Against Women
CERD	UN Convention on the Elimination of All Forms of Racial Discrimination
CoE	Council of Europe
CPT	European Committee for the Prevention of Torture
CPTA	Committee for the Prevention of Torture in Africa
CRPD	UN Convention on the Rights of Persons with Disabilities
ECHR	European Convention on Human Rights
ECPT	European Convention for the Prevention of Torture and Inhuman or Degrading Treatment or Punishment
ECtHR	European Court of Human Rights
EJIL	European Journal of International Law
EU	European Union
FIACAT	International Federation of Action by Christians for the Abolition of Torture
HMIP	Her Majesty's Inspectorate of Prisons
HRC	UN Human Rights Committee
HRLR	Human Rights Law Review
IAPL	International Association of Penal Law
ICC	International Coordinating Committee of National Human Rights Institutions
ICCPR	International Covenant on Civil and Political Rights
ICJ	International Court of Justice
ICLQ	International and Comparative Law Quarterly
ICRC	International Committee of the Red Cross
ICRMW	International Convention on the Protection of the Rights of All Migrant Workers and Members of their Families
IDA	International Disability Alliance
IMB	Independent Monitoring Board
LOIPR	List of Issues Prior to Reporting
MDAC	Mental Disability Advocacy Centre
NGO	Non-governmental organization
NHRI	National human rights institution
NI Unit	National Institutions Unit of the Office of the High Commissioner for Human Rights
NPM	National Preventive Mechanism

OAS	Organization of American States
ODIHR	Office for Democratic Institutions and Human Rights
OHCHR	Office of the High Commissioner for Human Rights
OMCT	World Organisation Against Torture
OPCAT	Optional Protocol to the Convention Against Torture and Other Cruel, Inhuman or Degrading Treatment or Punishment
OPCAT CG	OPCAT Contact Group
OSCE	Organization for Security and Cooperation in Europe
PRI	Penal Reform International
RCT	Rehabilitation and Research Centre for Torture Victims
SCAT	Swiss Committee Against Torture
SPT	Subcommittee on Prevention of Torture
UN	United Nations
UNCAT	United Nations Convention Against Torture and Other Cruel, Inhuman or Degrading Treatment or Punishment
UNHCR	United Nations High Commissioner for Refugees
UNMIL	United Nations Mission in Liberia
UNODC	United Nations Office on Drugs and Crime
UPR	Universal Periodic Review
WNUSP	World Network of Users and Survivors of Psychiatry

1

The Origins and Background of OPCAT

A. Introduction

The Optional Protocol to the Convention against Torture (OPCAT, or Optional Protocol) is unlike any of the other principal UN human rights treaties[1] in that it does not set out any additional substantive human rights commitments but is primarily focussed on establishing mechanisms to further the realization of the pre-existing commitment of States Parties to the UN Convention against Torture (the UNCAT) not to subject anyone to torture, or cruel, inhuman or degrading treatment or punishment.

The existence of a general obligation under international law not to subject anyone to torture, or cruel, inhuman, or degrading treatment or punishment is beyond doubt.[2] In addition to the strength of the prohibition, there is also a long history of the international community adopting innovative means of addressing torture. Although the prohibition was a central component of the human rights instruments which emerged in the years following the end of the second world war,[3] the resurgence of torture and the increased prominence that this received during the 1970s combined to create the international momentum that resulted in

[1] In this, it is of course similar to other Protocols to UN human rights treaties, such as the first Optional Protocol to the International Covenant on Civil and Political Rights (ICCPR), providing for the system of individual communications to the Human Rights Committee established by the principal instrument. In many ways, however, OPCAT is best understood as a free-standing treaty rather than as a Protocol to another, though a number of small but important connections to the UN Convention against Torture do exist within the text of the Protocol and as an Optional Protocol it is only open to Parties to the UNCAT. These connections will be considered in detail in Chapter 7, below.

[2] See, for example, Rodley, N, with Pollard, M, *The Treatment of Prisoners under International Law*, 3rd edn (Oxford: Oxford University Press, 2009), p 80 where, after an exhaustive survey of the materials, it says that 'it is safe to conclude that the prohibition of torture and other ill-treatment is one of general international law, regardless of whether a particular state is party to a treaty expressly containing the prohibition'. It is also noted that 'it appears that the General Assembly of the United Nations now accepts that the prohibition of torture is itself a norm of *jus cogens* or "a peremptory norm of general international law"' (ibid). There is now a wealth of authority supporting this proposition.

[3] See, for example, Article 5, UN Universal Declaration on Human Rights, GA Res 217A (III), adopted 10 December 1948 (UDHR); Article 3, Council of Europe Convention for the Protection of Human Rights and Fundamental Freedoms, 1950, ETS No 5; 213 UNTS 222 (ECHR); Article 7, International Covenant on Civil and Political Rights; Article 7, International Covenant on Civil and Political Rights, GA Res 2200A (XXI), adopted 16 December 1966, 993 UNTS 171 (ICCPR)—all of which address torture and ill-treatment in similar terms.

the adoption of the UN Declaration against Torture in 1975[4] and the Convention against Torture (the UNCAT) in 1984,[5] to which 147 States are currently party. The Declaration was based on a text originally discussed at the 5th UN Congress on Crime Prevention and established the concept that acts of torture ought to be criminal offences under domestic law, that where there are reasonable grounds to suspect that such acts have occurred the domestic authorities should investigate, and that, where appropriate, criminal proceedings should be brought.[6] This introduced a 'criminalizing' dynamic which was subsequently taken up, refined and expanded during the drafting of UNCAT itself.[7] In this, it follows the approach found in a number of other international conventions which had been adopted beforehand[8]—and which have been followed since[9]—in providing a definition of the forms of conduct to be tackled, requiring that States Parties make such conduct an offence subject to appropriate forms of penalty and obliging them, when persons suspected of having committed such offences are within their jurisdiction, either to submit their cases to the prosecuting authorities or, if requested, to extradite them to another State which wishes to do so.

This approach, summed up in the expression '*aut dedere aut judicare*'—extradite or prosecute—is a well-known technique of 'closing the net' on alleged offenders[10] and in the context of the UNCAT, its essential 'architecture' is as follows.

[4] Declaration on the Protection of All Persons from Being Subjected to Torture and Other Cruel, Inhuman or Degrading Treatment or Punishment, GA Res 3452 (XXX), adopted 9 December 1975 (Declaration against Torture).

[5] Convention against Torture and Other Cruel, Inhuman or Degrading Treatment or Punishment, GA Res A/RES/39/46, adopted 10 December 1984, 1465 UNTS 85 (Convention Against Torture or UNCAT).

[6] Declaration against Torture, Articles 7, 9, and 10. See Burgers, J and Danelius, H, *The United Nations Convention against Torture: A Handbook on the Convention against Torture and Other Cruel, Inhuman or Degrading Treatment or Punishment* (The Hague: Martinus Nijhoff, 1988), pp 13–18.

[7] This approach had been sanctioned by the UN General Assembly which had requested the Commission to develop a text on the basis of the 1975 Declaration. See UN GA Res 32/62, adopted 8 December 1977 and Nowak, M and McArthur, E, *The United National Convention against Torture: A Commentary* (Oxford, Oxford University Press, 2008), p 23. The principal draft used by the Working Group of the Commission was that of Sweden. This was largely modelled on the 1975 Declaration and its criminalizing approach but went beyond it by providing for the exercise of universal jurisdiction. The text of the initial Swedish Draft is reproduced in Nowak and McArthur, p 1216. The other principal draft submitted as a potential basis for discussion was that of the International Association of Penal Law (IAPL). It was similar to the Swedish Draft from a jurisdictional perspective but was more limited in scope, addressing only torture and not 'cruel, inhuman or degrading treatment or punishment'. See Nowak and McArthur, ibid p 1210.

[8] The models used for the Swedish Draft and others drawn on during the drafting process were chiefly the 1970 Hague Convention for the Suppression of Unlawful Seizure of Aircraft (860 UNTS 105), the 1971 Montreal Convention for the Suppression of Unlawful Acts against the Safety of Civil Aviation (974 UNTS 177), the 1973 New York Convention on the Prevention and Punishment of Crimes against Internationally Protected Persons (1035 UNTS 167), and the 1979 New York International Convention against the Taking of Hostages Convention (1316 UNTS 205).

[9] See, for example, the 1997 International Convention for the Suppression of Terrorist Bombings (2149 UNTS 256); the 1999 International Convention for the Suppression of the Financing of Terrorism (2178 UNTS 197); and the 2005 International Convention for the Suppression of Acts of Nuclear Terrorism (2445 UNTS 89).

[10] For a general exploration of these forms of treaty see Reydams, L, *Universal Jurisdiction: International and Municipal Legal Perspectives* (Oxford, Oxford University Press, 2004). See also

The definition of torture, for the purposes of the convention,[11] is given in Article 1(1), and provides:

For the purposes of this Convention, the term 'torture' means any act by which severe pain or suffering, whether physical or mental, is intentionally inflicted on a person for such purposes as obtaining from him or a third person information or a confession, punishing him for an act he or a third person has committed or is suspected of having committed, or intimidating or coercing him or a third person, or for any reason based on discrimination of any kind, when such pain or suffering is inflicted by or at the instigation of or with the consent or acquiescence of a public official or other person acting in an official capacity. It does not include pain or suffering arising only from, inherent in or incidental to lawful sanctions.

Article 4 provides for the criminalization of such acts, providing that:

1. Each State Party shall ensure that all acts of torture are offences under its criminal law. The same shall apply to an attempt to commit torture and to an act by any person which constitutes complicity or participation in torture.
2. Each State Party shall make these offences punishable by appropriate penalties which take into account their grave nature.

Moving on to the issue of jurisdiction, Article 5(1) of UNCAT first of all requires that States extend their jurisdiction in a range of situations reflecting the well-established jurisdictional 'heads' of 'territoriality', 'nationality', and 'passive personality'[12] before moving on to the controversial yet vital provision in Article 5(2) regarding the exercise of 'universal' jurisdiction, this providing that:

Each State Party shall likewise take such measures as may be necessary to establish its jurisdiction over such offences in cases where the alleged offender is present in any territory under its jurisdiction and it does not extradite him pursuant to article 8[13] to any of the States mentioned in paragraph I of this article.

Reydams, L, 'The Rise and Fall of Universal Jurisdiction' in Schabas, W and Bernaz, N (eds), *Handbook of International Criminal Law* (London: Routledge, 2010).

[11] For discussion of the scope of the definition of torture as found in Article 1 of UNCAT see, *inter alia*, *The Definition of Torture:* Proceedings of an Expert Seminar, Geneva 10–11 November 2001 (Geneva: APT, 2003); Evans, M D, 'Getting to Grips with Torture' (2002) 51 *ICLQ* 365; Nowak and McArthur, *Commentary*, n 7 above, pp 27–86; Rodley, with Pollard, *The Treatment of Prisoners*, n 2 above, pp 82–144; Rodley, N, 'The Definition(s) of Torture under International Law' (2005) *CLP* 467. See also APT/CEJIL, *Torture in International Law: A Guide to the Jurisprudence* (Geneva: APT and Washington: CEJIL, 2008).

[12] Article 5(1) provides that:

[e]ach State Party shall take such measures as may be necessary to establish its jurisdiction over the offences referred to in article 4 in the following cases:

(a) When the offences are committed in any territory under its jurisdiction or on board a ship or aircraft registered in that State;
(b) When the alleged offender is a national of that State;
(c) When the victim is a national of that State if that State considers it appropriate.

[13] Article 8 concerns the modalities of extradition, rather than the obligation to extradite which is found in Article 7(1).

Having provided for the establishment of the necessary definitional, criminal, and jurisdictional frameworks, Article 7(1) binds them together through the obligation to 'extradite or prosecute', providing that:

1. The State Party in the territory under whose jurisdiction a person alleged to have committed any offence referred to in article 4 is found shall in the cases contemplated in article 5, if it does not extradite him, submit the case to its competent authorities for the purpose of prosecution.

It is beyond the scope of this work to look generally at the many practical problems associated either with these jurisdictional provisions or other substantive provisions of UNCAT, though a more detailed examination of some of the provisions of UNCAT most relevant to an understanding of the Optional Protocol will be noted where relevant throughout this book.[14] This framework is presented in order to underline the extent to which the Convention against Torture is, in some ways, a hybrid instrument. Although from the outset it formed a key part of the 'canon' of international human rights treaties[15] it went significantly beyond existing instruments in the way in which it created obligations concerning the manner in which torture was to be addressed as a matter of domestic criminal law and, as will be seen, this finds echo in, and has practical implications for, the work undertaken within the framework of the Optional Protocol. It is only with the recently adopted International Convention for the Protection of All Persons from Enforced Disappearances that a similar approach has finally been taken in a subsequent UN human rights treaty dealing with a different subject matter.

Nevertheless, in common with the other principle UN human rights treaties—and unlike all the other 'terrorism' treaties[16] based on the '*aut dedere*

[14] Mention might, however, be made here of the particularly significant exploration currently before the International Court of Justice concerning the precise scope and substantive content of Article 7(1) itself in the case concerning *Questions relating to the Obligation to Prosecute or Extradite (Belgium v Senegal)*. This case concerns the failure of Senegal to extradite Mr Habre, formally President of Chad and who has been living in Senegal since1990, to face criminal charges in Belgium arising out of alleged acts of torture and crimes against humanity committed during his Presidency. The UN Committee against Torture (see below) had already determined that Senegal was in breach of its obligations under Article 5(2) by not being in a position to prosecute Habre for want of an appropriate domestic legal framework and under Article 7(1) for not having done so (see *Guengueng and others v Senegal*, CAT Communication No 181/2001). Although it has amended its domestic law, Senegal is yet to either prosecute or extradite Habre, as a result of which, Belgium, as a State seeking extradition, is claiming that Senegal is in breach of its obligations under the Torture Convention. In response to a request for an award of interim measures, the ICJ, whilst declining to make such an order on other grounds, has determined that it does, prima facie, have jurisdiction on the basis that there is a dispute concerning the interpretation and application of Article 7(1). See *Questions Relating to the Obligation To Prosecute Or Extradite (Belgium v Senegal)*, Provisional Measures, Order of 28 May 2009, ICJ Reports, 2009, not yet reported.

[15] The UNCAT has from the outset been serviced by and operated under the auspices of the UN Office in Geneva, now the Office of the High Commissioner for Human Rights, and understood to be a part of the human rights machinery of the UN—unlike the crime prevention and 'suppression' conventions which generally fall within the sphere of the UN office in Vienna.

[16] The Convention on Enforced Disappearances also establishes a treaty monitoring body—the Committee on Enforced Disappearances—but uniquely, in UN Human Rights instruments, Article

aut judicare' approach—the UNCAT establishes a monitoring body, the Committee against Torture (CAT), to which States are required to submit reports on a periodic basis[17] and which can consider individual and inter-state communications provided that the relevant consents have been given.[18] In addition to these fairly standard means of oversight, Article 20 of the UNCAT establishes what was at the time an extremely innovative procedure by which the CAT might undertake an inquiry *proprio motu* and consider conducting a visit to a State Party in cases where it decides, on the basis of reliable information, that there are 'well-founded indications that torture is being systematically practiced in the territory of a State Party . . . '.[19] Article 20 proved to be one of the most controversial in the convention and agreement on its inclusion was only reached at the very end of the drafting process in the UN General Assembly Third Committee when a proposal that parties be able to opt out of this procedure was adopted.[20] At the time of writing, only eight States have exempted themselves from the scope of Article 20.[21] Nevertheless, given its controversial nature, the CAT has proceeded with caution and has to date

27 of the Convention provides for a review of its effectiveness by the States Parties between four and six years after its entry into force in order to determine whether to transfer its monitoring functions to another body. The modalities for amendment are, however, such that they make this an unlikely outcome.

[17] See UNCAT Article 19. The Committee against Torture has adopted a variant on this procedure, by which it adopts in respect of each State a 'List of Issues Prior to Reporting (LOIPR)' and the State in question is invited to address these issues rather than submit a full 'periodic' report as provided for in Article 19. See 2007 Report of the Committee against Torture to the General Assembly, A/62/44, paras 23 and 24; 2009 Report of the Committee against Torture to the General Assembly, A/64/44, para 27.

[18] See UNCAT Articles 21 (inter-state communications) and 22 (individual communications). No use has ever been made of the inter-state procedure and, as of 30/11/2010, only sixty-four States had recognized the right of individual communication under Article 22. As of that date, a total of 429 cases had been lodged. 337 cases had been concluded, and of the 169 considered on the merits fifty-two had resulted in a finding of a violation (and nearly half of which concern Canada, Sweden, or Switzerland). The vast majority of cases brought concern the non-refoulement provision, UNCAT Article 3.

[19] Four other UN human rights treaties now expressly provide for an 'inquiry procedure' of this nature, these being Article 8 of the Optional Protocol to the Convention on the Elimination of Discrimination against Women; Article 6 of the Optional Protocol to the Convention on the Rights of Persons with Disabilities; Article 11 of the Optional Protocol to the International Covenant on Economic, Social and Cultural Rights and Article 33 of the International Convention for the Protection of All Persons from Enforced Disappearances. In addition, the Rules of Procedure of some treaty bodies embrace the possibility of conducting country visits as a part of their 'follow-up procedures'. See, for example, Human Rights Committee Rules of Procedure, Rule 101, concerning follow-up to individual communications (CCPR/C/3/Rev.8, 22 September 2005) and, indeed, the CAT itself: Rules of Procedure, Rule 114(4) (CAT/C/3/Rev.4, 9 August 2002).

[20] See UNCAT Article 28(1). For a discussion of the drafting see Nowak and McArthur, n 7 above, pp 659–673. See also Burgers and Danelius, *Handbook on the Convention against Torture*, n 6 above, passim; Ingelese, C, *The UN Committee against Torture: An Assessment* (The Hague: Kluwer Law International, 2001), ch 6.

[21] These being Afghanistan, China, Equitorial Guinea, Israel, Kuwait, Mauritania, Saudi Arabia, and Syrian Arab Republic. See Report of the Committee against Torture (forty-third and forty-fourth sessions), UN GA Doc A/65/44, Annex II. The length of this list has varied considerably over time. Initially most Eastern European group States, and other socialist States, made declarations but following the end of the cold war these have been withdrawn (one of the last to do so being Poland in 2008). For a detailed breakdown and analysis see Nowak and McArthur, n 7 above, pp 840–843.

carried out seven inquires under the Article 20 procedure,[22] these being in respect of Turkey,[23] Egypt[24], Peru,[25] Sri Lanka,[26] Mexico,[27] Serbia and Montenegro,[28] and Brazil.[29]

It is against this general background of procedural innovation in general and the controversy over the Article 20 procedure in particular that the development of the Optional Protocol to the Torture Convention (OPCAT) must be placed and understood.

B. The Origins of the Optional Protocol

The origins of the Optional Protocol lie in the belief that torture and ill-treatment can be prevented—or the risk of such treatment occurring can be lessened—by visits to places of detention undertaken by external independent observers with appropriate powers of access and recommendation. The story is now well known.[30]

[22] The only other Committee to have conducted such an inquiry to date is CEDAW acting under Article 8 of the Optional Protocol to the Convention on the Elimination of Discrimination against Women, in Mexico in 2003. The other inquiry provisions (see n 19 above) are of more recent origin and have yet to be used.

[23] The Committee commenced its inquiry regarding Turkey in April 1990, culminating in a visit which took place in June 1992. The CAT published its summary findings in November 1993. See CAT Annual Report, A/49/44 (1994) paras 172–177 and A/48/44/Add.1 for the summary account and Nowak and McArthur, n 7 above, p 684.

[24] This inquiry commenced in November 1991. Egypt declined permission for members to conduct an in situ visit and so the CAT produced a report on the basis of information submitted to it and published a summary account of this in May 1996. See CAT Annual Report A/51/44 (1996), paras 180–222 and Nowak and McArthur, n 7 above, p 685.

[25] This inquiry was initiated in April 1995 and resulted in a visit being conducted in September 1998. The summary findings were not published until May 2001. See CAT Annual Report A/56/44 (2001) paras 144–193 and Nowak and McArthur, n 7 above, pp 685–686.

[26] This inquiry was initiated in July 1998 and a visit took place in September 2000. Uniquely so far, the CAT concluded that whilst torture occurred, it did not amount to a systematic practice. Its findings were published in November 2001. See CAT Annual Report A/57/44 (2002) paras 123–195 and Nowak and McArthur, n 7 above, pp 686–688. The decision of the CAT on this matter prompted considerable criticism. See, for example, Rodley, with Pollard, n 2 above, p 218 where it is said that this conclusion 'defies analysis'.

[27] This inquiry was initiated in October 1998, with a visit taking place in August/September 2001. The Mexican authorities consented to the publication of the full report (along with its reply) in May 2003. See CAT Annual Report A/58/44 (2003) paras 147–153 and the report both of which are available as CAT/C/75. See also Nowak and McArthur, n 7 above, p 688.

[28] The CAT commenced its consideration in 1997 but deferred it until May 2000 due to the political situation. A visit took place in July 2002, resulting in a finding that torture had been systematic in Serbia prior to October 2000, during the presidency of Slobodan Milosevic. See CAT Annual Report A/59/44 (2004) 156–240 and Nowak and McArthur, n 7 above, p 689.

[29] The CAT initiated its inquiry in November 2002 and a visit took place, after a number of postponements, in July 2005. The Brazilian authorities consented to the publication of the full report (along with its reply) in November 2007. See CAT Annual Report A/63/44, paras 64–72 and the report, both of which are available as CAT/C/39/2.

[30] The most authoritative account of the early years is that given by the first Secretary General of the SCAT, Francois de Vargas, for which see de Vargas, F 'History of a Campaign' in International Commission of Jurists and the Swiss Committee against Torture, *Torture: How to Make the International Convention Effective* (Geneva: ICJ/SCAT, 1979). See also Evans, M and Morgan, R, *Preventing Torture: A Study of the European Convention for the Prevention of Torture and Inhuman or Degrading*

In the mid 1970s a retired Swiss banker, Jean-Jacques Gautier, inspired by the model of the ICRC, proposed that an international body be established by treaty which would have the right to conduct unannounced visits to places of detention and make recommendations to the State concerned with a view to better ensuring the prevention of torture and ill-treatment.[31] In 1970 Werner Schmid, a member of the Swiss Federal Parliament, had proposed that the Swiss Federal Council prepare an international convention for the protection of political prisoners. In 1971 the Federal Council commissioned the Henry Dunant Institute in Geneva to undertake such a study and they invited Gautier to contribute. In the end, it was Gautier who drafted the report's conclusion, recommending the establishment of such a body with a more generalized remit than political prisoners alone. Though coolly received by the Swiss Federal Council, the proposal garnered considerable public support, including that of Eric Martin, a former President of the ICRC, and in 1977 Gautier established the Swiss Committee Against Torture (SCAT)[32] which later that year established a group of experts under the Chairmanship of Professor Christian Dominicé which formed Gautier's ideas into a draft 'Convention Concerning the Treatment of Prisoners Deprived of their Liberty'.

It was shortly after this that the UN General Assembly requested that the UN Commission on Human Rights commence work on the drafting of the Convention against Torture[33] and as has been seen, in January 1978 drafts were tabled by both Sweden and the IAPL.[34] There were, then, two very different approaches 'in play' at that moment, though with very different levels of support: the criminalizing approach found in the Swedish and IAPL Drafts, a model which was already foreshadowed by the UN Declaration and the terms of UN GA Res. 32/62 itself, and the very different Gautier-inspired scheme based on visits to places of detention which, though lacking official backing, had attracted influential supporters. When the Working Group met to commence its work on the convention in February 1978 it decided to focus on the Swedish Draft and, rather than try to supplant one

Treatment of Punishment (Oxford: Oxford University Press, 1998), pp 106–112 which is based on interviews with de Vargas and which also forms the basis of this current account. For the more general background see Haenni, C, *20 Ans Consacrés à la realisation d'une idée* (Geneva: Association for the Prevention of Torture, 1997). For accounts of the drafting history of the Optional Protocol itself see Evans, M and Haenni-Dale, C, 'Preventing Torture? The Development of the Optional Protocol to the UN Convention against Torture' (2004) 4 *HRLR* 19; Nowak and McArthur, n 7 above, pp 4–7 and 935–1192; Rodley, with Pollard, n 2 above, pp 239–240. For the more general background see Haenni, C, ibid.

31 The letters and documents which reflect the development of Gautier's thinking over time on these issues have been published in Mischler (ed), *Jean-Jacques Gautier et la Prévention de la Torture: de l'Idée à l'Action: Recueil des Textes* (Geneva: Association for the Prevention of Torture/Institut Europe, Université de Genève, 2003).

32 In 1992 the SCAT was re-launched as the Association for the Prevention of Torture (APT) which subsequently took the lead in supporting the development of both the European Convention for the Prevention of Torture and the drafting of OPCAT. The APT continues to be the leading NGO working in the field of torture prevention and plays a leading role in supporting its practical application at both national and international levels.

33 See UN GA Res A/RES/32/62, adopted 8 December 1977.

34 See n 7 above.

model at the expense of the other, Niall McDermot (then Secretary General of the International Commission of Jurists) suggested to Gautier that his approach could be recast as an Optional Protocol to a Torture Convention, rather than as a rival model for such a convention.[35]

This approach was agreed upon at a conference convened by the Swiss University at St Gall in June 1978 and the text of a draft Optional Protocol was set out in the publication, *Torture: How to Make the International Convention Effective*,[36] which also contained commentary, comment, and endorsement by leading figures including not only Gautier himself but Martin and McDermott. Since details of the model proposed at that time were very different from that which formed the basis of later discussions and, of course, from the Optional Protocol as it is today, it will not be considered in detail. However, its essence is best summed up in the words of Gautier himself who considered it a relatively simple scheme in which:

> . . . an international committee elected by an assembly of the Member States of the Protocol would be empowered to send to the territory of each of these States on a regular basis delegates authorised to visit, without prior notification, any centre for interrogation, detention or imprisonment. The Committee will then inform the State concerned of the finding made by its delegates and will make an effort, if necessary, to bring about an improvement in the treatment of those in detention. In the event of disagreement as to the Committee's finding or as to the implementation of its recommendations, the Committee will be able publish its findings.[37]

Described in this fashion, the basic concept and idea is instantly recognizable as that found in the Optional Protocol today, even if much of the detail surrounding it is now very different and very much more complex than could possibly have been originally foreseen. The idea was, however, not yet 'on the table' as such as far as the official drafting process was concerned and it was not until 6 March 1980 that it became so, when Costa Rica submitted the draft of an Optional Protocol to the Working Group on the request of the ICJ and SCAT.[38]

The essence of the Costa Rica Draft, 1980 was as follows: States Parties to the Protocol would agree to 'permit visits . . . to any place . . . subject to the jurisdiction of a State Party where persons are held who have been deprived of their liberty for any reason'.[39] A Committee, initially comprising ten members, but subsequently rising to eighteen when the number of States Parties exceeded twenty-five,[40] would

[35] See McDermott, N, 'How to Enforce the Torture Convention' in *Torture: How to Make the International Convention Effective* (Geneva: ICJ/SCAT, 1979) pp 18–26.

[36] International Commission of Jurists and the Swiss Committee against Torture, *Torture: How to Make the International Convention Effective* (Geneva: ICJ/SCAT, 1979). See also above, n 30.

[37] Gautier, J-J, 'The Case for an Effective and Realistic Procedure' in *How to Make the International Convention Effective*, ibid, p 32.

[38] See Draft Optional Protocol to the Draft International Convention against Torture and Other Cruel, Inhuman or Degrading Treatment or Punishment, UN Doc E/CN.4/1409. This is also reproduced in Burgers and Danelius, n 6 above and in Nowak and McArthur, n 7 above, p 1452. Hereafter this will be cited as the 'Costa Rica Draft, 1980'.

[39] Costa Rica Draft, 1980, Article 1(1).

[40] Ibid, Article 4(1).

be elected by the States Parties from lists of candidates nominated by them.[41] Members would serve in their individual capacities for four-year terms,[42] and be eligible for re-election.[43] The Committee would arrange programmes of regular visits to each State Party and, in addition, 'such further visits as may appear necessary from time to time'.[44] Visits would be conducted by delegates, who might either be members of the Committee itself or be 'members of a panel of qualified persons chosen by the Committee from among the nationals of the States Parties'.[45] It was implicit in the draft that a country would be notified in advance both of the 'mission' itself and of the identity of the delegate(s) to be involved, but it was also clear that the delegates would be 'authorised to visit in all circumstances and without previous notice any place of detention within the jurisdiction of the State Party'.[46] Following a visit, the Committee would consider the report of its delegates, informing the State of its findings, and 'if necessary' make recommendations and initiate consultations 'with a view to furthering the protection of persons deprived of their liberty'.[47] Once again, the essential contours of the Optional Protocol as finally adopted can be seen clearly in this very first draft tabled at the UN.

This proposal, and particularly the use of delegates, also shows the influence of the practice of the ICRC but, despite its impressive lineage, the Costa Rica Draft, 1980 was stillborn. The wide-ranging right of access to any place of detention coupled with the possibility of its findings being made public was sufficient to ensure that, no matter how useful a mechanism it might be, it was well in advance of anything that the international community was prepared to accept. When one bears in mind the controversy over the considerably less intrusive Article 20 inquiry procedure, it is easy to see why those heading up the negotiations were wary of the draft and worried that, even as an Optional Protocol, it might not only be premature but might set back, or even undermine, the prospects for the convention itself.[48] Thus when Costa Rica submitted the proposal, it did so on the express understanding that it would not be considered further until the convention itself had been adopted.[49] As a result, moves towards the creation of a preventive visiting

[41] Ibid, Articles 3(2) and 5(1).

[42] Ibid, Article 6(1).

[43] Ibid, Article 5(3).

[44] Ibid, Article 8(2).

[45] Ibid, Article 9(1).

[46] Ibid, Article 10. Later on, this principle became commonly referred to as 'any time, any place, anywhere' (a catch phrase which may have a certain resonance for readers of a certain age).

[47] Ibid, Article 11(1). The Committee would be able to publish the findings and recommendations if the State concerned gave its consent or if, in the case of a disagreement with the State concerning the findings and recommendations, it considered it appropriate to do so (ibid, Article 11(2)).

[48] It is also worth remembering that at this time—1980—the system of State reporting was itself still something of a novelty, the full implications of which were unclear. Given that States were still experimenting with the experience of having their own accounts of their compliance with their treaty obligations subjected to international scrutiny by committee in Geneva, it is hardly surprising that there should be an even greater wariness of a system under which an international body would visit, unannounced, in order to examine the situation for itself at first hand.

[49] Burgers and Daneilus, n 6 above, p 28.

mechanism at the UN level stopped as soon as it started. Nevertheless, the idea was still 'on the table', even if it was not under active consideration and was clearly going to be returned to at some future date.

C. The European Convention for the Prevention of Torture

Much has been said about the relationship between the Optional Protocol to the UNCAT and its European counterpart, the European Convention for the Prevention of Torture (ECPT). In particular, there is great interest in the manner in which the work of the international bodies which they establish—the UN Subcommittee for the Prevention of Torture (SPT) under OPCAT and the Committee for the Prevention of Torture (CPT) under the ECPT—might impact on each other and these issues will be addressed in some detail later in this work.[50] It is certainly the case that both the establishment of the CPT and its practical experience have had a profound impact both on the detail of OPCAT as a legal instrument and on the work of the SPT as an international visiting body. However, it is sometimes forgotten that the origins of the ECPT are found in the hiatus in the drafting of the Optional Protocol itself. There were no moves towards there being a European Convention until the process at the UN had been halted, and to that extent it is fair to say that the European Convention represents the achievement at a regional level of the universal idea found in the Gautier proposal and the Costa Rica Draft, 1980. This is important, since, as will be seen, when the process of drafting the Optional Protocol was revived in the 1990s after the entry into force of the ECPT and the establishment of the CPT, it was sometimes thought that this was yet another example of European regional practice being extended to the global stage. This, however, was manifestly not the case. The idea all along was to establish a global rather than regional instrument and to that extent the European Convention acted as a proving ground for the idea, rather than being its precursor. For all these reasons, it is therefore important to take a short excursus into the development of the ECPT and to provide a brief overview of the experience of the CPT, in order to inform the examination of the drafting of OPCAT which is to follow.

1. Drafting the ECPT[51]

Less than a year after the tabling—and mothballing—of the Costa Rica Draft at the UN, the Parliamentary Assembly of the Council of Europe considered the Meier

[50] See in particular Chapters 7 and 8.

[51] For a full account of the drafting of the ECPT see Evans and Morgan, *Preventing Torture*, pp 112–141 (parts of which form the basis of this account). Other accounts include Cassese, A, 'A New Approach to Human Rights: the European Convention for the Prevention of Torture' (1989) 83 *AJIL* 130; MacDonald, R St John, 'The European Convention for the Prevention of Torture and Inhuman or Degrading Treatment or Punishment in Bello, E and Abjibola, B (eds) *Essays in Honour of Judge Taslim Olawale Elias* (Dordrecht: Martinus Mijhoff, 1992); Vigny, D, 'La Convention européene de

Report, which examined the progress being made towards the adoption of the UN Torture Convention.[52] The report, echoing criticisms previously made by Gautier, noted that provisions found in the Swedish Draft were 'quasi-judicial in nature and carried with them the usual drawbacks of complexity and slowness'. The report argued that the Optional Protocol offered a solution to these problems and that its approach was 'the right one for strengthening the effectiveness of the Convention'.[53] The advantages were considered to be that since it was, in principle, a cooperative and confidential model, States would not be on the defensive and that it permitted rapid action, unlike the other more protracted procedures, and the report and its conclusions were endorsed by the Parliamentary Assembly early in 1981.[54]

Later that year, and in the wake of motions raising questions of torture within Council of Europe countries, the Chair of the Legal Affairs Committee, Noel Berrier, submitted an 'Introductory Memorandum' concerning torture in which for the first time was formally introduced the idea that such a system be adopted at the regional level 'without waiting for the proposal to be implemented at the world level'.[55] Pandering somewhat to a sense of European complacency and superiority, the ICJ and SCAT offered to draft a regional convention or Optional Protocol to the ECHR which, when completed, was incorporated in the final version of the Berrier Report.[56] The Parliamentary Assembly duly adopted the report and called on the Council of Ministers to adopt the draft convention.[57] The Committee of Ministers responded by requesting its Steering Committee for Human Rights (CDDH) to consider the draft convention and submit proposals to it.[58] In March 1984 the CDDH delegated this task to a Committee of Experts[59] and in November 1986—a little over two and a half years later—the CDDH finalized the

1987 pour la prévention de la torture et peines ou traitments inhumains ou dégradants' (1987) 43 *Annuaire Suisse de droit international* 62; Decaux, E, 'La Convention européene pour la prévention de la torture et peines ou traitments inhumains ou dégradants' (1988) 34 *Annuaire français de droit international* 618.

52 See Council of Europe Doc AS/Jur (32) 22 of 8 December 1990. Mrs Meier was Rapporteur of the Legal Affairs Committee of the Parliamentary Assembly.

53 Ibid, para 13.

54 Council of Europe, Parliamentary Assembly Recommendation 909 (1981) on the International Convention against Torture, adopted 26 January 1981.

55 Berrier Report, Council of Europe Doc AS/Jur (33) 18 of 9 September 1981, para 13.

56 Ibid. The ICJ and SCAT had endorsed the idea of a regional convention, noting that 'it could serve to establish the viability and value of the system . . . Europe would once again lead the way, as it did with the ECHR' (letter from ICJ to the Clerk of the Parliamentary Assembly in Council of Europe Doc AS/Jur (24) 2).

57 Council of Europe, Parliamentary Assembly Recommendation 971 (1983) of 28 September 1983.

58 See Records of 366th Meeting of Ministers' Deputies, January 1984.

59 The Committee of Experts met in May and October 1984 and again in March and May 1985. A Drafting Committee met during that summer and its work considered by the Committee of Experts in October. The CDDH reviewed progress in November and the Committee held further meetings in February and July 1986 prior to the CDDH adopting the draft in October 1986. See Cassese, n 51 above, p 132 for further details.

text and transmitted it to the Council of Ministers which adopted the convention on 26 June 1987.[60]

It is neither necessary nor desirable to recount the drafting history of the ECPT in detail. However, three issues will be looked at briefly, either because of their direct relevance to OPCAT or because of the interest which they have for understanding its development and subsequent operation. These concern (a) the advisability of having a regional convention at all; (b) the nature of the membership and the use of 'experts'; and (c) the 'focus' of the convention.

(a) Should there be a regional convention at all?

Just as there had been concerns at the UN that discussions concerning the Optional Protocol might prejudice progress on the Convention against Torture itself, there were similar concerns at the outset of the discussions that a European initiative could also slow down or jeopardize the future adoption of such a mechanism by the UN. There were concerns that developing a European instrument might be seen as an attempt to entrench a European model and European approach in subsequent negotiations—something that did indeed prove to be a very real issue both as a matter of drafting and also as regards practice during the early years of OPCAT. Allied to this were concerns that if two rather different models were ultimately adopted, one at the European and another at the UN level, then there might be a difficulty in reconciling potentially incompatible approaches. Once again, experience has shown there to be some truth in this concern as well, as will be seen later.[61] However, the prevailing mood was that there was little real prospect of progress being made at the UN level. Moreover, there was a view that a global instrument was simply unrealistic anyway and that the future lay in regional mechanisms of this nature—and thus not only was a European approach appropriate in its own right, but it also could serve as a prototype for other regions.[62] Once the UN Convention was itself adopted in 1984 some questioned the need for the European initiative (seeing it as little more than a spur to the adoption of the UN instrument) but by then there was sufficient impetus behind the project for it to be carried forward in its own right and the rationale for the project was not seriously questioned again. What is, however, clear is that from the outset potential problems of practical

[60] European Convention for the Prevention of Torture and Inhuman or Degrading Treatment or Punishment (ECPT), CETS No 126.

[61] See Chapters 7 and 8.

[62] See Cassese, n 51 above, p 133. This has not been borne out by subsequent developments. There is no head of steam for additional regional conventions of this nature and, although the Committee for the Prevention in Torture in Africa has been constructed on the basis of the Robben Island Guidelines on Torture Prevention in Africa, this is a very different form of mechanism with a very different legal underpinning. See Niyizurugero, J-B and Lessène, G P, 'The Robben Island Guidelines: An essential tool for torture prevention in Africa' (2010) 6(2) *Essex Human Rights Review* 91 at 112. But cf the policy paper, 'Relationship between the African Commission on Human and Peoples' Rights Robben Island Guidelines and the Optional Protocol to the UN Convention Against Torture (OPCAT)' available at (<http://www.bristol.ac.uk/law/research/centres-themes/opcat/opcatdocs/rigrelationship-withopcat.pdf>. See also Chapters 7 and 8.

congruity with any eventual UN instrument were foreseen but, being at this stage abstract rather than real questions, they were left to the side.[63]

(b) Membership and experts

Both the Costa Rica Draft, 1980 and the ICJ/SCAT Draft found in Recommendation 971 envisaged that the 'Committee' or 'Commission' to be established by any new instrument would be comprised of a relatively small number of persons, who would issue recommendations on the basis of field work undertaken by delegates,[64] based on the model of the ICRC. As it turned out, the use of delegates proved increasingly controversial as further clarification was sought regarding their nationality, method of appointment and whether they could be refused permission to carry out a visit, and on what basis. In the light of these difficulties, the Committee of Experts decided that the new body should have seven members, rising to eleven once there had been more than fifteen ratifications and that it should be the members themselves who would undertake visits, but assisted if appropriate by other 'experts' drawn from a panel of qualified persons agreed upon by the body. The initial response from the ICJ, the SCAT and, indeed, the ICRC, was negative. They argued strongly that it would inappropriate for members to undertake visits, since they should be dealing with States on the basis of the information reported to them, and that a system of Delegates who would be professionally trained and employ a common approach was to be preferred. Nevertheless, the CDDH supported the view that the body should be small, and be assisted by experts drawn from a panel. Opposition continued, however, and in July 1986—almost at the end of the process—the Committee of Experts revived and adopted a suggestion which it had previously rejected, this being that each State Party should have a member in its own right, whilst also retaining the 'panel of experts' but expecting it to be called on less frequently given the increased pool of membership available to undertake visits. The CDDH endorsed this approach when it considered the matter in October 1986 but decided to eliminate the idea of a panel of experts entirely, replacing it with the laconic provision, now found in the convention text, that '[t]he Committee may, if it considers it necessary, be assisted by experts and interpreters'.[65]

The significance of this change can hardly be overstated. From the outset, the Gautier proposal, the Costa Rica Draft, 1980 and the Recommendation 971 Draft had all envisaged a small supervisory committee receiving reports from its experts and using them as a basis for its recommendations and dialogue. Indeed, a mere

[63] The relationship which was, understandably, of far greater concern to the drafters was that between any new Council of Europe body and the European Commission and Court of Human Rights. This has had a major and lasting legacy on perceptions of the nature of the CPT and of torture prevention more generally—and thus is of significance for an understanding of the SPT. See sub-section (c) below.

[64] See Costa Rica Draft, 1980, Article 4(1) proposing a Committee of ten, rising to eighteen and Recommendation 971, Draft, Article 4, proposing a Commission of five members.

[65] ECPT, Article 7(2).

twelve months before the text took on its final form the ICJ and the SCAT were arguing that it was extremely important that the members of the committee did *not* participate in visits at all. Yet due to the exigencies of the negotiations this model—consistently adhered to throughout—was abandoned at a very late stage for an alternative in which the members themselves would be 'the experts', supplemented as necessary by external assistance of a predominantly technical nature. The result was to create an international human rights treaty body which was 'field' oriented in its mandate and functioning. Rather than relying on information provided by others, the membership itself became the data collectors as well as the official interlocutors. It has now become a fixed point in the world of international preventive visiting of places of detention that the issuance of reports and recommendations and the ensuing dialogue with State authorities is to be carried out by those who have conducted the visits to places of detention personally. It is doubtful whether the full implications of this change were fully appreciated at the time. As will subsequently be seen, OPCAT also underwent a radical reorientation during the latter phases of its drafting in order to address problems in the negotiation process, which were vigorously opposed by some of the instrument's most influential supporters and which had an equally profound and positive impact on the final outcome.

(c) Nature and scope

Finally, there are a number of interesting points to be made regarding perceptions of the nature and scope of the convention and of the visiting mechanism it created. These concern the closely inter-connected questions of whether its focus was to be principally upon torture, what the purpose of visits actually was, and as a consequence, how such visits should be planned and conducted.

First, there was a surprising degree of ambiguity—or, perhaps, confusion—within the drafting process regarding the central question of what the convention was actually addressing. From the outset, the rhetoric surrounding the process was largely focused on torture alone. Although the Meier Report accepted that 'delegates appointed by the Committee would concern themselves not only with the problem of torture, but with any cruel, inhuman or degrading treatment' it nevertheless considered the Optional Protocol mechanisms to be primarily an additional means of calling States to account for the practice of torture which was a 'crime committed by pubic officials'. It noted that even if only those countries which did not practise torture ratified the convention, it would still be a useful instrument since 'political regimes can change . . . If a democratic government ratified the Convention, it would be difficult for a totalitarian government which replaced it to denounce the Convention subsequently.'[66] The justification for the Optional Protocol and the ECPT was, then, firmly rooted in the idea of combating any current instances of torture as a discrete phenomenon in a given political situation.

[66] See Meier Report, Council of Europe Doc AS/Jur, para 21.

This was also reflected in the commentary submitted by the ICJ and SCAT on their draft for a European convention, which was incorporated into the Berrier Report: in a passage worthy of being reproduced in full they presented the case for the adoption of the draft convention in the following terms:

> Torture does still exist in Europe and in recent years there have been serious allegations of such practices in Turkey, Greece, Northern Ireland, Italy, Portugal and Spain. Even if this were not the case, merely because at any particular time there have been no obvious cases of torture in a region this is not a sufficient reason to deny that region the means to prevent or fight such an occurrence in the future. Given certain conditions, torture can break out anywhere.[67]

Although prevention is mentioned, this is secondary to 'fighting the outbreak' of torture, and does not really consider inhuman or degrading treatment or punishment at all. Whilst the commentary does point out that 'on the spot visits... cannot but have a salutary effect on conditions of detention', this was a mere aside when compared to the focus on 'torture' *per se*.[68] The focus was first and foremost to be upon 'responding to torture'.[69] So what happened during the drafting process to change this?

In brief, it appears that a significant change in emphasis was the result of pressure from the European Commission and Court of Human Rights which were concerned that the new body would assume too prominent a role in investigating and determining whether a State had acted in a fashion which amounted to a breach of their obligations under Article 3 of the ECHR. Not only would this mean that the new body would be trespassing on what they considered to be their preserve but it might also result in divergent jurisprudence—and it has certainly proven to be the case that there has been considerable interest in the congruence of the jurisprudence of the Court with the work of the CPT.[70] The Commission and the Court therefore urged that the focus of the new convention should be shifted away from determining compliance with Article 3 and towards preventive and non-judicial approaches based on non-binding recommendations.[71] It was for this reason that the Committee of Experts introduced the word 'Prevention' into the title of the convention and into the name of the body it was to establish—and it is not found elsewhere in the text of the convention at all.

The original Assembly draft had provided that '[d]uring each visit, the delegates shall ascertain that detainees are being treated in conformity with Article 3 of the ECHR'.[72] This was clearly going to be unacceptable since is amounted to an invitation to determine whether a breach of the ECHR had

[67] See (1983) *ICJ Review* 50 and Council of Europe Doc AS/Jur (36) 2.

[68] Ibid.

[69] This focus was also reflected in the report adopted by the Parliamentary Assembly (Doc 5704, para 18) which again justified the adoption of the convention on the grounds that, though a part of the world 'least affected' by torture 'Europe is not immune to this evil'.

[70] This has generated a considerable literature over the years. See, for example, Murdoch, J, *The Treatment of Prisoners: European Standards* (Strasbourg: Council of Europe Publishing, 2006), pp 46–52.

[71] See Cassese, n 51 above, p 136.

[72] Assembly Draft, Article 9(6).

taken place. It was therefore proposed that this be replaced with a version in which the body to be established 'shall examine the conditions of detention with a view to improving, if necessary, the protection of persons deprived of their liberty from torture and from inhuman or degrading treatment or punishment'. However, the reference to 'conditions of detention' was removed by the Committee of Experts, to be replaced with the word 'treatment' in order to underline that conditions were only to be looked at when relevant to questions of ill-treatment. This was further underlined by the discussion in the CDDH which rejected the idea that the new body should consider matters relating to other ECHR rights such as correspondence, family life, and hygiene, on the grounds that this would be going beyond its remit and distract from the focus on torture and ill-treatment.

It is, then, clear that it was this process of 'distancing' the new body from influencing the interpretation and application of Article 3 which led to the emphasis being placed on the 'preventive' impact of its work and its task being seen as one of 'concerning itself with situations liable to give rise to torture' rather than with instances of torture as such.[73] Indeed, it is a quite extraordinary fact that the Explanatory Report to the Convention, in a section headed 'Main features of the System' has almost nothing to say about what the Committee is to do, but focuses almost exclusively on what it is not to do, which is to act judicially.[74] Moreover, it has nothing to say regarding what 'prevention' might entail.

The need to inject 'distance' between the judicial and non-judicial roles also affected the debate concerning the size and nature of the body's membership too. Whilst it was generally agreed that members should have relevant expertise, there were differences over what forms of expertise were relevant. Some favoured this being spelt out in some detail and believed that it should include references to matters such as medical and prison administration experience. Those favouring a small body supported by delegates tended to think this too limiting and believed that the text should be more open-textured. The Commission on Human Rights argued that members should be experts in the fields covered by the convention rather than 'human rights' specialists (by which was meant 'lawyers'), largely on the grounds that they would be more likely to focus on fact finding and less likely to stray into judicial determinations, something further buttressed by the decision to create a larger body itself engaged in fact finding. In the end, the text of the convention combines both, providing that the members should be 'known for their competence in the field of human rights or have professional experience in the

[73] Paradoxically, the use of this terminology also had the practical effect of encouraging the view that 'conditions of detention' should indeed be subject to its scrutiny, despite the negativity shown to this suggestion during the drafting process.

[74] This is reflected in the Explanatory Report to the Convention which, in para 17 hammers home the message that '[i]t is not for the Committee to perform any judicial junctions; it is not its task to adjudge that violations of the relevant international instruments have been committed. Accordingly, the Committee will refrain from expressing its views on the interpretation of those instruments either *in abstracto* or in relation to concrete facts.'

areas covered by this Convention'.[75] The Explanatory Report explains that '[i]t is not thought desirable to specify in detail the professional fields from which members . . . might be drawn. It is clear that they do not have to be lawyers [ie human rights specialists]' and it goes on to mention the desirability of members having experience in fields relevant to the treatment of persons deprived of their liberty in order to make 'the dialogue between the Committee and the States more effective and facilitate concrete suggestions from the Committee'.[76] And—it might have added—to reduce the likelihood of its making quasi-judicial findings.[77]

In short, the idea of 'prevention', far from being the driving force behind the convention, was used in order to emphasize the difference between the work of the two bodies, with a clear understanding that it was undoubtedly a 'useful supplement'.[78] The best that the Report could do to explain the meaning of Article 1, which provides that 'the Committee shall by means of visits, examine the treatment of persons deprived of their liberty with a view to strengthening, if necessary, the protection of such persons from torture and from inhuman or degrading treatment or punishment' was as follows:

> . . . the Committee shall not perform any judicial functions: its members will not have to be lawyers, its recommendations will not bind the State concerned and the Committee shall not express any view on the interpretation of legal terms. Its task is a purely preventive one. It will carry out fact-finding visits, and, if necessary, on the basis of the information obtained through them, make recommendations with a view to strengthening the protection of persons deprived of their liberty from torture and from inhuman or degrading treatment or punishment.[79]

Reading the text of the convention and the Explanatory Report today, one is left with a sense that there really was no very concrete idea as to what the Committee was actually going to do in practice, but a very firm idea of what it was not to do. As it happened, things turned out rather differently from what might have been expected.

[75] ECPT, Article 4(2). The use of 'this Convention' is significant, as it underlines the point that the Committee was not to stray into matters more properly associated with other EHCR articles.

[76] Explanatory Report, para 36.

[77] Nevertheless despite its rejection of a quasi-judicial role, the closest that either the text or the report comes to spelling out in anything other than the most general terms what sorts of activities the Committee might be involved in is found in its provisions on visits. After recalling that the purpose of the Committee is to undertake visits, the Explanatory Report suggests that the Committee should prioritize '*ad hoc*' visits which might be necessitated by particular sets of circumstances and, whilst not investigating individual complaints, it 'should be free to assess communications from individuals or groups of individuals and decide whether to exercise its functions upon such communications' (para 47). This suggests it would be appropriate for the Committee to respond to allegations but in a 'non-judicial' fashion, that is, by making recommendations aimed at strengthening the protection of persons deprived of their liberty. Once again there is a feeling that the job of the committee is to engage with particular instances of potential violations of Article 3, but in a manner which falls short of being judicial.

[78] To use the words found in the Explanatory Report, para 21, commenting on the Preamble to the Convention.

[79] Explanatory Report, para 25, commenting on Article 1 of the Convention.

2. The work of the CPT and some implications for the drafting of OPCAT

The European Convention entered into force in 1989 for 15 of the then 23 Member States of the Council of Europe. The CPT commenced its programme of visiting in 1989 and so has over twenty years of experience on which to draw.[80] During that time the geographic scope of its operation has expanded to embrace the now 47 Member States of the Council of Europe and by the end of 2010 it had conducted a total of 297 in-country visits of varying length and focus.[81] It is beyond the scope of this section to present and analyse its work during this time in any detail. Rather, the purpose of this section is to give a basic outline of its approach to its work, given its significance for the drafting of OPCAT. Inevitably, those involved in the drafting of OPCAT looked to the work of the CPT in order to understand what the implications of adopting such an instrument at the international level might be. Given that the ECPT was indeed something of a 'regional experiment', undertaken during the hiatus in the drafting of OPCAT, this was both perfectly understandable and perfectly appropriate. However, a number of important points tended to be overlooked.

First, and as has been seen, the ECPT is a very sparse text which actually says relatively little about what was to be expected of the mechanism it established. As a result, the model of 'preventive visiting' which it established was by no means a 'given'. It was (and remains) a potential model to follow but was not the only way of exercising such functions. Nevertheless, the CPT model became more of a benchmark than a reference point during the negotiations—and, indeed, has remained so for the SPT and others once OPCAT entered into force.[82] It is, then, fair to say that choices made by the CPT as regards both its methods and approach rapidly came to 'define' preventive visiting.[83]

Secondly, and related to this, it is often overlooked that the 'defining' work of the CPT as regards 'preventive visiting' was in its infancy when the process of drafting OPCAT recommenced in 1991. Moreover, relatively little was known of its real effectiveness and there was a tendency during the 1990s for supporters of the project to present the work of the CPT as an exemplar of success without there

[80] The CPT has given its own overview and reflection on its work in its publication *20 Years of Combating Torture*, pp 7–12, this being the 19th General Report of the CPT (CPT/Inf (2009) 27). For its most recent survey, covering the period to 1 August 2009 to 31 July 2010 see its 20th General Report (CPT/Inf (2010) 28).

[81] Of these, 179 are classified as 'regular' and 118 as '*ad hoc*' visits by the CPT. The relevance of this distinction is considered further below.

[82] For example, van Zyl Smit, D and Snacken, S, *Principles of European Prison Law and Policy* (Oxford: Oxford University Press, 2009), p 120 describe the OPCAT system as 'an interesting variation on the CPT's methods of work'.

[83] Cf Casale, S, 'A System of Preventive Oversight' (2009) 6(1) *Essex Human Rights Review* 9 at 10 who observes that whilst the CPT is currently the 'pre-eminent' example of a preventive visiting body, this may change in time and points out that the experience gained in a European context is not to be 'transposed facilely' to others. As the then President of both the CPT and SPT, Casale was ideally placed to make such an observation.

being a great deal of hard evidence to support this. As will be seen, the CPT has in fact changed its focus over the years in a number of subtle but significant ways as it has come to wrestle with differing challenges from those which faced it initially.

Thirdly, and related to this, is the point that the CPT operates within the framework of the Council of Europe which provides a very different institutional setting to that of the United Nations and which provides the operating framework for OPCAT. As will be seen, the tendency has been to see the very different UN context as a 'challenge' to be overcome in the realization of the 'preventive model' rather than as a discrete institutional setting within which to fashion a successful model of torture prevention.

Putting these factors together, one finds that a rather idealized—and possibly romanticized—vision of the CPT tended to be projected which offered up a model and manner of work which was neither expressly mandated by the convention itself nor dictated by the underlying concept on which it was based. Moreover, it was a model which was itself still a 'work in progress' and relatively untested in practice. This can be illustrated by looking at a number of key issues concerning the core practice of visiting, which show that the approach adopted by the CPT in practice did not necessarily fully map onto the expectations of the drafters or, in some ways, the letter of the text. Nevertheless, it is these approaches which became influential during the OPCAT drafting process and continue to influence perceptions today.

Article 2 of the ECPT provides that '[e]ach Party shall permit visits, in accordance with this convention, to any place within its jurisdiction where persons are deprived of their liberty by a public authority'. These are usually referred to as 'periodic' visits. This is supplemented by Article 7 which says that '[a]part from periodic visits, the Committee may organise such other visits as appear to it to be required in the circumstances', these being known as '*ad hoc*' visits. In the past, the Committee also utilized a third category of visits, known as 'follow-up' visits, which—as the name implied—were intended to pursue particular issues arising out of previous periodic visits. Over time, the difference between follow-up visits and *ad hoc* visits, and between follow-up and subsequent periodic visits has become blurred to the extent that the two-fold approach appears perfectly adequate from an operational perspective. However, in principle, follow-up visits are different to *ad hoc* visits: the former are 'checking' on the extent to which recommendations arising out of previous preventive visits have been implemented, whereas the latter are, in principle, 'responsive' visits undertaken in the light of particular concerns. Whilst now of little significance as far as the CPT is concerned,[84] the three-fold typology was in vogue during the 1990s and this has left its mark on OPCAT.

Similarly, the ECPT says nothing at all concerning the frequency or duration of visits and the Explanatory Report limits itself to observing that the Committee should 'ensure, as far as possible, that the different States are visited on an equitable

[84] Nevertheless, the three-fold categorization remains reflected in the CPT's Rules of Procedure. See Rule 31 (Periodic visits), 32 (Ad hoc visits), and Rule 33 (Follow-up visits), which were last updated in March 2008. See CPT/Inf/C (2008) 1.

basis'.[85] The CPT now spends in the order of 160 days per year conducting visits, typically conducting about ten 'periodic' visits lasting around ten days and a similar number of shorter 'ad hoc' visits.[86] This means that most countries will receive a 'periodic visit' roughly every five years, often interspersed with *ad hoc* visits. Periodic visits might themselves be limited to particular parts of a large country and may, in practice, be little different from an ad hoc visits. Indeed, some *ad hoc* visits have been as long, or longer, in duration than some of the shorter periodic visits.[87] Moreover, the balance has shifted over time towards conducting more *ad hoc* visits. Indeed, in more recent times the Committee has moved towards other forms of engagement with States altogether, including holding high level talks in countries without visiting places of detention at all.[88] Nevertheless, the general assumption—based on the early practice of the CPT—at the time of drafting OPCAT was that the work of such a body should be focused on conducting visits to places of detention with a frequency and duration which matched that found in the practice of the CPT.

It is also widely assumed that the text of the ECPT gives the Committee the right to conduct 'unannounced' visits to all places of detention and, as will be seen, this became a major issue in the drafting of the Optional Protocol. In fact, it does not. Indeed, it does the opposite. The original Parliamentary Assembly draft provided that visits were to take place 'without prior notice and at any time' but only following the notification of the State by the Committee that a visit was impending.[89] During the drafting process the words 'at any time' were dropped and Article 8 thus requires the Committee to 'notify the Government of the Party concerned of its intention to carry out a visit'.[90] The period of notification is not specified but the Explanatory Report suggests that the period in question might be 24 or 48 hours, adding that 'exceptional situations could arise in which the visit takes place immediately after the notification has been given'.[91] Whilst there is some ambiguity as to whether the report is referring to the visit as a whole or to particular places of detention, it seems clear that, read as a whole, the expectation was that the Committee would inform the authorities, in advance, of those places it wished to visit.[92]

[85] Explanatory Report, para 47.

[86] The CPT had previously aspired to move towards 200 days of visiting per year but this has proved to be an unrealistic goal.

[87] This is usually a factor of size. For example, the periodic visits to Andorra in February 2004 and to Monaco in March 2007 lasted only four days each (see CPT/Inf (2006) 32 and CPT/Inf (2007) 20 respectively) whereas the *ad hoc* visit to the Russian Federation in April 2010 lasted a week (Press Release, 26 April 2010).

[88] For example, two days of talks were held with Greece in January 2010 outside the framework of a visit. See 20th Annual General Report, CPT/Inf (2010) 28, para 19.

[89] Parliamentary Assembly draft, Article 8(1).

[90] Article 8(1).

[91] Explanatory Report, para 56.

[92] See ibid, para 58, which says that 'the fact that specific establishments are mentioned in the notification should not preclude the Committee from announcing that it also wishes to visit other establishments in the course of the visit'. This does not sound like a right to demand immediate access to places of detention.

Be this as it may, the approach subsequently adopted by the Committee, and accepted in practice, has been very different. The CPT adopted a three-stage process of notification. In the late autumn of each year it announces its programme of periodic visits for the coming year and informs the States involved of this. *Ad hoc* (or follow up) visits are never announced in this way, however. Shortly before a visit of any nature is to take place the country is informed of the proposed dates of the visit and the full composition of the delegation (this being required by Article 14(1) of the convention). Finally, a few days before the visit commences a provisional list of places to be visited is sent, though the Committee usually visits others in addition to these.[93] Arguably, this approach gives both far more and far less notice than was originally anticipated: more, in that a State may have many months' notice of a periodic visit, and a number of weeks' notice of any visit; less, in that the Committee reserves the right to decide to visit particular places of detention without giving any notice at all. Whatever the pros and cons of this approach, it does not reflect a belief that immediate and unannounced access to places of detention is an essential pre-requisite for the effective operation of the mechanism.

None of this should be taken to suggest that the approach of the CPT to the execution of its mandate is either inappropriate or ineffective. What it does do is illustrate that the Committee made important decisions concerning its working methods—the typology of visits, their duration, frequency, notification, etc—which had a major influence on the debates concerning OPCAT at the time and which still shape perceptions of its efficacy today. One cannot understand the dynamics surrounding OPCAT without an appreciation of the dynamics—and, perhaps, myths—surrounding the ECPT, however much one might wish otherwise.

[93] See Article 33 of the Rules of Procedure. This has been the practice from the outset. The Rules were originally adopted in November 1989 and the ability to phase notification was introduced to the Rules during their first revision in March 1990 before it had undertaken its first visit (which did not take place until May 1990).

2

Drafting OPCAT—Towards Deadlock: 1991–2000

A. The Return to the UN and its Consequences

The previous chapter traced the early years and formative influences on the development of OPCAT. It is now necessary to return to the UN, and pick up the story where it was left in 1981. As has already been said, the Costa Rica Draft Optional Protocol of 1980 was in a sense 'shelved' rather than 'tabled' but it was at least formally located within the processes of the UN. The Convention against Torture was adopted in December 1984 but there was to be no swift return to the Optional Protocol: in March 1986 the Commission decided to defer any further consideration of it until 1989,[1] when it decided to postpone the matter once again, this time until its forty-seventh session in 1991.[2] It was now nearly eleven years since the original draft had been tabled and in the meanwhile much had changed: the UN Convention was in force and the ECPT had demonstrated the workability of the proposed mechanism. Moreover, the UN had itself established and developed the mandate of its Special Rapporteur on Torture.[3] In the light of these developments, the ICJ and Swiss Committee against Torture took the initiative by convening a colloquium of international experts in Geneva in November 1990 which, with the blessing of Costa Rica, produced a revised draft that reflected these developments and the lessons learnt from them. This new draft was submitted to the Commission by Costa Rica in January 1991[4] and in March 1991 it was decided

[1] UN Commission on Human Rights Resolution 1986/56 on Torture and Other Cruel, Inhuman or Degrading Treatment or Punishment, 13 March 1986, E/CN.4/RES/1986/56.

[2] UN Commission on Human Rights Resolution 1989/104 on Postponement of Consideration of a Draft Optional Protocol to the Convention Against Torture and Other Cruel, Inhuman or Degrading Treatment or Punishment, 6 March 1989, E/CN.4/RES/1989/104. The reasons given for this postponement were that 'it would be advisable to take note, on the one hand, of the experience of the ECPT . . . and, on the other, of the work being carried out in other regions designed to establish regional systems of visits to places of detention'.

[3] The mandate was established by UN Commission on Human Rights Resolution 1985/33, adopted 13 March 1985, E/CN.4/RES/1985/33 and has been consistently renewed ever since, most recently for a period of three years, in UN Human Rights Council Resolution 8/8 on Torture and Other Cruel, Inhuman or Degrading Treatment or Punishment, adopted 18 June 2008.

[4] UN document E/CN.4/1991/66, reproduced in the Tenth Annual Report of the Working Group to the UN Commission on Human Rights, E/CN.4/2002/78, Annex II and in Nowak and McArthur, *The United Nations Convention against Torture. A Commentary* (Oxford, Oxford University Press, 2008), p 1453.

that the text would be considered at its session the following year. (This draft will hereafter be referred to as the 'Costa Rica 1991 Draft'.) Some sense of the frustration that these continual postponements were producing can be had from the written statement submitted to the Commission by a long list of NGOs shortly before its consideration of the draft in 1992 in which it was argued that it was high time that the draft be considered 'quite simply because the idea of a system of preventing torture through visits to places of detention is an idea to which nobody can reasonably object... Honestly, who—in such a forum as the Commission on Human Rights—could say that such an idea does not deserve to be examined?'[5]

The answer, it appears, was that many States did not think it to be an idea that ought to be examined. But after twelve years of delay, the Commission did ultimately agree to establish an open-ended working group to draw up a draft optional protocol 'using as a basis for its discussions the draft text proposed by the Government of Costa Rica'[6] and, in what became its regular practice, the ECOSOC authorized a two-week long meeting of the Working Group prior to the subsequent meeting of the Commission. The Working Group first met in October 1992 under Costa Rican Chair/Rapporteur-ship[7] and continued to meet annually, with its final session taking place in February 2002.[8] Following the change in the Chair in 1993, and in order to expedite progress, it was also decided at the second to seventh sessions to establish an Informal Drafting Group that would report to the Plenary of the Working Group.[9]

[5] Question of the Human Rights of All Persons Subjected to Any Form of Detention or Imprisonment, in Particular Question of a Draft Optional Protocol to the Convention against Torture and Other Cruel, Inhuman or Degrading Treatment or Punishment, written statement submitted by a coalition of NGOs, 4 February 1992, E/CN.4/1992/NGO/27, para 1(1). Nevertheless, powerful voices within the NGO community remained cautious. For example, Sir Nigel Rodley recounts that, as Head of Amnesty International's Legal Office in the late 1980s, he was 'lukewarm' and that on becoming Special Rapporteur for Torture in 1990 he remained so, whilst accepting that it was a good idea in principle. See Rodley, N, 'Reflections on Working for the Prevention of Torture' (2009) 6(1) *Essex Human Rights Review* 21 at 25.

[6] UN Commission on Human Rights Resolution 1992/43 on the Question of a Draft Optional Protocol to the Convention against Torture and Other Cruel, Inhuman or Degrading Treatment or Punishment adopted 3 March 1992, E/CN.4/RES/1992/43, para 1.

[7] The first Chair Rapporteur was Ms Odio Benito, prior to her being elected a Judge of the International Criminal Tribunal for the Former Yugoslavia, and subsequently followed by Mr Jorge Segura, from October 1993 to 1995, and Mr Carlos Pizarro, from October 1996 to 1998. Mrs Odio Benito resumed the Chair in October 1999 and saw the process through to its completion. Her clear commitment to ending her period as Chair at the end of 2002 may well have played a role in the successful outcome that year.

[8] The Working Group produced Annual Reports to the Commission on Human Rights, from which much of the following account of its work can be gleaned. The reports, year and session are as follows: first session (19–30 October 1992), E/CN.4/1993/28; second session (25 October–5 November 1993), E/CN.4/1994/25; third session (17–28 October 1994), E/CN.4/1995/38; fourth session (30 October–10 November, 1995), E/CN.4/1996/28; fifth session (14–25 October 1996), E/CN.4/1997/33; sixth session (13–24 October 1997), E/CN.4/1998/42; seventh session (28 September–9 October 1998), E/CN.4/1999/59; eighth session (4–15 October 1999), E/CN.4/2000/58; ninth session (12–23 February 2001) E/CN.4/2001/67; tenth session (14–25 January 2002) E/CN.4/2002/78.

[9] Mr Zdziskav Kedzia of Poland chaired this group at the second session in 1993, followed by Anne-Marie Pennegard of Sweden during the third–seventh sessions from 1994–1998. The bulk of the substantive work took place in the informal drafting group. As is standard UN practice, the Reports of

By way of explanation, it should be noted that the standard working practice at the UN is for initial working drafts to be examined and alternatives canvassed during what is known as the 'first reading'. This usually results in a set of draft articles which combine the agreed text with a number of alternative forms of wording relating to more contentious matters. These alternatives are contained in 'square brackets'. Sometimes entire articles may themselves be in square brackets. Nevertheless, at the conclusion of a first reading the general shape and orientation of the text is usually in a fairly advanced form, although nothing is set in stone. Once a full text has been adopted on 'first reading', the 'second reading' commences during which the task is to move through the previously adopted articles and progressively agree on text by eliminating bracketed material. Once again, however, there is no bar on introducing new material or ideas into the drafting process: indeed, it may prove necessary to do so in order to bring about a generally acceptable text. The entire process is undertaken, as far as possible, without votes being taken on matters under discussion.[10] At the end of the second reading, a complete draft can be adopted and transmitted to the Commission on Human Rights for further consideration within the UN system, hopefully culminating in the adoption of the instrument by the General Assembly.

Proceeding in this fashion, the Working Group was able to complete its first reading of the draft in October 1995. These will hereafter be referred to as the '1st Reading Articles'.[11] The second reading commenced in October 1996 and by the end of its eighth session in October 1999 considerable progress on a range of issues and some twenty-two articles had been adopted. These will hereafter be referred to as the '2nd Reading Articles'.[12] However, this seemingly encouraging picture is deceptive since little progress had been made on the key issues. The basic architecture of the draft revolved around a trade-off between permitting an international body of independent experts to visit all places of detention, to produce a report and to make recommendations which would form the basis of a dialogue with the State concerned, and the requirement that the Report, recommendations and dialogue be confidential. However, a number of States remained of the view that such an international visiting body would be overly intrusive and so its work should not only be confidential but should also be subject to a range of other limitations. As

the Working Group do not record such informal discussions but merely record their outcome, as reported to, and discussed in, Plenary Meetings of the Working Group. In consequence, considerable reliance must of necessity be placed upon unofficial notes taken by observers who were present at the informal sessions when reconstructing the tenor of the negotiations.

[10] The diplomatic conceit is that texts generated through a consensus process will be acceptable to the entire international community. This may well be so. Of course, it is equally true that the process permits States which may have no real interest in becoming a party to an instrument to influence its development, to significantly retard its progress, or even prevent it from being adopted at all.

[11] The 'text of the articles which constitute the outcome of the first reading' are to be found in Annex I to the 4th Report of the Working Group, E/CN.4/1996/28.

[12] The 'text of the articles which constitute the outcome of the second reading' are recorded cumulatively in the Reports of the Working Group. For the sake of convenience, reference will be made to the most complete set, which are to be found in Annex II B to the 10th Report of the Working Group, E/CN.4/2002/78.

dissension over the possible restrictions on the work of the international body increased, the likelihood of the project succeeding diminished and the drafting process drifted toward deadlock. Indeed, there appeared to be almost as much that divided the drafters as united them and eight years of work appeared to have produced little fruit.

In 1999 Ms Odio-Benito resumed the Chair/Rapporteur-ship of the Working Group and initiated a period of reflection on the fundamental aims of the Optional Protocol and issues which had arisen during the drafting process. This, combined with intensive inter-sessional consultations, served to pinpoint the principal areas of difficulty. The ninth session of the Working Group was scheduled to take place in October 2000 but this was delayed until February 2001 to allow more time for further informal discussions to be held both in Geneva and elsewhere. When the session did get under way it was presented with radically different proposal by Mexico (hereafter referred to as the 'Mexican Draft') on behalf of the Group of Latin American and Caribbean States (the GRULAC).[13] In outline, the draft, dated 13 February 2001, proposed that the focus of the Optional Protocol should be upon the role to be played by national as opposed to international visiting mechanisms in the prevention of torture. Rather than the visits to places of detention being carried out by an international body they should be carried out by national bodies and, to this end, States should establish a national system of preventive visits, to be supplemented by the international visiting body should this be necessary. Thus it was, at what proved to be a very late stage in the process, that the idea of OPCAT providing for 'National Preventive Mechanisms' was first introduced into the negotiations. This proposal provoked an immediate and hostile response both from some NGOs[14] and from some State representatives. Indeed, a few days after the tabling of the Mexican Draft, on 22 February 2002, Sweden, on behalf of the EU, submitted a number of alternative proposals to be incorporated into the revised drafts of the original Costa Rican proposal, which came to be known as the EU proposals[15] and which included the idea of a national mechanism but accorded it only a very subsidiary role.[16]

The result was that at the end of the 2001 meeting of the Working Group matters appeared even more complex than they had before. There were now three versions of the Optional Protocol 'on the table' offering radically different

[13] The 'Alternative preliminary draft optional protocol to the Convention against Torture and Other Cruel, Inhuman or Degrading Treatment or Punishment submitted by the delegation of Mexico with the support of the Latin American Group (GRULAC)'.This can be found in the 9th Report of the Working Group, E/CN.4/2001/67, at Annex I and in the 10th Report of the Working Group, E/CN.4/2002/78, at Annex II C. It is also reproduced in Nowak and McArthur, n 4 above, p 1460.

[14] The approach was strongly supported by the APT, FIACAT, and the ICRT but other leading NGOs following the process, including Amnesty International and Human Rights Watch, voiced significant reservations.

[15] The 'Proposal of new and revised articles to be included in the original draft optional protocol to the Convention against Torture and Other Cruel, Inhuman or Degrading Treatment or Punishment submitted by the delegation of Sweden on behalf of the European Union', E/CN.4/2001/WG.11/CRP.2. This can be found in the 9th Report of the Working Group, E/CN.4/2001/67 at Annex II; in the 10th Report of the Working Group, E/CN.4/2002/78 at Annex II D and in Nowak and McArthur, n 4 above, p 1470.

[16] See EU proposal, Article 15.

approaches, these being the Draft Articles deriving from the consideration previously given to the original Costa Rican proposal of 1991, the EU proposals for amendments to the those drafts, and the Mexican proposal. In time they were to be joined by yet another variant proposed by the USA[17] (which was a longstanding critic of the entire project). The negotiations were on a knife-edge and there was no clear sense of the direction in which progress could be made. Indeed, some believed that no further progress was possible and the session ended in considerable disarray. As it turned out the idea of combining the creation of an International Visiting Mechanism with a National Preventive Mechanism became the basis for the final refinement of the text, which occurred at a pace which took many by surprise.

In the months that followed, the Chair undertook a series of consultations which lasted into the tenth session of the Working Group, the first week of which was spent in a general discussion of the 'two-pillar' system. This was in many ways an unreal exercise since all concerned knew that the Chair had been devising a compromise proposal outside of the sessions, yet most were largely unaware of the precise nature of the text that they were shortly to be confronted with. That proposal was tabled in the second week of the session on 17 January 2002 and, despite the many criticisms made, remained virtually unchanged and was annexed to the 10th Report of the Working Group.[18] This was presented to the Commission in April 2002 and faced the challenge of a 'no-action' motion, tabled by the USA. This was defeated and, in a tense vote, the Draft was adopted by the Commission by 27 votes to 10 with 14 abstentions.[19] Critically, this meant that more than half the Commission had positively supported the text. There was still greater support at ECOSOC in July 2002[20] and at the 3rd Committee in November 2002.[21] When finally put to the General Assembly on 18 December 2002, Resolution 57/199 was adopted by 127 to 4 with 42 abstentions. Just one year earlier, twenty years of work appeared to have led to nothing but now the Optional Protocol had finally come into being.

But what of its content? And why was the radical 'twin-pillar' approach introduced so late in the day able to garner such support? The answers may be found in the manoeuvring that took place at the ninth session of the Working Group in 2001. Given the centrality of the discussions at that session to the final shape and structure of the Optional Protocol the remaining sections of this chapter will look at developments prior to that critical session. The following chapter will then look

[17] 'Alternative draft optional protocol to the Convention against Torture and Other Cruel, Inhuman or Degrading Treatment or Punishment submitted by the delegation of the United States of America'. This can be found in the 10th Report of the Working Group, E/CN.4/2002/78 at Annex II E and in Nowak and McArthur, n 4 above, p 1481. This was submitted on 16 January 2002 and, in truth, had little traction or bearing on the discussions, this coming just one day before the Chair presented her own outcome document and draft. The USA Draft is considered further at Chapter 3, n 29 below.

[18] See E/CN.4/2002/WG.11/CRP.1, reproduced in the 10th Report of the Working Group, E/CN.4/2002/78, at Annex I and in Nowak and McArthur, n 4 above, p 1486.

[19] UN Commission on Human Rights Resolution 2002/33.

[20] UN ECOSOC Resolution 2002/27.

[21] The text was approved in the 3rd Committee by 104 votes to 8 with 37 abstentions.

at what happened at that session, and how the text was finalized and came to be adopted in the manner already outlined above. Rather than offer a comprehensive chronological account of the development of each article, it seeks to present a picture of what the key issues were and how they were resolved, in the belief that this best assists in understanding the expectations regarding OPCAT as it entered into force.

B. The Principal Points of Agreement Prior to the 2001 Session and Their Place in the Final Text

The articles agreed upon during the course of the second reading prior to the ninth session chiefly related to the composition and election of the body to be established by, and the 'final clauses' of, the Optional Protocol. The 1991 Costa Rica Draft proposed the creation of a 'Subcommittee for the Prevention of Torture and other Cruel, Inhuman or Degrading Treatment or Punishment' (the Subcommittee)[22] that would be elected by the UN Committee against Torture from a list of candidates submitted by States Parties.[23] It was not to be a 'subcommittee' in the sense that it would be comprised of members of the CAT (although this was not precluded) but it would at least be a body largely of its creation. However, the nature of relationship between the CAT and the Subcommittee was a matter of some controversy and, although still called the 'Subcommittee',[24] it was agreed that members should be elected by the States Parties themselves[25] and this remained the case in the final text of the Optional Protocol.[26]

There had also been agreement on the proposed number of members, the nature of the qualifications and experience they were to possess, and their possible period of service. The 1991 Costa Rica Draft had suggested that the Subcommittee should have a maximum of twenty-five members and a minimum equal to the number of States Parties for as long as that remained less than twenty-five,[27] but it was agreed that this should be amended to ten members, rising to twenty-five following the 50th accession[28] and this too is now found in the final text.[29] This was itself a

[22] 1991 Draft, Article 2. [23] Ibid, Article 5.

[24] 2nd Reading, Article 2. A further question was whether the Subcommittee should be said to be a Subcommittee 'of the Committee against Torture'. It was ultimately agreed to retain this wording in the 2nd Reading Draft, Article 2 and this was retained in all subsequent drafts and is now found in OPCAT, Article 2(1). However, as Nowak and McArthur point out (Nowak and McArthur, n 4 above, p 914), there was considerable unease at there being too close a connection—as reflected in the decision on its election. It is, then, probably inaccurate to describe the Subcommittee as a 'subsidiary organ of the Committee against Torture' (as in Nowak and McArthur, n 4 above, p 908). Indeed, as the body has an autonomous legal basis and a distinct composition and identity, the use of the term 'Subcommittee' is potentially misleading and apt to confuse.

[25] Ibid, Article 6.

[26] Optional Protocol, Articles 2 and 7. The relationship between the CAT and the Subcommittee is explored in further detail in Chapter 7 below.

[27] 1991 Costa Rica Draft, Article 4(1).

[28] 2nd Reading, Article 4(1).

[29] Optional Protocol, Article 5(1).

compromise between those who felt that twenty-five was too large a number and those who felt that, given its involvement in field work rather than committee work, an even greater number of members would be needed, drawing on the model of the CPT which has one member per State Party.[30] It had always understood that members would serve in their individual capacities,[31] and this remains the case.[32] Similarly, there had been a longstanding agreement around the general proposition that members were to be chosen 'from among persons of high moral character, having proven professional experience in the field of the administration of justice, in particular criminal law, prison or police administration or in the various fields relevant to the treatment of persons deprived of their liberty'.[33] As regards the length of membership, it had been originally suggested that members merely be eligible for re-election if re-nominated,[34] but at the end of the first reading of the draft it was felt that some limitation was desirable, though it was left open whether members might be re-elected twice or only once.[35] This was resolved in favour of their only being eligible for re-election once,[36] arguably a surprising decision in the light of the experience under the ECPT, which having originally had the same

[30] For a summary of the discussions, see Nowak and McArthur, n 4 above, p 943.

[31] 1991 Costa Rica Draft, Article 4(4); 2nd Reading, Article 4(4).

[32] Optional Protocol, Article 5(6).

[33] Optional Protocol, Article 5(2) and see Nowak and McArthur, n 4 above, pp 937–949. Although there was general agreement around the idea that members should have professional competence in relevant fields, there were divergences concerning what those fields were and in what detail they should be set out. The reference to 'experience in the administration of justice' and 'criminal law' was first found in the 1st Reading, Article 4(2), replacing the narrower formulation of 'prison or police administration' found in the 1991 Costa Rica Draft, Article 4(2). The 1st and 2nd Reading Drafts, Articles 4(2) also referred to medical expertise and (as did the 1991 Costa Rica Draft, Article 4(2)) those experienced in the field of human rights. These formulations were retained in the Mexican Draft, Article 9(4) and the EU proposal, Article 5(2). The references to medical and human rights expertise were only dropped at the last minute in the Chair's Draft, Article 5(2). Whether this was a matter of presentation or substance is unclear, since both are doubtless capable of being embraced by the less prescriptive final element of Optional Protocol, Article 5(2) which provides for 'the various fields relevant to the treatment of persons deprived of their liberty'. Nevertheless, it is true that the 1991 Costa Rica Draft used this latter phrase in addition to its reference to experience in the field of human rights. It may be that, as in the debates concerning the ECPT, this was seen as being a coded reference to human rights lawyers, and that the final outcome was a coded signal that this form of expertise was not as important as the others mentioned. If it was, then it has had little impact on the composition of the Subcommittee which is dominated by lawyers with various forms of expertise. Optional Protocol, Article 5(3) also refers to equitable geographic distribution, representation of difference legal systems, and civilizations, whilst Optional Protocol, Article 5(4) refers to gender balance. Confusingly, Optional Protocol, Article 7 enjoins States to give 'primary' consideration to the criteria in, it appears, all of Optional Protocol, Article 5 when electing members. It is difficult to see how this can be done in practice. The 2nd Reading Draft was different, calling for primary consideration to be given to the criteria now found in Article 5(2), whilst calling for 'due' consideration' to be given to the other factors listed in what is now Article 5. It is perhaps to be regretted that functionally-oriented emphasis was not retained in the final text of the Optional Protocol but, once again, one doubts that it makes a great deal of difference in practice. The outcomes of elections to the SPT are considered further in Chapter 5, below.

[34] 1991 Costa Rica Draft, Article 5(4).

[35] 1st Reading, Article 6.

[36] 2nd Reading, Article 9; Optional Protocol, Article 9.

limitation was amended to permit the re-election of members to a third term of office.[37]

It had also long been understood that it might simply not be possible for members of the Subcommittee to carry out their work unaided. As has been seen, the 1980 Costa Rica Draft envisaged that much of the practical work would be undertaken by delegates acting on the authority of the Committee.[38] The ECPT provided an alternative model, of a system in which the visits to States Parties would be conducted by the members of the body itself, but assisted, if necessary, by other experts chosen for the task by the Committee.[39] In practice, experts have been—and still remain—a regular component of nearly all CPT visits from the outset of its work in 1990 and this was reflected in the revised 1991 Costa Rica Draft, which provided that missions would usually be carried out by at least two members but assisted by experts and interpreters if necessary.[40] Following the European model, experts were to be chosen by the Committee but their identity was to be released to a State prior to a visit, and the State could, in exceptional circumstances, object.[41]

This model proved quite unacceptable to many States in the Working Group, who felt the need to retain some degree of control over the range of persons who might conceivably have access to places of detention within their jurisdiction.[42] During the second reading, a compromise position emerged whereby each State Party would nominate up to five persons from which a list of experts would be compiled and from which the Subcommittee could draw, subject to a variety of procedural hurdles.[43] The final text reflects a somewhat simplified version of these rather convoluted provisions, the gist of which is that experts are to be drawn from a list prepared on the basis of proposals from States Parties, the UNHCHR, and the Centre for International Crime Prevention, with States able to propose no more than five experts (each, presumably).[44] A State might oppose the inclusion of an expert, 'whereupon the Subcommittee on Prevention shall propose another expert'.[45] This leans towards the sensibilities of the State, since experts can be

[37] See ECPT, Article 5(4)—this being the position following the entry into force of the Second Protocol to the ECPT on 1 March 2002 which provided for this. The Protocol had, however, been adopted back in November 1993 so the desirability of longer terms, as a matter of practice, was already known. Nowak and McArthur, n 4 above, p 970 point out that the Optional Protocol was the first UN human rights treaty to limit re-election in this way (though others have since followed this model, such as the Convention on the Rights of Persons with Disabilities, Article 34(7) and the Convention on Enforced Disappearances, Article 26(4)). It may be that the reason that this was retained had as much to do with sending signals concerning the issue of longevity of tenure found in other human rights treaty bodies than with what might have been operationally desirable for OPCAT. Nowak and McArthur, n 4 above, pp 970 and 975 are critical of this provision, and in particular the loss of 'institutional memory' that it causes and the criticism seems well founded.

[38] 1980 Costa Rica Draft, Article 9(1).

[39] ECPT, Article 7(2).

[40] 1991 Costa Rica Draft, Article 10(2).

[41] 1991 Costa Rica Draft, Article 11.

[42] See generally Nowak and McArthur, n 4 above, pp 1029–1030.

[43] 2nd Reading, Articles 13(3)(a), 14.

[44] Optional Protocol, Article 13(3).

[45] Ibid.

excluded without any particular justification being given, and thus obliging the Subcommittee either to engage in a potentially drawn out series of discussions or to simply proceed without the expert assistance which, *ex hypothesi*, it considers necessary. On the other hand, the Subcommittee should be able to ensure that its chosen experts are generally available to it, by virtue of the power of the UNHCHR to add names to the roster.[46]

These, then, represent the principal structural and organizational matters on which a consensus had emerged prior to the 2001 session and which, with minor variations, were carried over into the final text of the Optional Protocol. There was also agreement on a substantial number of ancillary matters such as the mechanics of elections,[47] adoption of rules of procedure,[48] procedures for amendment,[49] and denunciation[50] which are largely similar to those found in the CAT or other human rights treaties. Agreement had also been reached on the comparatively modest figure of twenty ratifications to trigger the entry into force of the Optional Protocol.[51] It had also been agreed that the Optional Protocol should provide for

[46] In practice, however, experts have been little used by the SPT. The SPT's First Annual Report indicates an assumption that two experts should participate in each visit (CAT/C/40/2, para 52). However, no experts accompanied its first visit, to Mauritius. Two experts accompanied its second visit, to the Maldives (CAT/OP/MDV/1, para 8), one its third visit, to Sweden (CAT/OP/SWE/1, para 8) and one its fourth, to Benin (CAT/OP/Ben/1, para 8) but it appears that experts have not been used thereafter—largely for budgetary reasons. See SPT, Second Annual Report of the Subcommittee on Prevention of Torture and Cruel, Inhuman or Degrading Treatment or Punishment, February 2008–March 2009, CAT/C/42/2, 7 April 2009, para 30 and Third Annual Report, CAT/44/2 para 34.

[47] See Optional Protocol, Article 7. The 1991 Costa Rica Draft, Article 5 proposed that the CAT elect members from a list nominated by States Parties. The 1st Reading, Article 5(1) had left open the question of whether the election of members should be by the States Parties or by members of the CAT themselves. Likewise, it left open the idea that the candidates for election be proposed by the CAT rather than States Parties. However, the 2nd Reading, Article 6 adopted the more orthodox position found in the UNCAT, Article 17 and other human rights treaties, this being that States Parties should themselves both nominate and elect the membership. This remained the position thereafter. For an overview see Nowak and McArthur, n 4 above, pp 957–966.

[48] See Optional Protocol Article 10, and cf UNCAT, Article 18. See Nowak and McArthur, n 4 above, pp 976–983. One significant addition was made in the Chair's final draft, this being the requirement in Article 10(3) that the Subcommittee and the CAT 'shall hold their sessions simultaneously at least once a year'. This certainly facilitates communication between the bodies and joint meetings have been held during the course of their simultaneous session, in November of each year. This meeting had been public but in November 2010, at the twelfth session of the SPT, it was held in camera for the first time. The scheduling of simultaneous meetings has the practical consequence of precluding a person from being a member of both the Subcommittee and the CAT.

[49] See Optional Protocol, Article 34, this being identical to UNCAT, Article 29. See Nowak and McArthur, n 4 above, pp 1172–1175, who also explore the practical difficulties which seeking to amend either instrument in accordance with these provisions would present.

[50] See Optional Protocol, Article 33, which is substantially similar to OPCAT, Article 31 and see Nowak and McArthur, n 4 above, pp 1166–1171. Not all of the UN human rights treaties contain a denunciation clause, but all drafts of the Optional Protocol had contained such a proposal and its inclusion was not particularly controversial.

[51] 2nd Reading, Article 19; Optional Protocol, Article 28. The 1991 Draft, Article 18(1) had proposed a threshold of ten; this was supported by a significant number of States in the Working Group and the 1st Reading, Article 18(2) left the figure unspecified. By the time of 2nd Reading, Article 19(2) a consensus had been reached on the figure of twenty, and this was reflected in all subsequent drafts. The lower figure would have had the perhaps unfortunate consequence of meaning that the membership of the Subcommittee might potentially have been limited to nationals of the

the establishment of a special fund 'to help finance the implementation of the recommendations made by the Subcommittee to a State Party'[52] and this too was reflected in the final text.[53] But at this point the consensus stopped and the most vital question of all remained unanswered: what was the proposed Subcommittee actually going to be able to do?

C. The Principal Points in Dispute Prior to the 2001 Session

It was always understood that the Optional Protocol was intended to establish an international mechanism that would have extensive and intrusive powers. The central difficulty was how to reconcile this with State sovereignty which in practical terms came down to the question of the extent to which national authorities might be able to exercise control over the activities of the visiting mechanism which it established. The 1991 Costa Rica Draft adopted the approach to this issue found in the ECPT and sought to strike a balance between the freedom of the international mechanism and the concerns of the State by trading 'sovereignty' against 'confidentiality'. In other words, the Subcommittee would have a near unrestricted right of access to places of, and persons in, detention[54] but the findings and recommendations of the Subcommittee would be confidential to the Subcommittee and the State concerned, unless that State authorized their publication.[55] States would, exceptionally, be allowed to delay access under tightly defined conditions[56] but the sense of symmetry was maintained by the Subcommittee being able, in similarly exceptional circumstances, to make public its findings.[57] The central aim of the exercise was to enable the Subcommittee to make its own first hand evaluation of the situation and to engage in a constructive dialogue with the State based on those findings, thus turning the usual pattern of human rights reporting mechanisms on its head. The rest was all rather secondary.

initial States Parties which might have had a negative effect on the prospects for future ratifications. See Nowak and McArthur, n 4 above, pp 1139–1144.

52 See 1st Reading, Article 16(bis) and 2nd Reading, Article 17(1). The 1991 Costa Rica Draft, Article 16(3) had not linked the use of the fund so much to the recommendations of the Subcommittee but to its work more generally. See Nowak and McArthur, n 4 above, pp 1122–1130.

53 Optional Protocol, Article 26. Whilst the basic concept had been agreed upon, it was slightly modified in the wake of the introduction of National Preventive Mechanisms into the OPCAT framework. Moreover, the details surrounding the 'Special Fund' have proved to be more difficult than might have been imagined and will be discussed in more detail in Chapter 9. It is interesting to note that this is one area in which OPCAT has influenced the CPT. The inclusion of this proposal sparked a debate regarding whether some sort of similar fund, aimed at the implementation of CPT recommendations, should be established. Although not done in quite these terms, a stream of funding has now become available which can be accessed for these purposes.

54 See 1991 Draft, Articles 1(1) and 12(2)(a)–(f) and 12(3).

55 Ibid, Article 14(3).

56 Ibid, Article 13.

57 Ibid, Article 14(2), which envisaged the Subcommittee having the right to publish without the consent of the State if 'the State Party fails to cooperate or refuses to improve the situation in the light of the Subcommittee's recommendations'.

However, after eight years of discussion, there was still no consensus on the key elements of this framework—there was no shared understanding concerning the basic obligation to permit visits to places of detention without the need for prior consent; the organization and modalities of constructing and executing the programme of visits and the conduct of visits. These unresolved issues represented the essence—the central core—of the Optional Protocol. It was, then, hardly surprising that the closely related issues of exceptional restrictions upon access to places of detention and the exceptional publication of its findings also remained unresolved. In addition, two further complexities had come to bedevil the process: respect for the provisions of national legislation and the question of reservations. The following sections will consider in further detail the nature of the difficulties that needed to be recognized and addressed.

1. The visiting programme

A fundamental problem concerned the basic question of the Subcommittee's having the right to unimpeded access to places of detention on demand. For some, this was the essential starting point of the discussion whereas for others permitting this would have been an unacceptable concession. This was a question on which views were becoming ever further apart, rather than narrowing, something which can most easily and graphically be illustrated simply by quoting the 'evolution' of the drafting texts, and noting the issues in square brackets, denoting a lack of agreement or alternative positions. The 1st Reading, Article 1(1) provided that:

> [a] State party to the present Protocol shall permit visits in accordance with this Protocol to any place in any territory under its jurisdiction where persons are deprived of their liberty by a public authority or at its instigation or with its consent of acquiescence are held or may be held [provided that full respect is assured for the principles of non-intervention and the sovereignty of States].

The concerns around State sovereignty are obvious here, but they become amplified in the complex—not to say convoluted—2nd Reading Draft, Article 1(2), which provided that:

> Each State Party agrees to permit visits, [in principle,] in accordance with this Protocol, to [any place] [places of detention][on any territory] under its jurisdiction [and control] where persons (may, based on reliable information [as determined by a competent and independent judicial authority of the State Party concerned] be deprived or) are [deprived of their liberty] [detained][including structures intended or used to house or transport such persons] by [or pursuant to an order of] a public authority [or at its instigation or with its consent or acquiescence].

As this shows, with the passing of time, there was more, rather than less, controversy surrounding this key issue and it had to be resolved if any progress was to be made. One attempt was to exploit the latent ambiguity in the word 'visit'.[58] To this

[58] An ambiguity which still remains: Nowak and McArthur, n 4 above, p 933 rightly note that OPCAT still uses this word 'in a double sense'.

end, during the seventh and eighth sessions of the Working Group a distinction emerged between *missions* and *visits*, with it being suggested that the Subcommittee would conduct *missions* to the territories of States Parties which would include *visits* to particular places of detention and whereas express prior consent would not be needed to undertake a *mission*, *visits* might be subject to greater restrictions or even be made conditional on the prior consent of the State.[59] Rather than solve the problem, however, this opened up a real Pandora's box since it dramatically increased the range of potential combinations of negotiating positions rather than assist in closing them down. Therefore, it came as no surprise that, not only did it fail to resolve the difficulties around Draft Article 1, but it also spilled over into other provisions concerning visiting. Again, this was vividly illustrated by the various bracketed elements 2nd Reading Draft, Article 8 which in part provided:

Article 8
2 (a) The subcommittee shall send a written notification to the Government of the State Party concerned of its [intention] [request] to organize a [mission] [visit], [followed by] [including] a list of places to the visited and the composition of the delegation. [The subcommittee may also visit other places as needed during its mission].

[(b) those [missions] [visits] shall be conducted after the consent of the State concerned and shall be mutually agreed upon between the Subcommittee and the State party in a spirit of cooperation]

...

3. [(a)] [Six months] Before a [mission] [visit] is carried out, the Subcommittee and the State party concerned shall, [if either of them so requests,] enter into consultations with a view to agreeing [without delay on the practical arrangements] [on the modalities] of the [mission] [visit].

At one extreme, this could resolve itself into a regime under which the Subcommittee would have had to notify the State of its intention to visit certain places of detention and the composition of the delegation, but would be free to visit others during the course of its sojourn. At the other extreme, the Subcommittee would have to request permission both to enter the State and visit places of detention, and discuss the details at least six months beforehand. These extremes were not merely theoretical possibilities[60] and it was proving impossible to reach

[59] It was argued that this distinction was found in the 1991 Costa Rica Draft and textually it is certainly true that that draft did indeed refer to both missions and visits. However, the use made of this terminological differentiation at this point in the negotiation did not reflect the original thinking, in which the terms appeared to have been considered as alternatives rather than reflecting different forms or phases of a programme of country engagement.

[60] For example, during the eighth session of the Working Group a group of delegations argued that 'it was possible to balance the sovereignty and legitimate concerns of States and the effectiveness of the protocol through the prior consent of the State to a visit', (Joint statement by the representatives of Algeria, China, Cuba, Egypt, Saudi Arabia, the Sudan, and the Syrian Arab Republic—see Report of the Working Group on the draft optional protocol to the Convention against Torture and Other Cruel, Inhuman or Degrading Treatment or Punishment on its eighth session, E/CN.4/2000/58, para 63.) One delegation went even further, arguing that the distinction between missions and visits should

agreement on the issue of 'whether the ratification of the protocol by a State Party implied that a standing invitation was extended to the Subcommittee or whether the Subcommittee should receive prior consent from the State Party before each mission'.[61]

A further problem in relation to the visiting programme concerned the distinction between *regular* and *ad hoc* visits. The starting point for the proponents of the Optional Protocol was that all States should be visited on a routine basis but that additional visits could be made outside of that programme if there were grounds for believing that it was appropriate to do so.[62] Predictably, this proved controversial, the concern being that the Subcommittee could decide to conduct frequent *ad hoc* visits to a State, or to a small number of States, whilst leaving the bulk of States Parties relatively untroubled by its attentions. Thus at the end of the first reading, the very question of conducting *ad hoc* visits at all was left open.[63] Two different means of circumscribing the potential impact of *ad hoc* visits then emerged. The first was to call for greater 'precision' in the grounds that could trigger such visits.[64] A second was to focus on the increasingly fashionable idea that in the conduct of all of its business the Subcommittee 'shall . . . be guided by the principles of confidentiality, impartiality, universality and objectivity'.[65] For some, this meant that no State ought to figure more prominently than another in the overall workload of the Subcommittee—there should be no singling out of States. Thus whilst prior consent might be given to *regular* visits, *ad hoc* visits might require such authorization.[66] This, of course, could mean that the Subcommittee might not be able to conduct missions or visits in precisely those States where the evidence suggested that they were most needed.[67]

be dropped and that irrespective of what they were called, 'all missions or visits should be conducted only with the prior consent of the State concerned' (ibid, para 65, statement by the representative of China).

[61] Report of the eighth session, ibid, paras 36–37.

[62] This distinction is found in the 1991 Draft, Article 8(1) and reflects the ECPT, Article 7(1). This distinction forms an important part of the CPT's working practice. As has been seen above, over time, *ad hoc* visits have assumed an increasingly important role and, arguably, now comprise the most significant element of its work.

[63] 1st Reading, Article 8(1) placed the entire question of the Subcommittee conducting *ad hoc* missions in square brackets.

[64] See, for example, Report of the eighth session, E/CN.4/2000/58, paras 33 and 60 (Cuba).

[65] See 2nd Reading, Article 3(3). This was finally reflected in the overarching provision now found in Article 2(3) of OPCAT, which provides that it will be guided 'by the principles of confidentiality, impartiality, non-selectivity, universality and objectivity'. For comment on this see Nowak and McArthur, n 4 above, p 918 who take a rather restrictive and functionally oriented approach to the practical implications of these terms.

[66] For an expression of this view see, for example, Report of the eighth session, E/CN.4/2000/58, para 39.

[67] It might also be wondered quite how such a system would differ from that provided for by UNCAT Article 20, under which the CAT may, if it considers it appropriate, seek the consent of a State to conduct a mission to a country and/or, visit places of detention. Presumably the difference would lie in the 'triggering threshold' which would probably be higher under UNCAT Article 20 than under OPCAT, but this is to enter into areas of very fine distinctions which would be difficult to navigate in practice.

2. Restrictions on access to persons in, or to places of, detention

Even if the Subcommittee were operating within a State Party, it is inevitable that circumstances might arise in which it was simply not prudent or possible for members to be able to have immediate access to places of detention. For example, there might be a riot within a prison, or general civil disorder in an area of the country that made it impractical to travel. No State can absolutely guarantee that access be assured at any time. This is simply common sense. What a State can do is undertake to do all in its power to facilitate access. However, the discussions within the Working Group tended to fix upon the self-evident impossibility of delivering upon absolute assurances of unimpeded access in order to justify an unnecessarily broad range of restrictions. At one extreme, this manifested itself in attempts to exclude entire categories of detention facilities from the scope of the Optional Protocol.[68]

A related argument was that visits to particular institutions or entire missions should be subject to postponement if the State objected to their taking place. This is not in itself objectionable provided that the grounds upon which an objection is made are appropriately cast and the negotiating texts did indeed seem to be suitably restrictive in their scope.[69] However, there was clearly a linkage in the eyes of some with the question of the extent of the general right of access to be exercised by the Subcommittee and this formed another pressure point inhibiting progress.[70]

A further crucial question that became entwined with that of access concerned the powers of the Subcommittee. After setting out a series of facilities which the State is to provide to the Subcommittee,[71] a wide-ranging set of general restrictions was placed on all visits.[72] As if this were not enough, some argued that the entire

[68] Thus it had been argued that Article 1 should contain a subsection to the effect that '[n]othing in this Protocol will be interpreted as allowing: (a) visits to any civil or military facility that the State considers in relation to strategic national interest; or (b) interference in the domestic affairs of Member States in a manner which exceeds the provisions of the present Protocol'. If this approach had been adopted the entire preventive scheme of the Protocol could have been undermined since it comes close to allowing each State to determine the facilities that would be subject to the Subcommittee's activities.

[69] In its final form, the text forming the basis for discussion provided:

> In exceptional circumstances, [in the context of a mission,] the competent authorities of the State Party concerned may make objections to the Subcommittee [or its delegation] against a particular visit [or mission]. Objections may only be made on [urgent and compelling] grounds of national defence, public [or individual] safety, natural disasters, serious disorders in [the place to be visited] [places where persons are detained] ... [which temporarily prevent the carrying out of a visit. The existence of a state of emergency as such should not be invoked by a State Party as a reason to object to a visit.]

Text of the Articles which Constitute the basis for future work, Report of the eighth session, E/CN.4/2000/58, Annex II, Article 13. See Optional Protocol, Article 14(2), for the manner in which these questions were ultimately resolved.

[70] Clearly, if the Subcommittee were to have extensive rights of access to places of detention during visits then there would be pressure for States to have greater scope to prevent such visits from taking place at all. On the other hand, if the Subcommittee's powers of access were to be heavily circumscribed by caveats and exceptions, then some States would be proportionately less concerned about their ability to prevent a mission or visit at the outset.

[71] See 2nd Reading, Article 12(1).

[72] Ibid, Article 12[(2)].

Optional Protocol system should be subject to the national legislation of the State concerned.[73] Although it was claimed that this was necessary to ensure compatibility with the domestic legal order, it was widely believed that this was really intended to facilitate further restrictions upon the functioning of the Subcommittee and was completely unacceptable to many.

Since the text of the Optional Protocol has been finalized there is nothing to be gained by considering the pros and cons of these arguments. How these problems were in fact resolved (or circumvented) will be considered below. The important point is that a dispassionate analysis of the negotiations shows just how little consensus existed around these fundamental questions after so many years of discussion. Despite the rhetorical commitments to the idea of an international visiting mechanism, there was still a deep-seated reluctance in many quarters to accept the fundamental principles that underpinned the draft. This is also borne out by the positions taken on a number of other principal points of contention.

3. The aftermath of a visit or mission

It had long been accepted that the confidential nature of the report and recommendations made by the Subcommittee would form an essential element of the architecture of the Optional Protocol system. But there was no meeting of minds regarding the process that led to the adoption of the report; the nature of the recommendations that the Subcommittee might make; and the circumstances in which the report—or a version of it—might be made public without the consent of the State concerned. There was widespread agreement within the Working Group that reports and recommendations should only be finalized after the views of the State had been taken into account.[74] But what forms of recommendations might the Subcommittee make? A debate emerged that centred on the idea that they should be 'technical' in nature. For some this implied that they should be detailed, focused, and capable of being translated into practical outcomes. For others, it meant that they should not be directed at the general thrust of the State's approach to the subject area concerned.[75] Once again, the malleable potential of such an approach was all too evident.

[73] The so-called 'Article X' provided that 'the provisions of this Protocol shall be applied in accordance with domestic legislation consistent with the Charter of the United Nations and other international obligations of the State'.

[74] 1st Reading, Article 14(1). This might be thought to prolong the process of adopting a report and be chiefly of benefit to the State by giving it a chance to seek to 'water down' the thrust of criticisms that might subsequently be placed in the public domain. However, since the Subcommittee might be able to extract some tangible action as the price for this, it might be a useful bargaining tool and a possible tool of prevention.

[75] See, for example, Report of the eighth session, E/CN.4/2000/58, para 45. There was, however, considerable support for the idea that recommendations should distinguish between those matters which States were themselves to address promptly, and those 'which were supposed to be progressively implemented by the States parties through technical assistance and cooperation financed by the special fund to be set up…' (Report of the eighth session, E/CN.4/2000/58, para 44). No great insight is needed to understand that differentiating between recommendations in this fashion would be problematic. It was, however, difficult to avoid the suspicion that the debate was at least in part a tactic by

Similar disagreements surrounded the question of whether, and under what circumstances, the content of the report might be made public without the consent of the State. It was generally accepted that this should be very much an exceptional procedure, as is in the practice of the CPT,[76] and that publication should be a 'last resort in cases of a failure or refusal to cooperate'.[77] The problem concerned who was to make that decision and the criteria upon which it was to be based. The draft text adopted at the end of the first reading provided that this would be decided by the Committee against Torture,[78] but this raised as many problems as it solved.[79]

4. Reservations

A final problem concerned reservations. It had become almost an article of faith in some quarters that the Optional Protocol should expressly exclude the possibility of reservations, either because of the intrinsic importance of its subject matter or because the essentially procedural nature of the instrument rendered reservations otiose. For some States, particularly the USA, the exclusion of a prohibition on reservations was held up as a non-negotiable *sine qua non*. Once again, it is not necessary to debate the issue—though it should be noted that the final text of the Optional Protocol does indeed exclude reservations.[80] What does need to be noted is that this was yet another difficult issue which stood in the way of progress.

which some sought to shift responsibility for failing to respond to recommendations from the addressee onto the international community, an impression reinforced by the argument that the Subcommittee should only be empowered to make 'feasible' recommendations (See 1st Reading, Article 14(1)).

[76] The CPT has to date issued only six public statements in accordance with the ECPT Article 10(2), two concerning Turkey (see Public Statement of 15 December 1992, CPT/Inf (93)1 and of 6 December 1996, CPT/Inf (96)34), three concerning the situation in the Chechen Republic (see Public Statements of 10 July 2001, CPT/Inf. (2001)15, and of 10 July 2003, CPT/Inf (2002)33 and of 13 March 2007, CPT/INF (2007) 17), and one concerning Greece (see Public Statement of 15 March 2011, CPT/INF (2011) 10).

[77] Report of the eighth session, E/CN.4/2000/58, paras 46–47.

[78] 1st Reading, Article 14(4).

[79] See, for example, Report of the eighth session, E/CN.4/2000/58, para 48. The problem was that the Subcommittee would have to make the initial finding that a threshold of non-compliance had been passed and the very fact of referring the matter to the CAT could itself be seen as a form of sanction. This process also creates a new problem: if the report and recommendations were still confidential to the State and the Subcommittee at this stage, on what material would the CAT base its judgment, or the State its representations? This throws into sharp relief the unresolved question of the relationship between the CAT and the proposed Subcommittee. As will be seen below, this problem remained unresolved in the final text of the Optional Protocol in which the CAT remains the body that authorizes public statements. See Optional Protocol, Article 16(4). There is as yet no indication that this question has had to be addressed or resolved in practice, though doubtless that time will come.

[80] Optional Protocol, Article 30. For discussion see Nowak and McArthur, n 4 above, p 1153. Although it is not necessary to discuss the merits, legally or politically, of either of these positions there might have been something to be said for simply leaving the matter to the outworking of the principles contained in the Vienna Convention on the Law of Treaties under which it could be concluded that reservations would be impermissible as incompatible with the object and purpose of the Optional Protocol, particularly as its provisions are procedural rather than substantive in nature. Other procedural instruments have, however, guarded themselves by the use of 'no reservations clauses' and the entire question remains contentious.

D. An Assessment of the Overall Situation

This, then, was the position prior to the ninth session of the Working Group in February 2001. Although progress had been achieved on many fronts, crucial components of the Optional Protocol remained controversial and this was, ultimately, a reflection of deep-seated political and philosophical differences between the States involved in the negotiation process. The way forward was far from clear. The options seemed to be limited. Finding a compromise between those pressing for a powerful international mechanism and those seeking to limit the intrusive capacity of the proposed body still remained a possibility; however, not only did that possibility seem to be receding but even if such a compromise were achieved it ran the risk of resulting in an Optional Protocol which actually satisfied no-one and which, in consequence, might become a dead letter for the want of adherents. A second option was to mothball the project for the time being and wait for a more auspicious moment to reopen the negotiation—but this was hardly an attractive option given that the proposal had been in circulation for over twenty years and under active negotiation within the Commission and Working Group for the previous eight years.

Moreover, a further issue—perhaps better thought of as an emerging realization—was that even if the Optional Protocol negotiations were to reach a satisfactory conclusion and the instrument to enter into force, a worldwide system of regular visiting was going to be both complex and expensive. Since the level of resources to be made available was likely to be quite limited each State Party was unlikely to be visited particularly often—indeed, a visit was likely to be so rare an experience that it could hardly be expected to significantly enhance the protection of detainees from torture and ill-treatment already provided by other international mechanisms. If this were the case, was there any point in continuing to devote time and resources to the enterprise?

3

The Text of OPCAT

The previous chapters have traced the origins of, the influences on, and the progress towards the adoption of the Optional Protocol until the end of 2000. The purpose of this chapter is two-fold. First, it aims to complete the 'historical narrative' by presenting the dramatic developments and radical re-orientation of the OPCAT project which took place during the ninth session of the Working Group in 2001 and how this was reflected in the Chair's text and the final version of OPCAT. In doing so, it aims to show how the new ideas introduced at that session were driven by the need to address the controversial issues identified in Chapter 2 and to demonstrate how they were finally resolved. The second aim, which is bound up with this, is to present the essential elements of OPCAT as an instrument, setting out the basic obligations which it places upon States Parties. To this end, the section of this chapter which presents the Chair's text will move beyond recounting the outcome of the drafting process and include some analysis, comment, and reflection on OPCAT itself.

Finally, and in order to complete the two-fold task, it is necessary to step back briefly from the text of the instrument itself in order to reflect on two important issues which, though rarely articulated within the drafting process, were always in the background—one of a conceptual nature, the other a more practical question—these being the 'concept' of prevention and the question of the 'standards' which would inform the work of the bodies operating within the OPCAT framework at both the international and national level. There is another reason why it is important to address these issues in the context of this chapter, and this relates to the scope and methodology of this book itself. As has been explained in the Authors' Preface, the book is the product of a research project focusing on perceptions and understandings of OPCAT by a range of key 'stakeholders' in the system which it establishes, through which it has been possible to gauge an understanding of a number of key issues affecting the operation of that system of prevention. To that end, the chapters which follow this will be more 'issue focused' and shaped by the material gained in the course of this research rather than presented as a systematic account of OPCAT as a system. As a result, there is no intention that all matters of potential interest be dwelt upon in those chapters. Yet the questions of 'what is prevention' and 'what are the standards' to be applied in the preventive endeavour are of such significance that they do deserve to be isolated and considered from a more generic standpoint than that permitted by the more empirically-based context of the subsequent chapters.

A. The 2001 Session: New Ideas and New Controversies

Returning to the drafting process, the previous chapter has shown that with the benefit of hindsight it is fair to conclude that by the end of the eighth session of the Working Group the negotiations based on the 1991 Costa Rica Draft had run into the ground.[1] Although a degree of consensus had been reached on a range of largely secondary questions, most of the primary issues were unresolved and positions were drifting further apart with every round of discussion. Crucially, there was no real political will in any quarter to drive the process forward and the only force preventing its collapse in the last four years was an unwillingness on the part of the States involved to be seen to be responsible for putting the negotiations out of their misery.[2] Then, unexpectedly, everything changed.

1. The Mexican Draft

All of the received wisdom surrounding the Optional Protocol was suddenly thrown into disarray when, on the second day of the ninth session, the delegation of Mexico, with the support of the GRULAC, presented its proposal for an alternative model which shifted the focus of the instrument away from the creation and operation of an international visiting mechanism. Instead, it proposed that the primary thrust of the instrument should be an obligation to establish, or maintain, a visiting mechanism at the national level which would fulfil the function that had previously been allocated to the international body.[3] If such a mechanism was not already in existence, States Parties would be obliged to 'establish a national mechanism at the highest possible level' within one year of becoming bound by the Protocol[4] and ensure that its independence was guaranteed[5] and that it was comprised of members possessing appropriate knowledge and skills.[6]

[1] Nowak and McArthur, *The United Nations Convention against Torture: A Commentary* (Oxford, Oxford University Press, 2008), p 7 sum it all up in the following fashion: 'The highly controversial and political discussions between Europe and most Latin American States on the one hand, and a broad variety of other States on the other, concerning primarily issues of State sovereignty, blocked any significant progress during the 1990s.' It is as fair a general summary as it is possible to make. However, the significance of the Optional Protocol being discussed at all ought not to be lost sight of. Even with no agreement, the discussions had the effect of validating the underlying concept.

[2] The NGO community, along with powerful voices within the ICRC, was crucial in applying pressure to keep the process alive during these difficult years. This often took quite innovative forms. By way of example, mention might be made of a major workshop organized by the APT in Geneva in 1999 which sought to compare, and learn lessons from, the experience of visiting mechanisms working in other fields, such as disarmament and under international environmental law. Key players involved in the OPCAT process were invited. The intended message was clear: that if such intrusive mechanisms could work in other spheres—and particularly in sensitive military and nuclear facilities—why could similar mechanisms not be possible in places of detention. See *Visits under Public International Law; Theory and Practice: Proceedings of an APT Workshop, Geneva, September 1999* (Geneva: APT, 2001).

[3] Mexican Draft, Article 1.

[4] Ibid, Article 3.

[5] Ibid, Article 4(1).

[6] Ibid, Articles 4 (2) and (3). The details are largely taken from the previously agreed text, but the need to ensure the adequate representation of ethnic groups and minorities was also included, a particularly important point for a national mechanism.

In order to comply with the Optional Protocol, the national mechanism would have to have certain minimum powers, including the ability to examine the situation of persons deprived of their liberty, to make recommendations to the competent authorities, to propose or comment on draft or existing legislation, and to take other initiatives complementary to the obligations undertaken in consequence of being a party to the UNCAT.[7] Crucially, the draft provided that the national mechanisms 'shall carry out visits' to places where persons are deprived of their liberty and, in order to do so are to be granted an impressive list of rights, embracing unrestricted access to: all relevant information concerning the numbers of persons in detention by or with the acquiescence of public authorities; all information relevant to treatment and conditions of detention; all places and premises where persons are deprived of their liberty; freedom to interview such persons without witnesses or other personnel; freedom to select places to visit; and unrestricted freedom to contact, inform, and meet the Subcommittee.[8]

As the mechanism would be the creation of national law and function on the national level, the question of balancing this intrusive regime against the dictates of State sovereignty ceased to be an issue. Thus a wide-ranging right of access was to be given to the national mechanism, with only a narrowly circumscribed power for the State to restrict visits, this being possible only '... in cases of absolute military necessity or serious disturbances in the place to be visited and then only as an exceptional and temporary measure ...'.[9] There should be no need for the national mechanism's reports and recommendations to be confidential,[10] and, although the draft was rather opaque on this point,[11] this seems to have been the intention.[12]

What was clear was that by placing the responsibility for conducting a programme of preventive visits on the shoulders of a national, rather than an international, mechanism, the Mexican Draft potentially cut through a broad swathe of thorny issues. But the philosophy underpinning the entire Optional Protocol process was that *international* visiting mechanisms should have a vital role to play in assisting in the protection of detainees and it was as clear as anything can be that it would be absolutely impossible to achieve a consensus on an Optional

[7] Ibid, Article 5(a)–(d).
[8] Ibid, Article 6(1)(a)–(g).
[9] Ibid, Article 6(2).
[10] Confidentiality would fly in the face of the common practice of many existing national inspection mechanisms whose reports and recommendations are in the public domain. It would also conflict with the 1991 Paris Principles, endorsed by the UN General Assembly in 1993, which stress the need for such bodies to be able to 'publicize its opinions and recommendations'. See UN General Assembly Res 48/134 on National Institutions for the Promotion and Protection of Human Rights, A/RES/48/134, adopted 20 December 1993, Annex, Methods of Operation (c).
[11] It merely provides that 'national mechanisms shall: (a) inform the competent authorities or their observations and make recommendations to them ...' (Article 7(1)(a)). Given that the minimum powers set out do not go beyond making recommendations addressed to the competent authorities, it could be concluded that States would not be obliged to permit a broader dissemination of observations and recommendations. However, the draft expressly requires that '[n]o personal data shall be made public without the prior consent of the person concerned ...' (Article 7(2)) and this could be taken to imply that other forms of materials might be placed in the public domain.
[12] Mexican Draft, Article 7(1)(b).

Protocol that abandoned this approach altogether. The Mexican proposal therefore provided for the establishment of an international body, still referred to as a Subcommittee of the CAT, which would exercise two discrete functions.

First of all, it would be 'responsible for supporting and supervising the work carried out by national mechanisms'.[13] In order to do so, it would have the power to provide the national mechanisms with assistance and advice.[14] It would also be able to make recommendations to the national mechanism concerning its operations[15] and to the State Party concerning the mechanism's establishment and functioning.[16] Clearly, the key issue here concerned the idea of the international mechanism exercising 'supervision' over the national mechanism. The stronger the powers of supervision, the more likely it would be that concerns relating to sovereignty would resurface. Moreover, the more powerful the element of international supervision, the more resistance there would be to the national mechanism itself enjoying extensive powers, since this might enable the international mechanism to intrude into the domestic sphere by dint of its supervisory capacity. In short, the inevitable corollary of international supervision was a degree of domestic reticence towards the national mechanism and the stronger the level of 'supervision', the weaker the powers of the national mechanism were likely to be. The Mexican Draft sought to strike the balance in favour of relatively weak supervision in order to allow for a relatively robust national mechanism.

The second function of the international body was directly in the spirit of the original Costa Rica Draft. The Mexican Draft empowered the international body to conduct visits itself, but only in two situations. First, there was an opt-in procedure under which States could accept the competence of the Subcommittee to carry out visits itself.[17] Those States not opting in to this procedure would therefore only be subject to scrutiny by their own national mechanism (though subject also to the form of international supervision outlined above). However, if the obligation to create an appropriate national mechanism was not fulfilled, or if that national mechanism proved to be ineffective or a sham, Article 22 of the Mexican Draft provided a 'default' mechanism, according to which

> The States Parties to the present Protocol undertake to accord the Subcommittee all the powers granted to national mechanisms for the prevention of torture under the provisions of articles 5 and 6 if, within two years of ratification of the present Protocol, a national mechanism has not started to visit places of detention.

This completed a radical package that offered a completely different way forward.[18] By placing the focus on national mechanisms, the Mexican Draft went a long way

[13] Mexican Draft, Article 2(1). [14] Ibid, Article 15(3).

[15] Ibid, Article 15(5). [16] Ibid, Articles 15(1) and (6).

[17] Ibid, Article 23. A minimum of five States would need to make declarations before the Article entered into force. This would have created a 'mini-regime' between a sub-set of States Parties which would have submitted themselves to international scrutiny in the manner originally intended.

[18] It was not, however, the only innovative alternative explored. For example, the idea of adopting an approach akin to that of the 1992 European Charter on Regional or Minority Languages (CETS No 148, in force in March 1998) in which different forms of obligation are undertaken from a 'menu' of options, was informally floated and received some discussion, but was not taken up (information on file

to disarm those critics of the Optional Protocol who were concerned at what they saw as the erosion of State sovereignty implicit in the original draft. It also addressed concerns that the human and financial resources that were likely to be made available to the Subcommittee would be so inadequate that the entire enterprise was likely to be ineffectual. Moreover, making the international mechanism an optional procedure meant that there was no need to dilute its powers to the point where it was almost worthless merely to achieve an acceptable compromise.

However, the principal difficulty with the Mexican Draft concerned the Article 22 'default' mechanism. Without such a mechanism, the chasm between the national and international elements of the Optional Protocol would be just too great for those who supported the original proposals calling for international scrutiny, since it would be all too easy for States to either do nothing or to simply create puppet or ineffectual bodies. But for others the very existence of even a residual power was objectionable, and all the more so because it would enable the international mechanism when acting 'in lieu of' the national mechanism to enjoy far greater powers of access and publicity than were likely to have been given to the international body on the basis of the draft previously under consideration.[19]

2. The EU proposals

Inevitably, the Mexican Draft provoked immediate controversy, not to say consternation. Rather than seeing it as a potential tool for breaking the deadlock into which the negotiations had stumbled, some long-standing supporters of the Costa Rica Draft and of a 'strong' international mechanism viewed the Mexican Draft with alarm, being suspicious of the true worth of some National Human Rights Institutions (NHRIs) and concerned at the way in which it relegated the visiting mandate of the international Subcommittee to being, in essence, an 'option within an option'.[20] Irrespective of the merits of these various positions, however, the tabling of the Mexican proposal had the immediate effect of galvanizing those

with the authors). Other alternative approaches involving progressive commitments were also mooted in NGO circles.

[19] Assuming that a default mechanism could have been agreed on in principle, the 'trigger' that activated it then becomes crucial and equally problematic. Under the Mexican Draft, Article 22 this would have been contingent on a failure to establish a functioning body within two years. However, the ineffectual operation of a national mechanism would not be a trigger. Any trigger mechanism that depended upon a subjective evaluation by the Subcommittee was likely to have been controversial since it would appear to be the gatekeeper to its own powers of intervention. Whether it would really have been possible for an international mechanism to conduct an effective visit in a State which refused to accept its legitimacy is doubtful.

[20] The NGO community found itself divided on its response to the Mexican Proposal. The APT (whose original *raison d'être* lay in the development of the original concept), FIACAT (International Federation of Christians against Torture), and IRCT (International Rehabilitation Centre for Victims of Torture) broadly supported the Mexican approach (though not all of its details) whilst Amnesty International and Human Rights Watch (HRW) were more hostile, as was reflected in the separate joint statements made to the Working Group (on file with the authors). The opposition of HRW might at least in part be explained by the fact that they were publishing a critical account of the work of national mechanisms in Africa at the time Mexican Proposal was tabled.

States within the EU Group who were supporters of the Costa Rica Draft but who in previous sessions had been unwilling to be seen to be taking a leading role in resisting its being progressively watered down.

It is difficult to avoid the conclusion that if the original version of the Costa Rica Draft had received such powerful support in 1991—or indeed, in 1980—as it appeared to have in 2001 then the negotiations might have been successfully concluded years earlier. Be that as it may, this resurgence in outward commitment towards the idea of a strong international visiting mechanism resulted in Sweden, on behalf of the EU, itself submitting its 'Proposal of new and revised articles to be included in the original Draft Optional Protocol' which, whilst recognizing that there might be a role for national mechanisms, placed its primary focus firmly on the international Subcommittee.

In its search for some common ground, the Swedish/EU proposal formalized the distinction between the overall 'mission' to a State and a 'visit' to a particular institution or facility within a State where persons were deprived of their liberty.[21] Whilst States would commit themselves to permitting missions to take place[22] they could object to a particular visit, but only on the basis of the same tightly circumscribed grounds as were found in the Mexican Draft for the postponement by a State of a visit by its own national mechanism.[23] The EU proposal also adopted in full the approach to the preparation and exceptional publication of reports by the Subcommittee that was found in the second reading.[24] The only concession made to those who were concerned about the overly intrusive nature of the visiting mandate of the Subcommittee was the insertion of an optional power to delay the commencement of a programme of visits (but not missions) for a maximum of two years after the entry into force of the Optional Protocol for the State in question.[25] This was hardly much of a concession, given the relatively low likelihood of a 'mission'—and therefore of 'visits'—taking place so swiftly after ratification in any case.[26] Finally, the reaction to the use of 'national mechanisms' might best be described as minimalist and hostile. There was a grudging acceptance that States could establish a visiting mechanism at the national level if they wished to do so, but not that they could offer an alternative to the international body. Rather, the EU proposal simply sought to ensure that if such bodies were created they would adhere to certain minimum guarantees of independence and

[21] EU proposal, Article 1(b) and (c).

[22] Missions might, however, be postponed should the CAT be due to conduct a mission under UNCAT, Article 20. See EU proposals, Article 12 (this being also found in 2nd Reading, Article 11).

[23] EU proposal, Article 3(3). Indeed, EU proposal, Article 3(4) included further safeguards that went beyond those provided for in the Mexican Draft and so was even more restrictive.

[24] EU proposal, Article 14 and see above, Chapter 2, Section D.

[25] EU proposal, Article 3(6).

[26] The CPT does now manage to visit States within one year of their becoming a party to the ECPT but in practice the SPT does not appear to seek to do so, doubtless because of the significant number of parties still awaiting a first visit. For example, none of the eight States which ratified in 2009 and 2010 will have been visited by the end of 2011, the visiting programme for which features Brazil which ratified in 2007, Mali which ratified in 2005, and Ukraine which ratified in 2006. This might change once all States Parties have received a visit, or if the nature of SPT visiting were to change—perhaps by making use of much shorter visits than is currently the case.

freedom of action.[27] It saw no positive role for them in the architecture of the preventive system to be created by the Optional Protocol. In many ways, then, the EU proposal offered a more robust international system than that found in the second reading outcome and it was a very long way indeed from the Mexican Draft. Positions were, it seemed, further apart than ever.

B. The Chair's Compromise Text: The Optional Protocol and What It Requires of States

The process that led up to the tabling of the Chair's text has already been outlined, as has the manner in which that text became adopted, with minimal alteration, as the Optional Protocol itself.[28] In presenting the essential elements of the Chair's text this section, in essence, is presenting the Protocol itself and setting out what it requires of States Parties. As was indicated at the opening of this chapter, this section will therefore serve a dual function. First, it will 'complete the story' of the development of the text, using the framework of presentation and tools of analysis which have been used in previous sections. Second, as it does this, it will highlight the key obligations of States Parties and introduce the key operative elements of the Protocol which will be explored in further detail in the subsequent chapters of this book and which primarily draw on an empirical methodology.

In terms of the competing approaches set out in the previous section, the Chair's text leaned heavily towards the EU conception of a strong international mechanism, but complemented this with an obligation to establish equally strong National Preventive Mechanisms (NPMs). In short, it borrowed and blended the more robust elements of both proposals and packaged them together in a manner which was sufficiently balanced to win support from (or, more accurately, avoid rejection by) either of the principal camps. Opposition to the package was limited to the die-hard opponents of the entire idea of the Optional Protocol, in particular the USA which produced a further variant scheme but which, as has already been noted, arrived so late in the day and was so far removed from any possible point of consensus that it received no serious scrutiny as an alternative model.[29]

As adopted, the Optional Protocol has seven parts. Part One sets out the general principles underlying the instrument. Article 1 sets out its fundamental objective, which is to 'establish a system of regular visits undertaken by independent

[27] EU proposal, Article 15.

[28] See above, Chapter 2, Section A.

[29] See above, Chapter 2, n 17. This proposal would have reduced the Subcommittee to a mere cipher, with a heavily circumscribed mandate to assist the CAT, national mechanisms, and States Parties at their request (Article 2). Similarly, it was proposed that national mechanisms 'may' be established under Article 1(2), that is, it contained no obligation that they exist. For a hostile critique of the Optional Protocol as adopted, written by a member of the UN delegation who presented and supported the US proposal, see Dennis, M, 'Human Rights in 2002; The Annual Session of the UN Commission on Human Rights and the Economic and Social Council' (2003) 97 *AJIL* 364 at 371–374.

international and national bodies' to places where persons are deprived of their liberty. As this makes clear, the Protocol seeks to achieve this by use of both international and national mechanisms and this is taken up by the following Articles: Article 2 providing for the establishment of an 'International Preventive Mechanism', the Subcommittee, whilst Article 3 obliges States to 'set up, designate or maintain at the domestic level one or several visiting bodies for the prevention of torture . . . (. . . national preventive mechanisms)'. Article 4(1) then provides that '[e]ach State Party shall allow visits . . . by the mechanisms referred to in Articles 2 and 3 to any place under its jurisdiction or control where persons are or may be deprived of their liberty . . . '. This, then, introduces the fundamental elements of the Protocol scheme: visits to places of detention to be undertaken by both national and international bodies.

Article 4(2) also goes on to define the scope of 'deprivation of liberty', which embraces 'any form of detention or imprisonment or the placement of a person in a public or private custodial setting, from which this person is not permitted to leave at will by order of any judicial, administrative or other authority'. This covers a very broad range of places, including not only all forms of police stations and prisons (including military detention facilities) but other places where people are detained by public order such as immigration centres and psychiatric hospitals. The list is not closed. Moreover, Article 4(1) extends the obligation to permit visits to places in which it is suspected that persons might be detained, as well as to places where persons are being held, or are suspected of being held, not by the State itself but with its consent or acquiescence. This, then, represents a broad approach to the concept of places of detention and deprivation of liberty.[30]

Moreover, the Optional Protocol puts all such places under both a national and international spotlight. It will be recalled that under the Mexican Draft the international Subcommittee would only be able to exercise a power to visit if the State in question had made an express declaration accepting its competence to do so or, if it had not done so, under the 'default clause' should an NPM not have been established, or not be functioning as it ought. The text of the Optional Protocol, however, makes acceptance of both the international and national mechanisms compulsory, except that under Part V of the Protocol (Article 24), a State may make a declaration upon ratification[31] postponing the implementation

[30] But cf Nowak and McArthur, n 1 above, p 932 who argue that whilst the definition of a place of detention in Article 4(1) is broad, the definition of 'deprivation of liberty' in Article 4(2) is narrower because whereas implied consent or acquiescence is all that is needed under Article 4(1) for a place to be a place of detention, an express act is needed by the public authority before a person can be deprived of their liberty under Article 4(2). The latter words of Article 4(2) are potentially troublesome but a purposive approach to interpretation allows the conclusion that those actually held in places of detention, as defined in Article 4(1), may also be considered to be persons 'deprived of their liberty' for the purposes of Article 4(2) since to do otherwise makes little sense: a person held in a place of detention can hardly be said not to be deprived of their liberty because that detention is unauthorized. Support for this approach is found in the APT, *Manual for Prevention*, p 73. The scope of Article 4 will be considered in detail in Chapter 4.

[31] There was a significant discrepancy between differing language versions of Article 24. The English, Arabic, Chinese, and French language versions provided that States Parties may make a declaration postponing the implementation of their obligations under either Part III or Part IV of the

of its obligations in respect of either the international or the national mechanism for a period of up to three years.[32] This 'opt out' provision was one of the key elements of the compromise package which comprises the Optional Protocol and it extends both in time and in scope the idea which was found in the EU proposal, which was to allow a two-year delay in the competence of the international mechanism to visit places of detention in the context of a mission. Despite being so major an issue in the negotiations and being so important an element of the final 'deal' relatively few States have in fact made Declarations under Article 24, and all of these have involved delaying obligations under Part IV, the NPM, rather than relating to their obligations under Part III concerning the Subcommittee.[33] This is perhaps unsurprising. If a State does not feel itself ready to assume its full range of obligations it is more likely that it will simply delay ratification, rather than ratify with a Declaration deferring its obligations for so comparatively short a period of time. The real attraction of Article 24, however, was that it provided a means of making both the national and international mechanisms, ultimately, 'compulsory' under the Optional Protocol and so had the great advantage of rendering the controversial 'default clause' redundant, meaning that the international mechanism would not have to pass judgment on the capacity or competence of the NPM in order to undertake a visit. Negotiating the 'trigger' for such interventions would have been extremely troublesome and an issue on which the Chair's text could easily have floundered had it been constructed in such a way as to require a clause of that nature.

Parts II and III of the Optional Protocol provide for the establishment and functioning of the Subcommittee. Part II (Articles 5–10) deals with establishment of the Subcommittee and the election of members and largely reflects the consensus reached during the second reading of the draft text prior to the 2001 session of the Informal Working Group—that is to say, that it would initially be comprised of ten members nominated and elected by States Parties, increasing to twenty-five

present Protocol 'upon ratification' (that is, at the time of ratification) whereas the Spanish and Russian language versions provided that they might do so at any point 'after ratification'. In 2010, at the request of the SPT, the UN Office of Legal Affairs expressed the view that the former was the proper reading of the text and the official versions of the Spanish and Russian texts were corrected, as of April 2010 and with retrospective effect, to reflect that understanding. See SPT, Fourth Annual Report of the Subcommittee on Prevention of Torture and Other Cruel, Inhuman or Degrading Treatment or Punishment (April–December 2010), CAT/C/46/2, 7 January 2011. See also n 33 below.

[32] Optional Protocol, Article 24. A further postponement of up to two years might be authorized by the UN Committee against Torture, this being one of the few specific roles that the CAT has under the terms of the Optional Protocol.

[33] Four States have made declarations under Article 24, three at the time of ratification and one subsequently. Germany made a declaration upon ratification in December 2008 for an unspecified period of time. It has, however, designated its NPM within the maximum three-year period. Romania postponed its obligations for a three-year period when ratifying in July 2009, as did Montenegro when ratifying in February 2009. Kazakhstan did not make a declaration when it ratified in October 2008 but according to the UN depositary it made such a declaration for an unspecified period in February 2010 which was accepted in May 2010 given the lack of objections from other States Parties. It will be recalled that there was a discrepancy between the Russian and English texts which has now been resolved in favour of the English version, meaning that such a situation will not arise in future. See also n 31 above.

following the 50th ratification of the Optional Protocol.[34] Part III (Articles 11–16) deals with the mandate of the Subcommittee and its *modus operandi* and reflects the manner in which the various controversies previously identified as being stumbling blocks at the time of the tabling of the Mexican proposal at the 2001 session were finally resolved. As these provisions are central to the work of the Subcommittee, they will be outlined at this point and explored in greater detail in subsequent sections of this book. Part IV (Articles 17–23) addresses the NPMs and so is novel, in the sense that it does not build on the outcome of prior discussion within the Working Group but represents the Chair's assessment of the place that such bodies should assume in the architecture of the Optional Protocol in the light of the Mexican Draft and subsequent consultations. The core of the Optional Protocol lies in the interplay between the international and national mechanisms, and essential features of Parts III and IV will be presented in the following subsections.

1. The Subcommittee and its visiting mandate

In its final form the Optional Protocol vests the Subcommittee with three discrete fields of competence.[35] Under Article 11(a) the Subcommittee shall '[v]isit the places referred to in article 4 [places where persons are deprived of their liberty] and make recommendations to States Parties concerning the protection of persons deprived of their liberty from torture and other cruel, inhuman or degrading treatment or punishment'. Under Article 11(b) it has a second sphere of competence in relation to the NPM and under Article 11(c) it is mandated to cooperate with other international, regional, and national mechanisms and institutions for the prevention of torture and other forms of ill-treatment. This section will look at the first of these, the second being considered in the following section concerning the NPMs. The third of these competencies will be considered later in a discrete chapter of this work.[36] A range of key outstanding questions relating to the *modus operandi* of the Subcommittee were identified above and narrowed down to a number of central issues and these will now be used as a framework for the presentation and further analysis of the visiting mandate of the Subcommittee.[37]

[34] The evolution of these articles has already been considered above and will not be repeated here. The practice associated with them will be considered in subsequent chapters.

[35] The SPT itself has stressed that it 'regards the three elements of its mandate as essential for the prevention of torture and other cruel, inhuman or degrading treatment or punishment'. See First Annual Report, para 8; Second Annual Report, para 8; Third Annual Report, para 12, referring to the three 'pillars' of its mandate. The 'three pillars of its [the SPT's] mandate' are not to be confused with the 'twin pillars' of OPCAT as a system, these being the NPMs and the SPT itself.

[36] See below, Chapter 6.

[37] Four areas of controversy were highlighted above. The fourth issue concerned the permissibility of reservations. Whilst the EU proposal contained a 'no reservations' clause (Article 19bis) the Mexican Draft did not. It has already been noted that Article 30 of the Optional Protocol does indeed follow the EU proposals on this point and prohibits the making of reservations and so it is unnecessary to consider the issue again at this point.

(a) The visiting programme

The main issues concerning the visiting programme was whether there was a need for express consent to a visit taking place, what forms of visit there might be and whether there was a distinction to be drawn between 'missions' and visits'. In its final form, the suggested distinction between 'missions' and 'visits' was abandoned and the Optional Protocol now provides in Article 13(1)[38] that the Subcommittee 'shall establish, at first by lot,[39] a programme of regular visits'.

Article 13(2) then provides that 'after consultations' the Subcommittee shall 'notify the States Parties of its programme in order that they may, without delay, make the necessary practical arrangement for the visits to be conducted'. It is unclear quite what 'consultations' are envisaged. Does it mean that the States Parties will be able to discuss and influence the programme of regular visits as determined under Article 13(1)? Presumably not. Does it mean that the actual implementation of that programme is to be undertaken after consultations with each State Party? Again, presumably not. It seems that the 'consultations', in reality, relate to those within the Subcommittee itself. It may well be that this was included as a 'nod in the direction' of those who still hankered after the need for a State Party to give its express consent to a visit, holding out the prospect of 'prior consultation' over the modalities of conducting a visit.[40] However, this would seem to be a chimera. The Optional Protocol is clear enough that regular visits can occur without any need for specific prior consent from the State to be visited and the purpose of notification is to allow the State to facilitate visits, not prevent them from occurring. It is equally clear, however, that the Subcommittee is unlikely to be able to conduct 'unannounced' visits to

[38] It must be said that the Protocol addresses this in quite a complex fashion. As has been seen, according to Article 1 the objective of the Optional Protocol is to establish a system of regular visits to places where persons are deprived of their liberty and this is to include visits by both the NPM and the Subcommittee. Article 4 then defines places of detention and persons deprived of their liberty. Part III concerns the Subcommittee and Article 11(a) requires it to 'visit the places referred to in Article 4' whilst Article 13 finally provides that 'the Subcommittee on Prevention shall establish, initially by lot, a programme of regular visits to the States Parties in order to fulfil its mandates as established in Article 11'.

[39] This, it should be noted, has not been taken to apply to the ordering of the entire programme of regular visits but to the choice of countries to be visited in its first year of operation. Nowak and McArthur, n 1 above, p 1027 say that this only applies to the first year programme, but there is no real textual or drafting basis for this, other than that this is what the CPT did when it was established. A ballot was conducted at the first session of the Subcommittee and the three countries drawn were Mauritius, the Maldives, and Sweden. See First Annual Report, para 14. One might reasonably wonder whether these would have been chosen as the initial tranche to be visited had it not been for the use of a ballot. Moreover, why choose three? In its first year the SPT in fact only managed to visit the first two of these States Parties, with the visit to Sweden taking place the following year. In the First Annual Report the SPT says it thought it ought to be undertaking eight visits a year, so why not draw the first eight? Be that as it may, the process is now said to be 'reasoned'. See First Annual Report, para 15. The selection of countries to be visited is considered further in Chapter 5 below.

[40] See, for example, Nowak and McArthur, n 1 above, p 1028 who suggest that the requirement of prior notification was a compromise formula, but falling short of requiring prior consent.

countries, in the sense that the State has no inkling at all that a visit is in prospect.[41]

A further—but far more critical—question is, however, still left open in the final text of the Optional Protocol: can the Subcommittee conduct unannounced visits to places of detention during the course of a regular visit, as is the practice of the CPT?[42] Article 14(1)(e) grants to the Subcommittee '[t]he liberty to choose the places it wants to visit . . . ' but this falls some considerable distance short of providing for a right of unannounced access to all places of detention. Article 14(3) provides for 'unrestricted access' to places of detention, but this does not necessarily mean 'unannounced access'. Moreover, since Article 13(2) requires States Parties to 'make the necessary practical arrangement for the visits to be conducted' it could be argued that this should be taken to apply not just to the visit to the country in general but also to visits to particular places of detention. It could therefore be argued that although it was obliged to grant 'unrestricted access' to the Subcommittee, a State was entitled to know of the places to be visited in advance in order that it might make such arrangements.[43] It has already been seen that, contrary to general assumptions, the ECPT is just as opaque on this point as is the final text of the Optional Protocol.[44] The difference is that the practice of the CPT, which certainly includes unannounced visits, had put this issue into stark relief and so it assumed a greater significance in the drafting process of OPCAT. It is, then, hardly surprising that a compromise text of this nature should be no less categorical on so significant a question—and, as with the CPT, the practice of States Parties under OPCAT has been to respect the right of the Subcommittee to access places of detention on an unannounced basis.

Probably the most difficult issue connected to visiting, however, concerned the capacity of the Subcommittee to be able to make visits outside of its regular programme. As has been seen, the CPT had the capacity to make short, '*ad hoc*' or 'follow-up visits' with very little notice and it was widely considered to be essential that the Subcommittee had similar powers. This is one area where the final text is considerably weaker than might have been expected. Rather than permit such visits as of right, Article 13(4) confines itself to providing that once a regular visit has taken place, it is possible for the Subcommittee to '*propose* a short follow-up visit to a regular visit'.[45] To whom this proposal is to be made is quite unclear from the text: it is certainly open to the interpretation that a follow-up visit may only take place with the express consent of the State concerned, though this is not

[41] Thus, for example, visas (or a visa waiver) may be necessary in order to enter the country. This largely precludes 'complete surprise', which would in any case normally not be conducive to a profitable visit.

[42] The CPT informs the State of a number of the places it intends to visit a few days before it arrives, but reserves the right to visit other places of detention in addition to these and it invariably does so in the course of its regular visits.

[43] The wording of the ECPT is much less equivocal, providing that the CPT might 'at any time visit any place' once it has notified a State of its intention to visit to it. See ECPT, Article 8(1).

[44] See above, Chapter 1 at nn 84–88.

[45] Optional Protocol, Article 13(4) (emphasis added).

an inevitable reading of a deliberately opaque provision.[46] It is worth noting that, in practice, the Subcommittee has begun to announce intentions to undertake unspecified follow-up visits as a part of its planned programme of work, and such visits have indeed been undertaken.[47]

To return to the problems that needed to be addressed, it can be seen that the text of the Optional Protocol rejected the need for prior consent for regular visits, but did so at the expense of *ad hoc* and follow-up visits, the former being excluded from the express scope of the Optional Protocol and the latter being potentially subject to consent. Although the distinction between 'missions' and 'visits' is not found in a formal sense within the text, its spirit lurks beneath and may give rise to some difficulties, as in the question of whether the text permits unannounced visits to places of detention, as opposed to unrestricted access to such places. Consent-based questions, then, continue to lie close to the surface of a text which, at first sight, seemed to have resolved these debates in favour of the international mechanism.

(b) Other restrictions on access to places of detention

As has been seen above, whilst it was generally accepted that visits to particular places of detention might be subject to postponement, some States within the Working Group which accepted that the Subcommittee should generally have a right to visit a country without prior consent had also argued that a State should be able to postpone the entire visit in certain circumstances. Given that the Mexican Draft did not provide for an automatic right for the international mechanism to visit, it had no cause to include this extreme provision. As such a right to postpone an entire visit was not found in the EU proposals either (albeit for different reasons), it was easy to predict that the Chair's compromise text would also not permit the State to postpone a visit in its entirety. As a result, the Optional Protocol limits itself to the general approach found in the ECPT, which is to permit States to object to a visit to a particular place of detention, 'on urgent and compelling grounds of national defence, public safety, natural disaster or serious disorder in the place to be visited, which temporarily prevent the carrying out of such a visit'.[48] This phraseology is not entirely free from ambiguity but its general thrust is clear enough: States may not prevent, they may only postpone a visit. Moreover, the reasons for the postponement must be specific to the place of detention and be of a nature that makes it imprudent or impractical for the visit to be carried out. This is underscored by the final clause of Article 14(2) which makes it clear that the mere fact that there is a state of emergency within a country

[46] Nowak and McArthur, n 1 above, p 1027 assert that the decision to undertake a follow-up is 'in the exclusive competence' of the Subcommittee. It is, however, difficult to locate the evidence for such a view.

[47] See for example, Third Annual Report, Annex IV, announcing a 'possible follow up visit, country to be determined'. A follow-up visit to Paraguay was in fact undertaken in September 2010, the regular visit having taken place in March 2009. At the time of writing, this remains the only follow-up visit.

[48] Optional Protocol, Article 14(2).

'shall not be invoked... as a reason to object to a visit' and there will be a heavy burden upon a State wishing to restrict the right of access on these grounds.

Given this robust approach to restrictions upon access in exceptional circumstances, it is not surprising that the final text rejected the idea that some entire categories of detention facilities be removed from the scope of the Optional Protocol. However, it must also be recalled that the programme of visits is more heavily circumscribed than many would have wished, and so the need for extensive exceptions to a probing regime of access was thereby lessened. It should also be remembered that Article 24 gives States the option to choose to exclude the international visiting mechanism in its entirety for up to a three years, though in fact no State has chosen to do so. Nevertheless, the outcome as regards restrictions upon access certainly leans towards the interests of the visiting mechanisms in enhancing access, rather than towards those of States which might be seeking to restrict or exclude it.[49]

(c) The aftermath

The third of the major areas of controversy concerned the capacities of the Subcommittee following a visit, with the principal issues being the role of the State in relation to the preparation of the report, the forms of recommendations that might be made, whether the report is confidential, and the circumstances under which the report might become public. Given the controversy over these questions in the Working Group, the robust and caveat-free nature of the final text relating to these issues might come as a surprise. Article 16 of the Optional Protocol simply provides that the Subcommittee is to 'communicate its recommendations confidentially to the State Party and, if relevant, to the national mechanism'. There is clearly no requirement for prior consultation with the State over the content of the report despite this having been the consensus position in the Working Group and reflected in the EU proposal.[50] The debates surrounding the nature of the recommendations that the Subcommittee might make also find no reflection in the final text: they are given a seemingly free hand. There was never any question of the reports being anything other than confidential and this remains the case.[51] As with the CPT, however, the report may be published by the Subcommittee at the request of the State concerned and, if the State makes a part of the report public, the Subcommittee may publish the report in full.[52] Moreover, OPCAT contains an important and innovative provision by which it may pass on the recommendations

[49] A further issue concerned restrictions upon the activities of the Subcommittee whilst undertaking a visit. Once again, the text rejected the idea of there being general restrictions, or of making the work of the Subcommittee 'subject' to national legislation, as some had wished—although Article 36(a) does require that members when conducting a visit '*respect* the laws and regulations of the visited state' (emphasis added), the scope of which is not clear. For a helpful discussion see Nowak and McArthur, n 1 above, pp 1188–1189.

[50] EU proposal, Article 14.

[51] Optional Protocol, Article 16(1).

[52] Ibid, Article 16(2).

and observations to the national mechanism should it consider it relevant to do so.[53] This certainly leans towards a perhaps surprising lessening of the bands of confidentiality.

Once again, it is likely that this surprisingly liberal approach is a consequence of the conjunction of the two texts having moved the ground of debate into new areas. Under the Mexican Draft the focus was on national mechanisms where there was clearly no need to restrict the forms of recommendations made on grounds of national sovereignty. Its minimalist approach to the international mechanisms meant that these questions were not looked at in detail. The EU proposal, however, mirrored the more robust ECPT approach. When put together in the Chair's text, the net effect was both to simplify the provisions and, in effect, to make them significantly more robust than would have seemed possible on the basis of the second reading outcome and previous discussions in the Working Group.

A final question to consider concerns the circumstances in which reports might be made public and on this point the text of the Optional Protocol does reflect the mood within the Working Group, which was that this would only be possible by a decision of the Committee against Torture itself, at the express request of the Subcommittee.[54] It seems implicit in this that the Subcommittee would be entitled to reveal its report and recommendations to the Committee against Torture, though whether this would be possible in all cases or only in those in which it was requesting permission to publish or make a public statement is not at all clear. This is yet another facet of one of the principal unresolved questions of the Optional Protocol—the relationship between the Subcommittee and the Committee against Torture, more on which will be said below.

2. The National Preventive Mechanisms

As has been explained, the emergence of the NPMs as a component of the Optional Protocol was the key to the ultimate success of the process. Although both the Mexican Draft and the EU proposals accorded NPMs very different roles within the structure of the Optional Protocol, their place in the final text was a foregone conclusion. The idea that national mechanisms have a role to play in protecting human rights was hardly controversial in the field of torture prevention at the time.[55] The novelty was to require States to utilize such mechanisms in combating torture as a matter of international legal obligation, rather than as a matter of

[53] Ibid, Article 16(1).

[54] Optional Protocol, Article 16(4).

[55] See, for example, Interim Report of the UN Special Rapporteur on Torture to the General Assembly, A/57/173, paras 36–45, and the Joint Declaration (appended as an annex to that report) issued on 26 June 2002 by the Special Rapporteur, the Committee against Torture, the Board of Trustees of the UN Voluntary Fund for the Victims of Torture, and the UN High Commissioner for Human Rights, urging support for the adoption of the Optional Protocol and endorsing its twin-pillar approach. The same bodies welcomed the adoption of the Optional Protocol in their Joint Statement of 26 June 2003, which encouraged States to ratify and establish national visiting mechanisms (see Annex I to the Interim Report of the Special Rapporteur on Torture to the General Assembly, A/58/120).

exhortation. As has been seen, whilst some thought the inclusion of NPMs in the draft of the Optional Protocol was merely a tactic by which to diminish the need for an international visiting mechanism, it quickly became apparent that there was an important role for both national and international mechanisms: both could be used as different means to a common end, mutually reinforcing each other and united by their being the product of a single legal instrument. But what, exactly, was a 'national preventive mechanism'? This is addressed in Part IV of the Protocol, the basics of which will be outlined here. The details of the expectations regarding NPMs, and the experience of operationalizing Part IV of the Protocol, will be considered in further detail later.[56]

It cannot be stressed sufficiently that the Optional Protocol does not require that State Parties establish any new human rights bodies or mechanisms. Rather, Article 17 requires that States 'maintain, designate or establish' within one year[57] of the entry into force of the Protocol[58] 'one or several independent national preventive mechanisms for the prevention of torture'. This was an essential element of the compromise package, as those States with such bodies would not have accepted any obligation that would have required them to duplicate what was already in existence. As a result, whether it is necessary for a State to create a new body depends upon how comprehensive a system of inspectoral bodies[59] is currently in place, their powers, and their independence.

Article 18 obliges the State to guarantee the 'functional independence' of the mechanisms and their personnel, and that their personnel have the abilities and resources necessary to carry out their functions.[60] Those functions are set out in Article 19 and, unsurprisingly, focus on the need to ensure that the mechanisms can exercise a preventive mandate through conducting regular visits to places of detention as defined in Article 4[61] and to make recommendations to the national authorities, based on UN norms, concerning the places, conditions, and forms of treatment encountered in the course of visits.[62] In addition, the NPMs are also to

[56] See below, Chapter 6.

[57] The period of one year was found in the Mexican Draft, Article 3 and carried over into the Chair's Draft and final text. It offers States which have not yet been able to establish or identify an NPM that accords with the OPCAT criteria a period in which to do so, during which they might be able to benefit from the assistance of the Subcommittee which in accordance with Article 11(b)(i) may 'advise and assist States Parties, where necessary, in their establishment'.

[58] Unless a Declaration has been made under Article 24 postponing the implementation of the obligations under Part IV.

[59] It is also worth noting here that the Optional Protocol does not require States to identify a single NPM, but permits the co-existence of 'one or several' such mechanisms within each State. As will be seen later, however, the tendency is to create a single NPM, or at the very least to have a single point of coordination of the various NPMs. All this tends to encourage the belief that a single mechanism or entity is to fulfil this function.

[60] In doing so, States 'shall give due consideration to the Principles relating to the Status and Functioning of National Institutions for the Promotion and Protection of Human Rights'. This is a reference to the 'Paris Principles' (see above n 10) which provide a starting point for the examination of the functional independence of the NPMs.

[61] Ibid, Article 19(a).

[62] Ibid, Article 19(b).

have a more general and more broad-ranging power to 'submit proposals and observations concerning existing or draft legislation'.[63] This takes the mandate of the NPM beyond that of a 'visiting body' by requiring that it also have systemic functions more akin to those more usually accorded to NHRIs than inspectoral bodies.

The State is then obliged to 'examine the recommendations of the national preventive mechanism and enter into a dialogue with it on possible implementation measures'.[64] This wording echoes that of Article 12(d) which requires the State to examine the recommendations of the Subcommittee and enter into dialogue with it. This is significant, since it means that the role of the NPM is not only to report and recommend, but also to engage in active follow-up of its recommendations with the State. Likewise, the State is required to respond to its recommendations in the same manner as it is to respond to the Subcommittee. It is also important to note that, unlike the output of the Subcommittee, the reports and recommendations of the national mechanisms are not said to be confidential. Since these reports are the product of a national system and not of the international body, there was no good reason why they should be confidential—and every reason why they should not be. Moreover, the Optional Protocol expressly requires that States publish and disseminate the Annual Reports of NPMs.[65] Clearly, it would be wrong to attempt to infer from this that either the Annual Report or other reports and recommendations should not be made public by the NPM itself.

Finally, the Optional Protocol expressly provides for a number of essential capacities that NPMs must enjoy if they are to be properly configured in accordance with OPCAT. These largely mirror the requirements for effective access to persons and places of detention which are to be enjoyed by the Subcommittee,[66] with Articles 20(a)–(c) providing for access to information concerning numbers of persons in, and places of, detention, access to all information referring to the treatment of detainees and of their conditions of detention and, critically, 'access to all places of detention and their installations and facilities'.[67] It also ensures that it has the opportunity to interview detainees, and any others who they believe have

[63] Ibid, Article 19(c).

[64] Ibid, Article 22.

[65] Ibid, Article 23. As Nowak and McArthur, n 1 above, p 1099 point out, it is not said to whom such reports should be addressed or what their focus should be. The basic question is whether the annual reports are those of the NPMs to the State concerning their findings, or whether what is envisaged is a report on the work of the NPM *as an NPM* and which would therefore cover rather different ground. As will be seen, this is a matter on which practice varies.

[66] Ibid, Articles 14(1)(a)–(e). The principal difference between Articles 14 and 20 is the omission of the word 'unrestricted' in the Article 20 equivalents. Thus whilst the Subcommittee enjoys 'unrestricted access' the NPM is only to be accorded 'access'. The Mexican Draft (Article 6) used the expression 'unrestricted access' but also allowed for exceptional restrictions. Whilst an exceptional restrictions clause is still found in Article 14, it is not found in the final version of Article 20. The net result is that whereas the Subcommittee has, in principle, 'unrestricted access', but subject to an exceptional limitation clause, the NPM only has 'access' but is not subject to limitation. Whilst the Chair's text doubtless reflects a compromise necessary to secure consensus, it is difficult to imagine that this difference will be of any great practical significance, though it would have been preferable for the wording to have been the same in both articles. See also Nowak and McArthur, n 1 above, p 1090–1091.

[67] Ibid, Article 20(d).

relevant information, in private and, in something of a 'belt and braces' measure, the Optional Protocol also confirms that the NPM enjoys 'the liberty to choose the places they want to visit and the persons it wants to interview'.[68]

Finally, the Optional Protocol requires that the NPMs have 'the right to have contacts with the Subcommittee on Prevention, to send it information and to meet with it'.[69] This is the counterpart to Article 11(b)(ii) which mandates the Subcommittee to '[m]aintain direct, if necessary confidential, contact with the national preventive mechanisms'. The web of relationships is then completed by Article 12(c), under which the States Parties undertake to 'encourage and facilitate contacts between the Subcommittee on Prevention and the national preventive mechanisms'. The obvious question is, of course, what is the purpose of these contacts, and the answer to this lies in the mandate of the Subcommittee. It may be recalled that one of the issues arising from the Mexican Draft was the degree of international scrutiny that the NPMs would be subject to. There was a concern that the Subcommittee could end up being as—or more—concerned with the manner in which the NPMs performed their functions as it was with the treatment of detainees and were this to be the case it could become a distraction from its core mission.[70]

In the final text, the role of the Subcommittee is projected as being that of general oversight, exercising something of a paternalistic interest in the operation and functioning of the mechanisms. As has been seen, in general terms, it is to '[a]dvise and assist States Parties, when necessary, in their establishment'.[71] As has already been noted, since States generally have a period of up to one year within which to designate their NPMs, there will often be a window of opportunity for the Subcommittee to engage with States Parties to the Protocol over the establishment of mechanisms appropriate for designation. But it is not a very large window and in reality most States which ratify have already considered this issue in some depth beforehand.[72] The Subcommittee is, therefore, just as likely to be advising States on the need to fill gaps, or to amend or strengthen the mandates of existing NPMs as it is to be advising on their designation. This is reflected in the second and third elements of the Subcommittee's mandate relative to the NPMs, which involve it offering them 'training and technical assistance with a view to strengthening their capacities' and 'to advise and assist them in the evaluation of the needs and the means necessary to strengthen the protection of persons deprived of their liberty . . .'.[73]

[68] Ibid, Article 20(e).

[69] Ibid, Article 20(d).

[70] Of course, this point of view begs the question of how the Subcommittee's core mission should be exercised. It could well be that focusing on the work of NPMs might be equally as significant as undertaking visits, and Article 11, setting out the mandate of the Subcommittee, certainly implies this.

[71] Ibid, Article 11(b)(i).

[72] As will be seen below, it is also the case that a great deal of activity now takes place concerning NPMs and most States prior to ratification have had contacts with Civil Society, and, through this, members of the Subcommittee itself.

[73] Ibid, Article 11(b)(ii) and (iii). This language rather suggests that the NPMs might be relatively weak and in need of development. This reflects the concern of some that national mechanisms were little more than a 'fig leaf' behind which States could hide. In truth, many NPMs are significantly more robust and influential domestically than the Subcommittee.

This likelihood is rendered a near certainty by the final element of the Subcommittee's mandate, which is to 'make recommendations and observations to the States parties with a view to strengthen the capacity and mandate of the National Preventive Mechanisms . . . '.[74]

3. Conclusion

The work of the Subcommittee in relation to NPMs is considered in detail later in this book. For the moment, however, enough has been said to demonstrate the profound impact that the Mexican Draft had on the final shape and structure of the Optional Protocol as a whole, and also on the mandate and *modus operandi* of the Subcommittee itself. It is fair to say that the implications of incorporating NPMs into the OPCAT framework was not been fully appreciated when the instrument was adopted. Whilst it certainly marked a significant improvement in the instrument as a whole, its implications for the practical work of the Subcommittee were substantially underestimated. It is difficult to avoid the conclusion that whilst the inclusion of NPMs added another major stream of activity to its mandate, for many the real thrust of the Subcommittee's work remained visiting States Parties and issuing its own recommendations. It is worth noting that the NPM dimension of OPCAT, and of the Subcommittee's mandate, had no parallel in the ECPT and so those who looked to the CPT for inspiration and guidance on how the Optional Protocol might work in practice tended to overlook the potential impact of its workload regarding NPMs prior to its entry into force. Whilst civil society was very active regarding the obligations of States concerning NPMs, it was only once the Subcommittee was established that the scale of the Subcommittee's tasks in relation to NPMs really became apparent.

C. The 'What' and the 'With What' Questions

At the beginning of this chapter the point was made that there were two issues which also needed to be addressed as a precursor to the chapters which are to follow, these being the 'concept' of prevention and the standards to be used in the preventive endeavour—questions which might rather glibly be called the 'what' and the 'with what' questions respectively. Given that the purpose of OPCAT is 'prevention' through the issuance of recommendations based on visits to places of deprivation of liberty, a proper understanding of both the 'concept' and the 'standards' to be applied might seem to be central to OPCAT and what it sets out to achieve. They certainly figured highly in initial thinking regarding OPCAT once

[74] Ibid, Article 11(b)(iv). There is something of a paradox in this final provision. The State is to ensure the functional independence of the NPMs, yet it is also to engage in a dialogue with the Subcommittee concerning its capacities and mandate. This might be unobjectionable, but when the Subcommittee addresses the State concerning the manner in which its NPMs are functioning, it must be careful to avoid encouraging the very form of State interference that the Optional Protocol is seeking to guard against.

the text had been concluded and as it entered into force. Yet as will be seen, as time has passed there has—perhaps paradoxically—become less and less interest in these questions and far more interest in more 'operational' dimensions of the system, and this is reflected in both the structure and the content of the chapters which are to follow. As a result, these questions have tended to slip from view. There are in fact good reasons for this, which relate to the nature of OPCAT as an essentially procedural instrument which does not establish any new normative commitments for States Parties. The operation of these procedures does, of course, have normative implications for States Parties but, for the moment at least, these are perceived as being of secondary importance compared to the establishment of effective NPMs and the functioning of the Subcommittee in accordance with the requirements of OPCAT as an instrument. The remainder of this section—and chapter—will illustrate this, taking as its starting point the text of OPCAT and then looking at the approach to these issues which have been adopted under it.[75]

1. The 'Concept of prevention'

The early drafts of what was to become the Optional Protocol were more focused upon the 'protection' of persons deprived of their liberty rather than 'prevention' and, in the context of the European Convention, the idea of 'prevention' was only introduced at a relatively late stage in the drafting process.[76] However, the obligation to prevent torture was already reflected in the working drafts which were to become UNCAT, Article 2(1), which provides that '[e]ach State Party shall take effective legislative, administrative, judicial or other measures to prevent acts of torture in any territory under its jurisdiction'.[77] In this, it merely mirrors the 1975 Declaration against Torture which also provides that '[e]ach State shall, in accordance with the provisions of this Declaration, take effective measures to prevent torture and other cruel, inhuman or degrading treatment or punishment from being practiced within its jurisdiction'.[78]

Quite what the scope of this is remains unclear. Article 2 is routinely referred to as setting out an obligation to prevent torture but it should be noted that it is rather more circumspect that this. Rather than oblige States to prevent torture, it obliges them to take 'effective legislative, administrative or other measures' in any territory under its jurisdiction to prevent act of torture. Moreover, unlike the 1975 Declaration, the UNCAT does not refer at this point to the prevention of cruel,

[75] It should be noted that the purpose of this section is limited to that mentioned here: to look at how the questions of the 'concept' of prevention and of 'standards' has been approached within the OPCAT framework. Although more general approaches will be drawn on to introduce and frame that discussion, there is absolutely no intention to consider the scope of preventive obligations or of 'standards' for prevention generally. Though very important issues, they lie well beyond the scope of this book.

[76] See above, Chapter 1, pp 14–17.

[77] This formulation was included as Draft Article 2(1) in the Revised Swedish Draft of February 1979 and was not subsequently changed. The initial Swedish Draft of 1978 did not include a reference to prevention at this point, although the IAPL of 1978 draft did so.

[78] Declaration against Torture, Article 4.

inhuman, or degrading treatment or punishment, the prevention of which is addressed separately in UNCAT, Article 16. The significance of this, for current purposes, is that the general architecture of the UNCAT is to set out a range of obligations regarding torture but then, by means of Article 16, to require that some—but not all—of these obligations also be applicable to the prevention of other forms of ill-treatment. Thus, whereas the UNCAT makes it clear that the obligations contained in Articles 10, 11, 12, and 13 of the convention apply to other forms of ill-treatment, it does not expressly require that the remaining obligations upon States regarding measures to address torture also apply to them as regards their undertaking to prevent cruel, inhuman, or degrading treatment or punishment.

The major 'omissions' from this list are usually considered to be Article 14, concerning the right to adequate redress (including compensation and rehabilitation) and Article 15 concerning the inadmissibility of statements made as a result of torture. Whilst UNCAT, Article 16 does not require that a State extend the protections offered by these and other obligations to situations other than torture,[79] it does not of course preclude their doing so.[80] It might be argued that it is inherent in the more general preventive obligation that they do so—but this of course begs the question of whether Article 2(1) and Article 16 do indeed amount to a more general obligation to prevent torture and/or other forms of ill-treatment, or whether the preventive obligation is limited to the realization of effective measures of a legal, administrative, or other nature which reflect the obligations provided for in the other substantive articles of the UNCAT itself.

[79] See, for example, *A and ors v Secretary of State for the Home Department* [2005] UKHL 71 (Lord Bingham, para 53; Lord Hoffman, para 97; Lord Hope, para 126); *R (Binyam Mohamed) v Secretary of State for Foreign and Commonwealth Affairs* [2010] EWCA Civ 65, para 14. See also n 80 below.

[80] Indeed, Article 16 says that Articles 10–13 shall apply to the prevention of other forms of ill-treatment 'in particular', rather than exclusively. Nowak and McArthur, n 1 above, p 539, stress that the words 'in particular' show that the reference to the list of articles in Article 16 is non-exhaustive. Nevertheless, there has never been any suggestion that the provisions concerning the criminalization of torture, the exercise of universal jurisdiction, or the extradition arrangements found in the UNCAT apply to cruel, inhuman, or degrading treatment or punishment and it seems unlikely therefore that a convincing argument can be made that others do so as a matter of obligation. In addition, Article 16(2) is a savings clause to the effect that the provisions of the Convention as a whole are without prejudice to the provisions of other instruments, which might offer a higher degree of protection. Thus the Human Rights Committee has argued that the exclusionary rule flows from both Articles 7 and 14 (right to a fair trial) of the ICCPR in General Comments no 20 and no 32 respectively (UN Doc HRI/GEN/1/Rev 9 (Vol II) p 200 at para 12 and p 248 at para 41). It has been argued that the exclusionary rule does extend to statements or evidence acquired as a result of inhuman or degrading treatment under Article 3 of the EHCR by virtue of ECHR Article 6 concerning the right to a fair trial. However, see now *Gafgen v Germany* [GC], No 22987/05, Judgment of 1 June 2010, in which the Grand Chamber of the ECtHR concluded that whether this was so would depend on whether or not the presentation of such evidence had an impact on the verdict or sentence, meaning that the simple fact of material having been presented in criminal proceedings which has been derived from ill-treatment short of torture does not in and of itself render a trial unfair (para 187). For discussion see Rodley with Pollard, *The Treatment of Prisoners under International Law*, 3rd edn (Oxford, Oxford University Press, 2009), pp 162–166. See also Greer, S 'Should Police Threats to Torture Suspects Always Be Severely Punished? Reflections on the *Gafgen* Case' (2011) 11 *HRLR* 67.

The CAT has addressed this in its General Comment No 2, on the 'Implementation of article 2 by States parties' by observing that:

[t]he obligation to prevent torture under Article 16 is wide ranging. The obligations to prevent torture and other cruel, inhuman or degrading treatment or punishment (hereinafter, 'ill-treatment') under Article 16, paragraph 1, are indivisible, interdependent and interrelated. The obligation to prevent ill-treatment in practice overlaps with and is largely congruent with the obligation to prevent torture. Article 16, identifying the means of prevention of ill-treatment emphasizes 'in particular' the measures outlined in article 10 to 13, but does not limit effective prevention to these articles, as the Committee has explained, for example, with respect to compensation in article 14. In practice the definitional threshold between ill-treatment and torture is often not clear. Experience demonstrates that the conditions that give rise to ill-treatment frequently facilitate torture and therefore the measures required to prevent torture must be applied to prevent ill-treatment. Accordingly, the Committee has considered the prohibition of ill-treatment to be likewise non-derogable under the Convention and its prevention to be an effective and non-derogable measure.[81]

This, then, appears to be a robust statement concerning the scope of the preventive obligation, deliberately blurring the boundaries between Article 2 and 16 in order to extend the reach of Article 16 to those embraced by Article 2(1). Yet on the other hand, the Comment adopts a more limiting approach. Rather than placing prevention at the heart of its architecture, it describes Article 2 as identifying principles which 'undergird the Convention's absolute prohibition against torture'[82] and says that, in order to ensure that the measures taken in pursuance of Article 2 'are in fact... known to prevent or punish acts of torture', the Convention 'outlines in subsequent articles obligations for the States party to take measures specified therein'.[83] This seems to limit the reach of the preventive obligation under Article 2 to those specific obligations as set out in the UNCAT, though it seems clear from other sections that the real intention is that the obligations set out in the text should be understood to represent the 'core minimum' which is known to have a preventive effect, but that the list of such preventive measures is not closed, since 'the committee's understanding of and recommendations in respect of effective measures are in a process of continual evolution'.[84]

The real tension that underlies this—and other—explorations of the concept of prevention is that between a generic, but open ended, 'obligation to prevent' on the one hand, and the existence of discrete obligations which have a preventive impact upon the other. As the structure of the UNCAT itself shows, it is often necessary to strike a balance between the existence of a preventive obligation and the inclusion of specific manifestations of what that entails *as a matter of legal obligation*. In the

[81] General Comment No 2, (adopted 2007) UN Doc HRI.GEN/1/Rev.9 (Vol II) p 376, para 3.
[82] Ibid, para 1. This is a rather odd proposition as, strictly speaking, the Convention does not contain such a prohibition *per se*.
[83] Ibid, para 2.
[84] Ibid, para 4.

text of the UNCAT this was resolved by it being reasonably clear what specific measures were to be required of States in fulfilment of their preventive obligations, and traces of this approach are still found in the CAT's General Comment. At the same time, and entirely understandably, the CAT has, in the light of its experience, sought to broaden the scope of its understanding of what prevention entails, but it has difficulty in projecting this as a matter of legal obligation for States Parties based on Article 2(1) alone. Thus in its General Comment it goes on to say that '[t]he provisions of Article 2 . . . constitute the foundation of the Committee's authority to implement effective means of prevention, including but not limited to those measures contained in the subsequent articles 2 to 16, in response to evolving threats, issues and practices'.[85]

Notably, the CAT does not say that States are obliged by virtue of their preventive obligation to implement such additional effective measures: rather, it is its own addressee. This caution is taken even further later in Part III of the General Comment setting out the 'Content of the obligation to take effective measures to prevent torture'.[86] After reiterating the importance of implementing the criminalizing obligations found in the text, the Comment notes that, in its concluding observations to States, it has 'articulated its understanding of what constitutes effective measures' and has 'recommended specific actions designed to enhance each State party's ability swiftly and effectively to implement measures necessary and appropriate to prevent acts of torture and ill treatment and thereby assist States parties in bringing their law and practice into full compliance with the Convention'.[87] This language falls a good way short of suggesting that such emergent ideas themselves form elements of the substantive obligation, though the section does conclude with the observation that '[a]s new methods of prevention . . . are discovered, tested and found effective, article 2 provides authority to build upon the remaining articles and to expand the scope of measures required to prevent torture'.[88] Since the preventive obligation is to 'take effective measures' this does hint at the emergence of additional obligations to those set out in the text, but the overall tenor and approach of the Comment is to present the content of a legal obligation to prevent by elaborating existing legal obligations and highlighting their preventive potential, reinforcing the primacy of the prohibition and seeing prevention as an ancillary measure.[89] Yet torture prevention is not about fulfilling international commitments concerning the prohibition of torture. This is the result of torture prevention. Torture prevention embraces—or should embrace—as many as possible of those

[85] Ibid, para 1.

[86] Despite the interconnectedness flagged in para 3, it is notable that this section is expressly devoted to 'torture' and UNCAT Article 2, though ill-treatment is occasionally referred to in passing.

[87] Ibid, para 12.

[88] Ibid, para 13.

[89] This is further reinforced by its seeing breach of the preventive obligation through the lens of the occurrence of an act of torture: 'If measures adopted by the State party fail to accomplish the purpose of eradicating acts of torture, the Convention requires that they be revised and/or that new, more effective measures be adopted' (para 4).

things which in a given situation can contribute towards lessening the likelihood or risk of torture and ill-treatment occurring.[90] The problem, as the CAT General Comment illustrates, is that it is very difficult to translate this desiderata into the language of legal obligation in a fashion which is sufficiently precise as to require compliance with so flexible and developmental a series of measures as are necessary to meet the needs of prevention.

It is against this background that the approach of the SPT to the 'concept of prevention' under OPCAT needs to be placed. It is clear that in its early years, the Subcommittee came under considerable pressure from civil society to articulate its understanding of what was meant by 'prevention', and various events and round-tables were organized in order to flesh this out.[91] The product of these activities, however, might be thought rather unexpected. In January 2010 the SPT released on its website a statement entitled 'The Approach of the Subcommittee to the concept of prevention of torture and other cruel, inhuman or degrading treatment or punishment under the Optional Protocol'.[92] Soon afterwards, this was published as Section IV B of its Fourth Annual Report headed 'Substantive Issues', the significance of which is that, according to the report, 'this section sets out its thinking on selected topics and may be taken to reflect the current approach of the SPT to the issues it addresses'.[93] It may, then, be taken as the official position of the Subcommittee on the issue. It is set out in Appendix VI of this book. It is of course clear from this that the Subcommittee has chosen not to take the route of offering a general concept of torture prevention. Rather, it has chosen to expand upon its approach to the realization of its own distinctive preventive mandate and sets out a series of principles which guides its thinking as it does so in practice. Hence the statement is described as the Subcommittee's 'approach' to the concept of prevention. It appears that the debate on that concept, so vibrant and urgent at the commencement of its work, has resolved itself in a rather unexpected fashion. It is

[90] It has been argued that there is in reality little difference between 'prevention' and 'protection' and that 'prevention is protection by another name'. See Rodley, N, 'Reflections on Working for the Prevention of Torture' (2010) 6(1) *Essex Human Rights Review* 21 at 29. There is a good deal of truth in this, but it remains the case that prevention casts a wide net, embracing more easily matters such as education and training which have a clear preventive nexus but may appear more tangential when viewed from the perspective of 'protection'. As Rodley says, 'It [prevention] has served the purpose of making palatable to States what might otherwise have been less palatable' (ibid).

[91] For example, there were a number of discussions around the concept of prevention emanating from the civil society grouping, the OPCAT Contact Group. Following extensive consideration within the Contact Group, and discussion with the SPT itself (at its request), a meeting was convened in May 2009 in Copenhagen where the various organizations discussed internal policy papers they had formulated on the topic and these were then presented and discussed with the SPT during its eighth and ninth sessions in June and November 2009. See Third Annual Report of the SPT, CAT/C/44/2, at para 17. In April 2010 the discussions surrounding the concept of prevention were taken to a wider forum through the initiative of one of the OPCAT CG organizations, the RCT, which organized a Research-Practice International Workshop on 'Prevention of human rights violations: conceptual and methodological issues' in April 2010 in Copenhagen which was attended by civil society, academics, and members of the SPT. For details of its outcomes see <http://www.uk.rct.dk/Link_menu/Activities/Previous_activities/Workshop_070410.aspx>.

[92] Doc CAT/OP/12/6.

[93] See Fourth Annual Report, CAT/C/46/2, para 4 and paras 102–107.

too soon to say whether, or in what form, this may be returned to, or whether that avenue of inquiry has served its purpose in clarifying how best to approach this facet of its work.

2. Standards

The previous subsection has looked at what the bodies established under OPCAT are to do. This subsection turns to the question of the standards which they might draw on in the doing of it. OPCAT itself has surprisingly little to say on the subject. Article 2(2) provides that in carrying out its work, the Subcommittee will be 'guided by the purpose and principles' of the UN Charter (which in this particular context hardly adds particular specificity) 'as well as the norms of the United Nations concerning the treatment of persons deprived of their liberty'.[94] Article 19(b) extends this to the NPMs, likewise providing that they should make their recommendations 'taking into consideration the relevant norms of the United Nations'. As these formulations make clear, neither the Subcommittee nor the NPMs are obliged to slavishly adhere to the 'relevant norms' in the sense of seeking to 'apply' them: rather, they are to take note of them as they go about their work.

The identity of the 'relevant norms' is of course open to debate. Nowak and McArthur point to its including the relevant provisions of other general human rights treaties, thereby including in addition to the fundamentals of the right to life, the prohibition of torture and ill-treatment and fair trial, and also matters such as 'the rights to privacy, freedom of religion, expression, equality and non-discrimination, the rights to food, water, shelter, clothing, health care and education'.[95] That such fundamental human rights, as set out in general human rights treaties, should indeed be applicable to persons deprived of their liberty is as a general proposition uncontroversial: the difficulty lies in how to apply them within the particularities of the criminal justice system, and how to best ensure their practical realization. To that end, the UN has adopted over many years a formidable array of non-binding declarations, principles, guidelines, and other instruments which are to be understood as being 'norms of the United Nations' for these purposes.[96] Illustrative examples include: the Standard Minimum Rules for the Treatment of

[94] The 1991 Costa Rica Draft, Article 1(1) had referred to the work of the Subcommittee being 'in accordance with international standards'. This was both too broad and too narrow: too broad in that it might import a whole swathe of standards into the work of the body which were not necessarily helpful to its particular task; too narrow in that it could potentially exclude standards not endorsed as such by the international community as a whole. Neither the Mexican Draft nor the EU proposal included such a reference at all. The Chair's Draft both broadened and narrowed: it broadened by expressly embracing 'norms' (which might be thought more embracing than more formally construed 'standards', though it is possible to understand this otherwise); it narrowed by focusing only on norms 'concerning persons deprived of their liberty'.

[95] Nowak and McArthur, n 1 above, p 916.

[96] See, for example Nowak and McArthur, n 1 above; APT, *Manual for Prevention*, pp 66–67. Both assume that Article 19(b), concerning the NPMs, is to be understood in the same way. See Nowak and McArthur, ibid, p 1082 and APT, ibid, p 99.

Prisoners;[97] Code of Conduct for Law Enforcement Officials;[98] Principles of Medical Ethics relevant to the Role of Health Personnel particularly Physicians, in the Protection of Prisoners and Detainees against Torture and other Cruel and Inhuman, Degrading Treatment or Punishment;[99] Body of Principles for the Protection of All Persons under Any Form of Detention or Imprisonment;[100] Basic Principles for the Treatment of Prisoners;[101] Rules for the Protection of Juveniles Deprived of their Liberty;[102] Principles on the Effective Investigation and Documentation of Torture and Other Cruel and Inhuman, Degrading Treatment or Punishment (Istanbul Protocol).[103] This is a non-exhaustive list and there are others besides.[104] It is already clear from the Subcommittee's published materials that it does indeed use such normative statements when it considers it appropriate to do so, and a number have been quoted directly in visit reports,[105] or had attention drawn to them in Annual Reports.[106]

These have been adopted over a long period of time, during which understandings and expectations have developed and so whilst it is appropriate that such documents provide inspiration, it would be inappropriate for them to provide limitation. The more interesting question is whether the Subcommittee and the NPMs might draw such inspiration from normative statements deriving from non-UN sources. Whatever might be the product of textual critique on this point,[107] both common sense and the evidence from practice suggest that this is the case, and it would, frankly, be absurd were it otherwise. Reduced to its most basic and pressing form, the real issue concerns the relevance of the extensive corpus of CPT standards for the work of the Subcommittee.[108]

[97] ECOSOC Res 663c(XXIV) (31 July 1957), amended by ECOSOC Res 2076 (LXII) (13 May 1977).

[98] GA Res 34/69 (17 December 1979).

[99] GA Res 37/194 (18 December 1982).

[100] GA Res 34/173 (9 December 1988).

[101] GA Res 45/111 (14 December 1990).

[102] GA Res 45/113 (14 December 1990).

[103] GA Res 55/89 (4 December 2000).

[104] The list of examples provided by Nowak and McArthur and the APT differ in some respects. There is little significance in this as they are merely illustrations. Behind these non-binding declarations, etc, lies another tier of guidance in the form of operational guides and handbooks, commentaries, etc which can also be usefully drawn on to amplify understanding of the range of possible approaches.

[105] See, for example, the use made of the 1988 Body of Principles (n 101 above) and the Standard Minimum Rules for the Treatment of Prisoners (n 98 above) in the visit reports on the Maldives, CAT/OP/MDV/1 and on Mexico, CAT/OP/MEX/1, which also drew on the Rules for the Protection of Juveniles Deprived of their Liberty (n 103 above). Subsequent published reports continue to draw on an ever widening range of material, including General Comments of the UN human rights treaty bodies and reports of the Special Procedures within the UN.

[106] See, for example, the 'Analysis of the Istanbul Protocol' in the Second Annual Report, CAT/C/42/2, Annex VII.

[107] Article 31, concerning the relationship with regional bodies calls, for the avoidance of duplication and the promotion of efficiency, which certainly implies the taking into account of each other's approaches, including each other's 'standards'.

[108] This is not to say that similar issues do not arise in relation to the material produced from other regional, and indeed, UN bodies but there can be no question that the corpus of standards generated by

At first sight, there is something odd about this being an issue at all: as has been seen in Chapter 1, the visiting mandate of the CPT was originally constructed, largely at the behest of the ECtHR, in such a way as to inhibit its having any standard setting or normative impact.[109] That notwithstanding, the CPT has produced a number of key statements of its standards which have been promulgated in various Annual General Reports and are now issued collectively in a publication, running to some ninety-six pages, simply entitled 'CPT Standards'.[110] They are exactly what they say they are: standards which the CPT draws on when making recommendations to States Parties in the context of its visit reports. These have not only been important in their own right but also in the generation of more widely applicable normative statements, such as the revised European Prison Rules.[111] What has been the impact of this on the work of the Subcommittee?

There are two dimensions to this. The first is that it is incontrovertible that the standard-setting work of the CPT has had a profound impact upon the approach taken by the Subcommittee not only in terms of visiting methodology but in terms of its basic approach to preventive safeguards. It is not the intention here to present and analyse that approach other than to say that it largely follows that of the CPT in calling for the erection of a range of 'preventive safeguards' for detained persons built around the 'trilogy' of immediate third-party notification, the right of access to a lawyer, and the right to an independent medical examination, accompanied by effective notification of these rights, all to be effective from the outset of detention, being understood as the moment at which a person is no longer 'free to leave'. A glance at the published SPT reports shows the extent of its influence on this fundamental matter.

In its statement of standards, the CPT has said that:

[t]he CPT attaches particular importance to three rights for persons detained by the police: the right of the person concerned to have the fact of his detention notified to a third party of

the CPT in the context of preventive visiting presents a particular issue, not least because of the overlap of membership, and initially leadership, across the two bodies.

[109] It is, then, ironic that it was a senior Judge of the European Court of Human Rights who, at a major conference held in November 2009 marking the 20th anniversary of the CPT, observed that 'the CPT's reports are very often valuable resources for us [the Court], not only when we are establishing the facts of cases.... But also in the development of the standards progressively being drawn up by the Committee, and which we are careful to adhere to on such matters as cell size.... The work of the CPT is truly indispensable.... In this context, I apologise if we sometimes misuse your reports and make a few mistakes.' See the Comments of Judge Francoise Tulkens, in Council of Europe/APT, *New Partnerships for Torture Prevention in Europe, Proceedings of the Conference, Strasbourg, 6 November 2009* (Strasbourg: Council of Europe, 2010) p 43.

[110] For the most recent version incorporating the latest statement, found in the 20th Annual Report and concerning the use of electrical discharge weapons, see CPT/Inf/E (2002) 1—Rev 2010. The core statements setting out the CPT's basic approaches were contained in its early reports and collected and analysed in Morgan, R and Evans, M, *Combating Torture in Europe: the Work and Standards of the CPT* (Strasbourg: Council of Europe Press, 2001). See also Murdoch, M, *The Treatment of Prisoners—European Standards* (Strasbourg: Council of Europe Press, 2006).

[111] See, for example, Council of Europe, Committee of Ministers Recommendation Rec(2006) 2 (11 January 2006) adopting the Revised European Prison Rules, the second preambular passage of which expressly has regard to the work of the CPT and 'in particular the standards it has developed in its general reports', reproduced in *European Prison Rules* (Strasbourg: Council of Europe Publishing, 2006), p 5.

his choice (family member, friend, consulate), the right of access to a lawyer, and the right to request a medical examination by a doctor of his choice (in addition to any medical examination carried out by a doctor called by the police authorities). They are, in the CPT's opinion, three fundamental safeguards against the ill-treatment of detained persons which should apply as from the very outset of deprivation of liberty, regardless of how it may be described under the legal system concerned (apprehension, arrest, etc).[112]

In the Subcommittee's visit report to Sweden, the only report so far by the Subcommittee related to a State Party to both the ECPT and OPCAT, it says that:

> [t]he SPT considers that the right to inform a close relative or another third party of their choice of the deprivation of liberty, the right of access to a lawyer and the right of access to a doctor are fundamental safeguards against ill-treatment which should apply from the very outset of deprivation of liberty. For the proper exercise of these rights, it is fundamental that the persons obliged to remain with the police are informed without delay of all their rights, including those mentioned above and the relevant procedural rights that the person concerned may exercise.[113]

The similarity in approach is unmistakable and the significance of these rights has been emphasized in similar terms in other published SPT reports.[114] Whether this amounts to the SPT 'applying' CPT standards is both irrelevant and beside the point. The point is that the SPT did not commence its work in a vacuum (and neither did the CPT) and drawing on the experience of others working in a similar field—whilst understanding and respecting differing approaches contexts—is both necessary and desirable, provided they remain open to reappraisal in the light of experience.[115]

The second dimension is whether the Subcommittee is itself to follow the route of issuing its own statements of 'Standards'. So far, it has not. Naturally, visit

[112] See CPT Standards, CPT/Inf/E (2002) 1—Rev 2010, p 6, this having originally been set out as its basic approach in its 2nd General Report in 1992 (see CPT/Inf (1992) 3, para 36).

[113] CAT/OP/SWE/1, para 43.

[114] See, for example, Maldives, CAT/OP/MDV/1, paras 94–112.

[115] The concern about standards was manifest in the organization of the major conference held in Strasbourg in 2009, 'New partnerships for torture prevention in Europe'. A working group was devoted to this topic, but, rather than search for commonality the view that emerged was supportive of the idea of searching for 'congruence', it being argued that

> . . . things 'cohere' when they come together, making for a richer whole than would have been the case if they had not. To that extent I do not see coherence as being the same as commonality or, indeed, convergence. However, I think it is difficult if not impossible to achieve coherence if the core values which are reflected in the work of the various bodies are fundamentally at odds with each other. The sense within the Working Group was that there was a real need to strive for convergence in our understanding of the key undergirding principles that guide the work of the different bodies. If they share a common underpinning, then there can be a coherence which embraces a diversity of different focuses and, indeed, potential approaches. Coherence in this sense implies that there be a shared goal and outcome, which in this case is the working towards the prevention of torture and ill-treatment. It does not necessarily mean that everyone involved in achieving that shared goal and outcome is doing the same thing, or doing the same thing in the same way or, perhaps more controversially, even applying exactly the same standards at one and the same time.

See Comments of the Working Group Rapporteur (Evans, M) in Council of Europe, *New Partnerships for Torture Prevention in Europe*, n 109 above, p 69 at p 72.

reports contain information, views, and recommendations from which is it possible to construct a compendium of the approaches which have been taken on issues it has addressed but until very recently so little material was in the public domain arising from visit reports that there has not been a sufficient body of material on which to draw in order to do so in a reliable fashion. This may soon be changing, and it remains to be seen whether, with this change, the Subcommittee itself chooses to take the lead in so doing, or leaves the task to others. What is notable is that in its most recent Annual Report it has begun to pass comment in general terms on a range of issues arising from its visits,[116] and holds open the prospect of its developing its thinking on such issues in future.[117] It may well be that the Subcommittee will, in time, proceed down a more 'standard'-setting avenue, but for the moment, and, unlike the CPT at a similar stage in its development, it has refrained from doing so at a systemic level.

[116] See, for example, the observations in Fourth Annual Report, Section III D, entitled 'issues arising from visits', which comments in brief and generically on a range of matters including overcrowding and pre-trial detention and systems of prisoner self-governance.

[117] This section is described in the following terms: 'This section is not intended to provide an exhaustive coverage of issues of interest or concern, nor is it intended to address the issues noted in a comprehensive fashion. Rather, it is intended to draw attention to issues which the SPT has encountered and upon which it is reflecting.' See Fourth Annual Report, para 3.

4

The Scope of OPCAT

While many might traditionally view 'places of detention' and 'places where people are deprived of their liberty' as applying to prisons or police cells, OPCAT provides protection beyond these to a potentially diverse range of places and situations. Article 1 of OPCAT sets out the objective of the instrument as being 'to establish a system of regular visits undertaken by independent international and national bodies to places where people are deprived of their liberty'. Article 4 then expands on this further:

1. Each state party shall allow visits . . . by the mechanisms referred to in articles 2 and 3 to any place under its jurisdiction and control where persons are or may be deprived of their liberty, either by virtue of an order given by a public authority or at its instigation or with its consent or acquiescence (hereinafter referred to as places of detention). . . .
2. For the purposes of the present Protocol, deprivation of liberty means any form of detention or imprisonment or the placement of a person in a public or private custodial setting which that person is not permitted to leave at will by order of any judicial, administrative or other authority.

With respect to the SPT, Article 12(a) requires the States Parties to 'receive the Subcommittee on Prevention in their territory and grant it access to the places of detention as defined in Article 4'. In addition, Article 14(1)(c) requires States to grant to the SPT 'unrestricted access to all places of detention and their installations and facilities', unless there are urgent and compelling grounds for the State objecting to such on grounds of national defence, public safety, natural disaster, or serious disorder.

At the national level, Article 19(a) requires that NPMs be granted minimum powers including 'to regularly examine the treatment of persons deprived of their liberty in places of detention as defined in article 4 . . . '. Similarly, Article 20(c) requires that States grant them 'access to all places of detention and their installations and facilities'.

As noted in Chapter 1, the inclusion of 'prevention' within the text of OPCAT arose from a desire to differentiate the SPT from existing judicial bodies. Although since the coming into force of OPCAT there has been considerable discussion about what a broader preventive mandate should entail, it is perhaps therefore not surprising that in fact attention has focused primarily on visits by NPMs, rather than other activities that could be undertaken such as awareness-raising, training, and commenting on legislation. As was seen in Chapter 3, the SPT has also recently moved away from attempting to define 'prevention' per se, but rather has outlined a preventive approach to its work and stressed the broader nature of the concept:

In this sense, the prevention of torture and ill-treatment embraces—or should embrace—as many as possible of those things which in a given situation can contribute towards the lessening of the likelihood or risk of torture or ill-treatment occurring. Such an approach requires not only that there be compliance with relevant international obligations and standards in both form and substance but that attention also be paid to the whole range of other factors relevant to the experience and treatment of persons deprived of their liberty and which by their very nature will be context specific.[1]

The SPT has thus set out 'Guiding Principles' on how it will itself perform its visits in the context of prevention.

This means that attention needs to be focused not so much on conceptual issues but on the actual manner in which the SPT and NPMs conduct their mandate. The key to this lies in determining the scope of OPCAT and, in particular, how 'deprivation of liberty' is to be understood since this dictates how far the mandate of the SPT and of the NPMs should extend.

A. 'Deprived of liberty'

Article 4 is very broad in terms of who may fall under OPCAT's protection. During the drafting of the Protocol there was division regarding the use of the terms 'detained' or 'deprived of their liberty' and 'many delegations pointed out that the latter term was more commonly used in the human rights arena and that "detained" could be too narrow'.[2] Yet the Protocol maintains the use of both 'deprived of liberty' and 'detained'.[3]

Other treaty bodies have taken a broad approach to the scope of the right to liberty and security of the person, the UN Human Rights Committee, for example, holding that Article 9(1) of the ICCPR 'is applicable to all deprivations of liberty, whether in criminal cases or in other cases such as, for example, mental illness, vagrancy, drug addiction, educational purposes, immigration control, etc.'.[4] Furthermore, 'persons deprived of their liberty' in Article 10(1) applies to

anyone deprived of liberty under the laws and authority of the state who is held in prisons, hospitals—particularly psychiatric hospitals—detention camps or correctional institutions,

[1] SPT, The approach of the Subcommittee on Prevention of Torture to the concept of prevention of torture and other cruel, inhuman or degrading treatment or punishment under the Optional Protocol to the Convention against Torture and Other Cruel, Inhuman or Degrading Treatment or Punishment, CAT/OP/12/6, 30 December 2010, para 3. See Appendix VI.

[2] Nowak, M and McArthur, E, *The United Nations Convention Against Torture: A Commentary* (Oxford: Oxford University Press, 2008), p 889.

[3] Edwards, A, 'The Optional Protocol to the UN Convention Against Torture and Refugees', (2008) 57(4) *ICLQ* 789–825 at 798.

[4] Human Rights Committee, General Comment No 8, Right to liberty and security of persons (Art 9), 30 June 1982, para 1.

or elsewhere. States Parties should ensure that the principle stipulated therein is observed in all institutions and establishments within their jurisdiction where persons are being held.[5]

Similarly, the UNHCR's definition of detention is less restrictive than that found in OPCAT,[6] such that the UNHCR 'accepts situations where the freedom of movement of a refugee is "substantially curtailed" and in doing so, it does not require a complete deprivation of liberty as otherwise required by international law'.[7]

How one defines these terms is not just an academic discussion. It has implications for what should fall within an NPM's jurisdiction at the national level and the SPT's internationally, particularly when one considers the areas which are often seen as less obvious, such as those relating to secure accommodation for the young or social care institutions. In addition, although these definitions under international law may be broad, domestically the law may not always reflect international obligations.

Although, legally, a State cannot use inconsistent national law as justification for failure to comply with its international obligations,[8] the NPM is likely to have to consider both OPCAT and relevant national legislation in its work. This may cause considerable challenges for the NPM when it attempts to determine the scope of its mandate. Even apparently restrictive national legislation, however, may be interpreted generously in practice depending on the attitude of the NPM or visiting body.

B. Public and Private: '... either by virtue of an order given by a public authority or at its instigation or with its consent or acquiescence', Article 4(1)

The inclusion of this phrase in Article 4(1) extends OPCAT's scope to detention by non-state actors but only if the State is aware of this and does not prevent it. On the face of it, if one took a liberal approach to 'consent or acquiescence', OPCAT could cover not only detention in private hospitals and care homes,[9] but also detention by, for example, paramilitary groups, those who traffic in persons, and in witch camps to name a few. Article 4(1) and (2), however, seem to contradict each other, with the latter being more restrictive than the first paragraph, as 'mere consent or acquiescence... would not be sufficient, as paragraph 2 seems to require an explicit

[5] Human Rights Committee, General Comment No 21, Replaces General Comment 9 concerning humane treatment of persons deprived of liberty (Art 10), 10 April 1992, para 2.

[6] 'Confinement within a narrowly bounded or restricted location, including prisons, closed camps, detention facilities or airport transit zones, where freedom of movement is substantially curtailed, and where the only opportunity to leave this limited area is to leave the country', UNHCR, Revised Guidelines on Detention, Guideline 1, para 1, see Edwards, n 3 above, 798.

[7] Edwards, n 3 above, 798.

[8] Vienna Convention on the Law of Treaties 1969, Article 27.

[9] Nowak and McArthur, n 2 above, p 931.

order of a public authority'.[10] In addition, Article 4(1) focuses on the place of deprivation of liberty, whereas Article 4(2) looks at the person whose liberty is deprived.[11]

The wording is borrowed from UNCAT and its Committee has held that there will be 'acquiescence' if the State fails to take action.[12] Similarly:

> The Committee has concluded that States parties are in violation of the Convention when they fail to fulfil these obligations. For example, where detention centres are privately owned or run, the Committee considers that personnel are acting in an official capacity on account of their responsibility for carrying out the State function without derogation of the obligation of State officials to monitor and take all effective measures to prevent torture and ill-treatment.[13]

Where those State authorities

> acting in official capacity or under colour of law, know or have reasonable grounds to believe that acts of torture or ill-treatment are being committed by non-State officials or private actors and they fail to exercise due diligence to prevent, investigate, prosecute and punish such non-State officials or private actors consistently with the Convention, the State bears responsibility and its officials should be considered as authors, complicit or otherwise responsible under the Convention for consenting to or acquiescing in such impermissible acts.[14]

So a failure by the State to prevent and protect against situations such as rape, domestic violence, female genital mutilation, and trafficking will incur State responsibility.[15] In this context, the SPT has noted in particular the prevalence of prisoner self-governance systems and reiterated that 'the state party remains responsible at all times for the safety and wellbeing of all detainees'.[16]

However, the remit of Article 1 of UNCAT will not extend as far as situations where, for example, paramilitaries hold control of a particular area and they do not have government support.[17] Consequently, it could be argued that neither will OPCAT apply.

Similarly, the European Court of Human Rights has held that rights extend to the private sphere.[18] The State must therefore provide 'effective protection of

[10] Ibid, p 932.

[11] Edwards, n 3 above, 798.

[12] *Dzemajl and others v Yugoslavia*, CAT/C/29/D/161/2000, UN Committee Against Torture (CAT), 2 December 2002, para 9.2.

[13] CAT General Comment No 2, Implementation of Article 2 by States Parties, CAT/C/GC/2, 24 January 2008, para 17.

[14] Ibid, para 18.

[15] Ibid.

[16] SPT, Fourth Annual Report of the Subcommittee on Prevention of Torture and Other Cruel, Inhuman or Degrading Treatment or Punishment (April–December 2010), CAT/C/46/2, 7 January 2011.

[17] *GRB v Sweden*, Communication No 83/1997, 15 May 1998.

[18] See *Refah Partisi (The Welfare Party) and others v Turkey* [GC], (2003) 37 EHRR 1 at para 103; also *von Hannover v Germany* (2005) 40 EHRR 1 at para 57; *X and Y v The Netherlands* (1986) 8 EHRR 235 at para 23; *Plattform 'Ärzte für das Leben' v Austria* (1991) 13 EHRR 204 at para 32. Campbell, A I L, 'Positive Obligations under the ECHR: Deprivation of Liberty by Private Actors' (2006) *Edinburgh Law Review* 399.

vulnerable persons, including reasonable steps to prevent a deprivation of liberty of which the authorities have or ought to have knowledge'.[19] Most human rights treaty bodies now take the view that the prohibition of torture, inhuman and degrading treatment and punishment also includes judicial corporal punishment[20] and as a result there is little doubt that the scope of OPCAT extends to settings in which such punishments may be administered.[21] Issues have, however, also arisen concerning the use of corporal punishment in other settings, such as schools and hospitals, and this raises the question of whether OPCAT applies in such contexts, that is to say, places where persons are to be found who may be susceptible to forms of corporal punishment which, though not judicially determined, might fall within the scope of UNCAT. Some such settings would not be controversial, such as prisons, secure homes, etc. Others would doubtless be more so, such as schools, orphanages, and hospitals[22] whether public or private.[23] As APT note, although the CAT was in the past more hesitant in its approach to judicial corporal punishment,[24] it is clear that it now considers corporal punishment in a broad range of settings to violate UNCAT[25] but whether this extends as far as situations in the home is not clear.[26] The ability of the SPT and NPM to visit such places and those under private control clearly

[19] *Storck v Germany*, para 102. As the Special Rapporteur on Torture has said: 'the prohibition of torture must be enforced in all sorts of institutions and States have to exercise due diligence to prevent, investigate, prosecute and punish such non-State officials or private actors', Interim report of the Special Rapporteur on torture and other cruel, inhuman or degrading treatment or punishment, A/63/175, 28 July 2008, para 51. See also, for example, Human Rights Committee, General Comment No 20, Replaces General Comment No 7 concerning prohibition of torture and cruel treatment or punishment (Art. 7), 10 March 1992, which provides (at para 13):

> States parties should indicate when presenting their reports the provisions of their criminal law which penalize torture and cruel, inhuman and degrading treatment or punishment, specifying the penalties applicable to such acts, whether committed by public officials or other persons acting on behalf of the State, or by private persons. Those who violate article 7, whether by encouraging, ordering, tolerating or perpetrating prohibited acts, must be held responsible. Consequently, those who have refused to obey orders must not be punished or subjected to any adverse treatment,

Also *A v UK*, European Court of Human Rights, No 25599/94, Judgment of 23 September 1998.

[20] See, for example, Human Rights Committee General Comment on Article 7, para 20; see also Human Rights Committee *Osbourne v Jamaica*, Communication No 759/1997, CCPR/C/68/D/759/1997 (2000); *Higginson v Jamaica*, Communication No 792/1998, CCPR/C/74/D/792/1995 28 March 2002; *Pryce v Jamaica* Communication No 793/1998,CCPR/C/80/D/793/1998 (2004). For the Inter-American Court see *Ceasar v Trinidad and Tobago* (Ser C), No 123 (2005) Judgment of 11 March 2005; for the African Commission on Human and Peoples' Rights see *Curtis Francis Doebbler v Sudan*, Communication 236/2000; and for the ECtHR see *Tyrer v UK*, Series A, No 26, 25 April 1978. See also Convention on the Rights of the Child, Articles 19(1) and 37(a), and General Comment of Committee on the Rights of the Child, General Comment No 8, 2006, para 18. For a full discussion see Rodley, with Pollard, *The Treatment of Prisoners under International Law*, 3rd edn (Oxford:Oxford University Press, 2009), ch 10.

[21] Indeed, the SPT has now addressed this by agreeing with the approach of the Human Rights Committee and the CAT: SPT, Report on the Visit to the Maldives, paras 26–29.

[22] See European Court of Human Rights. *Tyrer v UK*, n 20 above.

[23] See Human Rights Committee, General Comment No 20, 1992, para 5.

[24] APT, *Torture in International Law. A Guide to Jurisprudence* (Geneva: APT, CEJIL, 2008), p 37.

[25] Ibid, p 37; Concluding Observations on Saudi Arabia, UN Doc CAT/C/CR/28/5/, 2002, para 8(b).

[26] APT, n 24 above, p 38.

raises not only legal issues but considerable logistical and other challenges as well.[27] It is therefore important to consider other ways in which an NPM could monitor such situations.

Given that human rights treaty bodies have interpreted torture as having been committed in the context of enforced disappearances, this also adds another dimension to OPCAT.[28] Exactly what the mandate of NPMs and the SPT is in this context is therefore potentially very open ended.

C. '. . . are or may be deprived'/'installations and facilities'

OPCAT will cover places where individuals might be detained but there are none at the time of the visit.[29] 'Installations and facilities' could apply to

> all buildings belonging to the detention facility, the cells and living quarters of detainees, isolation and punishment cells, courtyards, exercise areas, kitchens, workshops, educational and medical facilities, sanitary installations, staff quarters, etc.[30]

The idea is to enable the visiting bodies to have

> a full impression of the conditions of detention and treatment of persons deprived of their liberty. They can visualise the layout of the detention facilities, their physical security arrangements, architecture etc., which all play an important part in the overall daily life of those persons deprived of their liberty and in the working environment of the staff.[31]

D. 'any place/all places of detention'

This broad definition and the reference to 'any place' mean that Article 4 broadens out the scope of OPCAT[32] and the SPT has made it clear that it envisages OPCAT as encompassing a non-exhaustive list of places of detention. Some of these will be outlined below.

1. Prisons, police, and pre-trial facilities

Detention in prisons, police cells, and other pre-trial facilities is what many imagine as the focus of OPCAT's attention. For example, it is clear from SPT reports that although it has visited other places of detention such as children's homes, drug

[27] See, for example UK Care Quality Commission, Inspection Report 2009/2010, Linden House; Clapham, A, *Human Rights in the Private Sphere* (Oxford: Oxford University Press, 1993), p 124.

[28] See also Convention on Enforced Disappearances, Articles 12(2)(b) and 17(2)(e); European Court of Human Rights, *Orhan v Turkey*, Appl No 25656/94, Judgment of 18 June 2002.

[29] Nowak and McArthur, n 2 above, p 932.

[30] Ibid, p 1042.

[31] IIHR/APT, *Optional Protocol to the UN Convention Against Torture and Other Cruel, Inhuman and Degrading Treatment or Punishment. A Manual for Prevention* (2005), p 93.

[32] Nowak and McArthur, n 2 above, p 926; see also IIHR/APT Manual, p 72.

rehabilitation centres, and psychiatric hospitals, the focus of its attention has been police stations and prisons.[33]

More specifically, taking into account CAT General Comment No 2, OPCAT also covers police cars and other means by which individuals are transferred:

> Additionally, if a person is to be transferred or sent to the custody or control of an individual or institution known to have engaged in torture or ill-treatment, or has not implemented adequate safeguards, the State is responsible, and its officials subject to punishment for ordering, permitting or participating in this transfer contrary to the State's obligation to take effective measures to prevent torture in accordance with article 2, paragraph 1.[34]

Interestingly, in a few States, police cells have not always been covered by their pre-existing independent national mechanisms, eg the UK and Georgia,[35] and some changes have been required in the reach of the national mechanisms in order to bring them into compliance with OPCAT.[36] This does not necessarily mean, in practice, that visiting bodies are permitted access to all such facilities, as the experience of the Independent Monitoring Board in the UK, for example, indicates.[37]

2. Refugee, asylum, and immigration centres

OPCAT visiting mechanisms should also cover refugee, asylum, and immigration centres.[38] This will encompass airports, being part of the territory of the State, and any holding cells therein,[39] border posts and international zones,[40] closed camps,[41]

[33] For example, in the Maldives the SPT visited: '12 police facilities, including police stations and police detention centres, and two prisons. It also visited two prisons under construction, an education and training centre for children, a home for children in need and one drug rehabilitation centre. In addition, the delegation visited the Maldives National Security Service training centre at Girifushi', Report on the Visit of the Subcommittee on the Prevention of Torture and other Cruel, Inhuman and Degrading Treatment or Punishment to the Maldives, CAT/OP/MDV/1, 26 February 2009, para 10. See also Report on the Visit of the Subcommittee on the Prevention of Torture and other Cruel, Inhuman and Degrading Treatment or Punishment to Mexico, CAT/OP/MEX/1, 31 May 2010, para 11.

[34] CAT General Comment No 2, para 19. See also interview with Miguel Sarre, member of the SPT, 5 June 2007.

[35] Interview with Giorgi Chkheidze, Georgian Young Lawyers Association (Georgia), 20 June 2007. See also New Zealand, 'one of the biggest gaps that we found was with regard to the inspection of police cells', interview with Stuart Beresford, New Zealand Ministry of Justice.

[36] However, visiting court cells remains a problem for the UK NPM.

[37] For example, the IMB in Bristol was only permitted access to the Command Suite on the invitation of the prison governor, The Independent Monitoring Board HMP Bristol, Annual Report 1 August 2009–31 July 2010, <http://www.imb.gov.uk/reports/Bristol_2009-2010.pdf>, paras 5 and 6.

[38] See Edwards, A, n 3 above; also HMIP, *Report on an unannounced full follow-up inspection of Campsfield House Immigration Removal Centre, 12–16 May 2008* by HM Chief Inspector of Prisons (HMIP, 2008); Northern Ireland Human Rights Commission, *Our Hidden Borders. The UK Border Agency's Powers of Detention* (NIHRC, April 2009).

[39] *Amuur v France*, Application 19776/92, European Court of Human Rights, judgment of 25 June 1996.

[40] Edwards, n 3 above, 808.

[41] APT, *The Optional Protocol to the United Nations Convention Against Torture: An Opportunity for Refugee and Migrant Rights Protection*, May 2009, p 2.

and extra-territorial processing or holding centres, namely those located outside the potential host country.[42] It could extend as far as places within airports or on airplanes where there have been allegations of extraordinary rendition.[43] Some of these areas may overlap with the mandate of the UNHCR, although, as noted in Chapter 7, the SPT has engaged with the UNHCR to share 'strategic information'.[44] Some NPMs are already visiting these types of facilities.[45]

3. Military detention facilities

Military detention facilities, often separate from prisons and the normal criminal justice system, will also be subject to OPCAT protection.[46] In practice, nationally it is often the case that such facilities are inspected by the military rather than external bodies. This will not be sufficient for OPCAT purposes. The SPT has already seen it as being within its mandate to visit military prisons.[47] As will be discussed further below, it is not just military detention facilities in the national territory of the State Party to OPCAT which are covered, but also those situated extra-territorially.

4. Mental health institutions

OPCAT also extends to mental health institutions.[48] In this context visits to those detained in hospital under mental health legislation should be covered.[49] Some private hospitals have beds which provide care in a secure setting.[50] The SPT has visited a number of psychiatric hospitals in the course of its country visits,[51] and many NPMs have the remit for these types of institutions. However, as will be

[42] Edwards, n 3 above, 816–820.

[43] See, for example, Irish Human Rights Commission, *'Extraordinary Rendition'. A View of Ireland's Human Rights Obligations* (Dublin: Irish Human Rights Commission, 2007), <http://www.ihrc.ie/download/pdf/ihrc_rendition_report_final.pdf>, p 18.

[44] SPT, Third Annual Report of the Subcommittee on Prevention of Torture, Cruel, Inhuman or Degrading Treatment or Punishment, CAT/C/44/2, 25 March 2010, para 63.

[45] See HM Chief Inspector of Prisons, *Detainees under escort at Manchester Detention Centre, Manchester Airport*. Report on one unannounced and one announced escort inspection, 3–4 September 2007, 2008.

[46] See also *Vuolanne v Finland*, UN Human Rights Committee, Communication 265/87, 7 April 1989 regarding military disciplinary procedure and detention in a guardhouse: 'The all-encompassing character of the terms of this article leaves no room for distinguishing between different categories of persons, such as civilians and members of the military', para 9.3.

[47] SPT, Report on the Visit of the Subcommittee on the Prevention of Torture and other Cruel, Inhuman and Degrading Treatment or Punishment to Mexico, CAT/OP/MEX/1, 31 May 2010.

[48] See attention to this issue by the Special Rapporteur on Torture, Report of the Special Rapporteur on the question of torture and other cruel, inhuman or degrading treatment or punishment, in accordance with Assembly resolution 57/200 of 18 December 2002, A/58/120, 3 July 2003, Part V.

[49] See, for example, Mental Health Act Commission, *Women Detained in Hospital*. A Report by the Mental Health Act Commission, March 2009; UN Human Rights Committee, *A v New Zealand*, 754/97.

[50] See, for example, UK Care Quality Commission, *Inspection Report 2009/2010*, Linden House.

[51] Report on the Visit of the Subcommittee on the Prevention of Torture and other Cruel, Inhuman and Degrading Treatment or Punishment to Mexico, CAT/OP/MEX/1, 31 May 2010.

discussed further below, this has prompted calls for greater medical expertise in the membership of those undertaking the visits.[52]

5. Care homes, foster homes, older persons, and other places

OPCAT's reach also includes, for example: care homes; foster homes; and homes for older persons and the young; youth justice residences, where children with disabilities may be placed; and other family residences.[53] The SPT has visited youth rehabilitation centres[54] and other places where minors have been detained.[55]

The broad definition in Article 4 means, in theory, that visiting bodies should also be able to visit secret places of detention, namely those identified by a joint UN report as where

> ...State authorities acting in their official capacity, or persons acting under the orders thereof, with the authorization, consent, support or acquiescence of the State, or in any other situation where the action or omission of the detaining person is attributable to the State, deprive persons of their liberty; where the person is not permitted any contact with the outside world ('incommunicado detention'); and when the detaining or otherwise competent authority denies, refuses to confirm or deny or actively conceals the fact that the person is deprived of his/her liberty hidden from the outside world, including, for example family, independent lawyers or non-governmental organizations, or refuses to provide or actively conceals information about the fate or whereabouts of the detainee.[56]

There are other types of detention which may be country or region-specific. For example, witch camps in Ghana, which its Human Rights Commission has visited and monitored, or even slum communities.[57] Yet, deprivation of liberty is broader

[52] Medical and psychiatric expertise is an issue that has also been raised by other international visiting bodies, see for example, European Committee for the Prevention of Torture, 13th General Report on the CPT's Activities, covering the period 1 January 2002 to 31 July 2003, CPT/CPT.Inf (2003) 35, at para 25.

[53] See, for example, Children's Commissioner of New Zealand, Annual Report 2008, presented to the House of Representatives pursuant to section 28 of the Children's Commissioner Act 2003 and section 150(3) of the Crown Entities Act 2004, 2008. See also Interim report of the Special Rapporteur of the Commission on Human Rights on the question of torture and other cruel, inhuman or degrading treatment or punishment, A/55/290, 11 August 2000, paras 11–12. See also Resolution 1995/41, 'Human rights and the administration of justice, in particular of children and juveniles in detention', Report to the fifty-second session of the Commission on Human Rights, the Special Rapporteur considered the issue of torture and children, E/CN.4/1996/35, paras 9–17.

[54] Report on the Visit of the Subcommittee on the Prevention of Torture and other Cruel, Inhuman and Degrading Treatment or Punishment to the Maldives, CAT/OP/MDV/1, 26 February 2009, paras 357–359.

[55] Report on the Visit of the SPT to Mexico, n 33 above.

[56] Joint study on global practices in relation to secret detention in the context of countering terrorism of the Special Rapporteur on the promotion and protection of human rights and fundamental freedoms while countering terrorism, the Special Rapporteur on torture and other cruel, inhuman or degrading treatment or punishment, the Working Group on Arbitrary Detention and the Working Group on Enforced or Involuntary Disappearances, A/HRC/13/42, 26 January 2010.

[57] The Ghanaian Human Rights Commission, for example, has visited and monitored these camps as part of its mandate, see Lilian Ayete Nyampong, 'Challenges facing the OPCAT in the Implementation of the OPCAT in the African Region Visiting places of detention-Methods, presentation', OPCAT in the African Region: Challenges of Implementation, Cape Town, South Africa,

still. For example, where an individual was banished, the Human Rights Committee found a breach of Article 10(1).[58] Article 9 also applies to house arrest.[59] There are limits, however. So, prohibition from travelling outside city limits[60] and compulsory residence orders[61] may not amount to deprivation of liberty within the context of Article 9(1) ICCPR. The implications for any national or international visiting mechanism are considerable, in terms of the practicalities and logistics of monitoring these types of situations. Whilst it is not being suggested that the SPT or NPMs prioritize these additional types of situations over others, it is clear that there should be an awareness of their existence and, depending on the context, consideration as to how their mandate can be carried out.

E. '... under its jurisdiction or control'

What is within the jurisdiction or control of a State has been the subject of considerable discussion and several high profile cases before the European Court of Human Rights, the UK House of Lords, and other judicial bodies.[62] The current position in international law would appear to be that the responsibility of a State, and thus for these purposes its jurisdiction, extends as far as areas and individuals over which it has effective control.[63] This is an approach that has been adopted by the CAT. UNCAT refers in Article 5(1)(a) to 'offences... committed in any territory under its jurisdiction' and the CAT has interpreted this as the Convention applying to those individuals or all areas where the State has 'de jure or de facto control'.[64]

It is worth noting that the French text of OPCAT refers to 'jurisdiction *or* control' ('... dans tout lieu placé sous sa juridiction ou sous son contrôle...'), although in accordance with international law principles, arguably the interpretation that provides greater protection for the individual should be adopted.

3–4 April 2008, p 6, see <http://www.bristol.ac.uk/law/research/centres-themes/opcat/docs.html#OPCAT-AfricanConference2008>.

[58] *Nqalula Mpandanjila et al v Zaire*, Communication No 138/1983, UN Doc Supp No 40 (A/41/40) at 121 (1986): 'because they were subjected to ill-treatment during the period of banishment', para 9.

[59] Human Rights Committee, General Comment No 28, para 14.

[60] *Celepli v Sweden*, Communication 456/91, CCPR/C/51/D/456/1991 26 July 1994, para 6.1.

[61] *Karker v France*, Communication 833/98, UN Human Rights Committee, CCPR/C/70/D/833/1998, 26 October 2000, para 8.5.

[62] See, for example, *Banković et al v Belgium et al* (Dec) [GC], no 52207/99, ECHR 2001-XII and *Ilaşcu and others v moldova and Russia* [GC], no 48787/99, ECHR 2004-VII before the European Court of Human Rights and, before the UK House of Lords, *R (Al-Skeini and others) v Secretary of State for Defence* [2007] UKHL 26, [2008] 1 AC 153; *R (Al-Jedda) v Secretary of State for Defence* [2008] 1 AC 332; *R (Al-Saadoon and Mufdhi) v Secretary of State for Defence* [2009] EWCA Civ 7.

[63] See *Application of the Convention on the Prevention and Punishment of the Crime of Genocide (Bosnia and Herzegovina v Serbia and Montenegro)*, Merits, Judgment of 26 February 2007, ICJ Reports 2007, paras 399–406.

[64] CAT General Comment No 2, para 7. See in relation to the US, Conclusions and Recommendations of the Committee Against Torture; United States of America, UN Doc CAT/C/USA/CO/2, 25 July 2006.

1. Nationally

The State will be responsible for acts occurring within its territory. There are a number of considerations here. Firstly, issues confront a range of States where there are federal or devolved administrations[65] and here both the federal and national State governments will be included within OPCAT's remit.[66] As the APT point out, however, there may be challenges in implementation across these States, including managing their respective jurisdictions.[67]

Furthermore, there are several examples of States which have dependencies or overseas territories over which the question of the applicability of OPCAT arises. According to the Vienna Convention on the Law of Treaties, 'a treaty is binding upon each party in respect of its entire territory'[68] but this may be affected by declarations as to its territorial scope made at the time of ratification or accession to the instrument. A number of States have limited the reach of OPCAT in this way.[69] This may generate some anomalies. For example, the CPT has been able to visit Aruba and the Antilles as a consequence of their being included within the scope of the Declaration made by the Netherlands when acceding to the ECPT, and has done so on a number of occasions.[70] However when ratifying OPCAT in 2010 the Netherlands did so only for the Kingdom in Europe, and so Aruba and the Antilles currently fall outside the scope of the SPT—and of course, of the obligation to have an NPM.

As regards the United Kingdom, there are also some potential anomalies. For example, the Channel Islands are Crown dependencies and therefore do not form part of the territory of the UK and so are not covered by OPCAT, although they are now covered by the ECPT.[71] The Isle of Man, however, is covered by OPCAT

[65] See Pollard, M, *Implementation of the Optional Protocol to the Convention against Torture and other Cruel, Inhuman or Degrading Treatment or Punishment (OPCAT) in Federal and other Decentralized States*, Discussion Paper for the Seminar 'The Optional Protocol to the UN Convention against Torture: Implementation in Federal States and Decentralized States' Sao Paulo, Brazil (22–24 June 2005), <http://www.apt.ch>.

[66] Interview with Stephen Blanks and Mr Michael Walton, the New South Wales Council for Civil Liberties (Australia).

[67] See Pollard, n 65 above, p 8.

[68] Vienna Convention on the Law of Treaties, Article 29.

[69] Denmark excluded the Faroe Islands when ratifying in 2004, but removed this restriction in 2005 before OPCAT had entered into force. New Zealand excluded Tokelau from OPCAT when ratifying in 2007.

[70] It has done so on several occasions, most recently in June 2006, for the Report on which see CPT/Inf (2008) 2. A further visit is due to be conducted during the course of 2011.

[71] On ratifying UNCAT the UK did extend its provisions to a number of overseas dependencies, these being Anguilla, British Virgin Islands, Cayman Islands, Falkland Islands (Malvinas), Gibraltar, Montserrat, Pitcairn, Henderson, Ducie and Oeno Islands, Saint Helena, Saint Helena Dependencies, and Turks and Caicos Islands. It subsequently informed the depositary in 1992 that it would henceforth apply to the Bailiwick of Guernsey, the Bailiwick of Jersey, the Isle of Man, Bermuda, and Hong Kong. When ratifying the European Convention in 1988 the UK initially extended it to the Bailiwick of Jersey and to the Isle of Man, extending this to Gibraltar a few months later but not extending it to include the Bailiwick of Guernsey until 1994. It should also be noted that some British overseas dependencies are excluded from the reach of the UNCAT (and hence OPCAT) and the ECPT, notably the British Indian Ocean Territory (BIOT), which includes the island of Diego Garcia, home to a major US military base which is used to support operations in that region.

whereas the other Crown dependencies are not. Other interesting issues will doubtless arise in time when some States ratify OPCAT: for example, Nauru is an independent State but houses a detention centre established through an agreement between the Nauru and Australian governments. Though at the time of writing neither is a party to OPCAT, Australia is a signatory. The detention centre was used to hold asylum seekers and others on behalf of the Australian government and there have been requests for visits to those places of detention on Nauru.[72]

2. Extra-territoriality

The extent to which OPCAT applies extra-territorially is a controversial one and an issue that has arisen for a handful of States, recently in the context of the detention of individuals by the forces of an OPCAT Member State in a country outside the national territory of that State. Examples include UK military activities in Afghanistan and Iraq and Canadian military activity in Afghanistan.[73]

Taking this case law as the basis on which OPCAT applies in these contexts and therefore whether the OPCAT Member State has a responsibility to ensure that its NPM can visit such places of detention, States argue that it depends on exactly where the individuals are in fact detained. If an individual is detained by the forces of an OPCAT Member State on its military base in a foreign State or in premises over which the State has control, such as diplomatic and consular premises and prisons, then this is within the territory and jurisdiction of the OPCAT Member State and OPCAT therefore applies. The UK House of Lords has interpreted the reference to 'within the jurisdiction' of the State in Article 1 ECHR to cover detention facilities at a British military base in Iraq.[74] Thus, Her Majesty's Inspector of Prisons has visited a British prison in Cyprus,[75] and has carried out inspections in Afghanistan.

The more difficult question arises with respect to those individuals who are detained in an area outside of the military base of the OPCAT Member State. There are strong reasons to hold treaty obligations of the State whose military is operating in that area to apply in those contexts.[76] The legal position must be

[72] Interview with Lachlan Murdoch, Deputy Director, STARTTS, Australia, September 2007.

[73] See *Amnesty International v Canada (Attorney General)*, 2008 FC 336 (CanLII), 3 December 2008.

[74] *Al-Skeini and others v Secretary of State for Defence, Al-Skeini and others v Secretary of State for Defence (Consolidated Appeals)* [2007] UKHL 26.

[75] Although this was prior to its designation as NPM under OPCAT HMIP, Inspection of HMP Dhekelia, 27–28 October 2004 by HM Chief Inspector of Prisons.

[76] For example, in its 19th Report of the Session 2005–2006 on the UN Convention Against Torture, the JCHR looked at the territorial applicability of UNCAT and noted that 'the government should expressly accept the application of all of the rights and duties in the Convention Against Torture to territory under the control of UK troops abroad', Joint Committee on Human Rights, The UN Convention Against Torture (UNCAT), 19th Report of the Session 2005–2006, HL Paper 185-I; HC 701-I, at para 73. CAT Conclusions and Recommendations of the Committee Against Torture; United Kingdom of Great Britain and Northern Ireland, Crown Dependencies and Overseas Territories, UN Doc CAT/C/CR/33/3, 10 December 2004.

examined from both international humanitarian as well as human rights law perspectives and they will apply concurrently in such circumstances.[77]

From an international human rights law perspective and States which are occupying another State, it turns around the issue of 'overall effective control',[78] the State being required to provide all 'substantive rights'.[79] Those OPCAT States who have effective control over places of detention outside their own territory 'are under an obligation' to allow visits by the NPM and SPT.[80] In respect of situations other than occupation, the situation is more complicated. If agents of the State exercise power over people, there will be responsibility.[81]

As the Parliamentary Assembly of the Council of Europe put it 'the extent to which Contracting parties must secure the rights and freedoms of individuals outside their borders, is commensurate with the extent of their control . . .'.[82] Such differentiated treatment has been recognized by the ICJ which required either territorial control or the exercise of sovereign rights in the territories occupied by Israel in order for the ICESCR to apply.[83]

More problematic are situations of detention outside of these contexts, in places where the State does not have effective control or which are not its premises. These may include the transfer of detainees to local authorities, holding individuals in vehicles or local buildings, or local police cells, unfortunately exactly the type of situations where there is an increased risk of torture and ill-treatment.

The Federal Court of Canada decided in December 2008 that the Canadian Charter did not apply to individuals detained in Afghanistan.[84] Detainees were held in a temporary detention facility in Afghanistan at Kandahar Airfield which is a NATO base. The Airfield is not within the control of the Afghan or Canadian State but is shared by Canada with other States which have security operations in Afghanistan, although the detention facilities were within Canadian control. The Court held that

[77] *Legal Consequences of the Construction of a Wall in the Occupied Palestinian Territory*, Advisory Opinion ICJ Reports 2004, para 106; *Coard v United States*, Case 10.951, Inter-Am CHR, Report No 109/99; Human Rights Committee, *General Comment 31: Nature of the General Legal Obligations Imposed on States parties to the Covenant*, UN Doc CCPR/C/21/Rev.1/Add.13 (26 May 2004); Concluding Observations of the Human Rights Committee: Israel, 21 August 2003, UN Doc CCPR/Co/78/ISR, para 11; SC Res 1265 (1999); Arts 72, 75 API.

[78] *Cyprus v Turkey*, Appl No 25781/94, European Court of Human Rights, 10 May 2001, para 77; *Loizidou v Turkey* (Preliminary Objections), European Court of Human Rights, 23 March 1995, Series A, vol 310, paras 62–64; *Bankovic and others v Belgium and 16 other Contracting States*, Appl no 52207/99, European Court of Human Rights, 12 December 2001, para 71.

[79] *Cyprus v Turkey*, ibid, para 77.

[80] Nowak and McArthur, n 2 above, p 932.

[81] *Ocalan v Turkey*, Appl No 46221/99, European Court of Human Rights, 12 March 2003, para 93.

[82] Parliamentary Assembly, Area where the European Convention on Human Rights cannot be implemented, Doc 9730, 11 March 2003, para 45.

[83] *Legal Consequences of the Construction of a Wall in the Occupied Palestinian Territory*, n 77 above, para 112.

[84] *Amnesty International Canada v Canada (Attorney General)*, 2008 FC 336 (CanLII), 3 December 2008.

the scope of the authority given to Canada by the government of Afghanistan to detain individuals on its soil is limited and specifically contemplates that Canada's actions in this regard be governed by international law. In addition, it is clear from a review of the documentation governing the relationship between Afghanistan and Canada that the rights to be accorded to detainees are those guaranteed by the Afghan constitution and by international law.[85]

This is a complex and controversial area. This discussion here serves simply to note that if OPCAT applies to these situations, then it is the obligation of the OPCAT Member State to provide its NPM with the capacity to visit these places of detention and therefore to have the required facilities such as professional knowledge and minimum powers as set out in Articles 18–20. In addition, the SPT will also have the power to do the same,[86] although there is a defence available to States, which does not apply to the NPM, in relation to visits by the SPT.

Conversely, Nowak and McArthur argue that 'if parts of a state's territory are occupied by another state... or administered by a UN transitional administration... or under the *de facto control of insurgent groups*... or governed by *de facto authorities*... the respective governments are not required to provide access to the places of detention in such territories'.[87] They would, however, still remain responsible under international law.

F. Article 14(2) Objection to a Visit by the SPT

States can object to a visit by the SPT if there are

urgent and compelling grounds of national defence, public safety, natural disaster or serious disorder in the place to be visited that temporarily prevent the carrying out of such a visit. The existence of a declared state of emergency as such shall not be invoked by the state party as a reason to object to the visit.[88]

Other human rights bodies have provided States with a 'very wide discretion' when it comes to national security.[89] However, Article 14(2) takes the ECPT as its model[90] but restricts it slightly. The State cannot object to the mission as a

[85] Ibid, paras 297 and 298.
[86] Article 14.
[87] Nowak and McArthur, n 2 above, p 932, italics as in original.
[88] OPCAT, Article 14(2).
[89] See Human Rights Committee, *Alzery v Sweden*, Communication No 1416/2005, CCPR/C/88/D/1416/2005, 10 November 2006, para 11.10. But these must be based on reasonable and objective grounds, *Vjatseslav Borzov v Estonia*, Human Rights Committee, Communication No 1136/2002, CCPR/C/81/D/1136/2002, 26 July 2004.
[90] ECPT, Article 9(1); see Nowak and McArthur, n 2 above, pp 1044–1045.

whole, only to a particular visit to a place of detention and this is clearly intended only to be a temporary objection.[91]

Although the prohibition of torture is absolute, this provision provides States with a modest degree of restraining power with respect to providing unrestricted access for the SPT to places of detention. From the information available, no State has so far sought to make use of this provision. It is important to note that the same restrictions do not apply with respect to the NPM, and therefore the NPM's access is unfettered even during such times.

G. Some Core Issues

The current approach of States and NPMs to the scope of OPCAT and the extent to which the breadth of places of deprivation of liberty is covered is mixed. This depends on a range of factors, including: whether the State has chosen an existing body as the NPM; how extensive or limited the visiting mechanisms that were available in the State before ratification of OPCAT; whether there is one single NPM or several; and whether those bodies are ombudsmen and/or NHRIs.

In general, where NHRIs or similar bodies have been chosen as the NPM, it is arguable that they are more likely to take a broader approach to the concept of deprivation of liberty and prevention than an ombudsman might. This is because they may be more closely tied to an ethos of human rights and less focused simply on visiting prisons and police cells as places of deprivation of liberty. However, this must be balanced against the extent to which it had the powers, and therefore the experience, to visit all places of detention.

1. Different approaches and requirements

Beyond prisons, and as evidence from the interviews and research we have conducted indicates, whilst many of the current visiting bodies cover a wide range of types of places of detention, it is often the case that certain areas may be omitted from the mandate of the existing visiting bodies and these are not always what one might expect. These have included the military and, perhaps more surprisingly, police stations.[92]

Overall, however, despite the breadth of places that could be visited under OPCAT, there is still the tendency to equate what is required with coverage, principally, of prisons and police cells. As a result, whilst in some situations visits to prisons and police cells might fit OPCAT requirements in terms of regularity, for example, and while the NPM may be visiting other places of detention such as

[91] Nowak and McArthur, n 2 above, p 1045.

[92] This was an initial stumbling block for the UK NPM. See also for Georgia, interview with Giorgi Chkheidze, Georgian Young Lawyers Association (Georgia) on 20 June 2007. See also New Zealand, initially, interview with Stuart Beresford, New Zealand Ministry of Justice.

psychiatric hospitals or migrant detention facilities, the latter may not be as frequent as OPCAT requires:

I guess their priority is police stations and prisons. Once there was this monitoring of psychiatric hospitals, it was some of kind of campaign initiated by the Public Defender but it was not like something happening on a regular basis, they did it once in a year and delivered the report.[93]

In part this is pragmatic. Of those institutions which are already in existence and which are then designated as an NPM under OPCAT they have frequently had as their primary (and often sole) focus criminal detention facilities. The addition of the OPCAT mandate requires some changes to their legislation. As will be seen in Chapter 6, there has been a trend by governments to fail to provide the necessary resources to existing institutions once they are designated as NPMs.

Broadening the scope of an existing body to cover a wider range of places of detention may also require a change in its ethos and approach. For example, an OPCAT visit will require more of a focus on torture prevention, whereas the NPM in its pre-NPM existence and in its non-OPCAT work may not have taken this stance. This is particularly the case for ombudsmen who may have taken a complaints-based approach which is often legalistic in attitude:

I mean how are you going to deal with them being the NPM? Will there be a special NPM part [in the report of the NPM]? Will there be a special part on torture or ill treatment? I don't know. I mean it's not been an emphasis. When you go to the prisons here and you ask medical staff or whoever, it's just not really considered.... I'd be interested to see how they're going to incorporate that role into the report that they are already doing.[94]

In some jurisdictions there are separate institutions for different types of detention. In the UK there are eighteen separate institutions forming the NPM covering a range of different types of detention. On the one hand this suggests a great deal of expertise specific to each context, something which one ombudsman or human rights institution is unlikely to be able to mirror, certainly not without many years of experience. However, such an approach may also lack consistency between the bodies and in the ethos or standards they apply.

2. Expertise

As noted in Chapter 1, what is deemed to be appropriate expertise for both the SPT and NPM has been the subject of debate even during the drafting of OPCAT. In practice, however, it is clear that a broad approach to the scope of OPCAT requires broad expertise in those members undertaking the visits. For example, visits by

[93] Interview with Giorgi Tugushi, OSCE field mission in Georgia (now Ombudsman of Georgia) (Georgia), 20 June 2007.

[94] Interview with Dorrit Rée Akselbo, Rehabilitation and Research Centre for Torture Victims (Denmark), 6 November 2007. This is not limited to ombudsmen, however: see change of name of the Board of Visitors in the UK to Independent Monitoring Boards.

lawyers alone to the range of institutions covered by OPCAT are not seen by many as sufficient to satisfy the requirement in Article 18(2) of professional expertise. Conversely, the lack of, for example, medical expertise among its members may dictate the extent to which the NPM may be willing to visit a psychiatric or other medical establishment.[95] These different demands may be accommodated if, as in the UK,[96] there are a range of different bodies carrying out visits to different places of detention, but may be more difficult to achieve where the NPM is only one institution.

This then raises the question of the extent to which different expertise is needed depending on the nature of the establishment or place of detention being visited. For example, should there always be a psychiatrist on the visiting team for a mental health institution? Should someone with a military background always be part of a visit to a military facility? Should there always be medical expertise on hand for all visits? There is certainly a perception that these are ideal, whether this relates to visits by the SPT or the NPM. This is in part because it provides the visiting team with the necessary 'expertise',[97] they are likely to get more respect as a result, and can be useful from the perspective of the need to ensure a dialogue with the State authorities.[98]

A further issue that has arisen in the context of expertise is the extent to which previous service users should form part of the visiting team. For example, a study of the examination of mental health and social care inspectorates recommended that the inspectors themselves be suitably qualified and experienced and that

> [i]n order to ensure credibility of the inspectorate's work, people who have experienced mental health services and services for people with intellectual disabilities should be actively recruited as inspectors. Inspectorates should identify groups of mental health service users and involve them in their work generally.[99]

This is a controversial issue that has been debated recently in the context of the CRPD, but less so with respect to OPCAT.[100] The question arises not only in respect of users of psychiatric institutions, for example, but also other places of detention, those who have been detained in juvenile facilities, those detained under immigration or refugee facilities, and soldiers in military facilities, even as far as

[95] Indeed, the most common concern so far has been to call for medical experts to be included in visits to places of detention, see interview with Diego Blazquez Martín, representative of the Spanish Red Cross and human rights professor of the University in Madrid (Spain), 21 November 2006.

[96] Indeed, it is in the case of the UK, which has separate institutions for visiting mental health and social care institutions, that the MDAC note the 'potential for overlap and confusion both within the system and for those trying to access it', Mental Disability Advocacy Centre (MDAC), *Inspect! Inspectorates of Mental Health and Social Care Institutions in the European Union 2006*, <http://www.mdac.info/documents/122_Inspect.pdf>, p 53.

[97] Interview with Diego Blazquez Martín, representative of the Spanish Red Cross and human rights professor of the University in Madrid (Spain) on 21 November 2006.

[98] APT, Guide, *Establishment and Designation of National Preventive Mechanisms* (Geneva: APT, 2006), p 51.

[99] MDAC recognizes the UK's 'widespread involvement of users and user groups in its inspectorate mechanisms', Mental Disability Advocacy Centre (MDAC), *Inspect!*, n 96 above, p 12 and p 53.

[100] Ibid, p 12.

those who have themselves been subject to torture or other forms of ill-treatment. So far this is not an issue that has received any real attention in the context of OPCAT but is a point worth considering.

Beyond the issue of experts, to what extent should the methodology of the visit itself differ depending on the type of place of detention being visited? Evidence suggests that visits to, for example, a military place of detention do not necessarily require an intrinsically different approach to a visit to a psychiatric hospital. As to whether the standards applicable to the variety of institutions differ, this is an issue that will be discussed below.

3. Coordination

There is no express requirement in OPCAT that there be coordination among elements of the NPM, if applicable, or between the NPM and non-NPM national bodies. With respect to the former, although it may not be an issue in many States which have only one institution as the NPM, in others where there are a variety of different bodies which form the NPM, the coordination among them becomes crucial. Indeed, the greater the number of institutions which constitute the NPM, the greater the need for coordination. This is even more the case when different institutions deal with different places of detention. The most notable examples in this context are New Zealand, where the NPM is composed of five institutions, and the UK, which is composed of eighteen. In New Zealand the five bodies are: the Human Rights Commission, the Ombudsmen, the Independent Police Conduct Authority, the Children's Commissioner, and the Inspector of Service Penal Establishments.[101] Apart from the New Zealand National Human Rights Commission, the others have existing powers to visit places of detention prior to their designation as NPM. The Human Rights Commission acts as the coordinating mechanism.

The UK is on the outer edges of the spectrum in its designation of eighteen institutions to form part of the NPM.[102] Whilst this has been lauded for its comprehensiveness—indeed few countries have this range of statutory or other institutions with specialist attention on different places of detention—it does make the case for coordination that much stronger.[103] In this context, Her Majesty's Inspectorate of Prisons (HMIP) has been selected as the coordinating mechanism for the entire NPM across the UK and has been provided with a small budget and one part-time member of staff to fulfil this role. Coordination is also an issue for federal or devolved States, where institutions exist across different parts of the country.[104]

[101] New Zealand Gazette, 21 June 2007, Notice Number 2667, 'Designation of Central National Preventive Mechanism', and 2668 'Designation of National Preventive Mechanisms', 21 June 2007, p 1816, <http://online.gazette.govt.nz/>.

[102] See <http://www.justice.gov.uk/guidance/opcat.htm>.

[103] See Law School, University of Bristol, *The Optional Protocol to the UNCAT.* Conference Report, Report on the First Annual Conference on the Implementation of the Optional Protocol to the UN Convention Against Torture (OPCAT), University of Bristol, 19–20 April 2007.

[104] APT, *The Optional Protocol to the UN Convention Against Torture in Federal and Decentralised States.*

Exactly what coordination entails, however, is very much open to debate. From interviews conducted with those NPMs already operating, this can be a light touch approach initially. This could include organizing meetings between the various constituent elements of the NPM to share information; acting as the focal point and point of liaison between the SPT and the NPM; providing information to each of the constituent elements on how other bodies operate; and compiling any annual report.[105]

However, evidence collected also indicates that in no situation has adding OPCAT requirements onto existing work, where the institution was already in existence before being designated as the NPM, meant that their workload or approaches have stayed the same. There has always been something additional required, whether this is, for example, through changing the internal structure of the organization,[106] taking on additional staff,[107] or adding a focus on torture specifically.[108] In the context of coordination, therefore, practice from those bodies who have started to carry out this function indicates that the obligation may in fact be more onerous and include: interpreting OPCAT responsibilities; identifying systematic practices and concerns across the range of the national constituent elements of the NPM;[109] and providing an oversight mechanism. The different bodies within the NPM may look to the coordinating body to provide some advice on how, for example, certain detainees should be treated or deciding whose remit they fall under.[110] This may also include identifying the potential conflict of roles and remits between the different elements of the NPM. There is also some call for the coordinating body to act as the expert on OPCAT nationally and to monitor the other bodies and their compliance with OPCAT. In a way, it could be argued that coordinating bodies should be undertaking activities which move the collective NPM towards a more coherent 'system' with regard to their methodologies and standards.

Consistency of approach between the different institutions, which may not be used to working under the same umbrella, is a challenging one. How a 'system' of preventive visiting. How this is achieved is more problematic, especially where there are bodies with years of experience operating in different contexts, which will be wary of what may be seen as interference in their operations. It will require the coordinating institution to identify, first, the respective scopes, methodology, and mandates of the different bodies, before it can come to any conclusions as to the need for consistency in approach.

105 See New Zealand Human Rights Commission, *Monitoring Places of Detention*.

106 For example, interview with Diego Blazquez Martín, representative of the Spanish Red Cross and human rights professor of the University in Madrid (Spain), 21 November 2006.

107 For example, Spain, '... they have a lot of work now and ... they would need more personnel and more money to be effective ...', interview with Diego Blazquez Martín, representative of the Spanish Red Cross and human rights professor of the University in Madrid (Spain), 21 November 2006.

108 For example, with respect to the Ombudsman in Denmark, see interview with Dorrit Ree Akselbo, Rehabilitation and Research Centre for Torture Victims (Denmark), 6 November 2007.

109 See, for example, New Zealand Human Rights Commission, *Monitoring Places of Detention*, p 9.

110 See, for example, interview with Commander Chris Griggs, Deputy Director of Legal Services, New Zealand Defence Force (New Zealand).

Who should take on this coordinating role is an additional difficulty. In practical terms, unless there is a requirement in the legislation or document establishing or designating the NPM, or within its existing remit, or the State specifically allocates the role to a particular institution, then there may in fact be no obligation on the various bodies of the NPM to coordinate. This applies equally to federal and devolved administrations:

they are separate . . . I mean they . . . have good coordination . . . They want cooperation but if they didn't have this commitment they are not compelled to do it.[111]

In addition, there may be some competition between the different elements of an NPM as to who should undertake this coordinating role, a role which may imply some sort of hierarchy among different bodies.

In the context of New Zealand, although the NHRC does not have a visiting mandate, it can provide the coordination: as an NHRI it provides the broader preventive and human rights angle which one might want to ensure that OPCAT is not just about the technicalities of visiting places of detention. In the UK, in contrast, the coordination is undertaken by HMIP which is also one of the visiting bodies.

Although not expressly mentioned in OPCAT, there is also the issue of coordination between the NPM and other relevant national bodies, both governmental and non-governmental, who may have a role or remit with respect to visiting places of detention or prevention of torture more generally but who are not officially designated as the NPM.[112] Some NPMs have already recognized this as being an issue. Thus, it is the coordinating body which can act as a link between government and civil society organizations who work on prevention of torture.[113]

4. Consistency in standards

At the outset of the coming into force of OPCAT there were concerns that where there were a number of bodies who make up the NPM, each would adopt different methodologies and different standards in their work. Even for an NPM which is comprised of only one body it may face challenges in dealing with differing standards across different sectors of its visiting mandate.

Furthermore, the legal standards relating to the protection of individuals who are detained may differ nationally depending on the context in which they are detained. For example, those detained in a military context are likely to have

[111] Interview with Diego Blazquez Martín, representative of the Spanish Red Cross and human rights professor of the University in Madrid (Spain), 21 November 2006.

[112] This could be implied, however, from Articles 19(b) and (c), and Article 22 OPCAT.

[113] 'It was really a big responsibility of the Public Defender to . . . take all the responsibility itself. There should be some kind of responsibility sharing process . . . Because of the pressure from the government also. Because we don't want to get to put all the responsibility on the Public Defender and to leave him alone in front of the official bodies . . .', interview with Giorgi Chkheidze, Georgian Young Lawyers Association (Georgia), 20 June 2007. See Okafor, O C and Agbakwa, S C, 'On Legalism, Popular Agency and "Voices of Suffering": The Nigerian National Human Rights Commission in Context' (2002) 24(3) *Hum Rts Q* 662–720.

different laws applicable to them than those detained in psychiatric institutions. The practice in applying those legal standards may also differ. As the UK's coordinating body, the HMIP, has stated in the context of a visit to the military corrective training centre in the UK

> we were mindful in this inspection of the particularities of an establishment run as part of the armed services.... It is clearly important that, during detention, service discipline and procedures are maintained and not undermined. However, it is equally important to recognise the particular vulnerabilities of those held in custody and to ensure that the safeguards required in international and domestic law are in place.[114]

The legal standards will include not only national laws, constitutional provisions, codes of conduct, and other practice documents, but also regional and international standards as well. What is applied in one State in one particular context may differ from another. For example, in the European context in some States the recently revised European Prison Rules are accepted as the applicable standards.[115] A range of different cultural contexts are likely to be apparent and any national and international visiting mechanism is going to have to take these into account.[116] Indeed, the SPT was initially criticized for doing just this, particularly in relation to the methodology it adopted on its visits, given that a number of SPT members were also concurrently or had previously been members of the CPT.[117]

In establishing its system of visits for the purpose of preventing torture, one of the hoped-for consequences of OPCAT, therefore, is that it will identify and iron out inconsistencies in standards between different categories of places of detention and detainees. This will require, however, a national assessment of what is available in any given context and as such should be the role of the NPM itself, if it is just one institution, or the coordinating body if there are several. The aim should be to identify best practice to enhance protection and prevention across the board.

However, in reality, few we spoke to saw variation in the applicability of standards as a concern on the ground, viewing it rather pragmatically. Some have mentioned the use of 'monitoring guides' such as that produced by the APT as being particularly helpful.

In addition, what the SPT applies in the national context when it visits a State may be different from what the NPM itself applies on its own visits. Absolute universality of standards may be difficult to achieve. As is hinted at in the Guiding Principles set out in its statement regarding its 'Approach to the Concept of Prevention', the SPT for its part will have a range of cultural, economic, and social differences to consider,[118] perhaps more so than the NPMs themselves. However,

[114] HMIP, Report on a Full Announced Inspection of the Military Corrective Training Centre, 14–18 June 2004, by HM Chief Inspector of Prisons, 2004, p 3.

[115] Law School, Conference Report, p 25.

[116] See, for example, in relation to the European CPT, ibid, p 25.

[117] These were Silvia Casale, Marija Definis Gojanovic and Zdenek Hajek, and Leopoldo Torres Boursaalt.

[118] See CAT/OP/12/6, para 5 (a): 'The prevalence of torture and ill-treatment is influenced by a broad range of factors, including the general level of enjoyment of human rights and the rule of law, levels of poverty, social exclusion, corruption, discrimination, etc...To that end, the SPT is deeply

initial concerns that the SPT would be too European in its approach, by modelling itself on the CPT, have proved in fact to be less of an issue, certainly for those outside Europe. Here many have seen the experience of the CPT as being useful to developing OPCAT and given the breadth of countries that the CPT covered, that it was in fact more international in its approach.[119]

H. Conclusion

Although the text of OPCAT is broad, how NPMs and the SPT are interpreting the scope of their mandate is still open to debate. A number of grey areas are appearing on the ground and it is now the role of the NPM and the SPT to identify those areas which lack protection and to make recommendations for their inclusion in the NPM's remit.

interested in the general situation within a country concerning the enjoyment of human rights and how this affects the situation of persons deprived of their liberty.'

[119] 'Basically all standards of CPT are mainly international standards because they cover 47 member states, so that's already a huge region', interview with Giorgi Tugushi, OSCE field mission in Georgia (now Ombudsman of Georgia) (Georgia), 20 June 2007.

5

The Role of the Subcommittee on Prevention of Torture (SPT)

As has been seen in the opening chapters, whereas the creation of an international visiting body was central to OPCAT from the outset, the idea of the Protocol requiring the establishment of national bodies of inspection came late in the day. The significance of the inclusion of NPMs within the OPCAT framework has, however, drawn attention away from the important shifts which also took place as regards the role of the international body itself, the final text being markedly different in some key aspects from that which was originally envisaged. In presenting the final text in Chapter 3, elements of the subsequent practice of the SPT were outlined and it is evident from what was said there that the SPT has already started to develop practices and emphases which might not necessarily have been fully foreseen or expected by those who concluded that text. Perhaps this is not surprising. As was noted previously, whilst there may have been clear ideas about what the SPT should *not* be doing, there was less clarity on what it *should* do. In this context, therefore, the SPT has had to define its own mandate and focus, complicated by the fact that it is not perceived as operating in the traditional vein of other UN treaty bodies by not receiving State reports or individual communications.[1] Instead, OPCAT charges the SPT with three main duties:[2]

1. to visit places of deprivation of liberty in the states parties to the OPCAT and make recommendations to the respective authorities with the aim of improving the prevention of torture and inhuman treatment;
2. to assist and advise states parties in setting up their own national preventive mechanisms (NPMs), which are to fulfil the functions of the national bodies referred above, and to assist these NPMs in their work;
3. to cooperate with other relevant UN organs and mechanisms as well as other international, regional and national institutions or organisations working towards the strengthening of the protection of all persons against torture and other forms of ill-treatment.

The purpose of this chapter is to build on and move beyond the account of the SPT given in Chapter 3 by examining further what these functions entail and how they

[1] See ICCPR, Article 40; ICESCR, Article 16; CERD, Article 9; CEDAW, Article 18; CAT, Article 19; CRC, Article 44; CMW, Article 73; CRPD, Article 35.

[2] OPCAT, Article 11.

have so far been interpreted by the SPT in practice. Issues that received considerable attention during the drafting of OPCAT, such as the relationship with the CAT, the number of members and their required qualifications and experience, how to deal with unannounced visits, and the issue of confidentiality have all come in for scrutiny, but not always in a manner or from a perspective which might have been envisaged. As the SPT moves from the 'old' Subcommittee of ten to the 'new' Subcommittee of twenty-five—more than doubling its membership—this is an opportune time to take stock of both its achievements and of the challenges which it has so far faced. In doing so, this chapter will draw extensively on the empirical work undertaken in the context of the research project on which this book is based in order that it be grounded in the experience, rather than in the text and theory, of the Subcommittee at work.

OPCAT entered into force following its 20th ratification in June 2006, and the election of the ten members of the Subcommittee took place in December of that year. In accordance with Article 9, the initial term of office of five of the members, chosen by ballot, was reduced to two years, in order to ensure a more regular rotation of membership. Following the 50th ratification in 2009 the membership increased to twenty-five, with elections taking place in October 2010 and the 'new' SPT of twenty-five meeting for the first time at the thirteenth session of the Subcommittee in February 2011.

Since the SPT's original inaugural meeting in February 2007,[3] it has held a further eleven sessions, in February, June, and November of each year.[4] By the end of 2010, the SPT had carried out visits to eleven States and one follow-up visit.

A constant source of frustration, certainly in the earlier years, has been an inadequate budgetary provision to service its visiting mandate and a lack of any budget at all to support its relationship with NPMs. The expectations placed on a newly formed human rights treaty body are considerable and, beyond an initial 'honeymoon period' of perhaps six or so months, one anticipates some visible policy and strategic direction. It was, then, disappointing that in this critical opening phase, when the SPT was faced with the need to determine what OPCAT actually required of an NPM and what the SPT's relationship should be with these novel national mechanisms, the Subcommittee was essentially without funds—and as a result suffered from a seriously impaired capacity—to engage in this task. During its first years, then, the main focus of the SPT's work appeared to be its own visits to States and places of detention, and the other aspects of how it engaged with its mandate, such as prevention, its work with NPMs, and with other regional and international bodies, were less visible. As the SPT has found its feet, however, there has been a marked increase in the number of policy documents and other forms of

[3] See <http://www2.ohchr.org/english/bodies/cat/opcat/sessions.htm>. Its members have participated in a range of other events, at the UN, regional, and national levels. Such engagements will be considered further in later chapters.

[4] According to Article 10(3), the CAT and the SPT are to hold at least one session per year simultaneously. In practice this has become the case with the November sessions.

guidance now emanating from it. It is therefore much easier, at this juncture, to get a sense of how the SPT now sees itself and how it sees OPCAT. At this point of transition from the 'old' to the 'new' SPT it is useful to provide in providing an account of what has been the practice so far, in order to inform future directions. It is to that expansion of membership that we shall turn first.

A. The Membership of the SPT

As has been said, according to Article 5(1) of OPCAT the initial membership of the SPT was to be ten members,[5] elected for a period of four years, staggered, with a possibility of their mandate being renewed once.[6] However, similar to provisions found in other UN treaties,[7] OPCAT also provides for an increase in membership once the number of States Parties crosses a given threshold,[8] which in the case of OPCAT rises to twenty-five members following the 50th ratification.[9] This threshold was reached in September 2009[10] and thus on 28 October 2010 elections of the SPT were held to elect an additional fifteen members to the SPT, combined with second re-elections[11] for the places of five of the SPT members whose mandates expired on 31 December 2010.[12] With this expansion of the membership to twenty-five, the SPT became the largest UN human rights treaty body.[13]

As noted in Chapter 2, the type of expertise and qualifications that should be required of an SPT member were an issue that taxed the drafters of OPCAT. The resulting text, Article 5(2), provides that the members are to be chosen from 'among the persons of high moral character, having proven professional experience in the field of the administration of justice, in particular criminal law, prison or police administration, or in the various fields relevant to the treatment of persons deprived of their liberty'.[14] There is also the requirement of equitable geographical

[5] For a list of current membership see <http://www2.ohchr.org/english/bodies/cat/opcat/membership.htm>. See also Appendix VII.

[6] OPCAT, Article 9.

[7] CEDAW, ICRMW, and CRPD.

[8] In case of CEDAW, the initial membership of eighteen members of the Committee on the Elimination of All Forms of Discrimination against Women expanded to twenty-three after the thirty-fifth ratification or accession to CEDAW (Article 17), while in the case of the ICRMW, the membership of the Committee of Rights of Migrant Workers expanded from ten to fourteen members after the forty-first ratification or accession (Article 72(1b). For the CRPD, the initial composition of twelve members of the Committee on the Rights of Persons with Disabilities, increased to eighteen members after an additional sixty ratifications (Article 34(2)).

[9] OPCAT, Article 5(1).

[10] Switzerland deposited its instrument of ratification on 24 September 2009, becoming the fiftieth State Party to OPCAT.

[11] First re-elections of half of the SPT members took place in 2008 and brought no changes to the composition of the treaty body as all those members whose mandates were about to expire successfully stood for re-election.

[12] See <http://www2.ohchr.org/english/bodies/cat/opcat/elections2010.htm>.

[13] Previously, the largest Committee had been the Committee on the Elimination of All Forms of Discrimination Against Women which is comprised of twenty-three members (CEDAW, Article 17).

[14] See, for example, CRC, Article 43(2).

distribution and representation of different forms of civilization and legal systems of the States Parties, in Article 5(3) of OPCAT,[15] and for due consideration to be given to gender representation.[16] Many of these provisions reflect those in other UN treaties, for example, that no two members can be nationals of the same State,[17] and that members serve in their individual capacity and are independent and impartial.[18]

We have already outlined previously[19] that the diversity of expertise required of the SPT as a collective was intended by those drafting the Protocol in part to reflect not only the broad nature of the scope of OPCAT and the type of places which the SPT can therefore visit, but also a desire to move away from a committee which was composed solely of lawyers. Whilst there is clearly some merit in ensuring a broad range of expertise on a committee of this nature and for it not to be dominated by one particular sector, there is a need for some balance. In fact, the membership of a human rights treaty body will ultimately determine its direction and its focus and, conversely, the membership should reflect the needs of that particular committee and what it is required to do in terms of its mandate. All human rights treaty bodies have jurisdiction over the interpretation of their founding treaties and this inevitably requires some legal background. In addition, States and NPMs often seek clarification and interpretation on the specific provisions of the treaty, and OPCAT is no exception. Some legal experience on the Committee is therefore necessary, but on its own may not be sufficient.

OPCAT's requirements for a breadth of experience in SPT membership were not very clearly reflected in its initial composition. Whilst there was some diversity of experience, with two of its ten members coming from the medical profession, many were disappointed with the fact that the other eight members of the SPT as initially elected had a legal background. At the end of the day, however, it is not at all clear whether this perceived lack of breadth of expertise has stifled the work of the SPT or not. Furthermore, and perhaps more importantly, the initial composition did not reflect a geographical balance, there being no members from Africa or the Asia-Pacific region.[20] The SPT was acutely aware of this issue—a problem, it must be emphasized, which was entirely out of its hands—and set out what it believed would make an equitable geographical distribution in an expanded Committee: three members from Africa, three from Asia, five from Western Europe, eight from Eastern Europe, and six from Latin America.[21] The SPT has shown itself to be continually mindful of this regional imbalance and the potential difficulty this may pose when the SPT is

[15] See, for example, CERD, Article 8(1).

[16] OPCAT, Article 5(4). See also, similarly, CRPD, Article 34(4).

[17] See, for example, ICCPR, Article 29(2).

[18] OPCAT, Article 5(6).

[19] See Chapter 2.

[20] The only State in the Asia-Pacific region which could have nominated anyone when OPCAT came into force was the Maldives, which ratified on 15 February 2006. Cambodia and New Zealand did not ratify until 14 and 30 March 2007 respectively.

[21] SPT, Third Annual Report of the Subcommittee on Prevention of Torture and Other Cruel, Inhuman and Degrading Treatment or Punishment, 25 March 2010, CAT/C/44/2, para 6.

advising States and NPMs: 'the SPT should set a good example for the NPMs'.[22] In terms of gender balance, while the initial membership was clearly not 'equitable', with only two out of ten being women,[23] compared with other UN treaty bodies it did not fare particularly badly.[24]

Given these concerns, expressed by those both within and outside the SPT, one might have hoped for some improvement when the potential for election of an additional fifteen members arose. There were thirty-one candidates for the elections in October 2010 and all those current SPT members whose membership expired on 31 December 2010 stood for re-election.[25] The potential pool from which to draw was clearly not that wide. The list of candidates alone could not hope to address fully the geographical imbalance, with only two candidates put forward by the States of the Asia-Pacific region, a predominance of legal backgrounds, and a disappointing although much improved proportion of around one third being women.[26]

In the end, the results of the elections for expanding the membership[27] do reflect some changes, albeit not particularly dramatic ones. Of the twenty-five members,[28] over two-thirds have a legal background, although there is diversity within this.[29] There is now some, although one could not say 'equitable', geographical balance, with one member from Asia,[30] two members from Africa,[31] and one from the Middle East and North African region.[32] The number of women on the Committee has significantly increased, with eight members now ensuring that the SPT is among the examples of treaty bodies displaying good, if not, best practice.

More concerning, however, is that some of the newly elected members hold government positions.[33] In terms of independence, as will be noted in relation to NPMs in Chapter 6, the same issues apply. Even if the members themselves can separate out their functions as government officials from those of the SPT, it does not give the appearance of independence. And it is this perception of bias which can have an impact on the legitimacy and integrity of the SPT overall.

Perhaps more interesting, and potentially again problematical, is the fact that some of the newly elected members are also members of the NPM in their home

[22] Interview with Miguel Sarre, SPT member, 5 June 2007.

[23] Reduced to one when Silvia Casale from the UK resigned in 2009 and was replaced by Malcolm Evans.

[24] Third Annual Report, n 21 above, para 6.

[25] See <http://www2.ohchr.org/english/bodies/cat/opcat/elections2010.htm>.

[26] See election, in accordance with articles 7 and 9 of the Optional Protocol to the Convention Against Torture and Other Cruel, Inhuman or Degrading Treatment or Punishment, of 5 members of the Subcommittee on Prevention to replace those whose terms are due to expire on 31 December 2010, and 15 additional members to the Subcommittee on Prevention in accordance with article 5; UN Doc CAT/OP/SP/8/Add.1 of 21 September 2010.

[27] See <http://www2.ohchr.org/english/bodies/cat/opcat/elections2010.htm>.

[28] For a list of members to the SPT, see Appendix VII.

[29] For example, experience on NPMs, or medical experience.

[30] Ms Aisha Shujune Muhammad from the Maldives.

[31] Mr Paul Lam Shang Leen from Mauritius, and Mr Fortuné Gaétan Zongo from Burkina Faso.

[32] Ms Suzanne Jabbour from the Lebanon.

[33] The SPT member elected in respect of the Former Yugoslav Republic of Macedonia is also Assistant Minister in the Ministry of the Interior.

State.[34] SPT members cannot participate in visits to their home States as part of the SPT delegation.[35] However, although the inclusion of NPMs on the inspecting body itself may undermine the appearance of independence, particularly if the specific NPM does not have a positive reputation, it may conversely engender greater respect from among the NPM community and may provide the other SPT members with some invaluable insights into how NPMs can operate.

The challenges now posed for the SPT with its expanded membership are several. First, those who have been sitting on the SPT must learn to accommodate a range of different, as yet unknown, viewpoints and approaches to their work. Issues which may have been settled by the previous membership, even after protracted debate, could well be open for discussion again. It will take some time for all the members to get to know each other. This may stall any new policy or strategic direction that the SPT could take for the immediate future. Practically, a broader geographical reach poses challenges for language. The 'old' SPT needed to use only English and Spanish as working languages. With the expansion of membership, this is set to rise, with French certain to be added and a possible need for others besides. This has budgetary and logistical implications. A report on a visit is likely to be drafted in one particular language. Translating this into other languages will take time and money but is crucial if all members of the SPT are to be able to appreciate fully and debate its contents. Finally, as the SPT itself notes,[36] the significant increase in the membership will require a larger secretariat able to serve effectively the expanding workload of the Subcommittee.

B. The Interpretation of Its Own Mandate and Rules of Procedure

In contrast with other UN treaty bodies which examine the measures of implementation taken by States Parties on the basis of information that a State Party submits and appraise to what extent these have been successful, the SPT is to compile such information itself through conducting visits to States Parties. On the basis of information gathered during such visits, the SPT is then to give recommendations to the State Party in question as to how prevention of torture and ill-treatment is best to be achieved.

The SPT has always presented itself as having a markedly different mandate: as a new generation UN treaty body[37] and an International Preventive Mechanism.[38]

[34] For example, the newly elected SPT members in respect of Armenia, Estonia, and New Zealand.

[35] 'No member of the SPT shall participate either in the conduct of a visit or in the consideration of a report on the visit to the State Party in respect of the nationality of which she or he was elected or of the State Party which nominated her or him. No member of the SPT shall participate in activities which may imply, or may be seen to imply, a conflict of interest with their capacity as independent and impartial SPT members', Rule 28, Rules of Procedure of the Subcommittee on Prevention of Torture and Other Cruel, Inhuman Degrading Treatment or Punishment, CAT/OP/12/3, 5 January 2011.

[36] SPT, Fourth Annual Report of the Subcommittee on Prevention of Torture and Other Cruel, Inhuman and Degrading Treatment or Punishment, CAT/C/46/2, 7 January 2010, para 109.

[37] SPT, First Annual Report of the Subcommittee on Prevention of Torture and Other Cruel, Inhuman and Degrading Treatment or Punishment, CAT/C/40/2, 14 May 2008, para 5.

[38] Ibid, para 6.

However until very recently, it provided little detail about its vision of how this is to translate in practice. In its first three annual reports the SPT explains its mandate as a three-pillar system: visits to States Parties; work with the NPMs, both in advising States about their establishment, and assisting those already established; and cooperation with the relevant UN and other international and regional bodies.[39] The SPT notes that all three of these strands are essential for the prevention of torture and ill-treatment. This however does not offer much more than is set out in the text of OPCAT and crucially does not give any guidance as to how the treaty body envisages the practical implementation of its mandate. It seemed peculiar to many observers that the SPT did not quickly make public its Rules of Procedure;[40] even the Committee on the Rights of Persons with Disabilities, which came into being after the SPT, published its Rules before the latter.[41] Indeed, it was very much expected that adoption of the Rules of Procedure would be the first key task that the SPT would undertake:

> [. . .] this first period, which is very important, because they [the SPT] are going to decide upon their internal rules and the way they are going to work and these are not minor things.[42]

The SPT, on the other hand, since its very First Annual Report stated that the Rules of Procedure had in fact been developed, but referred to these as a 'key internal working document'[43] without any further explanation as to the reasons behind the decision not to make them public. Finally, in January 2011, after nearly four years[44] and numerous requests from various stakeholders[45] the Rules were made public. This brief history is indicative of the struggle that the treaty body has had with 'finding its feet' in relation to a range of issues, including, but not limited to, the principle of confidentiality as embodied in Article 2(3) of OPCAT. The SPT exercised extreme caution in the first two or three years in relation to many aspects of its mandate, not even putting into the public domain such information as the notifications of designated NPMs. Such an overly cautious approach was also extended towards its Rules of Procedure which of course made it yet more difficult for various stakeholders to grasp exactly how they should be engaging with the SPT.

[39] First Annual Report, n 37 above, para 7, Second Annual Report of the Subcommittee on Prevention of Torture and Other Cruel, Inhuman and Degrading Treatment or Punishment, 7 April 2009, CAT/C/42/2, para 7; and Third Annual Report, n 21 above, para 11.

[40] Other UN treaty bodies have published their Rules: for the ICCPR see CCPR/C/3/Rev.8. (2005); for ICESCR see E/C.12/1990/4/Rev.1 (1993); for CEDAW see Annex I to A/56/38 (2001); for CERD see CERD/C/35/Rev.3 (1989); for the CAT see CAT/C/3/Rev.4 (2002); for CRC see CRC/C/4/Rev.1 (2005); and for the CMW see HRI/GEN/3/Rev.1/Add.1 (2004).

[41] See Rules of Procedure of the Committee on the Rights of Persons with Disabilities, 13 August 2010, CRPD/C/4/2; available at <http://www.ohchr.org/EN/HRBodies/CRPD/Pages/CRPDIndex .aspx>.

[42] Interview with Alejandra De Bellis, Ministry of Foreign Affairs, Uruguay, 8 March 2007.

[43] See para 60 of the Annual Report.

[44] See Rules of Procedure of the Subcommittee on Prevention of Torture and Other Cruel, Inhuman or Degrading Treatment or Punishment; UN Doc CAT/OP/12/3 of 5 January 2011.

[45] See, for example Letter of Comments on SPT's Third Annual Report by the OPCAT Contact Group of 31 August 2010; available at <http://www.bristol.ac.uk/law/research/centres-themes/opcat/ docs .html#otherdocs>.

Therefore, until the start of 2011, the only public sources of information about the SPT were its annual reports and visit reports which States Parties in question had requested the SPT to make public.[46] Then, in a flurry of activity towards the end of 2010 and early 2011, several key documents and policies were adopted by the SPT and made public almost immediately. These included not only its Rules of Procedure but also Guidelines on Visits,[47] the previously mentioned document outlining its approach to the concept of prevention, and the expanded Guidelines on NPMs. This significant change in approach can be explained not only by an increased confidence in its own work, but also by the desire to record for those new members some of the debates and issues that it had been facing till now. The result is that there is now much more information in the public domain which sheds light on the way the treaty body views each of the three pillars of its mandate, which will now be looked at further.

C. Pillar I: Visits to States Parties

The main vehicle for prevention envisaged in the text of OPCAT is the system of visits to places of deprivation of liberty by the SPT and by NPMs. In some ways this was the easiest part of the mandate to comprehend, from the perspective of the SPT. With some members of the SPT also holding membership of the CPT, they were already versed in CPT visits, and, with the perception that visits to States to inspect places of detention were exciting and challenging, the SPT was evidently very keen to embark on this practical aspect of its mandate by carrying out its very first visit only eight months after its first session, followed very closely by the second visit only two months later.[48] However, while OPCAT is rather detailed in prescribing that such visits are to take place,[49] there are a number of questions of detail that are of crucial importance: how are the countries selected; what does the SPT do on its visits; and how does it engage with the authorities?

1. Selection of the countries: criteria, types of visits, and frequency

Article 13(1) of OPCAT prescribes that in order to set up the programme of visits, the SPT is to choose the first States to be visited by lot. This is a slightly different construct when compared to the provisions of the ECPT,[50] where Article 7

[46] As per Article 16 of OPCAT; as of 10 March 2011, there are six public visit reports: Maldives (UN Doc CAT/OP/MDV/1 of 26 February 2009); Sweden (UN Doc CAT/OP/SWE/1 of 10 September 2008); Mexico (UN Doc CAT/OP/MEX/1 of 31 May 2010); Paraguay (UN Doc CAT/OP/PRY/1 of 7 June 2010), Honduras (UN Doc CAT/OP/HND/1 of 10 February 2010), and Benin (UN Doc CAT/OP/BEN/1 of 9 March 2011).

[47] Guidelines of the Subcommittee on Prevention of Torture and Other Cruel, Inhuman or Degrading Treatment or Punishment in relation to visits to States parties; UN Doc CAT/OP/12/4 of 18 January 2011. See Appendix III below.

[48] See First Annual Report, n 37 above, Annex III.

[49] OPCAT, Articles 12–16.

[50] CPT/Inf/C (89) 1 [EN]—Strasbourg, 26.XI.1987.

contains no similar stipulation as to how States are to be chosen. The provision was inserted so as to ensure that the SPT would not target or single out a particular State Party but rather treat all on an equal footing on the basis of principles of universality, non-selectivity, and impartiality, as set out in Article 3 of OPCAT.[51] Inevitably, the choice of first visits is going to be scrutinized closely by those outside the SPT, whether they be governments, NPMs, or civil society and some criticized the resulting selection of Mauritius, the Maldives, and Sweden,[52] not least because of the CPT's choice to visit Sweden.[53] Interestingly, a similar situation was also faced by the CPT when it chose its first countries to be visited by lot. However it managed to work around the problem by utilizing the *ad hoc* visits permitted under the ECPT.[54] This technique was not available to the SPT, nevertheless, there is no reason why the SPT might not seek to establish such a practice on the basis of the general obligation of cooperation imposed upon States Parties by OPCAT.[55] Although the SPT has not sought to do this, were it able to develop a practice akin to *ad hoc* visits the SPT would have at its disposal a rather useful tool should a situation arise in which it would be desirable for the SPT to act urgently.

While Article 13(2) of OPCAT requires that States Parties be notified about the programme of visits by the SPT 'after consultations', the aim of the provision is not to provide States Parties with a possibility to preclude a visit. Article 14(2) notes that even a state of emergency cannot be invoked as a reason for objecting to a visit[56] and thus the purpose of notification is to allow the State to facilitate the visit, not to prevent it from occurring.[57] The practice so far is consistent with this interpretation as no State has objected to a visit proposed by the SPT.

After having chosen the first three States by a lot, the SPT has proceeded with what it called 'a reasoned process'[58] for the selection of States to be visited. For the outsider, however, the criteria for selection remain somewhat unclear. In its First Annual Report the SPT indicated that such factors as the date of ratification, development of the NPM, geographical distribution, the size and complexity of

[51] Long, D, *Commentary on the Optional Protocol to the UN Convention against Torture* in *Optional Protocol to the United Nations Convention against Torture and Other Cruel, Inhuman or Degrading Treatment or Punishment. A Manual for Prevention* (2005) Publication of the IIHR and APT, 91.

[52] See First Annual Report, n 37 above para 14.

[53] The SPT visited Sweden in March 2008. In fact, the CPT's last visit to Sweden had taken place in January 2003. If there were a 'problem' of visiting 'duplication' here it was generated by the CPT when it announced later that year that it would itself be visiting Sweden again, and did so in June 2009.

[54] See ECPT, Article 7. An *ad hoc* visit was conducted to Turkey in the first year of the CPT's operation, which was in all regards the same as a periodic visit even though Turkey had not been one of the countries selected by lot for a visit that year. Permission to publish the Report on this visit, which took place in 1990, was finally given in 2007. See CPT/Inf (2007) 1.

[55] See OPCAT, Article 2(4).

[56] States may only postpone a visit to a particular place of detention on the grounds of national defence, public safety, natural disaster, or serious disorder: see Article 14(2).

[57] Evans, M D, 'The Place of the Optional Protocol in the Scheme of International Approaches to Torture and Torture Prevention and Resulting Issues' in H C Scheu and S Hybnerova (eds), *International and National Mechanisms against Torture* (University Karlova (Prague) Law School Publication, 2004), 39.

[58] First Annual Report, n 37 above, para 14.

the State, regional preventive monitoring, and urgent issues reported may be taken into consideration.[59] Very similar wording has been repeated in the Second,[60] Third,[61] and Fourth[62] Annual Reports, and in the latter two, 'development of NPM' has been substituted with 'establishment of NPM'[63] and 'date of ratification/development of NPMs'[64] respectively. Neither its Rules of Procedure,[65] the SPT's Guidelines on Visits,[66] nor information contained in the reports of visits undertaken so far provide any further insight on the factors that determine the choice. For example, if looking at the criteria for the development/establishment of an NPM, from the seven States that the SPT has so far chosen to visit, only two had set up their NPMs by the time of the SPT's visit: Mexico and Honduras. On the one hand this could suggest that the SPT is visiting States where the designation of the NPM is still open to debate. Indeed, an intervention by the SPT at this early stage of the process of establishing an NPM is seen as crucial by many:

> I would really urge the SPT to pay huge attention at this time to the quality of the NPMs that will be set up, to the extent of actually re-stating the criteria for the NPM to the relevant States, so that those contemplating something less than compliant know in advance that this will be noticed and responded to.[67]

This is indeed something that the SPT has acknowledged, expressing regret, for example, 'that it has not had the opportunity to engage more quickly with States in the early stages of their participation in the OPCAT system, and in particular during the process of establishing their NPMs'.[68] The reports of visits to the States so far, however, do not reflect any in-depth discussion with the State authorities or others on the NPM process which the SPT may have had during its visits. For example, the SPT devoted only three paragraphs to the NPM process in Paraguay in its 313-paragraph-long visit report,[69] despite the fact that the process here has been lauded by many as an example of good practice. Whilst, therefore, the SPT 'is attracted to a model in which it would seek to visit States Parties as soon as possible following their ratification of OPCAT in order to offer advice and assistance regarding the establishment of its NPMs',[70] it, conversely, also wishes to give some time to States to get to grips with their obligations under OPCAT by not visiting new States Parties straight away.

More interesting has been the choice of geographical regions: of the eleven States chosen so far, three have been from the African region (Benin, Liberia, and Mauritius),

[59] Ibid. [60] Second Annual Report, n 39 above, para 14.
[61] Third Annual Report, n 21 above, para 20. [62] Fourth Annual Report, n 36 above, para 112.
[63] Third Annual Report, n 21 above, para 20. [64] Fourth Annual Report, n 36 above, para 112.
[65] The Rules of Procedure do not deal with the visiting aspect of the SPT's mandate at all.
[66] Guideline 3 at para 4 only makes a broad reference to provisions of OPCAT that must be taken into account: 'In drawing up this programme, the Subcommittee shall have regard to the provisions of articles 1, 11, paragraph 1 (c), and 31 of the Optional Protocol.'
[67] Interview with Mary Murphy, Director of the Penal Reform International South Caucasus Regional Office (now Policy Director of the Penal Reform International) on 21 June 2007.
[68] Fourth Annual Report, n 36 above, para 44.
[69] See paras 56–58; CAT/OP/PRY/1.
[70] Fourth Annual Report, n 36 above, para 44.

four from Latin America (Mexico, Paraguay, Honduras, and Bolivia), one from Asia (Cambodia), one from the Middle East (Lebanon), and one from Europe (Sweden), and the 2011 plan of visits shows that the SPT intends to add Ukraine, Mali, and Brazil to the list of countries it has visited.[71] There is a clear desire, therefore, to have a regional spread, and the SPT has also been keen to make its mark on the regions where visiting mechanisms are perhaps less developed.[72] It also seems to be spending less time on visits in the European region, having actively chosen to visit only one European State (Ukraine),[73] possibly giving preference to the criterion of 'existing regional mechanisms' over that of the 'equitable geographical distribution'—given the operation of the CPT in Europe.[74] At the same time, it should be noted here that the SPT has engaged in a considerable number of other activities within Europe, including intensive meetings with NPMs in a number of countries and within the context of a number of programmes, as will be outlined later. It may well be that the range of alternative engagement opportunities in Europe is such as to make its overall portfolio of activities more 'balanced' than might be assumed from simply looking at the list of countries which have been formally and officially visited.[75]

There may therefore be other factors at play rather than a decision based on whether a regional mechanism has already visited the State in question. For example, the SPT visited Paraguay in May 2009 and then again on a follow-up visit in September 2010, when the State had already received the Inter-American Commission's Special Rapporteur on the Rights of Persons Deprived of Liberty only the year before.[76] Similarly, Bolivia was visited by the SPT in September 2010, when it had received two visits from the Inter-American Commission on Human Rights in 2006 and 2008.[77]

Even more puzzling is the final criterion for visiting a State Party advanced by the SPT: specific or urgent issues reported. This potentially runs the risk of a move towards an inquiry-like procedure, as carried out by the CAT,[78] or the urgent appeals system by the UN Special Rapporteur on Torture. It also runs contrary to

[71] Fourth Annual Report, n 36 above, para 111.

[72] For further discussion on the relationship between activities of regional visiting bodies and OPCAT see Chapters 7 and 8.

[73] Sweden was chosen by lot, see First Annual Report, n 37 above, para 14.

[74] Second Annual Report, n 39 above, para 55.

[75] Note, for example, the extensive range of activities conducted within European under the auspices of the European NPM project (for which see further below) and set out in the SPT's Fourth Annual Report, para 27:

> ... in the framework of the European NPM Project of the Council of Europe/European Union, with the APT as implementing partner, the SPT has participated in three thematic workshops: a) on the role of NPMs in preventing torture and other forms of ill-treatment in psychiatric institutions and social care homes in Italy in March 2010, b) on rights related to prevention of torture in Albania in June 2010, and c) on the preparation of visits in Armenia in October 2010, and three on-site visits and exchange of experiences: a) with the Polish NPM in Poland in May 2010, b) the Georgian NPM in Georgia in June–July 2010 and the Spanish NPM in Spain in November 2010.

[76] See <http://www.cidh.oas.org/PRIVADAS/visitas.htm>.

[77] Ibid.

[78] See CAT, Article 20.

the idea of a programme of regular visits as stipulated in Article 13(1) of OPCAT and may raise false expectations about the SPT mandate. Again, it is not possible to discern from the current approach of the SPT exactly what was envisaged here.

In addition to regular visits, Article 13(4) also provides for the possibility of a short follow-up visit after a regular visit if the SPT 'considers it appropriate'. This is something that the SPT carried out for the first time when it undertook a three-day visit to Paraguay in September 2010.[79] This is a very commendable development. Undeniably when the SPT visits a country, there is a certain momentum: for example, provisional NPMs were set up in both Mauritius and the Maldives in anticipation of the SPT's visit. There is a great danger of such momentum being lost once the SPT has left, especially given the fact that the report following the SPT's visit may remain confidential. It would, however, have been useful if the SPT could have furnished some explanation as to why a follow-up visit had been carried out only in respect of Paraguay and in general, what its criteria are for conducting follow-up visits.

The final issue in terms of the conduct of SPT visits is the stipulation in Article 13 that the visits of the SPT are to be regular. This raises the question of frequency and an interrelated point about resources, both human and financial. In its first Annual Report, the SPT estimated that with thirty-four States Parties at the time and ten members on the SPT, it would be able to visit each State Party every four to five years.[80] This is not dissimilar to other visiting bodies in frequency.[81] Struggling with inadequate budgetary provisions, in its Second Annual Report the SPT announced that it had had to limit its planned programme of visits to three visits per year, adding that it 'wishes to state categorically that it does not consider this periodicity of regular visits adequate to fulfil its mandate under the OPCAT'.[82] The concern over resources was also repeated in the Third Annual Report, noting that the SPT will need to maintain its three visits per year, but clarifying that:

> it [SPT] takes the view that, after the initial period of development, its visits programme in the medium term should involve 10 visits per 12-month period. This annual rate of visits is based on the conclusion that, to visit the 50 States parties effectively in order to prevent ill-treatment, the Subcommittee would have to visit each State party at least once every four to five years on average. In the Subcommittee's view, less frequent visits could jeopardize effective support to and reinforcement of national preventive mechanisms in the fulfilment of their role and the protection afforded to persons deprived of liberty.[83]

With the enlarged membership, the SPT has noted that its capacity to carry out more visits will change but that this must be matched by an increase in the SPT's secretariat.[84] Whether the target of visiting each State every four or five years is realistic remains to be seen, even with an enlarged membership. It is doubtful that

[79] <http://www2.ohchr.org/english/bodies/cat/opcat/spt_visits.htm>.
[80] First Annual Report, n 37 above, para 15.
[81] For example, the CPT considers 'regular' to be every five years.
[82] Second Annual Report, n 39 above, para 15.
[83] Third Annual Report, n 21 above, para 21.
[84] Fourth Annual Report, n 36 above, para 109.

it is. The more general question, however, is whether this matters as much as is generally assumed.[85] To the extent that it is desirable, it is arguable that regularity should depend on the specific context of the State Party, and the extent to which its NPM is fully operational and effective. There is little point in the SPT visiting a State which has a comprehensive and satisfactory national visiting system as frequently as it might visit one which does not. Whilst the SPT has provided some broad criteria to assist it in deciding which States to visit, it is likely to have to revisit this with the expanded membership, not least because the new members may not agree, but also because any choice must take into account the now different expertise and geographical backgrounds of the members of the SPT as a whole.

2. Content of the visit: choosing places of deprivation of liberty to be visited

The principal focus of the SPT on its visits to States Parties has been on places of deprivation of liberty. Exactly where it goes in the State, and when, therefore, depends on how it interprets 'places of deprivation of liberty' in Article 4 of OPCAT. As Chapter 4 notes, the definition in OPCAT is very broad and thus the potential reach of the SPT extends not only to 'traditional' establishments like prisons and police cells, but also to less conventional places such as psychiatric institutions, refugee camps, and centres for juveniles, immigration centres, and transit zones at international points, among others.

The SPT has reiterated this broad approach in its Guidelines on NPMs,[86] but in its own practice has been less ambitious, focusing principally on the more 'traditional' places.[87] For example, it was only on its fifth visit, to Mexico, that the SPT went to a psychiatric institution.[88] This has attracted criticism by civil society observers who consider that it may give the wrong impression to the NPMs that the human rights of the detainees in some places of deprivation of liberty are 'more important' than others as well as to indicate to professionals such as psychiatrists that their practices are not subjected to scrutiny.[89] Although, on the face of it, the limited type of places visited is a concern, in reality it can be explained by a variety of factors. Firstly, the expertise and background of members of the SPT will inevitably dictate where they visit. If there are no members with psychiatric experience, then the SPT may feel less comfortable visiting mental

[85] For an interesting discussion of the benefits of a 'random' approach based on the idea of the 'panopticon' see Schmidinger, P, 'Visiting Mechanisms to Eradicate Torture: A Foucaoultian Analysis' (2009) *Human Rights Review*; and 'Visiting mechanisms to implement human rights, or guerilla tactics in the progressive development of international law' (unpublished PhD Thesis, Oxford Brookes University, 2010).

[86] NPM Guidelines, Part VIII.

[87] See Hallo de Wolf, A, 'Visits to Less Traditional Places of Detention' (2009) 6(1) *Essex Human Rights Law Review* 103–137.

[88] Press Statement on Mexico visit of 12 September 2008: <http://www.unhchr.ch/huricane/huricane.nsf/view01/71676BFD91D1682CC12574C30007C555?opendocument>.

[89] Interview with Mr Oliver Lewis, Executive Director of the Mental Disability Advocacy Centre, 24 June 2008.

health institutions, for example.[90] Secondly, as noted in Chapter 4, given that the potential range of places within the scope of OPCAT is so extensive, the practical problems that this poses are prodigious. As a result, it is simply not realistic to expect the SPT to cover all forms of possible places of deprivation of liberty in the course of each of its visits. Lastly, it needs to be remembered that not all States do in fact have the full range of institutions to which Article 4 might relate. So separate institutions for the detention of the young, or care homes, or even specialist psychiatric hospitals, for example, may simply not exist in a particular State. Although the SPT could make use of the roster of experts, as envisaged by Article 13(3), which could supplement the 'gaps' in the expertise of the SPT, it is not realistic, for reasons of time, logistics, budget, etc,[91] to expect that this would allow it to visit examples of the full range of places that fall within the scope of its mandate.

As a result, the SPT has so far taken a pragmatic approach, and defined clearly at the outset of its report the scope of its attention. In Sweden, for example, it chose to focus on evaluating the basic safeguards for the prevention of ill-treatment at the early stage of deprivation of liberty by the police as well as of the remand prisoners held under restrictions;[92] in Mexico, it took a much broader approach.[93] This more sensible methodology will therefore inevitably be dictated by the demands of the particular State, concerns raised by civil society and others as to what deserves attention, as well as the capacity of any NPM to visit places of detention.

3. Preventive approach and visits

The preamble to OPCAT calls for wider 'educational and a combination of various legislative, administrative, judicial and other measures' implying that 'prevention' requires more than simply visits to places of detention. It is this broader approach which encompasses, for example, a thorough examination of the legal system, criminal justice system issues,[94] medical factors,[95] social care, and education that have led many to argue that the SPT should also be considering such aspects in carrying out its mandate.

As has been seen in Chapter 3, in the first few years of the work of OPCAT, many argued that the SPT should be providing guidance on what prevention means; this led some civil society organizations to discuss the idea of a definition of prevention and they encouraged the SPT to explore this with them in some

[90] See CAT/OP/SP/1 (2 November 2006) and CAT/OP/SP/1/Add.2 (14 December 2006).

[91] See Third Annual Report, n 21 above, paras 33–34.

[92] Report on the Visit of the Subcommittee on the Prevention of Torture and other Cruel, Inhuman or Degrading Treatment or Punishment to Sweden; CAT/OP/SWE1, 10 September 2008, para 6.

[93] Report on the visit of the Subcommittee on the Prevention of Torture and other Cruel, Inhuman or Degrading Treatment or Punishment to Mexico, CAT/OP/MEX/1, 31 May 2010, para 11.

[94] Interview with Ms Anhelita Kamenska, Latvian Centre for Human Rights, former member of the CPT, 15 May 2008.

[95] Conference Report of the First Annual Conference on the Implementation of the Optional Protocol to the UN Convention Against Torture (OPCAT) *The Optional Protocol to the UNCAT: Preventive Mechanisms and Standards*, Law School, University of Bristol, April 19–20, 2007, p 15.

detail.[96] In addition, some NPMs seemed to be unclear on this too and were looking to the SPT to clarify the meaning of prevention.[97]

From the outset, the SPT gave some indication of its thinking, outlining that preventive visiting should look at the 'legal and system features and current practice, including conditions, in order to identify where the gaps in protection exist and which safeguards require strengthening'.[98] It also described its preventive approach as forward looking, and an approach which, by the examination of both good and bad practices, it would seek to build upon existing protections in order to eliminate or reduce to a minimum the possibilities for abuse.[99] Though doubtless useful indicators, this did not amount to the form of concrete, practical guidance which many had been expecting or hoping for. The recently released statement on the 'Approach of the SPT to the Concept of Prevention'[100] seems to seek to strike a middle ground between these pressures. It rejects the move towards a formal definition of prevention but, by articulating a series of Guiding Principles, attempts to offer some very practical indications of how it seeks to go about its work when conducting visits, in the belief that this will act as a source of information and suggestion to others.[101]

The guidance to NPMs, however, is that they should be looking more broadly and that their mandate should extend beyond visits to a more preventive approach encompassing awareness raising and other activities. In practice, numerous NPMs have done this. For example, the Office of the Estonian NPM has decided that prevention means that it should 'identify systematic gaps in existing laws and practices of places of detention and second take measures to overcome them',[102] and that a visit to a place of deprivation of liberty is not an end in itself but rather a tool allowing for gaps to be identified. Visits should therefore be used in

[96] See Chapter 3, n 92.

[97] Interview with Ms Nele Parrest, Deputy Chancellor of Justice, Office of the Chancellor of Justice of Estonia (which had been designated as the Estonian NPM), 19 May 2008.

[98] First Annual Report, n 37 above, para 12.

[99] Ibid. The reports on visits to States Parties that have been made public also reflect this approach. See, for example, SPT Report on visit to Honduras, CAT/OP/HND/1, para 8, where it is said that:

> [v]isits by the Subcommittee are intended to examine the prison system and other public agencies with authority to detain, with the aim of identifying any gaps in the protection of the persons concerned and of determining, where appropriate, the safeguards needed to strengthen the system. The Subcommittee adopts a comprehensive preventive approach. By examining examples of good and bad practice, it seeks to help protect the life and the physical and mental safety of persons held in State custody and ensure their humane and dignified treatment, and to eliminate or reduce to the minimum the possibilities of abuse.

[100] 'The approach of the Subcommittee on Prevention of Torture to the concept of prevention of torture and other cruel, inhuman or degrading treatment or punishment under the Optional Protocol to the Convention against Torture and Other Cruel, Inhuman or Degrading Treatment or Punishment'; UN Doc CAT/OP/12/6 of 30 December 2010. See Appendix VI below.

[101] Ibid, para 4.

[102] Parrest N, *The Concept of Prevention*, Presentation in the Conference OPACT in the OSCE region: What it means and how to make it work?, Prague, Czech Republic, 25–26 November 2008; Available at <http://www.bris.ac.uk/law/research/centres-themes/opcat/opcatdocs/prague2008/presentationparrestnotes.pdf>.

conjunction with other measures, such as awareness raising and commenting on legislation.[103]

There is, however, something of a mismatch between words and deeds in the practice of the SPT itself. Although it articulates the need to adopt a broad approach to prevention, and has—with some success—urged others to do the same, it has focused its own preventive work primarily through conducting regular visits to States Parties.

4. Outcomes of a visit: the ongoing dialogue and follow-up

The aim of the visiting mandate in OPCAT is not to 'name and shame' States but rather is founded on the premise of cooperation whereby experts, based on what they have observed, can then make realistic, practical recommendations and enter into a dialogue with the authorities in order to resolve any problems detected.[104] To this end, and as required by OPCAT Article 16(1), following its visit the SPT issues a report to the State Party which remains confidential, unless the State Party in question requests its publication or publishes part of the report, in which case the SPT has the right to publish the remainder.[105] The report is not only to reflect the observations of the SPT, but also to give recommendations for the State Party in question on how to improve the situation in places of deprivation of liberty.[106] Certainly, in order to be credible these recommendations must be tailored to the individual country and take into account its institutions, cultural factors, and social realities.[107] The SPT and the State authorities are then to enter into a dialogue on the implementation of the recommendations. Thus a visit is not seen as the end of a process but rather as the start of a long-term engagement between the SPT and the State Party. This form of dialogue is a method utilized by the CPT as well as other bodies such as the ICRC which argues that:

> [d]ialogue provides a basis for a flow of objective information based on regular contact with prisoners and leads to the formulation of proposals for solutions. Permanent dialogue with all officials, irrespective of rank, is also a means of making the visit part of continuous process and helps furthermore to improve the feeling of proximity between the authorities, the law enforcement services and detainees.[108]

In the case of OPCAT and the SPT, it may be more of a challenge to maintain a permanent dialogue with the authorities, bearing in mind the frequency—or rather, the infrequency—of the SPT's visits to the country. Nevertheless, in its

[103] Ibid. [104] Pringle, p 8.

[105] OPCAT, Article 16(2). In practice, the SPT presents its initial observations to the authorities at a meeting on the final day of a visit, and these are subsequently transmitted to the State, prior to the finalization of the report proper. In this way the State acquires some immediate feedback, and the SPT an immediate opportunity to press for action to be taken on any urgent issues, whilst allowing more time for the construction and adoption of the full, and much more elaborate report.

[106] OPCAT, Article 16(1).

[107] Evans, n 57 above, p 33.

[108] Aeschlimann, A and Roggo, N, 'Visits to Persons deprived of their freedom: the experience of the ICRC', ICRC Resource Centre, 11 April 2007, <http://www.icrc.org>, p 5.

Fourth Annual Report and through the publication of its Guidelines on Visits, the SPT has clarified a number of issues relating to the outcome of its visits.

Firstly, the SPT has now explained its follow-up procedure, namely that the State Party is to provide a full account, within six[109] months,[110] of actions taken to implement the recommendations contained in the SPT's visit report. The SPT has also made public, both in its Annual Reports and on its website, State responses to visit reports, thereby drawing attention to those which have complied with the request and those which have not. It must be said that the evidence does not point strongly in the direction of there being a series of timely and vibrant exchanges. As at the end of 2010 the SPT had conducted eleven visits and one follow-up visit. The visit to Liberia was undertaken in December 2010 and the report had not been sent by the year end, so as of that date a total of ten reports had been adopted and transmitted. However, both of the other SPT visits conducted in 2010 took place in the early summer (Lebanon) and autumn (Bolivia) and although transmitted by the year end, clearly the six-month period had not yet elapsed.[111] This leaves a total of eight reports transmitted within a timeframe that means that a response should have been received. The actual situation at the end of 2010 was as follows:

- Mauritius was visited in October 2007. The Report remains confidential and no response has yet been received.
- The Maldives were visited in December 2007. The Report was made public in February 2009[112] but no response has yet been received.
- Sweden was visited in March 2008. The Report was made public in September 2008.[113] A reply was received which was made public in January 2009.[114]
- Benin was visited in May 2008. The Report was made public in March 2011[115] but no response has yet been received.
- Mexico was visited in August/September 2008. The Report was presented in June 2009 and made public in May 2010[116] but no response has yet been received.
- Paraguay was visited in March 2009. The Report was presented in August 2009 and made public in June 2010.[117] A reply was received which was made public in June 2010,[118] and a follow-up visit undertaken by the SPT in September 2010.

[109] It should be noted that the Guidelines on Visits do not specify that the reply from a State Party must come within six months but say that it must be provided 'within a stated period'. See para 33 of the Guidelines on Visits. The purpose of this is to allow for exceptional situations when information might be wanted more speedily.

[110] Fourth Annual Report, n 36 above, para 19.

[111] Ibid. However, according to the SPT website a response was received from Lebanon early in 2011.

[112] CAT/OP/MDV/1.

[113] CAT/OP/SWE/1.

[114] CAT/OP/SWE/1/Add.1.

[115] CAT/OP/BEN.1

[116] CAT/OP/MEX/1.

[117] CAT/OP/PRY/1.

[118] CAT/OP/PRY/1/ADD.1

- Honduras was visited in September 2009. The Report was presented, and made public, in January 2010.[119] No response has yet been received.[120]
- Cambodia was visited in December 2010. The Report remains confidential and no response has yet been received.

Thus at the end of 2010 responses had been received in just three of the eight cases due[121] although there is evidence of communication short of an official response taking place. In those cases where responses have been received, the SPT has taken further action, either by means of further written communications in the case of Mauritius and Sweden, or by means of a follow-up visit in the case of Paraguay.[122] Moreover, the SPT has made it known that it has been in touch with those States which have not furnished replies in order to encourage them to do so.[123]

The SPT rightly notes that the substantive aspects of the follow-up process are governed by the rule of confidentiality[124] but clarification over the procedural aspects is most welcome providing as it does some insight into the work of the treaty body and its dialogue with States Parties. Perhaps more crucially and more usefully, such information provides other interested parties, such as civil society and NPMs, with important information and enables them to engage with non-responding States Parties and thus assist the SPT with the follow-up process.

But what if there is no response? Formally speaking, the only sanction possible under OPCAT, according to Article 16, in the case of a State's refusal to cooperate with the SPT or failure to take steps to improve the situation in the light of the SPT's recommendations, is for the SPT to request the CAT to make a public statement on the matter or publish the report of the SPT. The sanction, which is in essence the same as that of the 'public statements' made by the CPT,[125] has not been used so far.[126]

Looked at as a whole, the overall pattern of engagement with States is quite encouraging. Half of the States have published the visit reports, there has been

[119] CAT/OP/HND/1.

[120] The situation concerning the Report on Honduras is unusual. The visit took place at a time of political turbulence concerning the legitimacy of the government. President Zalaya had left the country in June 2008 but returned during the period of the SPT visit. The Report, as published in January 2010, contains a brief response dated October 2008 to the observations of the SPT presented at the conclusion of its visit. See ibid, paras 18–25 and Annex, p 60.

[121] Since the receipt of the response of Lebanon this has improved to four out of nine.

[122] Fourth Annual Report, n 36 above, para 19.

[123] Ibid.

[124] Ibid.

[125] For which see Chapter 1 above.

[126] The SPT's Rules of Procedure do not address the issue of how this might work in practice. For example, must a decision to make a request of the CAT be taken by the full SPT in Plenary? Is it to be determined by the CAT in Plenary or the joint meeting? What information might the SPT make available to the CAT in support of its request? Will it be sufficient that no response or engagement has taken place? To what extent might the qualitative failure to engage with the SPTs substantive recommendations be a relevant trigger, and how might this be evaluated? And so on. As yet there are many questions but no answers. The relationship between the CAT and the SPT is considered further in Chapter 7.

active follow-up in at least three cases, and evidence of other forms of follow-up interaction in other cases. Moreover, the pace of publication of reports has accelerated, with three reports and one response being published during the course of 2010 alone.[127] Given that publication is a voluntary activity, and that the published reports are often critical in content, this is by no means a poor record. It is even more of a shame, therefore, that the SPT has not been able to visit more States during its first four years.

D. Pillar II: work with the NPMs

The SPT has a dual role in relation to NPMs: first, it is to advise States Parties on the establishment and strengthening of their NPMs; second, it is to engage with the NPMs themselves by advising and assisting these bodies in developing their mandates.[128]

Although novel when included in OPCAT, the idea of requesting States Parties to designate national institutions in order to assist in the fulfilment of international obligations has already been replicated in other UN treaties.[129] Through such a construct, as argued by Evans and Haenni-Dale:

> [...] in a way, those national mechanisms designated by the State become a part of the international framework of torture prevention, and the boundaries between the national and international suddenly become malleable and permeable.[130]

As this was the first instrument at the UN, and indeed regional, level to contain such an obligation, the SPT has been faced with the challenge of having to lead the way in defining its relationship with NPMs and in determining what makes for an effective and appropriate national institution.

As will be discussed further in the following chapter, whilst recognizing the centrality of NPMs to the success of OPCAT from the outset,[131] in its initial years the SPT appeared to struggle with its approach towards NPMs, both practically and conceptually.[132]

[127] A point made in the Fourth Annual Report, n 36 above, para 18.

[128] OPCAT, Article 11(b).

[129] States Parties to the UN Convention on the Rights of Persons with Disabilities are obliged to designate 'one or more focal points within governments' (Article 33 (1)) and to 'maintain, strengthen, designate or establish within the State Party, a framework, including one or more independent mechanisms' (Article 33(2)) to promote, protect, and monitor the implementation of the Convention. Similarly, the International Convention for the Protection of All Persons of Enforced Disappearances requires that its Committee 'cooperate with . . . all relevant State institutions, agencies or offices working towards the protection of all persons against enforced disappearances' (Article 28).

[130] Evans, M D and Haenni-Dale, C, 'Preventing Torture? The Development of the Optional Protocol to the UN Convention against Torture' (2004) 4(1) *HRLR* 54.

[131] First Annual Report, n 37 above, para 29.

[132] For a detailed analysis of NPMs see Murray, R, 'National Preventive Mechanisms under the Optional Protocol to the Torture Convention: One Size Does Not Fit All' (2008) 26(4) *Netherlands Quarterly of Human Rights* 485–516.

As has been seen in Chapter 3, OPCAT sets out a number of core requirements for NPMs relating to their composition and visiting mandate, but States Parties are left with considerable freedom as to how to achieve this within their own jurisdictions. Certainly this has the great advantage of allowing the flexibility which is necessary to create a mechanism that is suited for the specifics of the country and accommodates the local intricacies. Yet, coupled with the perceived innovative nature of the Protocol, this has meant that many looked to the SPT to provide guidance:

> The SPT has to take a more active role in this entire process of formation of domestic preventive mechanisms because they [the government] need some proper advice.[133]

The drafters of OPCAT seem to have predicted such a scenario in that the SPT is mandated to advise and assist States Parties in establishing their NPMs.[134] The SPT itself also recognised this and noted 'that contact during the period of leading up to the designation of an NPM and in its early days of operation is most often wanted by both States Parties and NPMs and is likely to have the greatest positive impact on the construction of an NPM system which conforms to the provisions of the OPCAT'.[135] It has also indicated that it could undertake visits in addition to its regular visits with the aim of advising and assisting States during the NPM establishment process,[136] although so far it has yet to do so.

Given the innovative element of the NPM, however, it is perhaps not surprising that it took the SPT several years to really get to grips with this aspect of its mandate. It was not until 2009 that the Subcommittee published the list of designated NPMs[137] and, as will be examined in the following chapter, the SPT has struggled with determining the difference between 'accrediting' and 'advising' or 'evaluating and assessing' an NPM.[138] Early on the SPT issued 'Preliminary Guidelines for the ongoing development of NPMs',[139] and these were both repeated[140] and amplified[141] in subsequent visit reports. At the end of 2010 the SPT consolidated and further developed its guidance in its revised NPM Guidelines, which will be looked at in more detail in the following chapter. In addition, the SPT has been willing to utilize its Annual Reports to clarify certain specific aspects relating to NPMs. Thus in its Third Annual Report the SPT made it clear that establishment of NPMs

[133] Interview with Giorgi Tugushi, OSCE field mission in Georgia (now Ombudsman of Georgia) (Georgia), 20 June 2007.

[134] OPCAT, Article 11(b) (i).

[135] Fourth Annual Report, n 36 above, para 44.

[136] Ibid, para 45.

[137] See Second Annual Report, n 36 above, p 11, n 18. Some, but not all, States informed the depositary of the identity of their NPM at the time of ratification or accession and where this is the case these are included as Declarations in the UN Treaty Database. This list is relatively short and does not include the majority of known designations, these being listed on the SPT website. The APT website also hosts a list of NPMs which at times varies somewhat from that on the SPT site, as not all designations which are known to have taken place are necessarily reported to the SPT Secretariat.

[138] See, for example, Third Annual Report, n 21 above, para 49.

[139] First Annual Report, n 37 above, para 28.

[140] See the Report on the Visit to Sweden, CAT/OP/SWE/1, para 41.

[141] See the Report on the Visit to the Maldives, CAT/OP/MDV/1, paras 71 and 72.

should complement existing systems of protection against ill-treatment and should not replace or duplicate the existing bodies.[142] In its Fourth Annual Report the SPT also reiterated that there is no one NPM model, but 'what is important is that the [NPM] model works well in the country of operation'.[143]

Overall, however, the engagement of the SPT with the issue of NPMs has been uneven. Even a brief examination of reports from visits to States Parties reveals that the Subcommittee is paying more attention to the visiting part of its mandate than that of the engagement with NPMs during the course of its visit. Fairly lengthy reports of about 300 paragraphs contain no more than a handful of paragraphs dedicated to NPMs.[144] The response of the SPT to challenging situations regarding the NPM designation has also been unconvincing. Thus, for example, in the case of Sweden, where at the time of the SPT visit the two institutions designated as NPMs—the Parliamentary Ombudsman (Riksdagens Ombudsmän) and the Chancellor of Justice (Justitiekanslern)—considered themselves unable to fulfil the mandate of the NPM. The Parliamentary Ombudsman had even openly opposed the designation and despite tensions running high, the SPT remained extremely brief in its country report on the NPM situation in Sweden: it took the SPT only seven paragraphs to explain the NPM situation, three to evaluate it, and six to give its recommendations.[145] It should also be noted that one of the six recommendations was a word-by-word replication of the Preliminary Guidelines set out in the First Annual Report.[146] In its recommendations concerning the NPM, while recognizing that it might need more time to study the specific situation of Sweden, the SPT made no more detailed recommendations than requiring Swedish authorities to 'examine their [the NPMs'] current mandates, to ensure that they are in a position to comply fully with all the requirements inherent to this [OPCAT] task'.[147]

In contrast to this part of the Report, the SPT dedicated almost 100 paragraphs to discussing police facilities and remand prisons, with recommendations intertwined within the descriptive part of the Report. These recommendations were specific and detailed,[148] and gave a fairly clear indication to the respective authorities as to what was expected of them. Perhaps unsurprisingly, the Swedish authorities in their reply to the SPT on the issue of the NPM simply reiterated that:

> [i]t is still the view of the Government that the role and tasks of these two institutions fit well with the role of the NPMs as laid down in the Optional Protocol.[149]

[142] Third Annual Report, n 21 above, para 50.

[143] Fourth Annual Report, n 36 above, para 62.

[144] See, for example, a report on a visit to Mexico, which consists of 350 paragraphs of which only about thirteen deal with the NPM, or a report on a visit to Paraguay, which consists of 313 paragraphs with only about four dedicated to the NPM.

[145] See Report of Visit to Sweden, CAT/OP/SWE/1, Section II.

[146] Ibid, para 41; replicated in para 142.

[147] Ibid, para 38.

[148] See for example, ibid, paras 48–49, where the SPT recommends that the police ensure that all persons detained are informed of their rights, and for those who do not speak the language, the list of rights are given orally through a translation.

[149] Replies from Sweden to the Recommendations and Questions of the Subcommittee on Prevention of Torture in its Report on the First Periodic Visit to Sweden CAT/OP/SWE/1/Add.1 on 26 January 2009, para 3.

The situation in Sweden has changed since the visit and indeed the two institutions now appear to be satisfied with their designation as NPMs. It could well be that the visit of the SPT focused the attention of the authorities to seek a solution, and perhaps the Swedish example is the most stark, being among the first States to be visited. Although later reports provide relatively little information on NPMs, however, together with the revised guidelines and, as will be noted in the subsequent chapter, a greater openness to receive NPMs during its sessions, the SPT is now showing itself to be more comfortable with this aspect of its mandate.

1. SPT as adviser to the NPMs

Perhaps inevitably, much of the focus of concern regarding NPMs has so far been upon the first of the SPT's roles in relation to NPMs, this being to advise and assist States in their establishment, as set out in Article 11(b)(i). This remains as much a focus for the Revised Guidelines on NPMs as it was for the Preliminary Guidelines which they replaced. Yet, as NPMs have started to function, it is the second aspect of the SPT's NPM mandate contained in Articles 11(b)(ii) and (iii) which becomes increasingly important, this being to maintain direct contact with the NPM and offer it training and technical assistance with a view to strengthening its capacities[150] and to advise and assist them in the evolution of the needs and means to strengthen protection against torture.[151] Such an approach appears very logical: as already argued earlier, the SPT would be extremely fortunate to be able to visit every State Party even every four to five years[152] and so it will be the NPM which will be the body carrying out the 'bulk of the work'. Indeed, the Subcommittee itself has recognized that:

> [u]nless the [national preventive] mechanisms are able to fulfil their role as the on-the-spot visiting mechanisms for the prevention of ill-treatment, the work of the Subcommittee will be seriously limited and adversely affected.[153]

There is, however, relatively little information about any direct work with NPMs that the SPT has been able to carry out. Certainly initially, serious budgetary constraints adversely impacted upon the ability of the SPT to discharge this strand of its mandate,[154] although, as will be seen in Chapter 6, this appears to be less of an issue now. A useful tool to this end has been the European NPM project,[155] a separate initiative outside of the SPT but which has drawn in members of the SPT to work directly with NPMs on the ground and assist them in developing their working methods. This has bolstered the ability of the SPT to engage directly with NPMs in their own States and although not a project of the UN, does provide

150 Article 11(b)(ii).
151 Article 11(b)(iii).
152 First Annual Report, n 37 above, para 15.
153 Ibid, para 29.
154 Third Annual Report, n 21 above, paras 12 and 74 in particular.
155 <http://unipd-centrodirittiumani.it/en/attivita/European-National-Preventive-Mechanism-against-torture-NPM-Project/458>.

members and NPMs with valuable opportunities for extensive interaction.[156] The Fourth Annual Report also draws attention to the attendance of NPMs at the sessions of the SPT[157] which offers further opportunities for discussion. It does, then, appear that the SPT is now in a position to embark on imaginative and more extensive forms of interactions with NPMs than has hitherto been possible. It remains to be seen whether the enlargement of the Subcommittee offers yet further possibilities.

E. Pillar III: Cooperation with Other UN and International and Regional Bodies

The SPT was not intended to work in a vacuum and the drafters of OPCAT recognized that there are other international and regional bodies charged with a similar mandate whose work may impact on that of the SPT. Article 11(c) requires the SPT to cooperate with these relevant mechanisms and Article 31 specifically refers to bodies established under regional conventions, encouraging these and the SPT to consult and cooperate with a view to avoiding duplication. This aspect of its mandate will be considered in Chapter 7 below.

F. Challenges Noted by the SPT

Even a fairly cursory reading of the four Annual Reports of the SPT reveals the considerable budgetary difficulties which the Subcommittee has had to face. In its First Annual Report the Committee stated:

> The full mandate clearly envisaged in the OPCAT has not yet been realised in practice due to limited budgetary and human resources, a situation which might not be uncommon during the initial phase of operations of a new body, but which must be resolved fully and permanently for the next phase of work. The SPT looks to the UN to provide the financial and human resources necessary for it to fulfil all elements of its mandate under the OPCAT.[158]

Even stronger language was employed in its Second Annual Report, where it concluded that the budgetary situation was such that the Subcommittee was 'not yet in a position to fulfil its Mandate'.[159] Similar sentiments are found in the Third[160]

[156] See Third Annual Report, n 21 above para 27. See also n 75 above.

[157] Fourth Annual Report, n 36 above, para 25, noting meetings with the NPMs of Albania at its tenth session in June 2010 and of Germany, Mexico, and Switzerland at its twelfth session in November 2010. However, care must surely be taken to ensure that such meetings do not evolve into the equivalent of a reporting procedure whereby NPMs, rather than States, present and are quizzed on their work. Such a development would not appear to reflect the spirit of OPCAT at all.

[158] First Annual Report, n 37 above, para 68.

[159] See Second Annual Report, n 39 above, para 75. See also paras 4, 5, 15, 16, 62–74.

[160] See, for example, Third Annual Report, n 21 above, paras 8–9 and 73–77.

and Fourth[161] Reports, although there are fewer references to the issue and the form of expressions used to articulate the concern are more restrained. In part, the concern over the budget can be explained by the principal mandate of the SPT being visits to States rather than sessions in Geneva:

> [T]his type of work in the field is completely new for the UN administration and we spent some time during the last fifteen or fourteen months to convince the UN that the special missions in the field require special consideration.[162]

In its first two years of operation the members of the SPT grappled with the problems common to all new treaty bodies, including acquiring an understanding of its own mandate, establishing its working practices, and getting to know each other. These challenges were exacerbated because of the novelty of its visiting mechanism within the UN context. There were some initial frustrations directed towards the UN treaty body system and the OHCHR for its perceived failure to comprehend what were perceived to be the proper needs of a body engaged in such work.

At the same time, it may also be the case that it has taken the SPT collectively some time to appreciate that the UN provides a very different operational context than that provided by the Council of Europe with its CPT, and to find its place within the larger and more complex organization that is the UN. Although budgetary issues will inevitably be an ongoing concern, an increased membership and increased budget should provide the SPT with renewed vigour in the implementation of its mandate.

G. Conclusion

In the first few years of the SPT's existence it has been quite clear that it is the visiting aspect of its mandate with which it is most at ease. When looking for initial guidance on how it should be operating, the SPT drew more on the European CPT experience rather than the other UN treaty bodies. Indeed, comparisons between the way in which the Council of Europe and UN operated were inevitable, but not often favourable to the latter. However, neither the UN nor the Council of Europe could provide some comparable experience to assist the SPT when it came to the NPM strand of its mandate and it is here that the SPT displayed, initially, considerable caution and reticence.

It is obvious that not all of the SPT's work is budget-sensitive, as demonstrated by the steps it has taken in formulating the Preliminary Guidelines for the Ongoing Development of NPMs and the Revised NPM Guidelines. Clearly the SPT has found the magnitude of the NPM strand of its mandate particularly challenging: as at the time of writing, the SPT had received notifications from twenty-seven States

[161] See, for example, Fourth Annual Report, n 36 above, para 42.
[162] Interview with Zbigniew Lasocik, SPT member, 22 November 2007.

Parties regarding the designation of their NPMs, and information through unofficial channels that there are more.[163] For a membership of ten to maintain and develop constructive relationships with so large a number of such very diverse NPMs clearly poses a challenge. It may be that the expansion in the membership will provide the human resources necessary to meet this, and it is noteworthy that, at this critical juncture, the SPT has flagged its intention to develop a more thoroughgoing system of Rapporteurships which may well facilitate this.[164]

The prospect of the expanded membership seems to have galvanized the existing members to push forward on various fronts: the Rules of Procedure and Visiting Guidelines have been made public, NPM Guidelines have been revised, Guidelines on Prevention have been adopted and it has amended the layout, reporting cycle and, most notably, the detail provided in its Annual Report.[165] This is a remarkable number of initiatives to have undertaken in the last few months before the first session of the expanded membership. The SPT has been keen to consolidate its practice to date. Beyond this, it seems fair to conclude that the 'winds of change' have been sweeping through the Subcommittee, blowing away the caution that it initially displayed and suggesting the emergence of a qualitatively very different SPT from that which has been seen so far.

[163] Fourth Annual Report, n 36 above, paras 20–22.
[164] Ibid, para 108.
[165] Ibid, paras 1–5.

6

The Role of NPMs

The existence of the SPT was always envisaged by those who drafted OPCAT, but national bodies with powers to visit places of detention were not. Ironically, as has been noted previously, although initially a compromise to State sovereignty[1] it is the NPM element of the Protocol which has subsequently been seen as raising the most potential for improved implementation by the State. Yet, equally, it is issues around NPMs which have generated the most interest and the most challenges. Although the existence of these independent yet official bodies which have been most often designated as NPMs, namely National Human Rights Institutions (NHRIs) and ombudsmen, is not new, placing them in such a central role under an international treaty is a novel approach.

The potential obligations imposed by this treaty on these institutions, which are required to be independent, raise a number of issues that have not been considered before. It is apparent from the interviews and research that we have conducted that there are considerable expectations placed on the NPM.

A. Introduction

Articles 1 and 17 provide for States to

> maintain, designate or establish, at the latest one year after the entry into force of the present Protocol or of its ratification or accession, one or several independent national preventive mechanisms for the prevention of torture at the domestic level. Mechanisms established by decentralized units may be designated as national preventive mechanisms for the purposes of the present Protocol if they are in conformity with its provisions.

Articles 19–22 set out a number of minimal powers and other tools that States should provide for these NPMs and Article 18(4) requires that when establishing an NPM due regard be paid to the Paris Principles, seen as the benchmark against which NHRIs are now measured.[2]

[1] Evans, M D, 'The OPCAT at 50' in Gilbert, G, Hampson, F, and Sandoval C (eds), *The Delivery of Human Rights: Essays in Honour of Professor Sir Nigel Rodley*, (Routledge, 2011), pp 85–113. See also Chapter 3 above.

[2] 'When establishing national preventive mechanisms, States Parties shall give due consideration to the Principles relating to the status of national institutions for the promotion and protection of human rights'.

State practice evidences a variety of approaches to the choice of body as NPM. Some States have chosen to establish new bodies, such as the National Observatory for the Prevention of Torture in Benin. Where there has been designation of existing bodies, these have been ombudsmen, NHRIs, and ombudsman plus models.[3] Some NPMs are a single institution, such as the Albanian Peoples' Advocate (Avokati i Popullit), while some are a combination of bodies, such as the eighteen member NPMs in the UK.[4]

As a result, it is quite clear that there are a wide variety of different approaches as to who is selected as an NPM institution and equally that one particular approach is not necessarily more appropriate than any other. As will be seen below, when considering all aspects of the NPM mandate, one size does not fit all and it very much depends on the context of the particular State in question. This, however, has left many in the dark, whether governments, potential and existing NPMs, or civil society, as to what these bodies should look like and how they should function. The SPT has begun to fill this gap, issuing, in December 2010, its 'Guidelines on National Preventive Mechanisms'.[5] These go beyond the 'Preliminary Guidelines for the Ongoing Development of NPMs' the Committee issued in its First Annual Report.[6] This first document was rather vague and added little to the text of OPCAT. It was not at all clear to whom they were addressed. The 2010 Guidelines provide some clearer practical guidance to States, NPMs, and others. Starting with 'basic principles' which underline the OPCAT provisions on independence, adequate resources, and mandate, the Guidelines then move on to 'basic issues regarding the establishment of an NPM', outlining the process by which an NPM should be selected, the membership, and how the State should practically designate it. A final section sets out guidance directed at both States and NPMs themselves on their operation, which again stresses the independence of the institution, and the need for the NPM to develop a coherent way of managing its work.

Although they focus primarily on the establishment and designation of the NPM, there is the promise of further guidelines being developed which will be 'addressing particular aspects of the work of NPMs in greater detail'.[7]

This chapter is structured around the range of expectations and factors being suggested from the interviews we conducted with members of the SPT, governments, members of potential and existing NPMs, civil society, and others. It highlights what role the NPM should play. As will be seen, the focus is primarily on the visiting aspect of the NPM's mandate, rather than looking also at any

[3] Such as those in Slovenia which designate the ombudsperson plus NGOs as the NPM, see <http://www.apt.ch>.

[4] See <http://www.justice.gov.uk/guidance/opcat.htm>.

[5] SPT, Guidelines on National Preventive Mechanisms, CAT/OP/12/5, 9 December 2010. These are reproduced in Appendix V.

[6] SPT, First Annual Report for the Subcommittee on Prevention of Torture and Other Cruel, Inhuman or Degrading Treatment or Punishment, CAT/C/40/2, 14 May 2008, part B. These are reproduced in Appendix IV.

[7] SPT, Guidelines on NPMs, n 5 above, para 4.

broader preventive function and it is worth noting a few points in relation to the latter here.

If one takes the Committee Against Torture's General Comment No 2 as a guideline, the obligation to prevent is 'wide-ranging' and requires States to

> eliminate any legal or other obstacles that impede the eradication of torture and ill-treatment; and to take positive effective measures to ensure that such conduct and any recurrences thereof are effectively prevented. States parties also have the obligation continually to keep under review and improve their national laws and performance under the Convention in accordance with the Committee's concluding observations and views adopted on individual communications. If the measures adopted by the State party fail to accomplish the purpose of eradicating acts of torture, the Convention requires that they be revised and/or that new, more effective measures be adopted. Likewise, the Committee's understanding of and recommendations in respect of effective measures are in a process of continual evolution, as, unfortunately, are the methods of torture and ill-treatment.[8]

Therefore, it is argued that beyond their visiting mandate, NPMs should be using publicity and awareness raising activities to highlight the issues of torture and OPCAT to those within the State. More specifically, it is also argued that the NPM should be raising awareness for those in detention so that they can then be made aware of their rights, as well as the existence of the NPM. This, in turn, can facilitate access by those detained to the NPM.[9]

Despite this much broader mandate of NPMs to look beyond the visiting aspect of its work, attention so far has been very much on the visits themselves. Whilst, therefore, there is evidence that being designated as an NPM under OPCAT can shift the ethos of an organization towards a more 'human rights' approach, there has been less attention paid to how an NPM can develop this broader concept of prevention in its work.

B. Visiting Powers and Mandate

Articles 19–21 set out minimal powers for the NPM:

Article 19

(a) To regularly examine the treatment of the persons deprived of their liberty in places of detention as defined in article 4, with a view to strengthening, if necessary, their protection against torture and other cruel, inhuman or degrading treatment or punishment;

(b) To make recommendations to the relevant authorities with the aim of improving the treatment and the conditions of the persons deprived of their liberty and to prevent

[8] Committee Against Torture, General Comment No 2, Implementation of Article 2 by States Parties, CAT/C/GC/2, 24 January 2008, para 4.

[9] Interview with Commander Chris Griggs, Deputy Director of Legal Services, New Zealand Defence Force, p 8.

torture and other cruel, inhuman or degrading treatment or punishment, taking into consideration the relevant norms of the United Nations;

(c) To submit proposals and observations concerning existing or draft legislation.

Article 20
In order to enable the national preventive mechanisms to fulfil their mandate, the States Parties to the present Protocol undertake to grant them:

(a) Access to all information concerning the number of persons deprived of their liberty in places of detention as defined in article 4, as well as the number of places and their location;
(b) Access to all information referring to the treatment of those persons as well as their conditions of detention;
(c) Access to all places of detention and their installations and facilities;
(d) The opportunity to have private interviews with the persons deprived of their liberty without witnesses, either personally or with a translator if deemed necessary, as well as with any other person who the national preventive mechanism believes may supply relevant information;
(e) The liberty to choose the places they want to visit and the persons they want to interview;
(f) The right to have contacts with the Subcommittee on Prevention, to send it information and to meet with it.

Article 21 provides for protection for those who communicate with the NPM and for confidential information collected by it to be privileged. Articles 22 and 23 require the State authorities to examine the recommendations of the NPM and enter into a dialogue with it and also to publish and disseminate the Annual Report of the NPM.

While the mandate of some NPMs may by and large comply with Articles 19–21 on paper, this is not the case for all NPMs.[10] Evidence from our research suggests that in the process of ratification of OPCAT gaps have been identified at the national level which have then, in some instances, been addressed. Thus, for example, in the UK, when considering the designation of the NPMs, the government recognized that police stations were not covered by any visiting mechanism at that stage. It sought to remedy this by extending the functions of Her Majesty's Inspectorate of Constabulary (HMIC) and Her Majesty's Inspectorate of Prisons (HMIP).[11]

For some ombudsmen whose remit was primarily based on responding to complaints, the designation as an NPM carries with it an additional challenge of how to relate this more reactive approach with the positive, proactive preventive

[10] For example, in relation to Kazakhstan, see letter from the Human Rights Implementation Centre, 14 September 2010, <http://www.bristol.ac.uk/law/research/centres-themes/hric/expertadvice>.

[11] See Database of UK NPM, <http://www.bristol.ac.uk/law/research/centres-themes/hric/hricnpmukdatabase>. However, gaps still remain: for example, coverage of court cells.

approach required of OPCAT.[12] In particular, complaints require investigation and OPCAT presupposes a dialogue between the NPM and the State which may sit uneasily with a more adjudicatory complaints process. Various ombudsmen have found ways around this, by for example setting up a separate unit within their body to deal with OPCAT specifically.[13] Indeed, receipt of complaints may help an ombudsman decide which institutions it should prioritize for visits on a preventive basis. For some it does not appear to be a problem[14] and indeed they see OPCAT as providing an opportunity for adopting a wider, rights-based approach to their work.

Furthermore, even where existing bodies, which are then designated as the NPM, have had the requisite powers as set out in OPCAT, the fact that they are undertaking OPCAT visits now adds a different strand to their mandate. As noted in Chapter 4, the national body may not always cover the scope required by OPCAT and certain places of detention, for example, mental health institutions or youth detention centres, may not have been visited with the regularity needed by OPCAT, when prisons and police stations were. Even if the institution(s) appears to have been carrying out the functions as required under OPCAT, its designation as an NPM has led some to look more at UN treaties in order to gain familiarity with a system of which they are now part, and to the International Coordinating Committee of NHRIs as a way of obtaining some form of peer support from other bodies experiencing this new role.

What is clear, therefore, is that designation of an existing body, even one with a mandate which closely resembles Articles 19–21 of OPCAT, will not be 'business as usual' for that body but will require additional resources to implement.

C. Independence

The linchpin for assessing the appropriateness of the choice of a particular institution as an NPM as well as what is seen as a factor in their effectiveness is independence. The first point of reference is often the Paris Principles, to which OPCAT refers.[15] OPCAT itself provides for the functional independence and independence of personnel in Article 18(1) and the SPT Guidelines stress the 'operational independence' and 'complete financial and operational autonomy' of the NPM.[16] What is independence, however, has been a concept that has taxed

[12] See Steinerte, E and Murray, R, 'Same but Different: National human rights commissions and ombudsman institutions as national preventive mechanisms under the Optional Protocol to the UN Convention against Torture' (2009) 6(1) *Essex Human Rights Review* 54–72. See also APT, *National Human Rights Commissions and Ombudsmans Offices: Ombudsmen as NPMs* (2008).

[13] Indeed, this is now something that the SPT advocates that the NPM do: 'where the body designated as the NPM performs other functions in addition to those under the Optional Protocol, its NPM functions should be located within a separate unit or department, with its own staff and budget', SPT, Guidelines on NPMs, n 5 above, para 32.

[14] For example, Denmark, see interview with Dorrit Rée Akselbo, Rehabilitation and Research Centre for Torture Victims (Denmark) on 6 November 2007.

[15] Article 18(4).

[16] SPT, Guidelines on NPMs, n 5 above, paras 8 and 12.

many. It is useful, therefore, to separate out factors that are within the control of the State and those within the control of the NPM itself.

1. Factors within the control of the State

Clearly, international law does not have a problem with addressing recommendations to States and making these part of a State's responsibility under the treaty to implement its obligations. Thus, factors that are within the control of the State such as the designation of the independent body, 'maintenance', 'establishment', guaranteeing the functioning independence thereof, funding and potential appointment of its members, and making available to it the necessary resources, should be the subject of recommendations by the SPT towards the State.

(a) Appointment of members of the framework

Firstly, considering the members of the NPM and their perceived relationship with government, the manner in which these members are appointed is central, namely that it 'gives them independence from influence or control of government the office is designed to investigate—the executive/administrative branch—and other government and nongovernmental bodies that could influence its activities'.[17] For existing bodies, who are then designated as the NPM, one needs also to examine the manner in which the members are appointed and recognize that if this is not sufficiently robust this could have an impact on the legitimacy of the body in carrying out its OPCAT functions. Yet one often finds where the appointment of members of statutory or constitutional bodies has been criticized, it is the members themselves that can often be the object of this criticism, rather than the government itself against whom such concerns should rightly be addressed.[18]

Research on NHRIs generally and OPCAT in particular argues that the process should be a 'transparent process that also involves both the legislature and civil society' and this requires 'wide consultation and include[s] a process for public nomination of candidates'.[19] The Paris Principles do not require them to be elected, but that the procedure of appointment

> affords all necessary guarantees to ensure the pluralist representation of the social forces (of civilian society) involved in the protection and promotion of human rights, particularly by powers which will enable effective cooperation to be established with, or through the presence of, representatives of: nongovernmental organisations responsible for human rights and efforts to combat racial discrimination, trade unions, concerned social and professional organisations, for example, associations of lawyers, doctors, journalists and eminent scien-

[17] Reif, L C, 'Building Democratic Institutions: The Role of National Human Rights Institutions in Good Governance and Human Rights Protection' (2000) 13 *Harvard Human Rights Journal* Spring, at 25. For further detailed discussion on the appointments process, see below.

[18] Livingstone, S and Murray, R, *Evaluating the Effectiveness of National Human Rights Institutions. The Northern Ireland Human Rights Commission with comparisons from South Africa*, on file with author, February 2005.

[19] Commonwealth Secretariat, *National Human Rights Institutions Best Practice*, Commonwealth Secretariat 2001, at 15.

tists; trends in philosophical or religious thought; universities and qualified experts; parliament; government departments (if they are included, these representatives should participate in the deliberations only in an advisory capacity).[20]

Other suggested criteria for an effective appointment procedure include: wide advertisement of the posts; the criteria on which staff and commissioners are appointed are to be made public; equal opportunities provisions apply; those who may be reticent or suspicious of such a body are encouraged to apply; there is a public nomination process; interviews are held in public; positions that become free should be filled quickly; and commissioners are appointed for a sufficient length of time.[21] The SPT Guidelines now reflect many of these points.[22]

There have been a number of examples of good practice in this regard. For example, in Paraguay and Honduras and in Spain, where an NGO coalition was set up specifically regarding OPCAT, initially to promote ratification but then to look at the NPM process and designation and has been part of negotiations with the government on this issue. Benin also had a consultation forum on the NPM.[23] It has also been seen as useful for civil society to do a scoping exercise of the range of national bodies available to carry out the NPM role.[24]

The Paris Principles require that

in order to ensure a stable mandate for the members of the institution, without which there can be no real independence, their appointment shall be effected by an official act which shall establish the specific duration of their mandate. This mandate may be renewable, provided that the pluralism of the institution's membership is ensured.[25]

Best practice for NHRIs suggests that members be appointed for fixed terms of five years with the possibility of reappointment, and that vacant positions should be filled quickly,[26] and a secure tenure implies that the less likely governments are to be able to remove members, the more likely they are to be perceived as independent and to feel comfortable to operate independently.[27] The SPT provides in its Guidelines on NPMs that 'the relevant legislation should specify the period of office of the member/s of the NPM and any grounds for their dismissal. Periods of office, which may be renewable, should be sufficient to foster the independent functioning of the NPM'.[28]

While appointment by the legislature has the advantage of at least giving the appearance of a more independent process, it is not that straightforward. It is naïve

[20] Paris Principles, para B.1.

[21] United Nations, *National Human Rights Institutions. A Handbook on the Establishment and Strengthening of National Human Rights Institutions for the Promotion and Protection of Human Rights*, Professional Training Series No 4, New York and Geneva, 1995.

[22] SPT, Guidelines on NPMs, n 5 above, para 16.

[23] See APT, *Civil Society and National Preventive Mechanisms under the Optional Protocol to the UN Convention Against Torture* (June 2008), <http://www.apt.ch>, p 5. Paraguay has also been cited as another example of an inclusive process.

[24] See APT, *Civil Society and National Preventive Mechanisms*, p 5.

[25] Paris Principles, para B.3.

[26] Commonwealth Secretariat, *National Human Rights Institutions*, n 19 above, at 16.

[27] Reif, 'Building Democratic Institutions', n 17 above, at 25.

[28] SPT, Guidelines on NPMs, n 5 above, para 9.

to assume that appointment by the legislature will necessarily entail a more objective process free from political manipulation:

> [A] major difficulty is that making a Parliamentary committee responsible for nominations inevitably means that the nominations will reflect the party political make-up of the committee. The danger is that party political considerations consequently overshadow criteria more germane to the nature of the body for which nominations are being considered.[29]

The issue of independence, therefore, is not straightforward. There is an inherent tension that is apparent here and throughout. On the one hand the independent body must be established or chosen by a government who, one assumes, is illustrating its commitment to human rights principles through doing so and in providing the resources for this institution to operate. On the other hand, the independent body must maintain a distance to enable it to function without government influence.

Yet, in practice, a national institution in this situation must maintain at the very least a working relationship[30] and preferably a close influential relationship with the State in order to be able to have access to the facilities that it needs to visit to conduct its work. One of the benefits of a statutory, constitutional, or 'official' designated body is that it is deemed to be closer to government than an NGO. In this sense it is not so easy to detach its involvement and relationship from government as it would be in the case of civil society organizations. In addition, the strength of a State body that OPCAT requires (ie through the requirement that it be established by government and requiring government to consider certain issues when establishing the independent body) is that it will have a status beyond that of a civil society organization and in this respect have some greater potential at least for influencing the government. A statutory or constitutional body it will be, yet one which is supposed to operate without government interference. To ignore its official status and the need for it to develop close relationships with executive and government bodies is to ignore the unique status of this type of institution and to ignore the very thing that makes it potentially more powerful than an NGO.

Government representatives on such a body could give access to government that would not be possible by others who did not maintain such a close relationship with it. If the individual in question is able to distance themselves from influence by the government, then the independence of the institution is not necessarily jeopardized. There is, of course, a risk that this will not happen and one would also imagine that the very reason a government chooses a particular individual to sit on such a body is precisely because that individual will act as a medium for its policies to be applied in practice. At the very least individuals appointed by government do not give the perception of independence and this inevitably has an impact on the credibility of the organization and the respect it is likely to achieve with civil society,

[29] Black Sash, Tilley, A, 'Process Problems May Haunt the HRC', *Democracy in Action* (1995), at 8.

[30] Interview with Lucy Richardson, Legal Adviser, New Zealand Ministry of Foreign Affairs, November 2007.

the public, media, and others.[31] The SPT agrees and requires that 'the state should ensure the independence of the NPM by not appointing to it members who hold positions which could raise questions of conflicts of interest'.[32]

(b) Financial autonomy

Great store is also set by the fact that, in this regard, the institution should have the power to investigate, report, manage its own budget, and appoint its own staff.[33] Funding is clearly an issue that affects the perceived independence of the NPM. This includes not only the need for sufficient resources to enable it to carry out its mandate, but also that it should be free to make decisions on how best to allocate funding for specific aspects of its work.[34]

The Paris Principles state:

> The national institution shall have an infrastructure which is suited to the smooth conduct of its activities, in particular adequate funding. The purpose of this funding should be to enable it to have its own staff and premises, in order to be independent of the Government and not be subject to financial control which might affect its independence.[35]

Various methods have been tried towards funding these types of institutions, for example, by funding them either wholly or partly by government, where the funding is determined by the relevant government department, or, which is often seen as the more attractive option, funding is determined by Parliament.[36] Yet even the latter is not without difficulties and does not always result in what the national body may deem to be adequate or 'necessary' funding or funding that has not been granted without some degree of influence.[37] It is therefore also necessary to consider whether the level of funding is determined by government, whether the NPM can apply for additional external funding if it so wishes, and whether it has the authority to allocate funding for various aspects of its mandate.

All of these factors play a key role in the perceived independence of the NPM yet they are issues over which those appointed have little control themselves. In this

[31] In the UK, Independent Monitoring Boards are part of the NPM but have traditionally been composed in part by magistrates. This raises some challenging issues, see letter to IMBs, <http://www.bristol.ac.uk/law/research/centres-themes/hric/index.html>

[32] SPT, Guidelines on NPMs, n 5 above para 18.

[33] Paris Principles, paras A.3 and B.2; Reif, 'Building Democratic Institutions', n 17 above, at 25.

[34] As the UK Parliamentary Joint Committee on Human Rights noted in its report on the Northern Ireland Human Rights Commission (NIHRC), 'A system which requires the NIHRC to present detailed proposals for a particular project for which it seeks additional funding allows for at least the potential for the Northern Ireland Office to withhold funding from projects on the basis of policy disagreements, or to influence the character of the project in the course of funding negotiations', Joint Committee on Human Rights, Fourteenth Report. *Work of the Northern Ireland Human Rights Commission*, 15 July 2003, HL 142, HC 132, para 39.

[35] Paris Principles, para B.2.

[36] For example, the funding of the Swedish Parliamentary Ombudsman comes from the Parliament, but it is entirely autonomous in how it uses it.

[37] See Murray, R, 'The Relationship between Parliaments and National Human Rights Institutions', in Morison, J, McEvoy, K, and Anthony, G, *Judges, Transition and Human Rights* (Oxford University Press: Oxford, 2007), pp 357–376.

regard, it must be the responsibility of the government or appointing body to uphold the independence of the individual members of the subsequent NPM, particularly when, post appointments, the criticism is more likely to be directed at the members themselves for their individual attributes, rather than the government or body for the way in which they were appointed. Governments, or whoever does the appointing, must take responsibility for their decisions.

2. Factors within the control of the NPM itself

As an international treaty the obligations under OPCAT fall to the State. However, given the way in which the NPM is conceived in the Protocol, that it should be an independent body, it is necessary to consider whether the institution itself should have obligations, if it should be accountable and to whom. On the one hand, where the institution does not have the list of powers, mandate, or resources as required by OPCAT, here one would hope that the SPT will engage strategically with the government to increase a national institution's capacity.

But what of the independent NPM which is failing to function effectively because of its own inability to do so? If the NPM is truly operating independently of government influence, what if its members have not spent their money wisely, or have failed to develop or carry out visits in an appropriate manner? What should be the role of the Committee here and to whom should it address its concerns?

If OPCAT and the NPM are to be meaningful then there may be circumstances in which the SPT needs to address its concerns to the NPM specifically. Indeed, the SPT has now recognized this in its visits to States where the report sets out recommendations towards the NPM itself, and in its Guidelines on NPMs which provide a number of 'points for NPMs' regarding their operation.[38]

(a) In fulfilling its remit

OPCAT requires the NPM to undertake visits to prevent torture. An NPM is not responsible for the conditions under which it is established and the manner of the appointment of its members, for example, but it should be accountable for how it performs its mandate, 'conscientiously and competently',[39] and for how it spends its money.

It is also crucial that the members of the NPM themselves want to be independent and in this regard have the responsibility to 'carry out all aspects of its mandate in a manner which avoids actual or perceived conflicts of interest'.[40] An NPM must also decide how best to spend its resources and allocate its budget. Given the extensive expectations that are likely to be placed upon it, it is crucial that it is

[38] SPT, Guidelines on NPMs, n 5 above, part III.B.

[39] Day, P and Klein, R, *Accountabilities. Five Public Services* (London: Tavistock Publications, 1987), at 236.

[40] SPT, Guidelines on NPMs, n 5 above, para 30.

strategic and identifies priorities for its work and that it maximizes the full extent of its powers. The SPT recognizes this in its Guidelines which call on NPMs to 'regularly review their working methods and undertake training' and 'establish a work plan/programme'.[41]

Despite the focus being primarily on visits, it is also clear from the research and interviews we conducted that there are expectations on the NPM to take a broader approach to its preventive mandate. This includes the suggestion that the NPM should be proactively making recommendations to State authoritie on prevention, as understood by Article 19(b) of OPCAT and should be making comments on draft and existing legislation,[42] among other things. The SPT has recommended to NPMs that in doing so, they should 'pay due attention to the relevant norms of the United Nations as well as the recommendations made by the SPT, if such recommendations are made public or communicated to the NPM in accordance with article 16 of OPCAT'.[43]

(b) In engaging with others

Independence does not mean that the independent body and the State have to be 'friends'.[44] As one person said to us, 'for some people he's a hero, and for others he's the devil'.[45] First, it is not just the need to maintain 'proper distance of the body to the controlled institutions'[46] but also to engage in a constructive dialogue,[47] and thereby 'monitor and control the authorities while at the same time building a relationship of cooperation and trust with them'.[48] Therefore, some have argued that the ability of the NPM to talk directly with the relevant minister is important.

Independence can be seen not only as directed towards the individual members of the body,[49] where one considers their integrity and impartiality, but also towards the NPM as a collective body: 'people in the institution are not the institution'.[50]

[41] Ibid, paras 31 and 33.

[42] Ibid, para 35.

[43] SPT, Report on the Visit of the Subcommittee on Prevention of Torture and other Cruel, Inhuman or Degrading Treatment or Punishment to Sweden, CAT/OP/SWE/1, 10 September 2008, para 40.

[44] 'The Optional Protocol to the UNCAT: Preventive Mechanisms and Standards, Conference Report, 19–20 April 2007, <http://www.bris.ac.uk/law/research/centres-themes/opcat/opcat2007.html>, p 22.

[45] Interview with Diego Blazquez Martín, representative of the Spanish Red Cross and human rights professor of the University in Madrid (Spain) on 21 November 2006.

[46] Suntinger, W, 'National Visiting Mechanisms – Categories and Assessment', Background Paper, APT, *Visiting Places of Detention. Lessons Learned and Practices of Selected Domestic Institutions*, Report on an Expert Seminar, Geneva, July 2003, Annex II, at p 91.

[47] OPCAT Conference Report, n 44 above, p 22.

[48] APT, *Visiting Places of Detention. Lessons Learned and Practices of Selected Domestic Institutions*, Report on an Expert Seminar, Geneva, July 2003, p 15. See also 'Note. Beyond Independent Directors: A Functional Approach to Board Independence' (2006) 119(5) *Harv L Rev* 1553–1575.

[49] OPCAT Conference Report, n 44 above.

[50] Interview with Diego Blazquez Martín, n 45 above.

Lastly, by referring to the Paris Principles OPCAT implies a relationship between the national body and other statutory or constitutional bodies in the jurisdiction and civil society:

(f) Maintain consultation with the other bodies, whether jurisdictional or otherwise, responsible for the promotion and protection of human rights (in particular, ombudsmen, mediators and similar institutions);

(g) In view of the fundamental role played by the non-governmental organizations in expanding the work of the national institutions, develop relations with the non-governmental organizations devoted to promoting and protecting human rights, to economic and social development, to combating racism, to protecting particularly vulnerable groups (especially children, migrant workers, refugees, physically and mentally disabled persons) or to specialized areas.[51]

The NPM cannot be seen to operate in isolation and an effective NPM is one which has close cooperation with and involvement of civil society:

> ...but the crucial thing is close co-operation with...NGOs because without strong involvement of NGOs in national preventive mechanism, there is no success.[52]

Furthermore, it is about developing relationships. An NPM can therefore act as an important and trusted[53] bridge between a variety of national actors, in particular between civil society and the State authorities. With the State authorities, however, the NPM can have 'direct contact', 'real influence', and 'make a difference'.[54] The NPM, therefore, could become the centre of a national torture prevention network.

Conversely, however, independence does not just mean independence from government but also independence from other stakeholders, whether those be Parliament, other statutory or constitutional bodies, or civil society. In practice, independent bodies that sit in this official watchdog position can find it difficult to mediate this space, having to develop allies in what are often seen as opposing camps of NGOs and government, yet not being able to class themselves as either. More consideration needs to be paid to the difficulties that holding such a position entails, not just from a legal responsibility point of view but also from the view of practically developing working relationships with various stakeholders in that particular jurisdiction.

A further task of the NPM should be to maintain direct contact with the SPT itself and the SPT sees this as a responsibility of the NPM itself: 'the NPM should seek to establish and maintain contacts with the SPT'.[55] The SPT has therefore called on NPMs to 'facilitate exchange of information in order to follow up the compliance of the reports of the SPT, if those reports are made public in accordance with article 16 of OPCAT'.[56]

[51] Paris Principles, para C(f) and (g).
[52] Interview with Zbigniew Lasocik, member of the SPT, on 22 November 2007.
[53] Interview with Diego Blazquez Martín, n 45 above.
[54] Zdenek Hajek, member of the SPT, on 22 November 2007.
[55] SPT, Guidelines on NPMs, n 5 above, para 39.
[56] Ibid.

The SPT has also underlined the role of the NPM with respect to ensuring a link between the SPT and its recommendations and their implementation by the State:

> As a body complementing, at a national level, the work of the SPT, the NPM is in a frontline position to ensure the continuity of the dialogue with the national authorities on the issues relating to prevention of ill-treatment.[57]

In its Guidelines on NPMs it specifically directs the NPM to 'actively seek to follow-up on the implementation of any recommendations which the SPT has made in relation to the country in question, liaising with the SPT when doing so'.[58]

(c) Integrity of institution's members

Despite what may be provided in the legal framework establishing the NPM, how effective the institution is and how well it is perceived will depend largely on the integrity of the individuals who sit on or work within the particular institution:[59] 'he's the kind of person that . . . you wouldn't try that sort of tack [with]',[60] 'he's a very respected person in his own right',[61] and the members of the NPM should be able to 'speak for themselves'.[62] Even if they are in fact appointed by government, how they act in practice may enhance an organization's credibility or independence. The individual themselves, despite, for example, how the NPM is funded, or how they have been appointed, must 'feel independent'.[63] It is also considered that the NPM should function in a 'professional' manner, namely that the individuals who are the members of the body should have the necessary expertise, act independently, and with integrity. In this context, therefore, they should understand 'what does monitoring mean and what should we achieve under this mechanism'.[64] Questions have arisen here on the extent to which lay visitors to prisons, for example, satisfy these criteria.

OPCAT makes reference in Article 18(2) to a certain degree of representativity in the membership of the NPM.[65] This has been interpreted as including, for example, the ability to speak a particular language, or membership of a particular ethnic group.[66] Particular jurisdictions raise particular concerns and in some

[57] Ibid. [58] Ibid, para 38.

[59] Ibid, para 30.

[60] Interview with Commander Chris Griggs, Deputy Director of Legal Services, New Zealand Defence Force (New Zealand).

[61] Interview with Dorrit Rée Akselbo, Rehabilitation and Research Centre for Torture Victims (Denmark) on 6 November 2007.

[62] Ibid.

[63] Interview with Bob Bywater-Lutman (New Zealand), Inspector of Penal Establishments of New Zealand Defence Forces, November 2007.

[64] Interview with Giorgi Chkheidze, Georgian Young Lawyers Association (Georgia) on 20 June 2007.

[65] This reads: 'They shall strive for a gender balance and the adequate representation of ethnic and minority groups in the country.'

[66] 'Well, [in] the Human Rights Commission, Commissioners always have a mixture of gender and ethnicity. The Children's Commissioner currently . . . is Maori. . . . People of other ethnicities have held that post in the past. So, . . . in the New Zealand context I think both gender and ethnicity are issues that these sort of bodies are very much aware of', interview with Richard Northey, Auckland City Council (New Zealand).

whether the NPM has members from a particular ethnic group on its membership can be crucial to its legitimacy. In others this idea of representation may be less relevant. One issue that has arisen in this context is the range of expertise available on the membership of the NPM. This issue will be examined further below.

Independence also means the ability to operate without influence, not just from government but also from others. An NPM which is seen as too easily influenced by NGOs and civil society may find it difficult to gain the ear of government:

> so for me the national preventive mechanism should be as independent as possible . . . this view is not necessarily popular because . . . most of the national preventive mechanisms are the . . . 'Ombudsman plus' [model] where the Ombudsman is nominated as [the] national preventive mechanism and . . . this Ombudsman is [then] . . . supported by NGOs'.[67]

Conversely, there is evidence that an existing body carrying out visits to places of detention, which is perceived as having the necessary independence and critical edge may not, for that very reason, be selected as the NPM.

Lastly, there is also evidence that designation itself may impact on the existing institution's independence. Although not a concern now, as noted in the previous chapter, this was an issue raised initially in Sweden on the designation of the Parliamentary Ombudsman and Chancellor of Justice, arguing that in so doing, the government was imposing certain tasks on an independent body.

D. Accountability and the Relationship with the SPT

If the NPM is to have some responsibilities under OPCAT, then to whom should it be accountable? Let's first examine whether this should be to the SPT. As noted in Chapter 3, the Mexican Draft presumed a 'supervisory' role for the SPT over the national visiting bodies. The final OPCAT text in Articles 11(b) and 12(c) in particular sets out the relationship that should be established between the SPT and the NPM. These provide for the SPT to

> (i) Advise and assist States Parties, when necessary, in their establishment;
>
> (ii) Maintain direct, and if necessary confidential, contact with the national preventive mechanisms and offer them training and technical assistance with a view to strengthening their capacities;
>
> (iii) Advise and assist them in the evaluation of the needs and the means necessary to strengthen the protection of persons deprived of their liberty against torture and other cruel, inhuman or degrading treatment or punishment;
>
> (iv) Make recommendations and observations to the States Parties with a view to strengthening the capacity and the mandate of the national preventive mechanisms for the prevention of torture and other cruel, inhuman or degrading treatment or punishment.

[67] Interview with Zbigniew Lasocik, member of the SPT, on 22 November 2007.

States should also 'encourage and facilitate contacts between the Subcommittee on Prevention and the national preventive mechanisms'.

The presumption by the SPT that it takes a non-confrontational approach to NPMs suggests that holding the latter to account is a challenge and places the SPT in an uncomfortable position. Indeed, as noted previously, the SPT was initially reluctant to even place a list of those NPMs which had been designated on its website for fear of being seen to give the stamp of approval to the State choice which may in reality be far from adequate in terms of its OPCAT obligations.

NPMs were, however, unclear about their role under OPCAT and they were looking for advice on how to proceed. Whilst NGOs such as the eminently respected APT could provide this support to a certain extent, NPMs and governments seemed to prefer that the SPT, as an 'official' body, provide this type of guidance. In addition, from the point of view of the NPM, being designated as a body under OPCAT then carries with it additional obligations and a different approach. It is apparent that designation causes the national body to look towards the UN system, perhaps more than it may have done previously. It therefore requires a familiarity with a complex treaty body system. As an OHCHR survey in 2009 noted, the awareness of treaty bodies and their mechanisms is 'moderate' among NHRIs and this is likely to be the case for existing bodies designated as NPMs.[68]

Furthermore, initially there was no opportunity for NPMs to engage with the SPT during its sessions. The SPT sessions are not carried out in the same way as other treaty bodies. It meets in private for most of its sessions, setting aside a few hours on one day to hear from the OPCAT Contact Group, a collection primarily composed of civil society organizations. Although the Contact Group does include members of an NPM,[69] this has occurred more by default than any deliberate attempt at inclusion and in fact there has been a general reluctance to expand membership this far. At the outset, therefore, NPMs or prospective NPMs were obliged to seek alternative means of engaging with the SPT.

As has been noted in Chapters 3 and 5, although the SPT has now risen to the challenge and found ways of engaging with NPMs, initially it did not do so. Instead, while it preferred to sit in the shadows, others stepped into the breach. The International Coordinating Committee of National Human Rights Institutions (ICC) and its Accreditation Committee examine applications from NHRIs to determine their extent of compliance with the Paris Principles and an additional range of documents which purport to elaborate on them.[70] The Accreditation Committee then provides the applicant NHRI with either 'A' status, 'Compliant

[68] See Office of the High Commissioner for Human Rights National Institutions Unit, Survey on National Human Rights Institutions. Report on the Findings and Recommendations of a Questionnaire addressed to NHRIs worldwide, July 2009, Geneva, Switzerland.

[69] For example, RCT as part of the Danish NPM.

[70] Guidelines for Accreditation and Re-Accreditation of National Human Rights Institutions to the International Coordinating Committee of National Human Rights Institutions, Version 3—April 2008; ICC Sub-Committee on Accreditation, General Observations, Geneva, April 2008, <http://nhri.net/default.asp?PID=608>.

with the Paris Principles', or 'B', 'Observer Status—Not fully in compliance with the Paris Principles or insufficient information provided to make a determination'. In recent years the process has become increasingly robust and arguably more independent[71] with reports now being received from the OHCHR National Institutions (NI) Unit and NGOs and others in order to assess compliance, rather than simply relying on the documentation provided by the NHRI itself. As a result some NHRIs have been downgraded from A to B status.[72] Each NHRI is also subject to review every five years. The process is not simply peer approval; it now has wider implications for the role that NHRIs can play in the broader UN and to some extent regional mechanisms. It is only A status institutions which are permitted to sit in the Human Rights Council, for example,[73] and although various mechanisms for participation exist at the regional level,[74] some of these are now happy to follow the ICC decision under this apparently more objective approach.

There is a close relationship between those bodies which are likely to be selected as NPMs and NHRIs and therefore potentially between the decisions made by the ICC and its accreditation committee and the way in which the SPT deals with NPMs. This is particularly so as there is clear evidence that States, NHRIs, and others use ICC accreditation as a reason why that institution should also be designated as an NPM under OPCAT.

While the SPT struggled to find its feet on NPMs, a difficulty arose whereby it was faced with the possibility that an NHRI may have been granted A status by the ICC, but may not be suitable for NPM designation. The SPT initially found it difficult to differentiate between 'accrediting' an NPM and providing information on its establishment or giving it advice. As some of the criteria required for accreditation by the ICC are the same as those required under OPCAT,[75] it might be natural to assume that an ICC accredited institution would automatically fit an NPM role. However, there are a number of reasons why this should not be presumed. For example, the minimal powers required of an NPM under OPCAT are not referred to in the Paris Principles, and there may be other institutions within a particular jurisdiction besides that which has been accredited by the ICC, which may be better suited for designation as the NPM.[76] As reflected in its Third Annual Report the SPT made it clear at a meeting with the NI Unit that 'the accreditation

[71] Decision Paper on the Review of ICC Accreditation Procedures for National Human Rights Institutions (NHRI) of March 2008, <http://nhri.net/2008/DecisionPaper-NHRI-March2008.DOC>.

[72] For example, Human Rights Commission of Sri Lanka, see Charter of the Status of National Institutions Accredited by the International Coordinating Committee of National Institutions for the Promotion and Protection of Human Rights, Annex I, A/HRC/7/70, <http://www.nhri.net>.

[73] Conclusions of the International Roundtable on the Role of National Human Rights Institutions and Treaty Bodies, Berlin, 23–24 November 2006, UN Doc HRI/MC/2007/3.

[74] See, for example, Asia Pacific Forum, <http://www.asiapacificforum.net/members/becoming-a-member>.

[75] OPCAT refers to the Paris Principles, Article 18(4).

[76] See OPCAT Research Team, Policy Paper on the Relationship between Accreditation by the International Coordinating Committee of National Human Rights Institutions and the Optional Protocol to the UN Convention Against Torture, 21 November 2008, <http://www.bristol.ac.uk/law/research/centres-themes/opcat/opcatdocs/iccaccreditationandnpms.pdf>.

of national human rights institutions in accordance with the Paris Principles is a supplementary mechanism but should not be used as a procedure for accreditation of national mechanisms in general, since it is for the Subcommittee to make such assessments in specific cases'.[77]

Fortunately, the SPT has moved beyond this initial reluctance to engage with the NPM issue and now treats designation as a simple statement of fact from the government, and displays that information on its website. Its Guidelines on NPMs also spell out that the chosen body 'be publicly promulgated as such at the national level'[78] and that the 'state should notify the SPT promptly of the body which has been designated as the NPM'.[79] This is not to say that negotiations may not take place behind closed doors on the appropriateness of choice of NPM or the extent to which the government has provided it with adequate OPCAT powers.

With the adoption of its new Guidelines on NPMs the SPT has now grasped this aspect of its mandate more fully. It now receives NPM delegations during its sessions and the EU NPM Project has provided further opportunities for members of the SPT to engage at the national level with NPMs. In its more recent reports on visits to States Parties the SPT has been more detailed in its recommendations regarding NPMs (albeit not as detailed as it is regarding places of detention which the SPT itself has visited), directing them both at the State and at the NPM itself.

It therefore appears to have made a crucial distinction between 'accreditation' of an NPM, which it does not consider necessary or appropriate, and an 'evaluation' or 'assessment' as to an NPM's suitability under OPCAT. As noted in its Guidelines on NPMs:

> Whilst the SPT does not, nor does it intend to formally assess the extent to which NPMs conform to OPCAT requirements, it does consider it a vital part of its role to advise and assist States and NPMs fulfil their obligations under the Optional Protocol.[80]

In addition to this international accountability, to what extent should an NPM be accountable domestically? When establishing the NPM the founding legislation will make reference to the body to which the institution should report with respect to its findings and use of financial resources. In many cases this may be the government itself, which of course undermines its independence. Other mechanisms that may be more appropriate include parliamentary scrutiny. But even the latter does not necessarily guarantee perceived independence.

Independence is therefore a multifaceted issue which requires a variety of different approaches. It is not simply a case of appointing members in a transparent fashion, providing the institution with appropriate funding and autonomy, although of course these are crucial as well. But it is also about the manner in

[77] SPT, Third Annual Report of the Subcommittee on Prevention of Torture and Other Cruel, Inhuman or Degrading Treatment or Punishment, 25 March 2010, CAT/C/44/2, para 61.

[78] SPT, Guidelines on NPMs, n 5 above, para 22.

[79] Ibid, para 23.

[80] SPT, Fourth Annual Report of the Subcommittee on Prevention of Torture and Other Cruel, Inhuman or Degrading Treatment or Punishment (April–December 2010), 7 January 2010, CAT/C/46/2, para 63.

which the NPMs conduct themselves, how they carry out their mandates and engage with others.

E. NPMs Should Ensure States Comply with the UNCAT and Other Relevant Legal Standards

OPCAT was established as a mechanism to ensure State compliance with UNCAT provisions. The system of visits provided for by both the NPM and SPT, therefore, is seen as achieving this ultimate aim. This has several strands. First, it would be presumed that it is the provisions of the UNCAT which the NPM will therefore apply when carrying out its OPCAT work:

> Well I think that they, as a minimum need to ensure that we are complying with the Convention Against Torture, which is implemented into New Zealand law by the Crimes of Torture Act. So that's the minimum standard. But I think also that the NPMs in New Zealand will go beyond that, certainly I know that the Inspector of Service Penal Establishments will go further than that.[81]

But this must be done in a realistic and pragmatic fashion. An NPM is also going to be faced with other international, regional, and national standards in its mandate under OPCAT. These may include binding as well as non-binding documents, such as the UN Minimum Standards[82] and there is a suggestion that the NPM can be benchmarking:

> I would imagine, although I don't know, that . . . because there's a central national preventive mechanism there will be a degree of co-ordination and I would think that that would mean that . . . benchmarking will occur that will ensure that . . . all people who are deprived of their liberty in New Zealand in whatever context . . . receive . . . minimum standards of treatment. But I think you know there is . . . a body of international standards out there, UN minimum standards are the ones that really immediately spring to mind but there are others as well . . . the NPMs will be ensuring that we do actually meet those standards'[83]

The challenge therefore arises as to how they marry these various documents in their work.

The introduction of the NPM element in OPCAT, now prompting a shift at the international level, is that it looks to the role of national bodies in monitoring human rights treaties,[84] and in so doing, the establishment or designation of the NPM will assist the State to implement its obligations under the UNCAT and other instruments. The NPM can therefore provide advice and recommendations

[81] Commander Chris Griggs, Deputy Director of Legal Services, New Zealand Defence Force (New Zealand).
[82] Ibid.
[83] Ibid.
[84] Carver, R, 'A New Answer to an Old Question: National Human Rights Institutions and the Domestication of International Law', (2010) 10(1) *HRLR* 1–32.

to those detaining authorities on how they should carry out any recommendations from the SPT or other international bodies.

This must not be confused, however, with the suggestion that has been made by some State authorities that the NPM should have an obligation to implement. It is the role of the *State* to implement and the NPM to *monitor implementation* of the UNCAT.

Related to this is the expectation that has arisen from the research but which is not reflected expressly in the text of OPCAT: the suggestion that NPMs should be filling any gaps that exist at the national level in terms of treatment of detainees. As one government official said to us:

> ... it's something which ... will ensure that if there are any gaps in the way that we treat our detainees that they get brought to the attention of the command and so that we can do something about it. I think you know if there are gaps in our treatment of detainees it's really not because of any desire to treat them badly or anything, it's just that we will not have known if there was a problem ... and so the inspector will be in a great position to bring any problems to our attention so that we can then do something about it.[85]

This also presumes that the NPM will identify any problems that have not been picked up on before:

> [B]ecause the inspector is going to be looking at these penal establishments more closely than they've been looked at before, it's possible that he'll pick up something which we weren't aware of and if that's the case then it would have been worthwhile.[86]

F. As a Forerunner to SPT Visits; Continuation of CPT Nationally; as a Small SPT on the Ground

Another function of the NPM which is apparent from speaking to representatives of those who have been designated as such, is that the NPM itself can act as the forerunner or taster for visits by international bodies. An NPM visit can therefore ensure that any changes required in a place of detention are amended before the SPT visits.[87] To a certain extent this is to be expected but it does rather, at the start of OPCAT at least, reflect the belief, as suggested in the earlier drafts of OPCAT, that the role of the SPT was to be more important and influential than that of the national body.

However, others who had had some experience of similar international visits, such as through the European CPT, saw it differently: the NPM was an extension of the CPT at the domestic level:

[85] Interview with Commander Chris Griggs, Deputy Director of Legal Services, New Zealand Defence Force (New Zealand).

[86] Ibid.

[87] 'And you know we want to do that because we want to make sure that when the UN committee does eventually show up, if it does, that we've got our house in order before they arrive', ibid.

But I mean the CPT has done quite a lot of good work in Denmark and they've put a lot of emphasis on the use of isolation and it's given a lot of press in Denmark and nobody likes that, so hopefully the NPM could be the national continuation of the CPT.[88]

Similarly, the NPM is therefore 'the prolonged hands of the SPT . . . I see them as a small SPT on a national level on the ground'.[89]

It is this triangular relationship, between the international bodies, the State, and the independent NPM which is said to be a unique contribution of OPCAT. In this sense, the NPM and SPT can reinforce each other with the NPM following up the recommendations of the SPT with the State.[90]

G. Have Expertise

Article 18(2) of OPCAT requires that the 'expert' members of the NPM be persons with the 'required capabilities and professional knowledge' and the SPT Guidelines on NPMs note that NPM members 'should collectively have the expertise and experience necessary for its effective functioning'.[91] Exactly what this expertise should be has been a matter of debate. There is a recognition that for many bodies who are designated as NPMs, such as NHRIs or ombudsmen, they will already have a legal mandate and therefore be staffed by lawyers, either entirely or principally. There is an understanding that some legal background is essential in work of this nature. Beyond this, however, the question has become: what other expertise is required of an NPM?

Firstly, it is important that this question is considered by looking at the NPM as a collective rather than the individual members of the NPM. It is hoped therefore that the NPM as an institution will have the necessary expertise to carry out its functions effectively. In the case of an NPM with a number of constituent parts, this may not be a problem. In the UK, for example, eighteen institutions make up the NPM covering a range of bodies with specific remits for inspection of prisons (HMIP), psychiatric institutions (Care Quality Commission), secure units holding children (Office for Standards in Education (OFSTED)), geographical coverage, and others. However, this is the exception rather than the rule and often this raises some challenges for single institution NPMs. In addition, attempting to ensure the breadth of expertise in one individual, an ombudsman, or a small number of members of an NHRI, for example, can be problematic and unrealistic. One therefore also needs to look at the staff composition of these institutions, in particular those who are undertaking the visits.[92]

88 Interview with Dorrit Rée Akselbo, Rehabilitation and Research Centre for Torture Victims (Denmark) on 6 November 2007.

89 Interview with Marija Definis Gojanovic, member of the SPT, on 19 April 2007.

90 'I mean the NPM can be really reinforced, have some kind of international support in their national work and as well the NPM can follow up the implementation of SPT recommendations after an SPT visit', interview with Barbara Bernath, APT, on 23 June 2008.

91 SPT, Guidelines on NPMs, n 5 above, para 17.

92 As noted by the SPT Guidelines: 'the NPM should ensure that its staff have between them the diversity of background, capabilities and professional knowledge necessary to enable it to properly fulfil its NPM mandate', SPT, Guidelines on NPMs, n 5 above, para 20.

This challenge has been approached in a number of ways. For example, some States, such as Slovenia, have adopted an 'ombudsman plus' model, where NGOs have become part of the NPM itself, and bring on board additional expertise from civil society organizations.[93] Beyond this more formal engagement, there is the possibility of involving specific experts in particular visits, such as the Consultative Council in Moldova,[94] or in the NPM itself.[95] In some smaller States they have faced difficulties in finding available local expertise and we are aware that proposals have been made in some States to hire experts from neighbouring States.

As to the type of expertise required, the SPT has suggested that the approach should be 'multidisciplinary' and involve, among others, the legal profession, 'the medical profession, children and gender specialists and psychologists'.[96] Medical expertise is considered crucial, as a way of helping to identify the practical signs of abuse. Psychiatric expertise is also considered particularly important given that OPCAT extends to mental health institutions such as psychiatric hospitals. There have been suggestions that an NPM membership should also include a military background when visiting military establishments.[97] The reason why this different expertise is important is put down to a need to understand and appreciate different environments and different purposes of detention:

> ... we have less of an expectation of privacy in the military anyway.... So, the whole purpose of the Services Corrective Establishment, which is why it's called that, it's not called a prison, it's quite different to a prison ... it's intended to be, like a very tough boot camp where they come in, have lost their discipline and we re-train them quickly, get them up to the right level and then we generally send them back to their units.[98]

There have also been calls for visiting members to have international expertise, namely expertise in human rights legal standards, arguably to enable them to apply consistency in approach in each visit.[99] More broadly, there should be 'appropriate knowledge' on the NPM,[100] to have experience in torture, specifically the preven-

[93] See APT, OPCAT database, <http://www.apt.ch/opcat>.

[94] APT, *Civil Society and National Preventive Mechanisms*, n 23 above, p 13.

[95] See, for example, Georgia's Special Preventive Group, <http://www.ombudsman.ge/index.php?page=777&lang=1&n=9>.

[96] See SPT, Report on the Visit of the Subcommittee on Prevention of Torture and Other Cruel, Inhuman and Degrading Treatment or Punishment to Sweden, CAT/OP/SWE/1, 10 September 2008, para 36. See also SPT, Guidelines on NPMs, n 5 above, para 20.

[97] 'I think this is particularly valid in the military context because he knows about commanding troops and looking after the welfare of troops ... and ... you know he's a kind of person who can really find out quite quickly what's going on in a military establishment', interview with Commander Chris Griggs, Deputy Director of Legal Services, New Zealand Defence Force (New Zealand).

[98] Ibid.

[99] For example, 'I mean they know about some of the standards but not a lot, and they're not applied in a very kind of unified way to each visit', interview with Dorrit Rée Akselbo, Rehabilitation and Research Centre for Torture Victims (Denmark) on 6 November 2007.

[100] 'It could be ... in that each of these, I mean the Children's Commissioner is only one person and ... they have staff but I am not aware of their range of skills they've got. The Human Rights Commission is somewhat larger ... one simply assumes that they would contract for somebody to accompany them ... on the visit that had the appropriate knowledge.... which is a resourcing issue as well as a judgement issue by those bodies. But of course ... the people who hold that particular office

tion of torture,[101] or someone who understands the system. These issues, as noted in Chapter 4, then impact on the interpretation of the scope of OPCAT in practice and the type of institutions then to be visited.

H. Large Expectations and Role Not Always Clear

Lastly, some caution must be exercised. The different approach of OPCAT when compared with other treaties and the potential that it therefore offers has led to considerable expectations being placed on the NPM, indeed expectations that are not reasonable or realistic. There are various issues that flow from this. NPMs are having now to try to clarify what their role is and what exactly is expected of them. Indeed, the role of the NPM, as noted above, is multifaceted and therefore not always that clear, particularly at the outset. To a certain extent, therefore, the NPM will have to carve out a role for itself. This may be very specific to that particular State and that particular NPM as it will depend on the existence of other stakeholders with functions that are relevant to OPCAT.

I. Additional Factors for an Effective NPM

There are therefore a number of suggestions arising from those we have spoken to in the course of our research as to how an NPM should operate. Ultimately, however, beyond compliance with the letter of OPCAT, there are a range of other factors which will determine the effectiveness of the NPM and its ability to have influence in the State. One difference between functioning as an OPCAT body and a non-OPCAT body, for those which were already in existence prior to their being designated as an NPM, is that OPCAT presupposes a rights-based approach to the work. This may then raise some challenges for institutions which are more complaints-driven. Some ombudsmen have faced this challenge:

> So it's actually a two-way street, too, we just cannot be confrontational or adversarial all the time because we want to think of ourselves as partners, because we have always emphasised the rights-based approach to governance, to development and all that. So we are trying to

would not have the full range of expertise, and none of these are medical people . . . ', interview with Richard Northey, Auckland City Council (New Zealand).

[101] '. . . in several countries . . . Ombudsmen are not well prepared to take this very difficult task. I'm not saying that they are not independent but they are not simply qualified . . . I mean they . . . don't have experience in prevention of torture. . . . even if they do similar things, this prevention of torture which is meant by the OPCAT is a very special task and and some of them are not even aware that they are supposed to co-operate with the Sub-Committee', interview with Zbigniew Lasocik, member of the SPT, on 22 November 2007.

convince government that when they look at all this and . . . their work it has to be done the rights-based way'.[102]

Interestingly, a further factor that renders an NPM effective in the eyes of many is whether it has the power of coercion, namely how strong its enforcement powers are. The more powerful its remit, the more it will be taken seriously.[103] As one government official said to us: 'if you're talking to somebody who has the power of deciding complaints against you, I'd be very cooperative . . . I'd be much more cooperative than if this guy just came to have a nice talk with you.'[104]

Stakeholders have to have trust and confidence in the NPM; this includes not only detainees but others. This then impacts on whether the NPM is approachable. In addition, the ability of the NPM to be effective will depend on the existence and effectiveness of other institutions and bodies within the State as well, such as the judicial system:

> I mean . . . where the judicial system has broken down, then to think that in the midst of this whole mess, you're going to throw in the OPCAT and create some kind of body that's independent . . . That's very difficult.[105]

Its effectiveness will also depend on those outside of the NPM itself, namely the goodwill of the government and the support and cooperation provided to it by others.[106]

Many we spoke to considered that the NPM must also be known and people made aware of its existence. In the end it may be down to the members of the NPM themselves and how they interpret their role.

J. Conclusion

The inclusion of NPMs within the OPCAT framework has been lauded as innovative and a real attempt to domesticate international human rights law. Rightly so. However, we must exercise some caution. As noted above, these institutions cannot be seen as the answer to all issues relating to the prevention of torture. Even if one is lucky enough to have an institution which on paper complies with OPCAT requirements, in reality, as research on the performance of NHRIs has shown, many other factors come into play in determining whether it has any impact on the ground. For those NPMs which also have non-NPM remits, they

102 Interview with Jake Mejia, Phillippines Human Rights Commission. See also Steinerte and Murray, 'Same but Different' n 12 above; APT, *National Human Rights Commissions and Ombudsmans Offices: Ombudsmen as NPMs*, 2008.

103 See, for example, interviews with Commander Chris Griggs, Deputy Director of Legal Services, New Zealand Defence Force (New Zealand) and Dorrit Rée Akselbo, Rehabilitation and Research Centre for Torture Victims (Denmark) on 6 November 2007.

104 Interview with Jens Færkel, Ministry of Foreign Affairs (Denmark) on 7 November 2007.

105 Interview with Dorrit Rée Akselbo, Rehabilitation and Research Centre for Torture Victims (Denmark) on 6 November 2007.

106 See interview with Stuart Beresford, New Zealand Ministry of Justice.

have got to balance their NPM commitments with their broader mandates. This may fit well if your broader mandate is a human rights one—the ethos may be the same. It may pose challenges if your broader mandate, as for example with ombudsmen, is premised more on receiving complaints on maladministration, and human rights has not been a primary focus of your work. For all institutions which have had this designation bestowed upon them, it is quite clear that with it come additional responsibilities, tasks, and therefore resource requirements. In some cases additional funding has been provided by States, in others OPCAT is seen as 'business as usual', particularly those who may already have been carrying out OPCAT-type visits.

Even for those institutions, however, OPCAT will require, at the very least, a link with the international body, the SPT. It may require a regularity of visits that was not there previously, particularly to places of detention that are less obvious such as mental health institutions, refugee and asylum centres, and youth detention facilities. It may require a totally different ethos, one which necessitates a greater understanding of the broader human rights framework, an education and awareness raising mandate. With the promise of NPMs come considerable expectations and a degree of pragmatism is required to ensure that these are not unrealistic.

7

OPCAT within the Broader UN and Regional Systems

In providing in Article 11(c) for the need for the SPT to 'cooperate, for the prevention of torture in general', with a broad range of UN, regional, and national institutions and organizations, OPCAT recognized the place of OPCAT within a broader human rights system. The very fact that OPCAT is an optional protocol to the Convention Against Torture (UNCAT) presupposes a particularly close relationship with this instrument and its Committee, and the first part of this chapter will examine whether this is in fact the case in practice. The second part of the chapter will examine the other bodies within the UN and regional treaties which may interact with the SPT and NPMs.[1]

A. OPCAT and the Convention Against Torture

All States Parties to OPCAT will also be party to UNCAT[2] and therefore subject to the remit of the Committee Against Torture (CAT). The preamble and various provisions of OPCAT make this clear and the overall aim of OPCAT was to complement the convention through the preventive visiting mechanisms, with 'further measures . . . necessary to achieve the purposes' of UNCAT,[3] and as part of State Party obligations under UNCAT to prevent torture.[4] OPCAT is thus intrinsically linked to the CAT. Indeed one of the reasons why States may ratify OPCAT is because 'this is definitely one of the ways of making [the CAT] more effective'.[5]

Formally, there are a number of ways that the CAT and SPT interact, as detailed in OPCAT. First, Article 10(3) requires that the SPT and the CAT 'shall hold their sessions simultaneously at least once a year'. The SPT and the CAT have met three

[1] SPT, Third Annual Report of the Subcommittee on Prevention of Torture and Other Cruel, Inhuman and Degrading Treatment or Punishment, 25 March 2010, CAT/C/44/2, para 10.

[2] OPCAT, Article 27(1)–(3).

[3] Preamble to OPCAT.

[4] CAT, Articles 2 and 16; Preamble to OPCAT.

[5] Interview with Lars Solskov Lind, Ministry of Justice (Denmark) on 6 November 2007. See also Preamble to OPCAT.

times[6] and the two committees have also appointed two of each of their members to facilitate contact between each other.[7] Meetings between the two Committees have been described as 'cordial and constructive'[8] and have identified a number of ways in which the two can support each other's work, including the CAT encouraging States to ratify OPCAT and contributing to the Voluntary Fund, and working together to deal with implementation.[9] Although the first joint sessions were in public, at the twelfth session, for the first time, it was held in private perhaps permitting a less formal and more detailed discussion of their respective relationships.

Secondly, Article 16(3) obliges the SPT to submit an annual report on its activities to the CAT and this is then included as an annex to the CAT Report. The chairpersons of both committees now present their reports to the General Assembly with the opportunity for discussions[10] and this has been seen as very useful in enhancing the profile of OPCAT and the work of the SPT.

Thirdly, Article 16(4) enables the CAT to step in, after it has been requested to do so by the SPT, where the State refuses to cooperate with the SPT under Articles 12 and 14 'or to take steps to improve the situation in the light of the recommendations' of the SPT. The CAT can then 'by a majority of its members, after the state party has had an opportunity to make its views known, . . . make a public statement on the matter or . . . publish the report of the Subcommittee on Prevention'. This provision has not yet been used and the SPT's Rules of Procedure are silent on this point. Similarly, Article 24(2) permits an extension to postponement of Part III or Part IV obligations by the CAT, after consultation with the SPT. Members of the UNCAT are also required to be informed if a State Party to OPCAT subsequently denounces the Protocol.[11]

Lastly, although not immediately visible from the face of OPCAT and UNCAT, it is in fact Article 20 of the CAT which may cause tensions between the two committees. Article 20 reads:

1. If the Committee receives reliable information which appears to it to contain well-founded indications that torture is being systematically practised in the territory of a State Party, the Committee shall invite that State Party to co-operate in the examina-

[6] For example, SPT's third session with thirty-ninth session of the CAT, SPT, First Annual Report of the Subcommittee on Prevention of Torture and Cruel, Inhuman or Degrading Treatment or Punishment, February 2007–March 2008, CAT/C/40/2, 14 May 2008; sixth session of the SPT with the forty-first session of CAT, see Second Annual Report of the Subcommittee on Prevention of Torture and Cruel, Inhuman or Degrading Treatment or Punishment, February 2008–March 2009, CAT/C/42/2, 7 April 2009, para 43; twelfth session of the SPT with the forty-fifth session of CAT, Fourth Annual Report of the Subcommittee on Prevention of Torture and Cruel, Inhuman or Degrading Treatment or Punishment, April-December 2010, CAT/C/46/2, 3 February 2011, para 33.

[7] SPT, First Annual Report, n 6 above, paras 32 and 33.

[8] Press Release, Committee Against Torture and Subcommittee on Prevention of Torture hold first meeting in Geneva, 20 November 2007, <http://www.unhchr.ch/huricane/huricane.nsf/view01/1EC7F431C8341C09C125739A0036955C?opendocument>.

[9] See, for example, 'Committee Against Torture meets with Subcommittee on Prevention of Torture to discuss synergies in their work', 17 December 2009, <http://www.ohchr.org/EN/NewsEvents/Pages/NewsSearch.aspx?MID=Sub_Committ_Torture>.

[10] SPT, Second Annual Report, n 6 above, para 45; SPT, Third Annual Report, n 1 above, para 56. GA Res 64/153, 18 December 2009.

[11] OPCAT, Article 33(1).

tion of the information and to this end to submit observations with regard to the information concerned.

2. Taking into account any observations which may have been submitted by the State Party concerned, as well as any other relevant information available to it, the Committee may, if it decides that this is warranted, designate one or more of its members to make a confidential inquiry and to report to the Committee urgently.
3. If an inquiry is made in accordance with paragraph 2 of this article, the Committee shall seek the co-operation of the State Party concerned. In agreement with that State Party, such an inquiry may include a visit to its territory.
4. After examining the findings of its member or members submitted in accordance with paragraph 2 of this article, the Commission shall transmit these findings to the State Party concerned together with any comments or suggestions which seem appropriate in view of the situation.
5. All the proceedings of the Committee referred to in paragraphs 1 to 4 of this article shall be confidential, and at all stages of the proceedings the co-operation of the State Party shall be sought. After such proceedings have been completed with regard to an inquiry made in accordance with paragraph 2, the Committee may, after consultations with the State Party concerned, decide to include a summary account of the results of the proceedings in its annual report made in accordance with article 24.

The challenge here concerns what information available to the SPT might be placed at the disposal of the CAT when it is considering whether to take action under Article 20. For example, if the SPT has been to a country but its report is still confidential, can the CAT nevertheless have sight of it? And how is the CAT to deal with information coming from the SPT that it has identified in the course of its visits which may point to torture or other abuse? The threshold of there being a 'systematic' practice is of crucial significance for the CAT under Article 20 but is of no particular significance from a textual point of view as regards the SPT. So does it matter if the SPT has not used such a term in its report? On the one hand, the CAT cannot be expected to ignore the findings of the SPT. On the other hand, this may be perceived as undermining the ability of the CAT to make its own decisions. The answers would seem to lie in each respecting the differing mandates and modus operandi of the other, rather than in developing more formal and hierarchical approaches to dealing with such issues when they arise, as they doubtless will in time.

Despite the tendency in the Protocol to suggest that the SPT will operate as a 'subsidiary' of the CAT, in fact in practice it has developed a life of its own and has not been seen as a 'sub-committee' at all, but as a body in its own right. From the perspective of the SPT, the CAT is seen as 'a brother committee':[12] 'we are two bodies, independent bodies coming from the same . . . convention with the help of OPCAT'.[13] As well as a recognition that there is 'inevitable overlap',[14] however,

[12] Interview with Miguel Sarre, member of the SPT, on 5 June 2007.

[13] Interview with Zdenek Hajek, member of the SPT, on 22 November 2007.

[14] Interview with Miguel Sarre, member of the SPT, on 5 June 2007.

there is the possibility of tensions between the two Committees, especially with the increased membership of the SPT and when financial resources for treaty bodies within the UN are scarce.

This overlap may have more to do with the scope of the places of detention that both can examine, rather than the approach in terms of methodology of each. As one member of the SPT said to us, when compared to NPMs: 'I think we have more wide open possibilities to interact with the countries than they do'.[15] Indeed, members saw the mandate of the CAT as being more reactive, whereas the SPT is more proactive.[16] But the biggest difference between the two bodies is the issue of NPMs and the relationship of the SPT with those NPMs. This particular part of its mandate then has an impact on what the SPT will do with respect to its visits to countries where its examination of the NPM will inevitably be a crucial part of its visit.[17]

The CAT, for its part, has made reference in its reports and observations to OPCAT, going into more detail than the other UN treaty bodies, as will be seen below. For example, in its Concluding Observations on Benin's report, the CAT commented on the bill establishing the NPM and the lack of mechanisms currently available in the country, calling on the State to 'grant all NGOs permanent access to detention facilities . . . '.[18] In its detailed Concluding Observations on Sweden's report the CAT specifically recommended that the State 're-examine' its decision to designate the Parliamentary Ombudsman's Institution and Chancellor of Justice as the NPM or provide them with the necessary resources to fulfil the OPCAT mandate.[19] As one might expect, this is in line with the SPT recommendations to the Swedish government after its visit to the country in March 2008.[20]

Despite the formal arrangements there are therefore a number of grey areas which could cause tensions between the SPT and the CAT. As will be noted below, many of these can be overcome with good working relationships between members of the two Committees and their respective secretariats. As the SPT develops its distinct separate identity, so it will develop specific relationships with other treaty bodies both at the UN and regional levels. This may have implications for the latter's relationship with the CAT.

[15] Interview with Miguel Sarre, member of the SPT, on 5 June 2007.

[16] Interview with Zdenek Hajek, member of the SPT, on 22 November 2007.

[17] Interview with Miguel Sarre, member of the SPT, on 5 June 2007.

[18] CAT, Concluding Observations Benin, CAT/C/BEN/CO/2, 19 February 2008, para 17. The SPT visited Benin shortly afterwards, in March 2008 but as the visit report has not been made public it is not possible to see the extent to which the SPT attempted to follow up on the CAT's concluding observations during the course of the visit, though it might be reasonably assumed that they did so.

[19] CAT, Concluding Observations Sweden, CAT/C/SWE/CO/5, 4 June 2008, para 25. See also detailed comments on Kazakhstan's report, Concluding Observations Kazakhstan, CAT/C/KAZ/CO/2, 12 December 2008, paras 22–23.

[20] Report on the Visit of the Subcommittee on Prevention of Torture and other Cruel, Inhuman or Degrading Treatment or Punishment to Sweden, 10 September 2008, CAT/OP/SWE/1.

B. Engagement with Other UN Bodies

Article 11(c) requires the SPT to engage with other international, national, and regional bodies that are 'working towards the strengthening of the protection of all persons against torture and other cruel, inhuman or degrading treatment or punishment' and this should be 'for the prevention of torture'. At the level of the UN, these bodies include other UN treaty bodies and in this context the meetings of the chairs of the treaty bodies are a good opportunity to discuss respective mandates.[21] Other treaty bodies have also mentioned OPCAT and the work of the SPT in their own reports. The Human Rights Committee has been welcoming the ratification of OPCAT[22] and noting that such a step would ensure better compliance with Article 7 of the ICCPR.[23] It has also shown some engagement with the NPM issue by recommending States Parties to OPCAT expedite the process of NPM designation[24] as well as noting a development of a particular type of NPM as a positive aspect in States' compliance with its obligations under the ICCPR.[25] In its Concluding Observations on the Spanish Report in January 2009, for example, it called on the State 'to speed up the process of adopting a national mechanism for the prevention of torture in accordance with the Optional Protocol . . . '.[26] Overall, however, the approach of the UN treaty bodies to OPCAT tends to be rather *ad hoc* and go little beyond recognizing the status of ratification or general encouragement to ratify the Protocol or designate the NPM.[27]

Inevitably OPCAT is likely to be of most interest to only a handful of the Special Procedures, namely the Special Rapporteur on Torture[28] and the Working Group on Arbitrary Detention. Indeed, the former has made specific reference to OPCAT and detailed comments regarding the NPM in a number of countries,[29]

[21] See, for example, SPT, Second Annual Report, n 6 above, para 50.

[22] See, for example, Concluding Observations Panama CCPR/C/PAN/CO/3 (17 April 2008), para 10; Concluding Observations Paraguay CCPR/C/PRY/CO/2 (24 April 2006), para 4.

[23] Concluding Observations Costa Rica CCPR/C/CRI/CO/5 (16 November 2007), para 4; Concluding Observations Czech Republic CCPR/C/CZE/CO/2 (9 August 2007), para 3.

[24] See, for example, Concluding Observations Spain CCPR/C/ESP/CO/5 (5 January 2009), para 13; Concluding Observations Georgia CCPR/C/GEO/CO/3 (15 November 2007), para 10.

[25] See, for example, Concluding Observations Austria CCPR/C/AUT/CO/4 (30 October 2007), para 3.

[26] Concluding Observations Spain, CCPR/C/ESP/CO/5, 5 January 2009, para 13. See also Concluding Observations Panama, CCPR/C/PAN/CO/3, 17 April 2008, para 10.

[27] For example, 'The Committee notes with satisfaction that Costa Rica ratified the Optional Protocol to the Convention Against Torture and other Cruel, Inhuman or Degrading Treatment or Punishment . . . ; this step should ensure better compliance with Article 7 of the Covenant', Concluding Observations Costa Rica, CCPR/C/CRI/CO/5, 16 November 2007, para 4; Concluding Observations Czech Republic, CCPR/C/CZE/CO/2, 9 August 2007, para B; Concluding Observations Paraguay, CCPR/C/PRY/CO/2, 24 April 2006, para 4.

[28] In Resolution 1985/33, the United Nations Commission on Human Rights decided to appoint an expert, a special rapporteur, to examine questions relevant to torture. The mandate was extended for three years by Human Rights Council Resolution 8/8 in June 2008.

[29] For example, Denmark, see Report of the Special Rapporteur on Torture and Other Cruel, Inhuman or Degrading Treatment or Punishment, Manfred Nowak, Mission to Denmark, A/HRC/10/44/Add.2, 18 February 2009, paras 24 and 25.

recommended ratification of OPCAT,[30] encouraged NPM designation,[31] met the designated NPMs during field missions,[32] scrutinized the appropriateness of the designated NPMs,[33] as well as examining the work the NPMs have carried out.[34] He has thus referred to the lack of sufficient resources for the operation of the NPM and the geographical reach of the NPM within the country.[35] Consequently, the SPT has described the 'close contact' that they have maintained with the Special Rapporteur.[36] The Working Group on Arbitrary Detentions has been less vocal with respect to OPCAT,[37] although it has recognized the need to cooperate with a range of UN bodies in fulfilling its mandate.[38]

With respect to other special procedure mandates, there has been very little attention to OPCAT specifically, although some of the comments are relevant to OPCAT-related issues, for example, calling on preventive measures against torture,[39] or the need to establish an 'independent oversight for the detention of immigrants'.[40] In contrast, the Human Rights Council, through the process of the

[30] See, for example, Follow-up to the recommendations made by the Special Rapporteur in the report of his visit to Jordan in June 2006 (A/HRC/4/33/Add.3, paras 72–73), para 19; Report of the Special Rapporteur on Torture and Other Cruel, Inhuman or Degrading Treatment or Punishment, Manfred Nowak, Mission to Indonesia A/HRC/7/3/Add.7 (10 March 2008), para 84.

[31] See, for example, Follow-up to the recommendations made by the Special Rapporteur in the report of his visit to Georgia in February 2005 (E/CN.4/2006/6/Add.3, paras 60–62), para 13.

[32] See, for example, Report of the Special Rapporteur on torture and other cruel, inhuman or degrading treatment or punishment, Manfred Nowak, Mission to the Republic of Moldova, A/HRC/10/44/Add.3 (12 February 2009), para 4.

[33] See, for example, Report of the Special Rapporteur on torture and other cruel, inhuman or degrading treatment or punishment, Manfred Nowak, Mission to Denmark, A/HRC/10/44/Add.2 (18 February 2009), para 25.

[34] See, for example, Report of the Special Rapporteur on torture, Mission to the Republic of Moldova, n 32 above, paras 73–74.

[35] Report of the Special Rapporteur on torture, Mission to the Republic of Moldova, n 32 above, paras 74, 78, and 88.

[36] SPT, Third Annual Report, n 1 above, para 60.

[37] Note, more recently, however, on its visit to Malta where it had discussions with the potential NPM, see May 2009 session of the SPT.

[38] 'The Working Group on Arbitrary Detention is not the only mechanism aware of the social reality in detention centres. Rather, other thematic special procedures, such as the Special Rapporteur on the independence of judges and lawyers, the Special Rapporteur on the promotion and protection of human rights while countering terrorism, or the Special Rapporteur on torture and other cruel, inhuman or degrading treatment or punishment, frequently visit prisons and other detention centres. However, and although a duplication of visits occasionally occurs, at present there appears to be no special procedures mandate that could address the full range of human rights enjoyed by detainees, and especially their right to rehabilitation, which can potentially be violated while in detention. Certainly, there is no special procedure of the Human Rights Council whose mandate provides for a global and comprehensive approach to the protection of all human rights of all persons deprived of their liberty. In fact, a paradox emerges: while important international standards such as the Standard Minimum Rules for the Treatment of Prisoners and the Basic Principles for the Treatment of Prisoners provide norms and standards on the rights of persons deprived of their liberty, no mechanism which monitors the compliance of these standards exists', Working Group on Arbitrary Detentions, Annual Report 2009, A/HRC/10/21, para 48.

[39] For example, Special Rapporteur on Terrorism and Human Rights, Mission to Spain, 2008, A/HRC/10/3/Add.2, para 62.

[40] Special Rapporteur on Terrorism and Human Rights, Visit to South Africa, 2007, A/HRC/6/17, Add.2, para 76.

Universal Periodic Review (UPR), has been engaging with the OPCAT-related issues. Thus States have been asking questions about OPCAT ratification,[41] and the NPM designation process[42] and OPCAT ratification has been among the recommendations in the outcomes of the UPR processes.[43]

More broadly, the SPT has established itself as a separate treaty body within the UN structure, attending and participating on an equal footing in inter-committee meetings between the various UN human rights treaty bodies. In this context, it is having to face the same discussions and debates that have arisen as part of the ongoing calls for treaty body reform, reflected in various Secretary General's reports,[44] and initiatives such as the Dublin Statement,[45] Poznan[46] and NGO responses to such.[47] As the SPT places itself as one of the UN human rights treaty bodies, so it exposes itself to reflection on its role, budget, mandate, and how this fits with existing bodies and within the broader UN structure.

Crucially, it is the relationship with the OHCHR which is also important to the actual operation of OPCAT, both the SPT and NPM aspects. First, as noted in Chapter 5, funding has been an issue for the SPT from its inception with its slightly different mandate and focus on visits and NPMs, creating some challenges for the OHCHR which has operated the budgets of treaty bodies on a 'traditional' model of sessions in Geneva. The expansion of members of the SPT and the potential for increased visits to States as a result provides further incentive for greater budgetary resources to be added to support the work of the SPT.

Secondly, OPCAT has been of particular interest to the National Institutions Unit (NI Unit), but it is only recently that there has been more detailed engagement between the two.[48] The NI Unit is the secretariat for the International Coordinating Committee of National Human Rights Institutions (ICC). As seen in Chapter 6, there have been some tensions between the ICC and its accreditation process and the SPT over how to deal with NPMs.

[41] UPR Report of the Working Group on the Universal Periodic Review. Czech Republic, A/HRC/8/33, para 33.

[42] UPR Report of the Working Group on the Universal Periodic Review. Ecuador, A/HRC/8/20, para 12.

[43] UPR Report of the Working Group on the Universal Periodic Review. The Netherlands (A/HRC/8/31), para 78(1); UPR Report of the Working Group on the Universal Periodic Review. South Africa (A/HRC/8/32), para 67(7).

[44] For example, Strengthening the United Nations: An Agenda for Change, A/57/387, 9 September 2002.

[45] 'The Dublin Statement on the Process of Strengthening of the UN Human Rights Treaty Body System', see <http://www.nottingham.ac.uk/hrlc/documents/specialevents/dublinstatement.pdf>, see also (2010) *Netherlands Quarterly of Human Rights*, 116; O'Flaherty, M, 'Reform of the UN human rights treaty body system: locating the Dublin Statement' (2010) 10(2) *HRLR* 319–335.

[46] The Poznan Statement on the Reforms of the UN Human Rights Treaty Body System, Poznan, 28–29 September 2010.

[47] See Dublin Statement on the Process of Strengthening the United Nations Human Rights Treaty Body System: Response by non-governmental organisations, November 2010.

[48] See Bristol OPCAT team, 'The Relationship between Accreditation by the International Coordinating Committee of National Human Rights Institutions and the Optional Protocol to the UN Convention Against Torture', November 2008, see <http://www.bristol.ac.uk/law/research/centres-themes/hric/index.html>.

It is important to bear in mind that institutions designated as NPMs may have other functions and a broader remit than just torture prevention. UN and regional treaty bodies may therefore be interested in making recommendations not relating to torture but to other aspects of the institution's mandate, but which impinge on OPCAT compliance. For example, the UN Committee on the Rights of the Child in its General Comment relating to the role of NHRIs, gives some guidance on what NHRIs should do in relation to children. This includes recommending that

> ... development of a broad-based NHRI that includes a specific focus on children is likely to constitute the best approach. A broad-based NHRI should include within its structure either an identifiable commissioner specifically responsible for children's rights, or a specific section or division responsible for children's rights.... It is essential that promotion and protection of children's rights is 'mainstreamed' and that all human rights institutions existing in a country work closely together to this end'.[49]

Similarly,

> In accordance with article 3 of the Convention states shall ... undertake visits to juvenile homes (and all places where children are detained for reform or punishment) and care institutions to report on the situation and to make recommendations for improvement.[50]

The difficulty then arises as to how to balance these requirements with OPCAT.

C. Engagement with Regional and Other Bodies

Article 11(c) specifically identifies regional bodies as those with whom the SPT should consult and cooperate. In addition, Article 31 provides:

> The provisions of the present Protocol shall not affect the obligations of states parties under any regional convention instituting a system of visits to places of detention. The Subcommittee on Prevention and the bodies established under such regional conventions are encouraged to consult and cooperate with a view to avoiding duplication and promoting effectively the objectives of the present Protocol.

This provision is clearly a reference to the work of the European Committee for the Prevention of Torture (CPT), on which, as noted in Chapters 1 and 2, much of what OPCAT aims to achieve is based. This Committee was created within the Council of Europe (CoE) through the adoption of the European Convention for the Prevention of Torture and Inhuman or Degrading Treatment or Punishment (European Convention) in 1987.[51] Pursuant to Article 1, the CPT is mandated to

[49] UN Committee on the Rights of the Child, General Comment No 2 (2002), The Role of Independent National Human Rights Institutions in the Promotion and Protection of the Rights of the Child, CRC/GC/2002/2, 15 November 2002, paras 6–7.

[50] Ibid, para 19(s).

[51] CPT/Inf/C (2002) 1 [EN] (Part 1)—Strasbourg, 26.XI.1987.

> ... by means of visits, examine the treatment of persons deprived of their liberty with a view to strengthening, if necessary, the protection of such persons from torture and from inhuman or degrading treatment or punishment.

Every State Party is to allow such visits[52] and at the end of the visit, the CPT is to issue recommendations to the relevant authorities.[53] Thus in many respects the CPT's mandate resembles that of the SPT and indeed the main difference lies with the fact that the European Convention does not provide for the establishment of the NPMs. However, since OPCAT has entered into force, the CPT has started to engage with the issues that arise from OPCAT's system. Thus, while not directly encouraging States to ratify OPCAT,[54] the CPT has met with the SPT,[55] a number of its members are also members of the SPT, and the CPT has engaged with the NPMs during its visits, even following up on the work the NPMs have done,[56] whilst not always acknowledging that the particular body is working in the capacity of NPM.[57]

As Nowak and McArthur note,

> [F]or states that are party to both instruments, i.e. the ECPT and CAT, two crucial questions will be raised at the moment of ratifying the OP: what added value will the Protocol have for such states and how will the different preventive mechanisms cooperate with and complement each other?[58]

In terms of added value, in the context of Europe, this can be a difficult question to answer. From interviews conducted in the course of the research, there is some suggestion that the role of the SPT in terms of its visits to places of detention may be rendered obsolete by the existence of the CPT.[59] However, what is also clear is that where the SPT and OPCAT add value is in relation to the NPMs.[60] The SPT in the European context therefore was seen as a rather weaker form of the CPT when it came to visiting places of detention, but it was in relation to its advisory

[52] Article 2 of the European Convention for the Prevention of Torture and Inhuman or Degrading Treatment or Punishment.

[53] Article 10.

[54] Summary and Recommendations for the Conference OPCAT in the OSCE region, November 2008, p 2.

[55] SPT First Annual Report, n 6 above, para 37; Second Annual Report, n 6 above, para 54.

[56] Report to the Albanian Government on the visit to Albania carried out by the European Committee for the Prevention of Torture and Inhuman or Degrading Treatment or Punishment (CPT) from 16 to 20 June 2008; CPT/Inf (2009) 6; para 17.

[57] In the case of Denmark, for example, the CPT commended the visiting methodology of the Danish Parliamentary Ombudsman without mentioning that this institution has been designated as the Danish NPM. See Report to the Government of Denmark on the visit to Denmark carried out by the European Committee for the Prevention of Torture and Inhuman or Degrading Treatment or Punishment (CPT) from 11 to 20 February 2008; CPT/Inf (2008) 26; para 13.

[58] Nowak, M, and McArthur, E, *The United Nations Convention Against Torture* (Oxford, Oxford University Press, 2008), p 1154.

[59] See, for example, interview with Emils Plaksins, Office of the Representative of the Government of the Republic of Latvia before International Human Rights Organizations, Ministry of Foreign Affairs of the Republic of Latvia (Latvia) on 16 May 2008.

[60] APT, *Added Value of the Optional Protocol for States Parties to the European Convention for the Prevention of Torture*, Position Paper on the Optional Protocol to the UN Convention Against Torture, 3 March 2003, p 3.

capacity on NPMs and the role of the NPMs that OPCAT had value. Furthermore, national legislation implementing OPCAT may be modelled on the ECPT and role of the CPT.[61]

For some States, adding another visiting body to those that are already available, in particular the CPT, leads to a feeling of 'visiting fatigue' by the institutions subject to those inspections as well as by government. In part this comes from a lack of understanding of the different mandates of the SPT and OPCAT, but is also due to an expectation that these bodies will coordinate their visits,[62] even if this is lacking in practice. However, ratification of the ECPT did not seem to have been a reason for not ratifying OPCAT and experience with the CPT visits was raised on several occasions as a reason why visits by the SPT should not be the same.[63]

More generally, the EU Member States have committed themselves to 'support actively the work of the relevant actors (... the Subcommittee for the Prevention of Torture...). The EU will pro-actively contribute to ensure that the existing international and regional safeguards against torture and ill treatment are strengthened and effectively implemented'.[64] There are now a variety of mechanisms under the Council of Europe and its Commissioner for Human Rights has also undertaken various initiatives with respect to 'independent national human rights structures'[65] and sees working with them as a key part of his mandate.[66] Thus, during his visit to Moldova in 2009, for example, the Commissioner looked into the issues relating to persons deprived of their liberty by the police by visiting a number of places and talking to those deprived of their liberty as well as the authorities.[67] In his report the Commissioner issued some recommendations to the State also concerning the Moldovan NPM, referring to it specifically as the NPM.[68]

A 'European NPM Project' is an important innovation in this regard, financed by the EU and the Council of Europe. The purpose behind this project is to provide support for NPMs within Europe and enable them to meet collaboratively. A number of workshops have been held under its auspices and various briefing

[61] For example, Sweden, see SPT, Report of the Visit of the Subcommittee on Prevention of Torture and Other Cruel, Inhuman or Degrading Treatment or Punishment to Sweden, CAT/OP/SWE/1, 10 September 2008, para 22.

[62] 'I guess—that they work together and, and don't visit the same country at the same time or, ... in the same year, or, ... maybe they do but then there is something really ... terrible going on probably. But, in general, we expect that they coordinate their activities', interview with Jacob Struyker Boudier, Ministry of Justice (the Netherlands) on 19 May 2008.

[63] For example, 'we'll have to see how that goes, but, well, we have developed a fruitful co-operation with the CPT so I don't see why that shouldn't happen to the OPCAT subcommittee', ibid.

[64] Guidelines to EU Policy Towards Third Countries on Torture and Other Cruel, Inhuman or Degrading Treatment or Punishment, General Affairs Council of 18 April 2008, p 4.

[65] For example, see 5th Round Table of National Human Rights Institutions, Ombudsmen and the Council of Europe Commissioner for Human Rights Dublin, 16–17 September 2008.

[66] The Commissioner shall 'facilitate the activities of national ombudsmen or similar institutions in the field of human rights', Resolution 99(50) on the Council of Europe Commissioner for Human Rights, adopted by the Committee of Ministers on 7 May 1999 at its 104th session, Article 3(d).

[67] See Report by Thomas Hammarberg Commissioner for Human Rights of the Council of Europe Following his visit to Moldova—25–28 April 2009; Strasbourg, 17 July 2009, CommDH(2009)27

[68] Ibid, para 42.

papers and other outputs raise the possibility of a 'European' approach being developed towards NPMs. The possibility of visits from experts and members of the SPT—although not as an official SPT visit—to NPMs within States may provide some additional support and source of advice for NPMs but does raise some challenges for the SPT itself and how it will operate alongside such projects. The need to ensure consistency in the delivery of the advice and approach and for the SPT to maintain the global perspective, as the European NPM Project takes on a life of its own, may prove particularly difficult.

Beyond Europe, the added value of OPCAT comes with its universal reach. Although no other region has the extensive visiting powers that the CPT does, many have mechanisms and procedures which are of relevance to the work of the SPT and the NPMs.

The African Charter on Human and Peoples' Rights (ACHPR) makes reference in Article 5 to the prohibition of torture, cruel, inhuman, or degrading punishment and treatment.[69] Prompted by the NGO—the APT—the African Commission adopted in 2002 the Guidelines and Measures for the Prohibition and Prevention of Torture, Cruel, Inhuman or Degrading Treatment or Punishment in Africa (Robben Island Guidelines).[70] A Follow-up Committee was established by the resolution. This complements and adds to other mechanisms under the ACHPR, including a Special Rapporteur on Prisons and Other Conditions of Detention, an office initially supported heavily by the NGO Penal Reform International and which visited places of detention across a variety of African States.[71] The Follow-up Committee's mandate was broader, namely:

- To organise, with the support of interested partners, seminars to disseminate the Robben Island Guidelines to national and regional stakeholders.
- To develop and propose to the African Commission strategies to promote and implement the Robben Island Guidelines at the national and regional levels.
- To promote and facilitate the implementation of the Robben Island Guidelines within Member States.
- To make a progress report to the African Commission at each ordinary session.[72]

It did not propose that the Follow-up Committee visit places of detention, and this was not the focus of its work initially, this being carried out by the Special Rapporteur whose mandate includes:

[69] Article 5 reads: 'Every individual shall have the right to the respect of the dignity inherent in a human being and to the recognition of his legal status. All forms of exploitation and degradation of man, particularly slavery, slave trade, torture, cruel, inhuman or degrading punishment and treatment shall be prohibited.'

[70] ACHPR/Res 61(XXXII)02: Resolution on Guidelines and Measures for the Prohibition and Prevention of Torture, Cruel, Inhuman or Degrading Treatment or Punishment in Africa (2002), adopted thirty-second Ordinary Session, October 2002.

[71] See Murray, R, 'Special Rapporteurs', in Evans, M D and Murray, R, *The African Charter on Human and Peoples' Rights*, 2nd edn (Cambridge: Cambridge University Press, 2008).

[72] Resolution on Guidelines, n 70 above, para 3.

1. Conducting an examination of the state of prisons and conditions of detention and making recommendations for their improvement;
2. Advocating adherence to the African Charter and other relevant international human rights norms;
3. Examining the national laws and making recommendations concerning their compliance with international norms;
4. At the request of the Commission, making recommendations on any communications filed with the Commission related to the subject-matter of the mandate;
5. Proposing to States any urgent action which needs to be undertaken;
6. Conducting studies into conditions which contribute to detention and proposing preventative measures;
7. Coordinating his activities with those of other Special Rapporteurs and working groups.[73]

The Special Rapporteur has in fact undertaken visits to a number of States in Africa, including follow-up visits to some countries and places of detention.[74] Although the mandate is potentially broader, the Special Rapporteur has focused primarily on prisons and police stations.

As part of 'mechanisms for oversight', States are required, under paragraph 43 of the Robben Island Guidelines to

[s]upport the adoption of an Optional Protocol to the UNCAT to create an international visiting mechanism with the mandate to visit all places where people are deprived of their liberty by a State Party.

In addition, paragraphs 41 and 42 also provide that States should

[e]stablish, support and strengthen independent national institutions such as human rights commissions, ombudspersons and commissions of parliamentarians, with the mandate to conduct visits to all places of detention and to generally address the issue of the prevention of torture, cruel, inhuman and degrading treatment or punishment, guided by the UN Paris Principles Relating to the Status and Functioning of National Institutions for the Protection and Promotion of Human Rights.
Encourage and facilitate visits by NGOs to places of detention.

Although the section in the Robben Island Guidelines obviously now needs updating given the coming into force of OPCAT, this provides a clear role for the African Commission's Committee in the context of OPCAT, its mandate being '[t]o develop and propose to the African Commission strategies to promote and implement the Robben Island Guidelines at the national and regional levels' as well

[73] As set out in an appendix to the Report of the Special Rapporteur on Prisons and Conditions of Detention to the 21st Session of the African Commission on Human and Peoples' Rights, Tenth Activity Report 1996–1997, Annex VII, paras 3–5.

[74] For example, Mali: Prisons in Mali: Report of the Special Rapporteur on Prisons and Conditions of Detention, Report on a Visit 20–30 August 1997, by Professor E V O Dankwa, Series IV, No 2 (*Documents of the African Commission*, p 625); Mali Prisons Revisited: Report of the Special Rapporteur on Prisons and Conditions of Detention in Africa, Report of a Visit, 27 November to 8 December 1998, Series IV, No 4.

as to 'promote and facilitate the implementation of the Robben Island Guidelines within Member States'.[75]

In 2008, the Follow-up Committee started to visit places of detention itself and at the African Commission's forty-sixth session decided to change its name to the Committee for the Prevention of Torture in Africa (CPTA).[76] In the meantime the Special Rapporteur, in part due to lack of funds, has not carried out any visits to places of detention and in the Chair of the CPTA also rode over the mandate of Special Rapporteur. The Special Rapporteur did, however, in 2008, make it clear that there were a variety of different ways in which his office could engage with the SPT, including using the relationships developed by the African Commission with African States and alerting it to any sensitivities; making documentation and studies available to the SPT; as well as looking at the possibility of joint missions.[77]

In relation to the NPMs, there are again parallel developments at the African Commission and AU level which also tie into the OPCAT requirements. The African Commission on Human and Peoples' Rights has a procedure for working with NHRIs by enabling them to apply for affiliated status,[78] although this has been little used in actual practice.[79] In order to acquire affiliated status, the NHRI has to indicate its compliance with the Paris Principles and although the procedure for determining this is not as robust as that which is now before the ICC, there have been occasions when the African Commission has postponed an application due to concerns about the independence of the institution.[80]

In the Americas, Article XXV of the American Declaration of the Rights and Duties of Man protects from arbitrary arrest and the requirement that anyone deprived of their liberty 'also has the right to humane treatment during the time he is in custody'.[81] Article 1 of the Inter-American Convention on Human Rights provides for a general prohibition on torture requiring States to 'prevent and punish torture'. In addition, the Inter-American Commission has not only adopted the Principles and Best Practices on the Protection of Persons Deprived of Liberty in

[75] Resolution on the Guidelines and Measures for the Prohibition and Prevention of Torture, Cruel, Inhuman or Degrading Treatment or Punishment in Africa (Robben Island Guidelines), thirty-second session, Banjul, The Gambia, October 2002.

[76] ACHPR/Res158(XLVI)09.

[77] See OPCAT in the African Region: Challenges of Implementation, Summary and Recommendations from Conference held 3–4 April 2008, Cape Town, South Africa, <http://www.bris.ac.uk/law/research/centres-themes/opcat/opcatdocs/africaconference2008report.pdf>, p 6. The chair of the Follow-up Committee attended the SPT session in June 2009.

[78] Resolution on Granting Affiliate Status to National Human Rights Institutions, 31 October 1998.

[79] Despite twenty-one NHRIs acquiring this status, and their now having an opportunity to present a joint statement at the opening ceremonies of the sessions of the African Commission, their involvement with the Commission has gone little beyond this and few of those twenty-one appear to have made active use of their status.

[80] For example, in relation to Nigeria.

[81] American Declaration of the Rights and Duties of Man, adopted by the Ninth International Conference of American States, Bogotá, Colombia on April 1948. See also Article XXVI, right 'not to receive cruel, infamous or unusual punishment'.

the Americas,[82] but has also appointed a Special Rapporteur on the Rights of Persons Deprived of Freedom.[83] The Special Rapporteur has a mandate to 'verify the respect for the dignity and the fundamental rights and guarantees of persons deprived of liberty in Member States of the Organization of American States'.[84] The Special Rapporteur has visited a number of different places of detention and gone beyond prisons and police cells, to visit for example, a detention centre for minors[85] and a neuropsychiatric hospital,[86] although his focus is still the former traditional places of detention.

There has been interaction between the Inter-American system and the SPT already, including an invitation extended to the Executive Secretary of the Inter-American Commission to visit the SPT's second session[87] and conversely a member of the SPT has attended a session of the Inter-American Commission in March 2008.[88] A meeting between the Inter-American Commission, CAT, SPT, and the NGO, APT to discuss cooperation was held in March 2008,[89] and some members of the SPT also have a close relationship with the Inter-American system,[90] in part aided by the strong Latin American membership of the SPT. Where the SPT has carried out visits to Latin American States, for example, to Mexico in September 2008 and Paraguay in March 2009, it was not clear to what extent it made use of information from the Special Rapporteur of the Inter-American Commission and his visits to those States. The Inter-American Special Rapporteur is not bound by the same restrictions of confidentiality as the SPT.

With respect to the Organization for Security and Co-operation in Europe (OSCE), in 2005 it adopted a Ministerial Council Decision on Upholding Human Rights and the Rule of Law in Criminal Justice Systems,[91] in which it stressed 'the need to strengthen procedural safeguards to prevent torture as well as to prosecute its perpetrators, thereby preventing impunity for acts of torture, and

[82] See Principles and Best Practices on the Protection of Persons Deprived of Liberty in the Americas, OAS Doc. OEA/Ser/L/V/II.131 doc 26.

[83] Resolution of the General Assembly of the OAS, OAS Doc AG/RES/2037 (XXXXIV-0/04), of 8 June 2004.

[84] Inter-American Principles, Principle XXIV.

[85] See Order of the Inter-American Court of Human Rights of 3 July 3 2007, Provisional Measures regarding Brazil, *Matter of Children Deprived of Liberty in the 'Complexo do Tatuapé' of FEBEM*.

[86] See website of the Special Rapporteur found at <https://www.cidh.oas.org/PRIVADAS/visitas.htm>.

[87] See SPT, First Annual Report, n 6 above, para 38.

[88] Summary of the Thematic Meeting on the Implementation of the Optional Protocol to the Convention Against Torture and other Cruel, Inhuman or Degrading Treatment or Punishment before the Inter-American Commission on Human Rights requested by the APT, 7 March 2007, available at <http://www.apt.ch/region/americas/MemoCELS.pdf>.

[89] See Press Release No 10/08, by the Inter-American Commission on Human Rights, 'IACHR Concludes its 131st Period of Sessions', available at <http://www.cidh.org/Comunicados/English/2008/10.08eng.htm>.

[90] Mr Victor Rodríguez Rescia, for example, is a consultant for the Inter-American Institute for Human Rights.

[91] Ministerial Council Decision No 12/2005 on Upholding Human Rights and the Rule of Law in Criminal Justice Systems of 6 December 2005.

calling upon participating States to give early consideration to signing and ratifying the Optional Protocol to the Convention against Torture', a commitment that has been displayed in its involvement in a number of events around and relating to OPCAT.[92] The field missions provide the OSCE with direct presence in various countries and these have in fact been instrumental in bringing about the ratification of OPCAT as well as the establishment of the NPMs in some countries.[93] The SPT has met with the Office for Democratic Institutions and Human Rights (ODIHR) of the OSCE and participated in events organized by the latter.[94]

In addition, Article 32 of OPCAT makes express reference to the relationship with the International Committee of the Red Cross (ICRC). This provides:

> The provisions of the present Protocol shall not affect the obligations of States Parties to the four Geneva Conventions of 12 August 1949 and the Additional Protocols thereto of 8 June 1977, nor the opportunity available to any State Party to authorize the International Committee of the Red Cross to visit places of detention in situations not covered by international humanitarian law.

Torture is prohibited under the Geneva Conventions and breaches international humanitarian law, and if there is an international armed conflict the ICRC can visit places of detention where prisoners of war, civilians detained, or other protected persons may be detained.[95] In situations of non-international armed conflict and internal violence, the treaty basis for ICRC engagement is not express yet in practice States have permitted it to visit. The ICRC operates through a policy of strict confidentiality, underlying its impartial and independent approach.[96] As Nowak and McArthur note, some of the original drafts of OPCAT suggested that the ICRC be given preference although this is not the approach eventually adopted by Article 32 which stresses complementarity.[97] In practice the relationship between the ICRC and the CPT and the Special Rapporteur on Torture has not been problematic.[98]

At present, although we understand that the ICRC visits places of detention under UK military control, this does not satisfy the OPCAT criteria as it is not a body established, maintained, or designated by the UK itself.[99] There is a belief that any body which is designated as the NPM with responsibility for such places of detention extra-territorially should also be one that understands the specific circumstances of the military context of detention.

[92] See Prague event, November 2008; HDIM seminars May 2009, see <http://www.bristol.ac.uk/law/research/centres-themes/opcat/index.html>.

[93] For example, in Moldova and Armenia: APT, Database, <http://www.apt.ch/opcat>.

[94] See, for example, SPT, Second Annual Report, n 6 above, para 56.

[95] Common Article 3 to the Geneva Conventions.

[96] Nowak and McArthur, *The United Nations Convention Against Torture*, n 58 above, p 1161.

[97] Ibid, p 1162.

[98] Ibid, p 1165.

[99] OPCAT, Article 17.

Finally, there are the field mission offices of OSCE,[100] UN OHCHR,[101] UNDP,[102] and UNHCR which can also undertake visits to places of detention. In relation to some of these, this may facilitate access to places of detention. As the OHCHR in Uganda said: 'we . . . at OHCHR have a very open and a good agreement with the government which allows us . . . to visit places of detention without notice except military installations for which we require 24 hour notice'.[103] In States where there has been conflict, the UN peacebuilding missions also provide some visiting mechanism to places of detention.[104] The SPT has also initiated discussions with the UN Office on Drugs and Crime (UNODC).[105]

The SPT has decided to forego visiting some places of detention on its visits, given that they have recently been visited by the UNHCR.[106] The UNHCR has responsibility for supervising the UN Refugee Convention of 1951[107] and has looked at the issue of detention[108] and UNHCR staff can visit places of detention. In terms of how this interacts with OPCAT, the latter can perhaps fill some of the gaps left by UNHCR. As Edwards notes, the UNHCR is often not able to access detainees and faces a range of obstacles in following up cases.[109] However, this needs to be balanced against the very broad geographical reach and large number of staff that it has on the ground and the need for effective NPMs. This leads Edwards to conclude that 'it is envisaged that the UNHCR will remain the primary international monitor of both the legality of detention policies as well as general conditions of detention of asylum-seekers and/or refugees, not least in the short

[100] The OSCE has established a Focal Point for Human Rights Defenders and National Human Rights Institutions in 2007 which provides training, organizes events relating to freedom of association and assembly, and assists in capacity building for these institutions, see <http://www.osce.org/odihr/29028>.

[101] See interview with Maarit Kohonen- Sheriff, Representative/Head of Office UN OHCHR (Uganda) on 9 April 2008.

[102] See, for example, 'EU, UNDP, OHCHR Conduct Workshop on International Experiences on the Implementation of the UN Convention against Torture and its Optional Protocol', Ashgabat, 15 July 2010, <http://www.undptkm.org/index.php?option=com_content&task=view&id=884&Itemid=43>.

[103] Interview with Maarit Kohonen- Sheriff, Representative/Head of Office UN OHCHR (Uganda) on 9 April 2008.

[104] For example, in Liberia it is the United Nations Mission in Liberia (UNMIL) that provides this.

[105] See SPT, Fourth Annual Report, n 6 above, para 35.

[106] For logistical reasons, and in order not to duplicate efforts, the delegation did not visit any migrant detention centres, which were the subject of a recent assessment by the United Nations Special Rapporteur on the subject, Report on the Visit of the Subcommittee on the Prevention of Torture and other Cruel, Inhuman and Degrading Treatment or Punishment to Mexico, CAT/OP/MEX/1, 31 May 2010, para 11.

[107] Statute of the UNHCR, Article 8.

[108] UNHCR, Revised Guidelines on Applicable Criteria and Standards Relating to the Detention of Asylum Seekers, February 1999.

[109] Edwards, A, 'The Optional Protocol to the UN Convention Against Torture and Refugees', 57(4) *ICLQ* (2008) 789–825, at 821.

term due to the low number of OPCAT ratifications from major refugee-hosting countries'.[110]

Taking into account the respective limitations and practical difficulties faced by the UNHCR, NPMs, and the SPT in the context of asylum seekers and refugees, some degree of coordination between them is crucial.[111] This may require building on the capacity of the UNHCR, as the body remaining in the country, to follow up recommendations made by the SPT after a visit, bearing in mind the restraints of confidentiality of the SPT, and sharing of information on areas of priority to be visited, as well as ensuring that experts on refugees are included on visits under OPCAT.[112]

D. Some Common Issues

1. Confidentiality

Articles 2(3), 11(1)(b)(ii), and 16 of OPCAT imply that confidentiality should underpin much of the work of the SPT, although less so the work of the NPMs.[113] With respect to engagement with other universal and regional bodies, this presents some challenges for the SPT in particular.

Initially this posed a difficulty for the SPT which took a restrictive approach to what was confidential and therefore how this impacted on its engagement with other bodies. As one of the members of the SPT said to us: 'we still don't know... we are still thinking about... the way of cooperation. And the problem is in that confidentiality because SPT's very strictly bound by that confidentiality.'[114]

Questions were initially asked such as: does Article 16 mean that the SPT is not going to be able to engage with other bodies as well as it might, and does this conflict with Article 11(c) and cooperation? As Edwards notes, Article 11(c) should

> take priority in view of the overarching prevention purpose of the Optional Protocol. Confidentiality could consequently be interpreted to apply to those outside, but not those inside, this inner circle of international bodies. Additionally, the UNHCR might take advantage of the OPCAT arrangements by informing them of particular detention facilities that need inspection. In the interests of asylum seekers and refugees, a two-way dialogue between the UNHCR and the OPCAT mechanisms ought to be established.[115]

In its Fourth Annual Report the SPT notes the important interrelationship between confidentiality and constructive dialogue but takes a more pragmatic approach that this 'is a means to an end', particularly if States request publication of the report of the visit. It also reiterated that confidentiality did not apply to all the work of the SPT, in that it did 'not consider either its activities or the approaches which it takes to its work to be confidential as such'.[116]

110 Ibid, 822.
111 Ibid, 823.
112 Ibid.
113 However, see Article 21(2).
114 Interview with Marija Definis Gojanovic, member of the SPT, on 19 April 2007.
115 Edwards, n 109 above, 823.
116 SPT, Fourth Annual Report, n 6 above, para 48.

2. Standards/norms

There has been some concern expressed that the legal norms applicable by the NPMs in carrying out their visits may not be the same as those applied by the SPT. Where States were subject to more than one visiting body, in particular in the context of Europe where the CPT has a remit, there was a concern that the recommendations made by the SPT compared with the CPT would be different. There is some recognition that the European CPT itself is careful in how it approaches different States and in this context there is no reason why the SPT should not be similarly sensitive.[117]

In fact, some have little concern regarding any inconsistency in approach, choosing to focus instead on what may be seen as best practices:

> I think that the purpose is the same, isn't it? And for example in our work, even though we are acting in a framework of OPCAT we are continuously using the CPT materials, the guidelines, the handbook, in order to . . . to establish what are the best practices and the best standards. So I think it's a good mixture.[118]

Given the composition of the SPT and the fact that there are members of the CPT who sit on the SPT, there were initial concerns that it would adopt a European approach to its mandate. On the one hand this did not pose a problem for some, as illustrated by the comment that 'the European model is the most developed one so good experience and good case studies might be transmitted to the national . . . reality'.[119] For some, however, this perception that the SPT was modelling its visits on the CPT model was not considered appropriate.[120]

The various regional guidelines adopted also display some inconsistency in their approach to the concept of deprivation of liberty. The EU Guidelines take Article 1 of the CAT as the definition but then go further to state that 'ill treatment means all forms of cruel, inhuman or degrading treatment or punishment, including corporal punishment, which deprives the individual of its physical and mental integrity'. The Guidelines also include mention of the death penalty and call on States to 'ban secret places of detention', and make specific reference to 'groups requiring special

[117] 'The CPT tries not to compare apples and oranges, so it doesn't compare the Russian prison system with that of the Spanish system or the Scandinavian system', interview with Stuart Beresford, New Zealand Ministry of Justice.

[118] Interview with Nele Parrest, Office of the Chancellor of Justice of Estonia (Estonia) on 19 May 2008.

[119] Interview with Giorgi Chkheidze, Georgian Young Lawyers Association (Georgia) on 20 June 2007.

[120] For example, 'one of the objections was well, there seems to be . . . a transplantation of the European mechanism on the international state, and . . . one of the objections (and I don't think this is a very genuine one) was to say "well, what worked regionally . . . probably doesn't work internationally"', interview with Ben Saul, Director of the Sydney Centre for International Law & The Faculty of Law at the University of Sydney (Australia). See also, 'many of [the SPT members] have just fallen back to what they feel comfortable with, which for the CPT members is the CPT style', interview with Mark Thompson, Association for Prevention of Torture, on 23 June 2008.

protection', namely: 'women, children, refugees, asylum seekers, internally displaced persons, migrants and other groups'.[121]

Similarly, the Inter-American Principles provide that deprivation of liberty is:

> [a]ny form of detention, imprisonment, institutionalization, or custody of a person in a public or private institution which that person is not permitted to leave at will, by order of or under de facto control of a judicial, administrative or any other authority, for reasons of humanitarian assistance, treatment, guardianship, protection, or because of crimes or legal offenses. This category of persons includes not only those deprived of their liberty because of crimes or infringements or non compliance with the law, whether they are accused or convicted, but also those persons who are under the custody and supervision of certain institutions, such as: psychiatric hospitals and other establishments for persons with physical, mental, or sensory disabilities; institutions for children and the elderly; centers for migrants, refugees, asylum or refugee status seekers, stateless and undocumented persons; and any other similar institution the purpose of which is to deprive persons of their liberty.[122]

The Principles are broadly similar to Article 4 of OPCAT; however, there are minor inconsistencies—for example, whereas the Principles only cover official detentions, OPCAT also deals with unofficial detention if the State acquiesces.[123]

3. The need for consistency in engagement with NPMs

Many see the key contribution of OPCAT as being the NPM. States who have ratified OPCAT and those who have a good knowledge of the instrument recognize the importance of the NPM element to the Protocol. Whilst visits by other UN and regional bodies to places of detention raise the potential for duplication, this is perhaps easier to overcome with detailed and up-to-date information being passed between the various bodies. What is seen as more problematic is how each engages with the NPMs within specific States and how to ensure consistency in approach between the different bodies. At present this does not appear to have happened under the UN system and where the different bodies are referring to OPCAT they are taking their lead from the SPT and have been consistent in their approach. When considering the approach of the ICC and regionally, however, cracks have already appeared. With the increase in States Parties to OPCAT and the increase in numbers of visits by the SPT and of NPMs designated, the ability of the individual UN and regional bodies to keep up-to-date information and advice on the NPMs is made more difficult.

Part of the difficulty in ensuring consistency is that it is unlikely, and indeed undesirable, for the SPT to take a straightforward approach to what is required of an NPM. Some of the information the SPT gains on the NPM may be deemed to

121 EU Guidelines, pp 8–9.

122 Inter-American Commission on Human Rights, Principles and Best Practices on the Protection of Persons Deprived of Liberty in the Americas, Approved by the Commission during its 131st regular period of sessions, held from March 3–14, 2008, General Provision.

123 See, OPCAT Research Team, The Inter-American Commission on Human Rights Principles and Best Practices on the Protection of Persons Deprived of Liberty in the Americas and the Optional Protocol to the Convention Against Torture, August 2009, <http://www.bristol.ac.uk/law/research/centres-themes/opcat/opcatdocs/iacmhrprinciples.pdf>.

be confidential, some of it may be very context-specific. The role of the SPT is to 'advise and assist' NPMs,[124] not to condemn them. How it approaches a particular body within the context of OPCAT may differ from what is important from the perspective of other UN and regional bodies.

The Inter-American Principles, for example, provide little detail on the bodies that should visit places of detention, making no reference in its Principle XXIV to the need for them to be independent, expert, and regular in their visits, nor additional powers such as commenting on legislation. As the Inter-American Commission does not possess a procedure akin to affiliated status before the African Commission, there are relatively few opportunities for the Commission to consider institutions such as NHRIs or NPMs. The Organization of American States (OAS) has made some moves in this regard with the adoption of a number of resolutions on Strengthening of the National Human Rights Systems of the Member States and Support for the Work of Defenders of the People, Defenders of the Population, and Human Rights Attorneys or Commissioners (Ombudsmen)[125] which encourage 'the establishment of forums for dialogue between institutions of the kind to which this resolution refers and the pertinent organs of the inter-American system, in order to strengthen their contribution to the democratic order in the Hemisphere'.[126] The President of the Inter-American Commission has also noted his engagement with ombudsmen in order to 'exchange views on possible cooperation with national human rights institutions, in order to strengthen the Inter-American system and in particular to enforce the decisions of the Court and the Commission itself'.[127]

Similarly, Article 33 of the Convention on the Rights of Persons with Disabilities (CRPD) requires States to set up government focal points and a national monitoring framework, involving civil society organizations, one element of which should comply with the Paris Principles. In some states it is possible that the Article 33 framework could also be the NPM under OPCAT.

Although, on the whole, statements from other regional bodies have not contradicted the approaches adopted by the SPT, there is a concern that without future strategic regular interaction and engagement between the various bodies and the SPT this may not always be the case. Fortunately, the increasingly confident stance taken by the SPT as reflected in its newly adopted Guidelines suggest that it is now prepared to provide some guidance to States, NPMs, and others on what issues should be considered when establishing and designating these national bodies.

[124] OPCAT, Article 11(1)(b)(iii).

[125] See Resolutions of the General Assembly of the OAS, OAS Doc AG/RES. 2132 (XXXV-O/05) and AG/RES. 2221 (XXXVI-O/06) of 7 June 2005 and 6 June 2006 respectively on Strengthening of the National Human Rights Systems of the Member States and Support for the Work of Defenders of the People, Defenders of the Population, and Human Rights Attorneys or Commissioners (Ombudsmen).

[126] Ibid, para 4.

[127] Address by the President of the Inter-American Commission on Human Rights, Florentin Melendez, at the Opening of the 130th Regular Session 9 October 2007 collected in Annex 3 to the Annual Report of the Inter-American Commission on Human Rights 2007, OAS Doc OEA/Ser.L/V/II.130, Doc 22, rev 1, 29 December 2007.

Although the advice in the guidelines is still general and permits States and NPMs to create a system which is context- and country-specific, this approach, with the promise of more guidance to come, does mean that other UN and regional treaty bodies will have somewhere to look in the future for advice on NPMs.

E. Conclusion: The Need for Systematic and Strategic Engagement

There appears to be an implied agreement between the various torture prevention bodies of the need for collaboration and avoidance of duplication in the fulfilment of their respective mandates. This seems, on the surface at least, not to be hindered by sensitivities over protecting one's turf. This collaborative attitude has enabled informal relationships to be developed among those involved in the various treaty bodies and special procedures so resulting in their engaging with each other and keeping each other informed of their work.

The SPT has now created regional rapporteurs from among its members who then take on responsibility and are the focal point for Africa, Asia, Europe, and Latin America.[128] Going further, the SPT has now set out, in its Fourth Annual Report, a 'template for forms of co-operative activities' to build upon such relationships. This details a range of activities in which it can cooperate with various bodies and includes: promotion and awareness raising, exchange of information, coordination of visits and engagement with NPMs, participating in events and other respective activities, and collaboration on shared events and other activities.[129] This illustrates an attempt to take a more coherent approach. However, it needs to go further. Neither the SPT nor other UN or regional bodies have moved into a more systematic and strategic engagement where each has mapped out their respective strengths and weaknesses and identified how they can usefully support each other. While OPCAT is still new, it has the potential to carve out a niche for itself and as a relatively unknown entity, people will be looking closely at the SPT to see where it will make its mark. However, as has been said elsewhere 'the distinctiveness of [OPCAT] can be overstated and, over time, is in any case likely to become less marked'.[130]

Beyond the relationship with the CAT, which is formally set out in OPCAT, whether and how these different bodies engage with the SPT has more to do with interpersonal relationships and whether the same members sit on the same bodies, than any strategic decision to discuss their respective agendas and mandates in a regular way.

On the one hand, this may not be a problem. Indeed, as noted above, it is quite clear that the different bodies are aware of the existence of OPCAT and raise questions about it during their examination of State reports, under the Universal Periodic Review (UPR) process, and on country visits. The references tend to be

[128] See SPT Fourth Annual Report, n 6 above, para 12.
[129] Ibid, paras 112–114.
[130] Evans, M D, 'The OPCAT at 50', in Gilbert, G, Hampson, F and Sandoval, C (eds), *The Delivery of Human Rights: Essays in Honour of Professor Sir Nigel Rodley* (Routledge, 2011) p 113.

rather general, often simply referring to the ratification or otherwise of OPCAT, and perhaps designation of NPMs, rarely to anything more. The Special Rapporteur on Torture and the CAT are exceptions to this, having made reference in their reports and making more strident comments regarding OPCAT implementation.

A mapping out of respective strengths and weaknesses of the range of bodies will identify that certain bodies have more of an impact than others in certain circumstances. For example, it was noted in the Netherlands that initially the CPT was not taken seriously by the Dutch authorities and only became relevant once the European Court of Human Rights started to use CPT findings in its decisions. There are concerns, therefore, that the SPT would also not be taken seriously.

There is a need to recognize that each institution must in some way add value to the system as a whole. Some are bound by confidentiality which means that their ability to speak out is limited (SPT, CPT, ICRC), but others are not (such as the SRT and the CoE Commissioner for Human Rights). Conversely there needs to be an acknowledgement that just as publicity of findings and reports can be beneficial, at times confidentiality may be a very useful tool in achieving pragmatic results. The UN level may 'add clout' to findings of regional bodies which operate closer to the ground. Looking at the UNHCR, for example,

> the size of the UNHCR is to be compared to a single sub-committee established under the OPCAT made up of 10 members, who may add specialist experts to its team for particular visits. The UNHCR operates in 111 countries and has over 6000 staff. Clearly the SPT's capacity to engage with all the various forms of detention will be limited, and a prioritising exercise will have to be undertaken by the SPT, not only in relation to which countries to visit but also the particular types of detention facilities to be visited once there.[131]

There needs to be some recognition of the differences of focus between the various bodies: some mandates focus on broader elements of the situation in a particular country (like the SRT), others on specific incidents in particular places of detention (the SPT, CPT, etc), while others have a permanent presence in the State (NPMs, ICRC, OSCE and OHCHR field offices). Others only visit rather infrequently (like the CoE Commissioner for Human Rights). Certain of these bodies are crucial during times of crisis or conflict (such as the ICRC).

Once this mapping exercise has been carried out, it may then help to develop strategic links between the various bodies, so that each can identify where they can build on their own weaknesses and each other's strengths. This will require, however, a degree of honesty on the part of the individual SPT members and those of other treaty bodies, as well as a willingness to recognize their own restrictions and not to engage in a turf war.

Beyond this mapping exercise, there are a number of activities that can be considered which can enhance engagement between the SPT and others. First, it would be important to increase the opportunities for further meetings between various members of these bodies and their secretariats which would allow further discussion of the intricacies of their various mandates.

[131] Edwards, n 109 above, 821–822.

Secondly, in a very practical sense, there is a need to develop a tool which would allow for an easy reference for the existing bodies on each other's work.[132] The existing bodies should not only ascertain the work that has been carried out by others, but also exchange information on the planned activities and thus coordinate their future efforts.

Thirdly, each international and regional body needs to carefully consider the ways in which they can engage with NPMs themselves, either through procedures and fora set up for NHRIs or by adopting alternative methods.

Fourthly, detailed, up-to-date, and reliable information on the nature of the NPM in each State Party to OPCAT is crucial and needs to be made available not only to the SPT but also to all the other relevant bodies so as to enable international and regional bodies to make a judgement as to their suitability and whether they can rely on them as an objective source of information. The international and regional bodies can then vary their approach to the NPM depending on the context. The international and regional bodies, however, should refrain from making any pronouncements on the appropriateness of the States Parties' choice in respect of the NPM, and instead recognize that OPCAT charges the SPT with such a function.

Lastly, the opportunity to conduct joint missions between the SPT and the regional bodies is worth examining. On the one hand, this could ensure there is no duplication and that resources are pooled. On the other, the methodology of the SPT and the regional body may differ, there are issues of confidentiality which confront the SPT and which may not confront the regional bodies, and whereas the SPT has an automatic mandate to enter a State and its places of detention once the State has ratified OPCAT, for the other regional mechanisms consent from the State is required. Thus, what on the face of it may appear to be a simple process of joining forces may in reality pose more problems than it solves. The other possibility is to use the regional bodies as experts for specific visits. Again this opens up the challenge of conflict of interests and there would need to be very clear terms of reference and guidelines for the involvement of such experts in SPT visits.

The system of prevention of torture that OPCAT puts in place is not intended to work in isolation. Rather, the instrument was adopted in acknowledgement of the shortcomings that have emerged in the existing system and the SPT and NPMs have been added to the web of various international, regional, and national bodies that work in the field of prevention of torture and other forms of ill-treatment. It is thus essential that all these actors recognize each other's existence and actively explore avenues for effective collaboration.

132 See the website developed by the members of the Law School of the University of Bristol: <http://www.humanrightsvisits.org>.

8

Regional Trends towards Ratification and Implementation of OPCAT

As has been illustrated in the previous chapter, OPCAT operates in the context not just of the UN but also of regional mechanisms. The other aspect of a regional approach that arises from our research is the perceptions, expectations, and approaches that are emerging around the globe as States from different regions become parties to OPCAT, start implementing the instrument, or decide to stay away from it all together. Our research reveals that there are some common patterns around the world and also some fine nuances of detail that are different. It has emerged that not all States have the same perceptions of what OPCAT ought to entail and certainly did not share the same vision about the modalities of the torture prevention system that the instrument was to put in place:

> The idea that an independent international institution could come to visit unannounced, without any warning... was of course quite a novelty to many of the states.[1]

Whilst any conclusions drawn about regional variations can inevitably be accused of being sweeping generalizations, it has become apparent to us that there are a number of regional 'trends' and patterns worthy of note. An awareness of such may help inform the strategy then to be employed in particular regions:

> So I think there's a huge regional imbalance when you discuss the OPCAT. You can see it from how many countries in Asia have ratified compared to Latin America. And I mean I think it's great; I think there's going to be some really good lessons learned coming out of Latin America but, again, I think, comparing them to Asia is extremely difficult.[2]

A. Reasons For and Against Ratification

First, and perhaps most obviously, there is a correlation between the presence (or absence) of regional human rights mechanisms, especially mechanisms tailored to address the issue of torture and ill-treatment through visits, and the desire of States to become party to OPCAT. However reasons for ratifying OPCAT, NPM

[1] Interview with Jens Faerkel, Danish Ministry of Foreign Affairs, 7 November 2007.

[2] Interview with Dorrit Rée Akselbo, Rehabilitation and Research Centre for Torture Victims (RCT) (Denmark), 6 November 2007.

choices, and expectations of OPCAT and the SPT are more complex than that. Across all regions there has been considerable international NGO involvement. The Association for the Prevention of Torture (APT), Rehabilitation and Research Centre for Torture Victims (RCT), and others have made great efforts to look in particular at States which may be more reticent to ratify and have channelled their energies appropriately. Although their work can account perhaps for specific State ratifications, there is however no evidence to suggest that regional trends are down to NGO involvement or otherwise.

At the time of writing there are 57 States Parties and 21 signatories to OPCAT;[3] about one third of all UN Member States. Furthermore, examination of the regions according to the UN regional groupings reveals that there are ten African States, six Asian States, sixteen Eastern European States, thirteen Latin American and Caribbean States, and twelve Western European and Other States that are currently parties to OPCAT.[4] On the face of it, these figures represent rather minor differences among the regions. However, these UN statistics can be confusing and if these numbers are converted into more 'user friendly' categories, it emerges that there are thirty States Parties from the Europe and Central Asia region,[5] thirteen from the Americas,[6] eleven from Africa (although mostly West Africa) and the Middle East,[7] and only three States Parties from the Asia Pacific[8] region. Even examining the twenty-one additional signatories,[9] there are ten from Europe and Central Asia,[10] one from the Americas,[11] eight from Africa and the Middle East,[12] and two signatories from the Asia Pacific.[13] This means there are no States Parties or signatories from North America, and the Caribbean region and other large regions such as South Asia (with one State Party, the Maldives) and the Far East (with only one State Party, Cambodia, and one further signatory, Timor Leste) are under-represented. Consequently, a disparity among the regions emerges which warrants closer examination.

[3] See <http://treaties.un.org/Pages/ViewDetails.aspx?src=TREATY&mtdsg_no=IV-9-b&chapter=4&lang=en>.

[4] SPT, Fourth Annual Report of the Subcommittee on Prevention of Torture and Other Cruel, Inhuman or Degrading Treatment or Punishment (April–December 2010), CAT/C/46/2, 7 January 2011, para 7.

[5] Albania, Armenia, Azerbaijan, Bosnia and Herzegovina, Croatia, Cyprus, Czech Republic, Denmark, Estonia, Former Yugoslav Republic of Macedonia, France, Georgia, Germany, Kazakhstan, Kyrgyzstan, Liechtenstein, Luxembourg, Malta, Montenegro, Netherlands, Poland, Republic of Moldova, Romania, Serbia, Slovenia, Spain, Sweden, Switzerland, Ukraine, and United Kingdom.

[6] Argentina, Bolivia, Brazil, Chile, Costa Rica, Ecuador, Guatemala, Honduras, Mexico, Nicaragua, Paraguay, Peru, and Uruguay.

[7] Benin, Burkina Faso, Democratic Republic of Congo, Gabon, Lebanon, Liberia, Mali, Mauritius, Nigeria, Senegal, and Togo.

[8] Cambodia, Maldives, and New Zealand.

[9] See <http://treaties.un.org/Pages/ViewDetails.aspx?src=TREATY&mtdsg_no=IV-9-b&chapter=4&lang=en>.

[10] Austria, Belgium, Bulgaria, Finland, Iceland, Ireland, Italy, Norway, Portugal, and Turkey.

[11] Panama.

[12] Cameroon, Republic of Congo, Ghana, Guinea, Madagascar, Sierra Leone, South Africa, and Zambia.

[13] Australia and Timor-Leste.

As was noted in the previous chapter, Europe is seen as having the most advanced network of regional human rights mechanisms which prohibit torture and ill-treatment. Twenty-eight of the States who are party to the ECPT are also parties to OPCAT (with a further ten being signatories). As a result, in the Council of Europe (CoE) area, the ratio of OPCAT ratifications is very high, with only nine States not being even signatories.[14] It is worth mentioning that during its twenty-five years of operation, the CPT has conducted 177 periodic visits and 118 *ad hoc* visits—totalling 295 visits to States Parties—and published 244 reports.[15] With the Commissioner for Human Rights also undertaking visits, these States are therefore accustomed to regular visits by a regional body. During our interviews, we observed two trends emerging among such States. First, there were those who perceived the ratification of OPCAT to be a natural step forward given the practice of CPT:

Maybe that's why in Europe it's been easier because they [countries] know of the CPT and a lot of countries see that the CPT has had quite a good effect. So that's made it easier for people to understand why the OPCAT is needed.[16]

Secondly, prevalent among the States of the region that chose to refrain from ratifying OPCAT is the approach of 'one at a time': instead of being subjected to the jurisdictions of various mechanisms, the State would work with one, striving to implement the recommendations made, before considering joining another:

[T]he authority and expertise of the CPT experts cannot be disputed. The CPT has carried out regular visits and already identified a number of issues, which we have to address. Although many of these issues are part of the legacy of the post-Soviet penitentiary system, and we cannot claim that the present state of affairs is perfect, we are constantly working to improve the situation in the penitentiaries.[17]

Additionally, the origins of which can be traced to the practice in relation to the CPT visits, over the years ECPT States have developed a practice of requesting the publication of their reports by the CPT, which is now considered to be a customary rule under the ECPT.[18] Sweden, being the only ECPT State that has so far also been visited by the SPT,[19] requested the publication of its report[20] and despite being the third country overall to receive a visit by the SPT, was the first to request

[14] These are: Andorra, Greece, Hungary, Latvia, Lithuania, Monaco, Russia, San Marino, and Slovakia.

[15] See <http://www.cpt.coe.int/en/about.htm#Statistics>.

[16] Interview with Dorrit Rée Akselbo, Rehabilitation and Research Centre for Torture Victims (Denmark), 6 November 2007.

[17] Interview with Emils Plaksins, Office of the Representative of the Government of the Republic of Latvia before International Human Rights Organizations, Ministry of Foreign Affairs of the Republic of Latvia (Latvia), 16 May 2008.

[18] Murdoch, J, *The Treatment of Prisoners. European Standards* (Strasbourg: Council of Europe Publishing, 2006), p 43.

[19] The SPT has announced that it will visit Ukraine during 2011, which will make it the second country to be visited by both the SPT and CPT. See 'UN Subcommittee on Prevention of Torture concludes twelfth session, announces programme of work in the field for 2011' UN Press Release of 19 November 2010.

[20] Report on the visit of the Subcommittee on Prevention of Torture and Other Cruel, Inhuman or Degrading Treatment or Punishment to Sweden, UN Doc CAT/OP/SWE/1 10 September 2008.

the publication of the SPT's report.[21] It was also the first State to request the publication of its replies to the recommendations of the SPT.[22] This may point towards the possibility that the practice adopted by States Parties to the ECPT may now be extended also to OPCAT. It will be interesting to observe whether Ukraine, which will become the second CPT State to receive a visit by the SPT, will follow the same practice.

The existence of the CPT in particular has therefore been the reason for both ratifying OPCAT and for refraining from doing so:

> [. . .] for other countries, which are not subject to any other regional monitoring mechanisms, the SPT has a very important role. In our [European] regional context I see it rather more as taking a complementary role.[23]

In the Americas, of the 35 OAS Member States,[24] thirteen are parties to OPCAT with one further signatory. Thus over a third of the OAS Member States are parties to OPCAT. Moreover, if focusing exclusively upon the South American continent, only four States are not parties to OPCAT: Colombia, Guyana, Suriname, and Venezuela,[25] and among the Central American States only Belize and El Salvador have not ratified.[26]

The popularity of OPCAT in South and Central America reflects that in Europe. States in the Americas appear to be following the example of Sweden in the publication of reports of visits of the SPT (Mexico,[27] Paraguay,[28] and Honduras[29]). How can this be explained? Certainly, the existence of visiting bodies in the region is a possibility, but the Inter-American Commission Special Rapporteur simply cannot be said to have the same depth of experience and visibility as the CPT has in Europe. A further explanation is that States such as Costa Rica and Mexico played a central role in the drafting of OPCAT and this may have heightened awareness of

[21] The first country that was visited, Mauritius, has never requested the publication of the report; the Maldives, being the second country to be visited (10–17 December 2007) requested the publication on 23 February 2009: Report on the visit of the Subcommittee on Prevention of Torture and Other Cruel, Inhuman or Degrading Treatment or Punishment to Maldives, UN Doc CAT/OP/MDV/1 of 26 February 2009. Sweden was visited 10–14 March 2008 and requested the publication of the report on 23 July 2008.

[22] Replies from Sweden to the Recommendations and Questions of the Subcommittee on Prevention of Torture in its Report on the First Periodic Visit to Sweden, UN Doc CAT/OP/SWE/1/Add.1 of 30 January 2009.

[23] Interview with Anhelita Kamenska, Latvian Centre for Human Rights (Latvia), 15 May 2008.

[24] See <http://www.oas.org/en/member_states/default.asp>.

[25] The overseas territories of the Falkland Islands and South Georgia and South Sandwich Islands (United Kingdom) and French Guiana (France) are not included here.

[26] Panama has been a signatory to OPCAT since 22 September 2010.

[27] Report on the visit of the Subcommittee on Prevention of Torture and Other Cruel, Inhuman or Degrading Treatment or Punishment to Mexico, UN Doc CAT/OP/MEX/1 of 31 May 2010.

[28] Report on the visit of the Subcommittee on Prevention of Torture and Other Cruel, Inhuman or Degrading Treatment or Punishment to the Republic of Paraguay, UN Doc CAT/OP/PRY/1 of 7 June 2010.

[29] Report on the visit of the Subcommittee on Prevention of Torture and Other Cruel, Inhuman or Degrading Treatment or Punishment to Honduras, UN Doc CAT/OP/HND/1 of 10 February 2010. It remains to be seen if the fourth State in the region which has received a visit from the SPT, Bolivia, will follow the practice of its neighbouring States.

OPCAT. Indeed, it was the Mexican Draft which initiated the idea of national visiting bodies.[30]

In contrast, African States have been less willing to ratify OPCAT. There are only ten ratifications and a further eight signatories from the region. Three States in Africa have received a visit from the SPT and only Benin has recently agreed to publication of the report.[31] There are quite a significant number of National Human Rights Institutions (NHRIs) and similar bodies in African States, some of which already visit places of detention, suggesting that the reticence to ratify OPCAT may have less to do with the NPM element and more to do with the international visiting body, the SPT. There is also an underlying concern that the treaty body should be aware of the specific African context:

> So again the problem that we are faced with is Parliament and the Minister, they are well aware of the problem. We know our prisons are over-crowded. We know that our medical care is not on an international standard. The question is how do we solve it? [. . .] in the African context there is an element of variance. Meaning that when you go, for instance, let's say to your rural areas, in the Eastern Cape, and you look at medical care, the nearest hospital to the local community is 500km away. So when you look at medical care in prison you must be mindful of the conditions in the area as well. [. . .] So you know, is this abnormal or is this normal? [. . .] Of course you have over-arching standards in terms of a constitution. There's definitely 'nos' and 'yeses'. But then also you look at the local standards as well and say how they are involved.[32]

Although there exists no comparable regional human rights instrument for the Middle East and Asia Pacific regions, they are not without their treaties and mechanisms. The League of Arab States' 2004 Arab Charter on Human Rights[33] prohibits 'physical or psychological torture or . . . cruel, degrading, humiliating or inhuman treatment' in Article 8 and provides further obligations for States,[34] and although the Association of South East Asian Nations (ASEAN)[35] has yet to adopt a regional human rights treaty or declaration, its Inter-Governmental Commission on Human Rights is charged with a wide human rights mandate.[36] The fact that a

[30] See Chapter 2.

[31] SPT, Fourth Annual Report, n 4 above, para 18 and CAT/OP/BEN.1.

[32] Interview with Gideon Morris, Director of Corporate Services, Judicial Inspectorate of Prisons; member of the 'Section 5 Committee' (South Africa), 9 April 2008.

[33] Adopted 22 May 2004, entered into force 15 March 2008, reprinted in (2005) 12 *IHRR* 893. The 2004 Charter is a revised version of the original Charter which was adopted in 1994, Member States of the Arab League are: Algeria, Bahrain, the Comoros, Djibouti, Egypt, Iraq, Jordan, Kuwait, Lebanon, Libya, Mauritania, Morocco, Oman, Palestine, Qatar, Saudi Arabia, Somalia, Sudan, Syria, Tunisia, United Arab Emirates, and Yemen.

[34] Article 8(2) reads: 'Each State party shall protect every individual subject to its jurisdiction from such practices and shall take effective measures to prevent them. The commission of, or participation in, such acts shall be regarded as crimes that are punishable by law and not subject to any statute of limitations. Each State party shall guarantee in its legal system redress for any victim of torture and the right to rehabilitation and compensation.'

[35] ASEAN was established in 1967 and has ten Member States, of which only Cambodia is a party to OPCAT.

[36] See Terms of Reference of ASEAN Intergovernmental Commission on Human Rights, available at <http://www.aseansec.org/DOC-TOR-AHRB.pdf>.

cohesive regional human rights instrument and mechanism has proved elusive in both these regions may go some way to explaining the very low number of States Parties to OPCAT.[37] The suspicion with which States here may view international scrutiny is reflected in the desire on the part of the two States who have received visits from the SPT so far for their reports to remain confidential.[38] It was different in the case of the Maldives, however, which was the second country ever to receive a visit from the SPT, and which requested the publication of its report.[39]

Any broad conclusions that can be drawn from this overview of regional ratification can only be tentative, but they do suggest some correlation between the existence or absence of a regional human rights mechanism, especially one which has a visiting capacity, and the 'popularity' of OPCAT in the region. Countries of the CPT region are accustomed to the idea of opening up their places of deprivation of liberty to the scrutiny of an external, regional expert body which may freely choose to visit any such places without interference from the State. The practice of the CPT over the twenty-five years of its operation has developed so far that publication of its often critical reports does not pose a challenge to States but is rather perceived as a part of a mature constructive dialogue. It is therefore perhaps not surprising that such States saw the SPT as being something very similar to the CPT:

> The SPT is a committee to prevent torture. We have the CPT already but with the SPT we would probably get more of the same [. . .]. I doubt very much if it [SPT] would make much difference here [in Denmark].'[40]

This is markedly different in the regions where there are no visiting bodies where the perceived intrusions on State sovereignty that such visits may entail may impact on whether OPCAT is ratified or not:

> Yeah, I think from my perspective, the key reason really is Federal Australian governments' hostility towards outside experts visiting Australian detention facilities. I mean, there's this view, the current government, it is quite suspicious of, and sceptical of, the value of more human rights reporting mechanisms, but it stems really from this kind of general hostility towards foreigners telling us what to do.[41]

While the research we have carried out suggests that this correlation is a fairly strong one, there are also discrepancies within the regions and this warrants further examination of reasons in favour of or against the ratification of OPCAT.

[37] Among the countries from the Middle East, only Lebanon is a party to OPCAT, with no additional signatories; while in Asia Pacific, Cambodia, New Zealand, and Maldives are the only three States Parties to OPCAT, with Timor Leste and Australia being two further signatories.

[38] Cambodia in December 2009 and Lebanon, in June 2010, SPT Fourth Annual Report at para 18.

[39] Report on the visit of the Subcommittee on Prevention of Torture and Other Cruel, Inhuman or Degrading Treatment or Punishment to Maldives, UN Doc CAT/OP/MDV/1 of 26 February 2009.

[40] Interview with Jens Færkel, Ministry of Foreign Affairs (Denmark), 7 November 2007.

[41] Interview with Dr Ben Saul, Director of the Sydney Centre for International Law & The Faculty of Law at the University of Sydney (Australia).

B. The Added Value of Being Parties to OPCAT

Although one can explain the relatively easy acceptance of OPCAT in the European region as being due to CPT experience, conversely it does beg the question: if the SPT and CPT are so similar, why ratify OPCAT at all? In another words, what is the added value of OPCAT? Here, several reasons arise from the interviews we conducted. Firstly, ratification of OPCAT was seen as setting an example to States in other regions of the world:

> The way we see it here in the Ministry of Foreign Affairs, torture does not really have anything to do with Denmark. But Denmark will take the lead in torture prevention. If we don't ratify the Protocol, others will not take it seriously.[42]

This was an interesting rationale that also featured not just in Europe but in other regions among the States that see themselves as being at the forefront of human rights protection. For them, being a party to OPCAT is more of a symbolic act, a way to support or promote the need for torture prevention strategies.[43] This was particularly the case for those States that consider themselves to be leaders of a particular region.

Secondly, certainly in the European context, many States saw the advantage of OPCAT being a universal instrument as opposed to the regional character of the ECPT: 'Because when you are talking about foreign experience, it's a really good forum for discussion of the negative and positive achievements in case studies from different countries.'[44] For many States across the 'CPT region' becoming a party to OPCAT was also about not being complacent in their fight against torture and ill-treatment. Becoming a party to OPCAT is viewed as providing a 'fresh pair of eyes' to ascertain that the approach adopted in the country in terms of torture prevention is a correct one.[45]

The fact that the SPT is a UN body which would be applying international standards was noted in other regions such as Africa where OPCAT could therefore assist the State in reaching its international obligations:

> Because we can measure how we perform within the boundaries of the country, so the SPT would kind of say, 'But, you know guys, you are doing well,' or, 'You're not close to international norms and standards, you need to . . . ' So I would say that international perspective would definitely be something that the SPT would be able to bring to us.[46]

[42] Interview with Jens Færkel, Ministry of Foreign Affairs (Denmark), 7 November 2007.

[43] Interview with Commander Chris Griggs, Deputy Director of Legal Services, New Zealand Defence Force (New Zealand).

[44] Interview with Giorgi Chkheidze, Georgian Young Lawyers Association (Georgia) on 20 June 2007.

[45] 'It's always good to have fresh eyes on a subject. Just because Denmark believes that we're doing fine with the CAT [. . .] it's always it's nice to have a second opinion. So I think that would be the most important role of the SPT in relation to Denmark, to have the second opinion', interview with Lars Solskov Lind, Ministry of Justice (Denmark) on 6 November 2007.

[46] Interview with Gideon Morris, Director of Corporate Services, Judicial Inspectorate of Prisons; member of the 'Section 5 Committee' (South Africa), on 9 April 2008.

Historical contexts also emerged as a reason for becoming party to OPCAT and this was a common theme across all regions with the exception of Asia Pacific. In Europe, it was the memories of the second world war that were still alive in people's minds,[47] in Africa, the legacy of apartheid and in the Americas, dictatorships and military rule.[48] OPCAT is therefore reflective of a path towards greater protection of human rights and democracy within the State. This was further bolstered by the perception of the value that is brought by the 'double-tier of protection' offered by OPCAT with its national and international bodies. With respect to the former, most regions have regional human rights mechanisms and many States have their own NHRI or other institutions dealing with issues of torture and ill-treatment prevention. But it is the obligation to designate an NPM which provides many with the hope that State commitment and implementation of the Protocol will continue beyond ratification.[49]

Furthermore, the SPT then was seen as a way of focusing governments' attention on the prevention of torture and ill-treatment. The SPT and NPMs, however, are sometimes not seen as distinct entities, in fact one will reinforce the other and the SPT can provide international expertise in assisting the development of the capacity of the NPM to engage with torture prevention issues:

> [...] that instead of just going about in your own little world, in your own country thinking everything is perfect, it's nice to have the second opinion. So definitely I think the two tier system is a value. And if we could come to a situation where there could be a good communication between the two, that would probably make it even more valuable.[50]

Finally, the scope of OPCAT, especially in terms of Article 4,[51] was noted as an important contributing factor towards the added value of OPCAT in the Americas[52] and Africa.[53] In Europe this was less so, given that the approach of the CPT

[47] 'We also had cases of torture during the Second World War and we had also witnessed it ourselves' interview with Dorrit Rée Akselbo, Rehabilitation and Research Centre for Torture Victims (Denmark), 6 November 2007.

[48] 'Well perhaps first we should start saying that Uruguay has a long record and tradition on human rights protection and promotion. This was unfortunately interrupted during the period of long dictatorship. That's very important to have in mind that torture precisely was often occurring during this period. [...] So when we came back to democracy in 1985, the Convention against Torture was one of the priorities for us', interview with Alejandra de Bellis, Ministry of Foreign Affairs (Uruguay), 8 March 2007.

[49] '[...] the NPM, it takes away one of the general criticisms on international instruments which is, "Well we sign it and so what?" The situation "We sign it and then we file it." And the NPM will help so that it does not happen with OPCAT', interview with Gideon Morris, Director of Corporate Services, Judicial Inspectorate of Prisons; member of the 'Section 5 Committee' (South Africa), on 9 April 2008.

[50] Interview with Lars Solskov Lind, Ministry of Justice (Denmark) on 6 November 2007.

[51] As outlined in Chapter 4.

[52] 'Because at the moment, the existing mechanisms in Uruguay are more focused on prisons. So this [the wide visiting mandate of the SPT and NPMs] will be very, very useful', interview with Alejandra de Bellis, Ministry of Foreign Affairs (Uruguay), 8 March 2007.

[53] 'Of course the benefit of extending it [visiting] to other places of detention ... what's happening in those places [other types of detention places] I don't know. And after OPCAT now all of a sudden we're all aware of that we don't know', interview with Gideon Morris, Director of Corporate Services, Judicial Inspectorate of Prisons; member of the 'Section 5 Committee' (South Africa), on 9 April 2008.

to 'deprivation of liberty' has been broadened out to what are seen as less traditional places of detention.[54]

C. Trends in the Choices for NPMs

As was examined in Chapter 6, the provisions of OPCAT leave considerable room for manoeuvre to States Parties in terms of choosing which institution(s) are to perform the task of the NPM. However, an examination of the approaches adopted by States reveals some interesting differences and trends across the regions.

European States have predominantly designated their existing institutions as NPMs, the most 'popular' choice being that of the ombudsman. Indeed, of the thirty European and Central Asian States that are parties to OPCAT, twenty-one have designated their NPMs and of these, fifteen have designated their ombudsman offices, either alone or together with other entities, to fulfil the duties of the NPM.[55] The most common explanation for this approach is the perception held by the respective governments that the ombudsman institutions already carry out similar functions to those envisaged for the NPM and thus the institution can be designated as an NPM without any changes in either legislation or practice.[56]

This then leads to a further common attitude of 'business as usual', namely, the designation of existing institutions as NPMs without the provision of additional financial resources. This has been a point of criticism from a number of NPMs, whether those be within Europe or elsewhere:[57]

An additional challenge for those States that choose to designate existing ombudsmen institutions as their NPMs has been the need for such institutions to adapt to the pro-activeness of a preventive mandate. This was another criticism by the SPT in relation to the Swedish NPM[58] and it has been noted as a challenge in other regions too.

Conversely, in the Americas and on the African continent, however, it was noted that NPMs ought to also assist with the complaints handling system as there are no other mechanisms that have direct access to people deprived of their liberty.

[54] Evans, M and Morgan, R, *Preventing Torture. A Study of the European Convention for the Prevention of Torture and Inhuman or Degrading Treatment or Punishment* (Oxford: Oxford University Press, 2001), p 194.

[55] See <http://www.apt.ch/index.php?option=com_k2&view=item&layout=item&id=767&Itemid=267&lang=en>.

[56] Interview with Dorrit Rée Akselbo, Rehabilitation and Research Centre for Torture Victims (Denmark), 6 November 2007.

[57] Report on the visit of the Subcommittee on Prevention of Torture and Other Cruel, Inhuman or Degrading Treatment or Punishment to Maldives, UN Doc CAT/OP/MDV/1 of 26 February 2009, para 69.

[58] 'When conducting their activities as NPMs, their visiting methodology should reflect a preventive approach, which, although complementary, differs substantially from their current, complaint-driven activities.' See Report on the visit of the Subcommittee on Prevention of Torture and Other Cruel, Inhuman or Degrading Treatment or Punishment to Sweden, UN Doc CAT/OP/SWE/1 of 10 September 2008, para 38.

African States have been keen to ensure that their NPMs reflect their regional and national characteristics, even if that would include aspects of their mandate that are not necessarily prescribed by OPCAT:

> I think the South African concept like any other country, to have the elements of uniqueness and I would, you understand, hopefully that we would not lose that through the NPM mechanism. [...] Because the requirements of the NPM would basically be a group of specialists, let's say five or six people that would go around the country and visit prisons once a year or twice a year. Now that would add value but on the other side it would, in terms of the grassroot presence and prisoners, helping them with their day-to-day complaints may be lost in the process. So that... uniqueness of the South African system should not be lost.'[59]

Of the eleven States that are parties to OPCAT in Africa, only four have designated their NPMs and of these, Mali and Mauritius have designated their respective NHRIs,[60] while Senegal[61] and Nigeria[62] have created entirely new entities for the purposes of their NPMs (National Observer for Places of Deprivation of Liberty (Observateur National des Lieux de Privation de Liberté) and National Committee against Torture respectively).

In the Americas, of the thirteen States Parties, only four have designated their NPMs[63] and some, such as Chile and Uruguay, have used the need for the establishment of an NPM as an opportunity to establish an NHRI.[64] Some, such as Costa Rica and Mexico, have appointed their existing NHRIs as their NPMs. Yet others are establishing entirely new entities for the purposes of their NPM.[65] Yet it is the process of selecting NPMs which has received considerable focus in the Americas, perhaps spearheaded by the approach of Paraguay.[66] As the SPT remarked:

59 Interview with Gideon Morris, Director of Corporate Services, Judicial Inspectorate of Prisons; member of the 'Section 5 Committee' (South Africa), 9 April 2008.

60 <http://www2.ohchr.org/english/bodies/cat/opcat/mechanisms.htm>.

61 Ibid.

62 Penal Reform International 'Nigerian government approves National Committee on Torture'; available at <http://www.penalreform.org/news/nigerian-government-approves-national-committee-torture>.

63 Ombudsman office for Costa Rica; National Committee for the Prevention of Torture for Honduras; National Human Rights Commission for Mexico; National Institute for Human Rights for Uruguay <http://www2.ohchr.org/english/bodies/cat/opcat/mechanisms.htm>.

64 Please note that the NHRI for Chile is still to be established. See APT 'List of designated NPMs' available at <http://www.apt.ch/index.php?option=com_k2&view=item&layout=item&id=767&Itemid=267&lang=en>.

65 For example, Honduras, and potentially Paraguay and Bolivia.

66 See also Honduras, as the SPT remarked:

> The Subcommittee commends the process that led to the adoption of the National Preventive Mechanism Act. This process has been cited as exemplary because of the open, transparent and inclusive involvement of various actors. Special mention should be made of the role played by the legislature, the offices of the attorneys for human rights and civil society organizations. The Subcommittee is pleased to note that the national preventive mechanism was established by law, as a prerequisite for its institutional stability and functional independence.

The SPT expresses its satisfaction at the process that led to the adoption of the draft legislation setting up the National Preventive Mechanism (MNP). This process has been described as a model for the open, transparent and inclusive participation of a wide range of stakeholders. The SPT is also satisfied with the current content of the MNP bill, which meets the minimum requirements of the Optional Protocol to the Convention against Torture and Other Cruel, Inhuman or Degrading Treatment or Punishment (OPCAT), including financial independence of the NPM.[67]

Such an open process is less apparent in the European context, with the SPT commenting, for example, on Sweden:

[T]he SPT can already anticipate that there will be a need for a profound re-examination, including consultations with the Parliamentary Ombudsmen and the Chancellor of Justice as well all other relevant stakeholders, as to the decision originally taken by the government to designate these institutions as the NPMs.[68]

D. Some Concluding Thoughts

Despite some initial concerns, as outlined in Chapter 3, that it was going to be difficult to identify which standards would be suitable in any given context, in practice this has been a relative non-issue. Whilst many felt that the SPT ought to be careful and try to employ some sort of 'universal' standard across all States so as not to give the impression of too 'European' an approach, equally it was considered more important that it tailor its advice to the particular State and provide practical guidance on how emerging issues could be addressed.

Our research in fact identifies several points. Firstly, there is an expectation that the SPT, having global coverage, will be able to draw examples from other countries from the relevant region and beyond to provide specific advice on how particular problems can be addressed in a useful, practical manner:

I would say especially again the benefit of the SPT in terms of the dialogue part is that they will have a perspective that's not limited to one country only. So they could come in on the basis of best practices and say, 'You know what? We've seen this problem also in Mauritius. And the way that they dealt with it is A, B and C.'[69]

See Report on the visit of the Subcommittee on Prevention of Torture and Other Cruel, Inhuman or Degrading Treatment or Punishment to Honduras, UN Doc CAT/OP/HND/1 of 10 February 2010 at para 262.

[67] Report on the visit of the Subcommittee on Prevention of Torture and Other Cruel, Inhuman or Degrading Treatment or Punishment to the Republic of Paraguay, UN Doc CAT/OP/PRY/1 of 7 June 2010 at para 56.

[68] Report on the visit of the Subcommittee on Prevention of Torture and Other Cruel, Inhuman or Degrading Treatment or Punishment to Sweden, UN Doc CAT/OP/SWE/1 of 10 September 2008 at para 37. See also similar approaches in Denmark and Estonia.

[69] Interview with Gideon Morris, Director of Corporate Services, Judicial Inspectorate of Prisons; member of the 'Section 5 Committee' (South Africa), 9 April 2008.

Secondly, the SPT is perceived as a body that would accumulate 'best practices' from around the world and through its 'continuous dialogue' enable pragmatic solutions to be reached together with States.

More generally, it is clear that through regional events and fora, such as the EU NPM Project and gatherings of NHRIs, for example, regional pressure and regional approaches have developed. The particular consultative process adopted by Paraguay was taken as an example of good practice by many and set a benchmark across the Americas, influencing others in how they should approach designation.

The very poor ratification rate in the Asia Pacific region, despite its high profile and active NHRI forum, can in part be explained by the same reasons that have prevented the adoption of an Asia-Pacific instrument as well as a suspicion about international scrutiny of places of detention.[70]

All regions seem to share the view that OPCAT and its treaty body, the SPT, ought to embrace its international character. In broad terms however, the angle of this argument differed, especially between Europe and Africa. In Europe, while recognizing that SPT's mandate is closely modelled upon that of the CPT, it was noted that the CPT is in a much more privileged position in terms of availability of resources and the need for the SPT to avoid duplication was underlined. As one interviewee put it:

> [...] I consider that maybe the main activity of the SPT will be coordination of the domestic mechanisms because I'm not sure how many visits they can come up with during the year, especially when SPT will start monitoring activities. CPT wants to reach 200 visits during the year and SPT will be much less and also to put in place effective domestic mechanisms it has to be a priority for this committee in order to be in touch with these domestic bodies to get the information.[71]

The seeds of an approach whereby the SPT would differ in its approach across different regions of the world are there. But conversely, what emerges from this is the principle of complementarity which will manifest itself differently in various regions. In Europe, it is about ensuring that the SPT does not duplicate CPT, which may perhaps dictate a greater focus on the NPM rather than the SPT visits. In Africa and the Asia-Pacific, in contrast, it may be that both the SPT's visits and the NPMs will be the more problematic elements.

[70] Harding, R and Morgan, N, 'OPCAT in the Asia-Pacific and Australasia' in *Essex Human Rights Review*. Special Issue. Part II, Vol 6, No 2; at pp 142–146.

[71] Interview with Giorgi Tugushi, OSCE field mission in Georgia (now Ombudsman of Georgia) (Georgia), 20 June 2007.

9

Conclusion: Emerging Trends and the Future of OPCAT

Although it is early days to make a comprehensive assessment of how OPCAT is working in practice, this unique instrument has already had some impact on a variety of different levels. Whilst more research and analysis needs to be carried out, therefore, on how those institutions designated or created will function in practice as NPMs under a treaty remit, and how the SPT will manage with an increased membership, this does not preclude a discussion at this stage of some underlying issues that need to be borne in mind, not only for the implementation of OPCAT but also for the implementation of similar treaties and mechanisms. Some degree of stocktaking is all the more pertinent given the increase in membership of the SPT and the likelihood of there being some delay in progressing many issues further while the new members find their feet and the current members deal with the different dynamics of an expanded committee.

It is worth mentioning a few issues which have at various stages so far in the existence of OPCAT prompted some discussion. Early confusion over when exactly States could use Article 24 of OPCAT[1] to postpone their obligations under Parts III and IV of the instrument have been resolved with the clarification from the SPT of the consistency between the languages of the text.[2] Although there have been a few examples of States making use of this provision,[3] as the SPT gains increased confidence and as there are more examples available of NPMs which have been designated and are already functioning, the lack of clarity as to what an NPM is may become less of an issue and therefore less reason for States to use Article 24. Similarly, some discussion among NGOs about the concept of prevention[4]

[1] Article 24 reads: '1. Upon ratification, States Parties may make a declaration postponing the implementation of their obligations under either part III or part IV of the present Protocol.

This postponement shall be valid for a maximum of three years. 2. After due representations made by the State Party and after consultation with the Subcommittee on Prevention, the Committee Against Torture may extend that period for an additional two years.'

[2] See SPT, Third Annual Report of the Subcommittee on Prevention of Torture, Cruel, Inhuman or Degrading Treatment or Punishment, CAT/C/44/2, 25 March 2010.

[3] For example, Kazakhstan, Romania and Montenegro, see <http://www2.ohchr.org/english/bodies/cat/opcat/mechanisms.htm>; SPT, Fourth Annual Report of the Subcommittee on Prevention of Torture and Other Cruel, Inhuman or Degrading Treatment or Punishment (April-December 2010), CAT/C/46/2, 7 January 2011, para 22.

[4] A conference was held in Copenhagen on the concept of prevention, see <http://www.uk.rct.dk/Link_menu/Activities/Previous_activities/Workshop_070410.aspx>.

suggested in the early stages that this may be something the SPT could provide clarification on and perhaps a definition. The SPT has chosen to adopt a more practical approach, outlining principles emanating from the concept which will assist it in its work on visits and its relationship with NPMs and States.[5] Rather than being bogged down with formulating definitions of prevention this approach seems sensible.

A. Expansion of Membership of OPCAT

In October 2010 the number of States Parties to OPCAT reached the fifty mark thus prompting the implementation of Article 5(1) which increases the membership of the SPT from ten to twenty-five. New members were elected on 28 October 2010.[6]

This has various implications. First, it will inevitably impact on the manner in which the SPT itself operates. The SPT has taken several years to operate as a team and learn of each other's approaches and their role within the broader UN structures. More than doubling its existing membership, introducing different backgrounds, experiences, and expectations not only provides opportunities but also potential tensions. As the SPT itself notes, one of its first tasks 'will be to get to know each other and to consider how best to utilise the enhanced range of skills and experience that it will then possess'.[7]

The need for expertise on a range of other issues such as different contexts of visiting (refugees/asylum, military, etc) or national institutions more generally was something many hoped would be picked up with the appointment of new members, as could a broader geographical reach. The SPT has already been criticized for its Euro-centric membership and approach, through the inclusion of several members of the CPT. Indeed, there are now three members from Africa, whereas previously there were none, and some have direct experience with NPMs.

Lastly, the increase in membership provides the opportunity for more visits to take place, with less demands on each member, and for more engagement to take place nationally with NPMs and others beyond the formal visiting structure. The presence of an SPT member in every continent offers considerable promotional opportunities for OPCAT.

To a certain extent the SPT may have to backtrack and start from basics to get others on board and up to speed. This may mean that any innovation will be stalled for a couple of years until they find their feet.

[5] SPT, The approach of the Subcommittee on Prevention of Torture to the concept of prevention of torture and other cruel, inhuman or degrading treatment or punishment under the Optional Protocol to the Convention against Torture and Other Cruel, Inhuman or Degrading Treatment or Punishment, CAT/OP/12/6, 30 December 2010. See Appendix VI.

[6] For a list of members of the SPT see Appendix VII.

[7] SPT, Fourth Annual Report, n 3 above, para 107.

B. Expertise on OPCAT

The initial years of OPCAT has shown that all actors—the SPT, NPMs, governments, and civil society—are still finding their way with respect to the exact nature and content of the Protocol. This is no different from any newly established instrument or treaty. On the face of it the SPT has worked closely with civil society organizations and, through the OPCAT Contact Group, been open to assistance from them in identifying important issues and helping to draft policies, among other things. While this is very much to be encouraged and implies a potential for fruitful collaboration into the future, there are also concerns and risks associated with it. First, it is not at all clear how much the SPT itself might have initiated this interaction with civil society if the latter had not been so willing to offer its assistance. Second, whilst initially many looked to whatever source of information they could find on OPCAT and how it should function, now there is evidence of a shift to the need for a more 'official' take on OPCAT and it is the SPT to which they look at the international level. There is a perception that the SPT holds the expertise and can be consulted on all aspects of OPCAT,[8] in particular the NPM elements, yet the SPT itself is still learning the extent and potential of the instrument and has shown some hesitancy in putting itself forward to undertake this role. The SPT has to demonstrate its usefulness in the provision of advice and knowledge on OPCAT:

> I mean if they, if the SPT, since we don't know exactly how they're going to function... I mean if they do become this body that everybody hopes, that can give recommendations and advice and, once they start to pick up on, on different trends of NPMs and problems and difficulties, maybe they will be able to, to give that like sense of expertise that will add the value of torture prevention.[9]

As OPCAT becomes more established and as more NPMs are designated, so there will be increased attention to the instrument. New projects such as the European NPM project and other activities and events will generate their own documentation and discussions. It is crucial that there is consistency in the approach to OPCAT and its implementation.

If the SPT does not step up to the challenge of establishing itself as a central player in OPCAT then it risks losing credibility. The SPT has been very cautious in its approach to many aspects of OPCAT, in particular to NPMs and its role in relation to them. It has held back from issuing comments and policies for fear of appearing to take a stance which would not be compatible with what it has seen as its essentially advisory and dialogue function. Its hesitancy at the outset, when NGOs such as the APT and others have managed to address a range of issues relating to OPCAT quickly and competently, despite their novelty, could damage

[8] 'You know, if there are difficulties then hopefully they will become that body that they can consult and ask if they have difficulties or issues or . . . ', interview with Dorrit Rée Akselbo, Rehabilitation and Research Centre for Torture Victims (Denmark) on 6 November 2007.

[9] Ibid.

its new reputation if it does not now respond. Similarly, where the SPT fails to respond more forcefully to challenges raised by NPMs, civil society is likely to step into the breach. While most civil society organizations operating in this area, such as the APT and members of the OPCAT Contact Group, among others, have huge integrity and respect, this cannot be said for all civil society organizations and the importance of the SPT setting benchmarks cannot be underestimated.

Added to this, it is clear from the research we have conducted that the expectations resting on the SPT are immense. As to the role that the SPT is perceived to play, this has ranged from maintaining an ongoing relationship with NPMs, providing extra external support for NPMs,[10] providing NPMs with relevant training, to being a 'crucial partner' to the NPM itself. As one person said to us: an 'international body with a different view and perhaps different standard can interact with . . . the national one'. Clearly the SPT cannot fulfil all of these expectations and it is therefore to the NPM at the national level that it is hoped many will start to look as potential experts on OPCAT.

C. A 'System' of Prevention Through Visits

There has been a tendency, as one might expect, with the excitement of a new instrument, to focus attention solely on it. However, it must not be forgotten that OPCAT is part not only of the UNCAT, but also of a line of international treaties and procedures within the UN. It adds to existing regional mechanisms and also national ones, beyond those formally designated as NPMs under OPCAT. The expectations on the SPT and NPMs are high. There is a presumption that, as with any new instrument or new institution, it can deliver alone on the broader aim within which it is established, in this case, the prevention of torture. Yet it is not realistic to presume that one institution, whether that be the SPT at the international level, or the NPM at the national level, will be able to achieve this single-handedly. It needs to be placed within the broader context of factors that play a part in torture prevention. These include criminalization of torture, education, etc, and extend as far as a democratic State system and an independent judiciary.[11]

As outlined in Chapter 7 there is a clear need now to become more strategic in how OPCAT fits within the existing structures. These require an honest consideration not just by the SPT and NPMs as to their strengths and weaknesses but also an audit of what is available internationally, regionally, and nationally, to identify where they each fit, how they can avoid duplication, and how they can dovetail and support each other's work. This can sometimes be difficult, with each institution often competing for space, trying to identify its own niche and role. As we have seen, when it comes to

[10] 'Because . . . this dialogue . . . is a space where . . . an international body with a different view and perhaps different standard can interact with . . . the national one helping them to . . . implement it at a national level', interview with Alejandra de Bellis, Ministry of Foreign Affairs (Uruguay) on 8 March 2007.

[11] See, for example, CAT General Comment No 2, Implementation of Article 2 by States Parties, CAT/C/GC/2, 24 January 2008, at Part IV.

designation of NPMs, the vast majority of national bodies are vying for selection, with only a few arguing for non-inclusion. These turf wars should not blur the identification of which institutions and bodies are best suited to particular tasks.

D. Budget and Financial Resources

From the start of the operation of the SPT, discussions were dominated by tensions with the secretariat of the OHCHR for increased funding for the SPT. It is perhaps not surprising that the new committee posed some challenges for the OHCHR as its approach did not fit the more 'traditional' mandate of the other human rights treaty bodies. A core part of the SPT's mandate was visits to States, not simply holding sessions in Geneva. As noted in Chapter 5, it was also clear during the early months that NPMs were going to be a crucial part of the SPT's work if OPCAT was to work effectively, yet funding for this aspect of the SPT's work had not been factored into its budget.

Whilst many of these issues now appear to have been dealt with, there is the broader matter of the impact of this on the relationship with the secretariat and the OHCHR in general. In terms of the ability of the SPT, and indeed any UN treaty body, to function effectively it is crucial that both the OHCHR and the treaty body work to maintain a close and collaborative relationship.

As the UN human rights system considers wider issues of reform,[12] and the treaty bodies have moved towards more harmonization in their working methods, the multiplicity of bodies raises challenges for all of them with respect not only to their 'efficiency and effectiveness'[13] but also to implementation and follow-up at the domestic level. This will have implications for the mandate of the SPT, in particular its visiting function and how this fits with other treaty bodies and special procedures not only at the UN but regionally. As budgets become more strapped, so the need will be increased for the SPT and other treaty bodies to maintain a unique identity which has an impact.

With respect to implementation of OPCAT at the national level, a new resource is now available under Article 26 of OPCAT. This provides:

1. A Special Fund shall be set up in accordance with the relevant procedures of the General Assembly, to be administered in accordance with the financial regulations and rules of the United Nations, to help finance the implementation of the recommendations made by the Subcommittee in Prevention after a visit to a State Party, as well as eduction programmes of the national preventive mechanisms.
2. The Special Fund may be financed through voluntary contributions made by Governments, intergovernmental and non-governmental organizations and other private or public entities.

[12] See, for example, Dublin Statement on the Process of Strengthening the United Nations Human Rights Treaty Body System, November 2009, and Response by non-governmental organizations, November 2010.

[13] Ibid, para 5.

A small number of significant contributions have now been made to the Fund, thus providing some further resources to assist national actors in the implementation of OPCAT obligations and indirectly to assist the SPT in the fulfilment of its remit. Inevitably, however, questions now arise (and as yet remain unanswered) over how this money will be disseminated: who will administer it; and how much input the SPT is likely to have in any decision-making in this regard? Should the Fund be open only to applications by States or also to NPMs, and maybe others?

E. Standards and Accommodating Regional Differences

First, subsumed in all of this—and something which has arisen on various occasions—is the issue of 'standards' and which of them are applicable at any one time by the visiting bodies, whether that is the SPT or the NPMs. Exactly what legal 'standards' are being applied—whether these are treaty provisions, or soft law documents—not only by the SPT but also by NPMs on their visits has been open to question.

In its reports on visits to States, the SPT refers to a variety of different instruments and documents including the UNCAT, ICCPR, and findings of the Human Rights Committee, the Committee on the Rights of the Child,[14] as well as national laws, the constitutions of the State concerned and soft law documents.[15] As to whether there is consistency of approach or methodology, and what benchmarks the SPT is using when compiling its reports and during its visits, is not always clear.

Similarly, at the national level, it is apparent that NPMs themselves are referring to a variety of different standards during their visits and in carrying out their mandates. These range from the use of national legislation and the constitution[16] to reference to the ECHR,[17] the UNCAT, and the UN Standard Minimum Rules for Non-Custodial Measures, among others.[18]

The issue of language here is also an important one. Translation of reports from visits and other documents is not always consistently done and as a result it is not unusual for members of the SPT and others to be unable to read and understand

[14] For example, Report on the Visit of the Subcommittee on Prevention of Torture and Other Cruel, Inhuman or Degrading Treatment or Punishment to the Maldives, CAT/OP/MDV/1, 26 February 2009, paras 27 and 28.

[15] For example, Body of Principles for the Protection of All Persons under Any Form of Detention or Imprisonment, A/RES/43/173 (9 December 1988), see Report of the Visit of the SPT to Maldives, ibid, p 22.

[16] See, for example, New Zealand Human Rights Commission, Monitoring Places of Detention. Annual Report of activities under the Optional Protocol to the UN Convention Against Torture (OPCAT), 1 July 2008–30 June 2009, December 2009, p 11; 2009 Annual Report of the People's Advocate of Albania, Activity of the People's Advocate on the Role of the National Mechanism on Prevention of Torture.

[17] See, for example, Estonian Chancellor of Justice, 2009 Overview of the Chancellor of Justice. Activities for the prevention of torture and other cruel, inhuman or degrading treatment or punishment, Statistics of Proceedings, Tallinn, 2010, p 11.

[18] New Zealand Human Rights Commission, Monitoring Places of Detention, n 16 above, p 23.

the reports that they subsequently adopt. This has huge implications for ensuring consistency in standards and approach across regions and findings of the SPT.

Secondly, as noted in Chapter 8, OPCAT, with its global reach, has highlighted some differences between the regions. For example, it is arguable that the concept of deprivation of liberty holds different meanings for different areas. Europeans may be influenced heavily by the approach adopted by the CPT, for example, whereas other regions appear to have thought little of its applicability beyond prisons and police stations. Similarly, whereas Europe and to a certain extent the Americas and Africa have become more comfortable with the idea of an international visiting body to their places of detention, having had the CPT, various Special Rapporteurs, and others, the Asia-Pacific States may find this more of a challenge. Furthermore, at the domestic level, where States already have national visiting bodies in place which they then simply designate as the NPM, albeit perhaps with some slight changes to its mandate or budget, other regions where this type of body is novel have found the establishment of an NPM more difficult.

However, on the ground we have heard few concerns about the applicability of standards in this variety of different contexts. NPMs and the SPT appear to have taken a pragmatic approach to the issue, recognizing that they are not operating in a vacuum and perhaps displaying that their function is first and foremost operational, assisting in the implementation of already existing standards and drawing upon the variety of different documents available as and when necessary, rather than setting new ones.

F. Influence and Lessons for Other Treaties

Lastly, there is a tendency with many human rights treaties to see them in isolation, as distinct entities operating alone with a core group of NGOs, and other civil society organizations and others surrounding them, whose focus is closely linked to that of the relevant committee. Yet as Chapter 8 makes clear, no human rights treaty operates in a vacuum and OPCAT is no exception. Created as an optional protocol to an existing treaty, it has in fact taken on very much a life of its own. It is crucial that the *system* within which it was created is now brought more to the fore and that the SPT, NPMs and others recognize the interaction between OPCAT and other mechanisms.

This may be obvious when considering how OPCAT relates to treaties such as the CAT or even the ICCPR and ICESCR, and regionally, the CPT, but less so when one considers treaties such as the ICERD or the new Convention on the Rights of Persons with Disabilities (CRPD). In fact it is to OPCAT which this newer treaty and its Committee on the Rights of Persons with Disabilities may look when it considers Article 33. This reads:

> National Implementation and Monitoring
>
> 1. States Parties, in accordance with their system of organization, shall designate one or more focal points within government for matters relating to the implementation of the present Convention, and shall give due consideration to the establishment or designa-

tion of a coordination mechanism within government to facilitate related action in different sectors and at different levels.

2. States Parties shall, in accordance with their legal and administrative systems, maintain, strengthen, designate or establish within the State Party, a framework, including one or more independent mechanisms, as appropriate, to promote, protect and monitor implementation of the present Convention. When designating or establishing such a mechanism, States Parties shall take into account the principles relating to the status and functioning of national institutions for protection and promotion of human rights.
3. Civil society, in particular persons with disabilities and their representative organizations, shall be involved and participate fully in the monitoring process.

A provision which found its way into the convention largely due to the efforts of NHRIs[19] inevitably places these institutions in an important position with respect to the treaty's monitoring and implementation. It is this focus not just on international monitoring but also on domestic monitoring which makes a clear link between OPCAT and the CRPD.[20] A number of factors that have played a part in OPCAT so far are likely to be of interest to the newer CRPD and its Committee who will be three years behind OPCAT and SPT in experience. These include: the relationship between the CRPD Committee and the national institutions established under Article 33; how the CRPD Committee will manage this relationship; how it will engage with designated national bodies who may be less than perfect when it comes to Article 33 requirements; how it should use the information and accreditation status accorded by the ICC when it comes to evaluating the role of national frameworks under the convention; and how practically it should liaise with the national bodies, whether that be simply through the State reporting procedure that the convention provides, by giving them space at its sessions as other treaty bodies have done, or taking on board some of the ways in which the SPT has sought to approach these bodies on visits, for example.

There has already been a suggestion within the context of the CRPD and Article 33 to look for potential 'models' for these independent national frameworks. However, as this book has shown, whilst this was an approach advocated by many in the first year or so of OPCAT's existence there is now a recognition that 'one size does not fit all' and that, just as under OPCAT, the institutions designated under Article 33 must be tailored to the specific political and social context of the jurisdiction in which they will function. Issues of coordination between the

[19] Asia Pacific Forum, *Disability Issues Paper*, 12th Annual Meeting of the Asia Pacific Forum of National Human Rights Institutions, Sydney, Australia, 24–27 September 2007, p 3.

[20] See <http://www.un.org/esa/socdev/enable/rights/ahcstata34sscomments.htm#nhri>; Quinn, G, 'Resisting the "Temptation of Elegance": Can the Convention on the Rights of Persons with Disabilities Socialise States to Right Behaviour?', in O M Arnardottir and G Quinn (eds), *The UN Convention on the Rights of Persons with Disabilities: European and Scandinavian Perspectives* (Leiden: Martinus Nijhoff, 2009), pp 39–40. See Bristol OPCAT project team, The Optional Protocol to the UN Torture Convention and the UN Convention on the Rights of People with Disabilities: some common issues, 15 December 2009, <http://www.bristol.ac.uk/law/research/centres-themes/opcat/opcatdocs/opcatcrpd.pdf>.

government and independent elements of Article 33 bodies are likely to be similar to those faced under OPCAT. Article 33 and the CRPD in general provide for a central role for civil society organizations. Whilst this is less visible in the text of OPCAT, it is clear that the role of civil society has been crucial to the drafting, adoption, and development of OPAT so far. How civil society organizations have worked together to engage with the SPT through, for example, structures like the OPCAT Contact Group may provide some useful lessons for the CPRD where the divisions between NGOs around issues of disability are often stark and entrenched.

While the division between those institutions which should be responsible for implementation and those responsible for monitoring is more clearly laid out in the CRPD, it is already apparent that a distinct line between the two is unlikely to be easily drawn.[21] Although OPCAT does not make such a distinction, there have been attempts by governments to 'hand over' responsibility for implementation of OPCAT and torture prevention generally to the NPM once it has been established. Lastly, just as governments have a tendency to argue for 'business as usual' with respect to the mandate and resources of an NPM post-designation under OPCAT, so there may be a desire to follow the same approach with respect to Article 33 of the CRPD. As with OPCAT, where no NPM has so far seen its existing mandate and/or resources as satisfactory to fulfil its OPCAT requirements, so this must be guarded against under the CRPD. Besides these very practical points, however, there is also a range of issues where the relationship between the two treaties is interlinked on a more substantive level such as through dealing with the rights of persons detained in mental health institutions. How the CPRD and OPCAT and how any national institution designated under either or both interrelate in these contexts and how their respective Committees engage on these issues requires further consideration.

And this model of focusing on the domestic structures in human rights treaty monitoring and implementation is not confined to the torture and disability fields and has already been picked up in other treaties, such as the Convention on Disappearances.[22] Even where there are no provisions in the treaty itself, the relevant Committees are now issuing recommendations that national institutions have a role in monitoring implementation of the treaty.[23]

[21] Asia Pacific Forum, *Disability Issues Paper*; UK Parliamentary Joint Committee on Human Rights, *The UN Convention on the Rights of Persons with Disabilities*, First Report of Session 2008–09, HL Paper 9, HC 93, 4 January 2009, para 101.

[22] Article 12 refers to the ability of competent national authorities to carry out investigations and Article 17(e) guarantees access by 'competent and legally authorised authorities' to places where persons are deprived of their liberty. In addition, Article 17(3) reads: 'Each State Party shall assure the compilation and maintenance of one or more up-to-date official registers and/or records of persons deprived of liberty, which shall be made promptly available, upon request, to any judicial or other competent authority or institution authorized for that purpose by the law of the State Party concerned or any relevant international legal instrument to which the State concerned is a party.'

[23] 'NHRIs should ensure that their composition includes pluralistic representation of the various elements of civil society involved in the promotion and protection of human rights. They should seek to involve, among others, the following: human rights, anti-discrimination and children's rights non-governmental organizations (NGOs), including child- and youth-led organizations; trade unions; social and professional organizations (of

Given increased attention by the OHCHR to the role of NHRIs generally and the trend towards considering implementation and impact, these types of national mechanisms—which the NPMs in OPCAT are spearheading—may well become the norm in new instruments. OPCAT provides valuable lessons for their potential effectiveness.

G. Conclusion

Lastly, what is the bigger picture? Issues that appeared at the start and prior to the adoption of OPCAT to be pressing have in fact proved little more than an interesting diversion. Concern about the applicability of universal standards and what they should be, the methodology that NPMs and the SPT should be employing when they are actually carrying out visits to places of detention, the need for a clearer understanding of the concept of prevention or even a definition, have proved to be of little more than academic interest. Instead, our research has highlighted, through the people we have spoken to and the discussions that have taken place at various OPCAT events, that it is in fact other issues which are more relevant and pertinent to the actual operation of OPCAT at the international and national levels. The role of NPMs has assumed a significance and importance beyond what even the original drafters had contemplated. There are other new factors, such as continued discussion on revision of working practices of UN human rights treaty bodies, which will inevitably impinge on the future operation of OPCAT. Initially many pronounced on the uniqueness of OPCAT and its NPM element but in fact this is becoming less obvious with the entry into force and adoption of new treaties which mimic the national implementation element in particular. Similarly, the visiting mandate which dictates much of the SPT's work is now considered an attractive option to many members of UN human rights committees as a possible direction that they may wish to take in their work. In that sense what is important now is not whether OPCAT offers anything unique or different but that those who are tasked with its monitoring and implementation do it well.

> doctors, lawyers, journalists, scientists, etc); universities and experts, including children's rights experts. Government departments should be involved in an advisory capacity only. NHRIs should have appropriate and transparent appointment procedures, including an open and competitive selection process',

UN Committee on the Rights of the Child, General Comment No 2 (2002), *The Role of Independent National Human Rights Institutions in the Promotion and Protection of the Rights of the Child*, CRC/GC/2002/2, 15 November 2002, para 12.

APPENDIX I

Optional Protocol to the Convention against Torture and Other Cruel, Inhuman or Degrading Treatment or Punishment

Adopted on 18 December 2002 at the fifty-seventh session of the General Assembly of the United Nations by resolution A/RES/57/199.

Protocol is available for signature, ratification and accession as from 4 February 2003 (ie the date upon which the original of the Protocol was established) at United Nations Headquarters in New York.

Preamble

The States Parties to the present Protocol,

Reaffirming that torture and other cruel, inhuman or degrading treatment or punishment are prohibited and constitute serious violations of human rights,

Convinced that further measures are necessary to achieve the purposes of the Convention against Torture and Other Cruel, Inhuman or Degrading Treatment or Punishment (hereinafter referred to as the Convention) and to strengthen the protection of persons deprived of their liberty against torture and other cruel, inhuman or degrading treatment or punishment,

Recalling that articles 2 and 16 of the Convention oblige each State Party to take effective measures to prevent acts of torture and other cruel, inhuman or degrading treatment or punishment in any territory under its jurisdiction,

Recognizing that States have the primary responsibility for implementing those articles, that strengthening the protection of people deprived of their liberty and the full respect for their human rights is a common responsibility shared by all and that international implementing bodies complement and strengthen national measures,

Recalling that the effective prevention of torture and other cruel, inhuman or degrading treatment or punishment requires education and a combination of various legislative, administrative, judicial and other measures,

Recalling also that the World Conference on Human Rights firmly declared that efforts to eradicate torture should first and foremost be concentrated on prevention and called for the adoption of an optional protocol to the Convention, intended to establish a preventive system of regular visits to places of detention,

Convinced that the protection of persons deprived of their liberty against torture and other cruel, inhuman or degrading treatment or punishment can be strengthened by non-judicial means of a preventive nature, based on regular visits to places of detention, Have agreed as follows:

Part I
General principles

Article 1

The objective of the present Protocol is to establish a system of regular visits undertaken by independent international and national bodies to places where people are deprived of their liberty, in order to prevent torture and other cruel, inhuman or degrading treatment or punishment.

Article 2

1. A Subcommittee on Prevention of Torture and Other Cruel, Inhuman or Degrading Treatment or Punishment of the Committee against Torture (hereinafter referred to as the Subcommittee on Prevention) shall be established and shall carry out the functions laid down in the present Protocol.
2. The Subcommittee on Prevention shall carry out its work within the framework of the Charter of the United Nations and shall be guided by the purposes and principles thereof, as well as the norms of the United Nations concerning the treatment of people deprived of their liberty.
3. Equally, the Subcommittee on Prevention shall be guided by the principles of confidentiality, impartiality, non-selectivity, universality and objectivity.
4. The Subcommittee on Prevention and the States Parties shall cooperate in the implementation of the present Protocol.

Article 3

Each State Party shall set up, designate or maintain at the domestic level one or several visiting bodies for the prevention of torture and other cruel, inhuman or degrading treatment or punishment (hereinafter referred to as the national preventive mechanism).

Article 4

1. Each State Party shall allow visits, in accordance with the present Protocol, by the mechanisms referred to in articles 2 and 3 to any place under its jurisdiction and control where persons are or may be deprived of their liberty, either by virtue of an order given by a public authority or at its instigation or with its consent or acquiescence (hereinafter referred to as places of detention). These visits shall be undertaken with a view to strengthening, if necessary, the protection of these persons against torture and other cruel, inhuman or degrading treatment or punishment.
2. For the purposes of the present Protocol, deprivation of liberty means any form of detention or imprisonment or the placement of a person in a public or private custodial setting which that person is not permitted to leave at will by order of any judicial, administrative or other authority.

Part II
Subcommittee on Prevention

Article 5

1. The Subcommittee on Prevention shall consist of ten members. After the fiftieth ratification of or accession to the present Protocol, the number of the members of the Subcommittee on Prevention shall increase to twenty-five.

2. The members of the Subcommittee on Prevention shall be chosen from among persons of high moral character, having proven professional experience in the field of the administration of justice, in particular criminal law, prison or police administration, or in the various fields relevant to the treatment of persons deprived of their liberty.
3. In the composition of the Subcommittee on Prevention due consideration shall be given to equitable geographic distribution and to the representation of different forms of civilization and legal systems of the States Parties.
4. In this composition consideration shall also be given to balanced gender representation on the basis of the principles of equality and non-discrimination.
5. No two members of the Subcommittee on Prevention may be nationals of the same State.
6. The members of the Subcommittee on Prevention shall serve in their individual capacity, shall be independent and impartial and shall be available to serve the Subcommittee on Prevention efficiently.

Article 6

1. Each State Party may nominate, in accordance with paragraph 2 of the present article, up to two candidates possessing the qualifications and meeting the requirements set out in article 5, and in doing so shall provide detailed information on the qualifications of the nominees.
2. (a) The nominees shall have the nationality of a State Party to the present Protocol;
   (b) At least one of the two candidates shall have the nationality of the nominating State Party;
   (c) No more than two nationals of a State Party shall be nominated;
   (d) Before a State Party nominates a national of another State Party, it shall seek and obtain the consent of that State Party.
3. At least five months before the date of the meeting of the States Parties during which the elections will be held, the Secretary-General of the United Nations shall address a letter to the States Parties inviting them to submit their nominations within three months. The Secretary-General shall submit a list, in alphabetical order, of all persons thus nominated, indicating the States Parties that have nominated them.

Article 7

1. The members of the Subcommittee on Prevention shall be elected in the following manner:

   (a) Primary consideration shall be given to the fulfilment of the requirements and criteria of article 5 of the present Protocol;

   (b) The initial election shall be held no later than six months after the entry into force of the present Protocol;

   (c) The States Parties shall elect the members of the Subcommittee on Prevention by secret ballot;

   (d) Elections of the members of the Subcommittee on Prevention shall be held at biennial meetings of the States Parties convened by the Secretary-General of the United Nations. At those meetings, for which two thirds of the States Parties shall constitute a quorum, the persons elected to the Subcommittee on Prevention shall be those who obtain the largest number of votes and an absolute majority of the votes of the representatives of the States Parties present and voting.

2. If during the election process two nationals of a State Party have become eligible to serve as members of the Subcommittee on Prevention, the candidate receiving the higher number of votes shall serve as the member of the Subcommittee on Prevention. Where nationals have received the same number of votes, the following procedure applies:

   (a) Where only one has been nominated by the State Party of which he or she is a national, that national shall serve as the member of the Subcommittee on Prevention;

   (b) Where both candidates have been nominated by the State Party of which they are nationals, a separate vote by secret ballot shall be held to determine which national shall become the member;

   (c) Where neither candidate has been nominated by the State Party of which he or she is a national, a separate vote by secret ballot shall be held to determine which candidate shall be the member.

Article 8

If a member of the Subcommittee on Prevention dies or resigns, or for any cause can no longer perform his or her duties, the State Party that nominated the member shall nominate another eligible person possessing the qualifications and meeting the requirements set out in article 5, taking into account the need for a proper balance among the various fields of competence, to serve until the next meeting of the States Parties, subject to the approval of the majority of the States Parties. The approval shall be considered given unless half or more of the States Parties respond negatively within six weeks after having been informed by the Secretary-General of the United Nations of the proposed appointment.

Article 9

The members of the Subcommittee on Prevention shall be elected for a term of four years. They shall be eligible for re-election once if renominated. The term of half the members elected at the first election shall expire at the end of two years; immediately after the first election the names of those members shall be chosen by lot by the Chairman of the meeting referred to in article 7, paragraph 1 (d).

Article 10

1. The Subcommittee on Prevention shall elect its officers for a term of two years. They may be re-elected.

2. The Subcommittee on Prevention shall establish its own rules of procedure. These rules shall provide, inter alia, that:

   (a) Half the members plus one shall constitute a quorum;

   (b) Decisions of the Subcommittee on Prevention shall be made by a majority vote of the members present;

   (c) The Subcommittee on Prevention shall meet in camera.

3. The Secretary-General of the United Nations shall convene the initial meeting of the Subcommittee on Prevention. After its initial meeting, the Subcommittee on Prevention shall meet at such times as shall be provided by its rules of procedure. The Subcommittee on Prevention and the Committee against Torture shall hold their sessions simultaneously at least once a year.

PART III
Mandate of the Subcommittee on Prevention

Article 11

1. The Subcommittee on Prevention shall:

(a) Visit the places referred to in article 4 and make recommendations to States Parties concerning the protection of persons deprived of their liberty against torture and other cruel, inhuman or degrading treatment or punishment;

(b) In regard to the national preventive mechanisms:

(i) Advise and assist States Parties, when necessary, in their establishment;
(ii) Maintain direct, and if necessary confidential, contact with the national preventive mechanisms and offer them training and technical assistance with a view to strengthening their capacities;
(iii) Advise and assist them in the evaluation of the needs and the means necessary to strengthen the protection of persons deprived of their liberty against torture and other cruel, inhuman or degrading treatment or punishment;
(iv) Make recommendations and observations to the States Parties with a view to strengthening the capacity and the mandate of the national preventive mechanisms for the prevention of torture and other cruel, inhuman or degrading treatment or punishment;

(c) Cooperate, for the prevention of torture in general, with the relevant United Nations organs and mechanisms as well as with the international, regional and national institutions or organizations working towards the strengthening of the protection of all persons against torture and other cruel, inhuman or degrading treatment or punishment.

Article 12

In order to enable the Subcommittee on Prevention to comply with its mandate as laid down in article 11, the States Parties undertake:

(a) To receive the Subcommittee on Prevention in their territory and grant it access to the places of detention as defined in article 4 of the present Protocol;

(b) To provide all relevant information the Subcommittee on Prevention may request to evaluate the needs and measures that should be adopted to strengthen the protection of persons deprived of their liberty against torture and other cruel, inhuman or degrading treatment or punishment;

(c) To encourage and facilitate contacts between the Subcommittee on Prevention and the national preventive mechanisms;

(d) To examine the recommendations of the Subcommittee on Prevention and enter into dialogue with it on possible implementation measures.

Article 13

1. The Subcommittee on Prevention shall establish, at first by lot, a programme of regular visits to the States Parties in order to fulfil its mandate as established in article 11.

2. After consultations, the Subcommittee on Prevention shall notify the States Parties of its programme in order that they may, without delay, make the necessary practical arrangements for the visits to be conducted.

3. The visits shall be conducted by at least two members of the Subcommittee on Prevention. These members may be accompanied, if needed, by experts of demonstrated professional experience and knowledge in the fields covered by the present Protocol who shall be selected from a roster of experts prepared on the basis of proposals made by the States Parties, the Office of the United Nations High Commissioner for Human Rights and the United Nations Centre for International Crime Prevention. In preparing the roster, the States Parties concerned shall propose no more than five national experts. The State Party concerned may oppose the inclusion of a specific expert in the visit, whereupon the Subcommittee on Prevention shall propose another expert.
4. If the Subcommittee on Prevention considers it appropriate, it may propose a short follow-up visit after a regular visit.

Article 14

1. In order to enable the Subcommittee on Prevention to fulfil its mandate, the States Parties to the present Protocol undertake to grant it:
   (a) Unrestricted access to all information concerning the number of persons deprived of their liberty in places of detention as defined in article 4, as well as the number of places and their location;
   (b) Unrestricted access to all information referring to the treatment of those persons as well as their conditions of detention;
   (c) Subject to paragraph 2 below, unrestricted access to all places of detention and their installations and facilities;
   (d) The opportunity to have private interviews with the persons deprived of their liberty without witnesses, either personally or with a translator if deemed necessary, as well as with any other person who the Subcommittee on Prevention believes may supply relevant information;
   (e) The liberty to choose the places it wants to visit and the persons it wants to interview.
2. Objection to a visit to a particular place of detention may be made only on urgent and compelling grounds of national defence, public safety, natural disaster or serious disorder in the place to be visited that temporarily prevent the carrying out of such a visit. The existence of a declared state of emergency as such shall not be invoked by a State Party as a reason to object to a visit.

Article 15

No authority or official shall order, apply, permit or tolerate any sanction against any person or organization for having communicated to the Subcommittee on Prevention or to its delegates any information, whether true or false, and no such person or organization shall be otherwise prejudiced in any way.

Article 16

1. The Subcommittee on Prevention shall communicate its recommendations and observations confidentially to the State Party and, if relevant, to the national preventive mechanism.
2. The Subcommittee on Prevention shall publish its report, together with any comments of the State Party concerned, whenever requested to do so by that State Party. If the State Party makes part of the report public, the Subcommittee on Prevention may publish the report in whole or in part. However, no personal data shall be published without the express consent of the person concerned.

3. The Subcommittee on Prevention shall present a public annual report on its activities to the Committee against Torture.
4. If the State Party refuses to cooperate with the Subcommittee on Prevention according to articles 12 and 14, or to take steps to improve the situation in the light of the recommendations of the Subcommittee on Prevention, the Committee against Torture may, at the request of the Subcommittee on Prevention, decide, by a majority of its members, after the State Party has had an opportunity to make its views known, to make a public statement on the matter or to publish the report of the Subcommittee on Prevention.

Part IV
National preventive mechanisms

Article 17

Each State Party shall maintain, designate or establish, at the latest one year after the entry into force of the present Protocol or of its ratification or accession, one or several independent national preventive mechanisms for the prevention of torture at the domestic level. Mechanisms established by decentralized units may be designated as national preventive mechanisms for the purposes of the present Protocol if they are in conformity with its provisions.

Article 18

1. The States Parties shall guarantee the functional independence of the national preventive mechanisms as well as the independence of their personnel.
2. The States Parties shall take the necessary measures to ensure that the experts of the national preventive mechanism have the required capabilities and professional knowledge. They shall strive for a gender balance and the adequate representation of ethnic and minority groups in the country.
3. The States Parties undertake to make available the necessary resources for the functioning of the national preventive mechanisms.
4. When establishing national preventive mechanisms, States Parties shall give due consideration to the Principles relating to the status of national institutions for the promotion and protection of human rights.

Article 19

The national preventive mechanisms shall be granted at a minimum the power:

(a) To regularly examine the treatment of the persons deprived of their liberty in places of detention as defined in article 4, with a view to strengthening, if necessary, their protection against torture and other cruel, inhuman or degrading treatment or punishment;

(b) To make recommendations to the relevant authorities with the aim of improving the treatment and the conditions of the persons deprived of their liberty and to prevent torture and other cruel, inhuman or degrading treatment or punishment, taking into consideration the relevant norms of the United Nations;

(c) To submit proposals and observations concerning existing or draft legislation.

Article 20

In order to enable the national preventive mechanisms to fulfil their mandate, the States Parties to the present Protocol undertake to grant them:

(a) Access to all information concerning the number of persons deprived of their liberty in places of detention as defined in article 4, as well as the number of places and their location;

(b) Access to all information referring to the treatment of those persons as well as their conditions of detention;

(c) Access to all places of detention and their installations and facilities;

(d) The opportunity to have private interviews with the persons deprived of their liberty without witnesses, either personally or with a translator if deemed necessary, as well as with any other person who the national preventive mechanism believes may supply relevant information;

(e) The liberty to choose the places they want to visit and the persons they want to interview;

(f) The right to have contacts with the Subcommittee on Prevention, to send it information and to meet with it.

Article 21

1. No authority or official shall order, apply, permit or tolerate any sanction against any person or organization for having communicated to the national preventive mechanism any information, whether true or false, and no such person or organization shall be otherwise prejudiced in any way.
2. Confidential information collected by the national preventive mechanism shall be privileged. No personal data shall be published without the express consent of the person concerned.

Article 22

The competent authorities of the State Party concerned shall examine the recommendations of the national preventive mechanism and enter into a dialogue with it on possible implementation measures.

Article 23

The States Parties to the present Protocol undertake to publish and disseminate the annual reports of the national preventive mechanisms.

PART V
Declaration

Article 24

1. Upon ratification, States Parties may make a declaration postponing the implementation of their obligations under either part III or part IV of the present Protocol.
2. This postponement shall be valid for a maximum of three years. After due representations made by the State Party and after consultation with the Subcommittee on Prevention, the Committee against Torture may extend that period for an additional two years.

Part VI
Financial provisions

Article 25

1. The expenditure incurred by the Subcommittee on Prevention in the implementation of the present Protocol shall be borne by the United Nations.
2. The Secretary-General of the United Nations shall provide the necessary staff and facilities for the effective performance of the functions of the Subcommittee on Prevention under the present Protocol.

Article 26

1. A Special Fund shall be set up in accordance with the relevant procedures of the General Assembly, to be administered in accordance with the financial regulations and rules of the United Nations, to help finance the implementation of the recommendations made by the Subcommittee on Prevention after a visit to a State Party, as well as education programmes of the national preventive mechanisms.
2. The Special Fund may be financed through voluntary contributions made by Governments, intergovernmental and non-governmental organizations and other private or public entities.

Part VII
Final provisions

Article 27

1. The present Protocol is open for signature by any State that has signed the Convention.
2. The present Protocol is subject to ratification by any State that has ratified or acceded to the Convention. Instruments of ratification shall be deposited with the Secretary-General of the United Nations.
3. The present Protocol shall be open to accession by any State that has ratified or acceded to the Convention.
4. Accession shall be effected by the deposit of an instrument of accession with the Secretary-General of the United Nations.
5. The Secretary-General of the United Nations shall inform all States that have signed the present Protocol or acceded to it of the deposit of each instrument of ratification or accession.

Article 28

1. The present Protocol shall enter into force on the thirtieth day after the date of deposit with the Secretary-General of the United Nations of the twentieth instrument of ratification or accession.
2. For each State ratifying the present Protocol or acceding to it after the deposit with the Secretary-General of the United Nations of the twentieth instrument of ratification or accession, the present Protocol shall enter into force on the thirtieth day after the date of deposit of its own instrument of ratification or accession.

Article 29

The provisions of the present Protocol shall extend to all parts of federal States without any limitations or exceptions.

Article 30

No reservations shall be made to the present Protocol.

Article 31

The provisions of the present Protocol shall not affect the obligations of States Parties under any regional convention instituting a system of visits to places of detention. The Subcommittee on Prevention and the bodies established under such regional conventions are encouraged to consult and cooperate with a view to avoiding duplication and promoting effectively the objectives of the present Protocol.

Article 32

The provisions of the present Protocol shall not affect the obligations of States Parties to the four Geneva Conventions of 12 August 1949 and the Additional Protocols thereto of 8 June 1977, nor the opportunity available to any State Party to authorize the International Committee of the Red Cross to visit places of detention in situations not covered by international humanitarian law.

Article 33

1. Any State Party may denounce the present Protocol at any time by written notification addressed to the Secretary-General of the United Nations, who shall thereafter inform the other States Parties to the present Protocol and the Convention. Denunciation shall take effect one year after the date of receipt of the notification by the Secretary-General.
2. Such a denunciation shall not have the effect of releasing the State Party from its obligations under the present Protocol in regard to any act or situation that may occur prior to the date on which the denunciation becomes effective, or to the actions that the Subcommittee on Prevention has decided or may decide to take with respect to the State Party concerned, nor shall denunciation prejudice in any way the continued consideration of any matter already under consideration by the Subcommittee on Prevention prior to the date on which the denunciation becomes effective.
3. Following the date on which the denunciation of the State Party becomes effective, the Subcommittee on Prevention shall not commence consideration of any new matter regarding that State.

Article 34

1. Any State Party to the present Protocol may propose an amendment and file it with the Secretary-General of the United Nations. The Secretary-General shall thereupon communicate the proposed amendment to the States Parties to the present Protocol with a request that they notify him whether they favour a conference of States Parties for the purpose of considering and voting upon the proposal. In the event that within four months from the date of such communication at least one third of the States Parties favour such a conference, the Secretary-General shall convene the conference under the auspices of the United Nations. Any amendment adopted by a majority of two thirds of the States Parties present and voting at the conference shall be submitted by the Secretary-General of the United Nations to all States Parties for acceptance.

2. An amendment adopted in accordance with paragraph 1 of the present article shall come into force when it has been accepted by a two-thirds majority of the States Parties to the present Protocol in accordance with their respective constitutional processes.
3. When amendments come into force, they shall be binding on those States Parties that have accepted them, other States Parties still being bound by the provisions of the present Protocol and any earlier amendment that they have accepted.

Article 35

Members of the Subcommittee on Prevention and of the national preventive mechanisms shall be accorded such privileges and immunities as are necessary for the independent exercise of their functions. Members of the Subcommittee on Prevention shall be accorded the privileges and immunities specified in section 22 of the Convention on the Privileges and Immunities of the United Nations of 13 February 1946, subject to the provisions of section 23 of that Convention.

Article 36

When visiting a State Party, the members of the Subcommittee on Prevention shall, without prejudice to the provisions and purposes of the present Protocol and such privileges and immunities as they may enjoy:

(a) Respect the laws and regulations of the visited State;

(b) Refrain from any action or activity incompatible with the impartial and international nature of their duties.

Article 37

1. The present Protocol, of which the Arabic, Chinese, English, French, Russian and Spanish texts are equally authentic, shall be deposited with the Secretary-General of the United Nations.
2. The Secretary-General of the United Nations shall transmit certified copies of the present Protocol to all States.

APPENDIX II

Rules of Procedure of the Subcommittee on Prevention of Torture and Other Cruel, Inhuman or Degrading Treatment or Punishment

In accordance with article 10, paragraph 2, of the Optional Protocol to the Convention against Torture and Other Cruel, Inhuman or Degrading Treatment or Punishment (hereinafter "Optional Protocol"), the Subcommittee on Prevention of Torture and Other Cruel, Inhuman or Degrading Treatment or Punishment (hereinafter "the SPT"), adopts the following Rules of Procedure[1]:

Part one
General rules

I. Sessions

Rule 1
Dates of sessions

1. Regular sessions of the SPT shall be convened according to these Rules at dates decided by the SPT in consultation with the Secretary-General of the United Nations (hereinafter "the Secretariat"), taking into account the calendar of conferences as approved by the General Assembly.
2. The SPT shall set the dates of future regular sessions in advance on an ongoing basis, in consultation with the Secretariat. Amendment to the agreed dates of future regular sessions shall be possible only after consultation with members at least six months in advance of the date concerned.
3. The SPT and the Committee against Torture and Other Cruel, Inhuman or Degrading Treatment or Punishment (hereinafter "the CAT") shall hold at least one session a year simultaneously, in accordance with article 10, paragraph 3, of the Optional Protocol.
4. In addition to regular sessions, special sessions shall be held at dates agreed by the SPT in consultation with the Secretariat.

Rule 2
Place of sessions

Sessions of the SPT shall normally be held at the United Nations Office at Geneva. Another venue for a session may be designated by the SPT in consultation with the

[1] These Rules of procedure will be complemented by separate SPT Guidelines on visits.

Secretariat, taking into account the calendar of conferences approved by the General Assembly and Rule 16.

Rule 3
Notification of sessions

The Secretariat shall notify the members of the SPT of the date, duration and place of each session as early as possible, and not later than two months prior to the session concerned, such date being in accordance with the dates agreed in advance by the SPT (see Rule 1).

Rule 4
Draft agenda and draft order of business

1. The provisional draft agenda and the draft order of business for a session shall be prepared by the Secretariat, in consultation with the Bureau of the SPT, no later than one month prior to the session. They shall be transmitted in the working languages of the SPT at least two weeks before the opening of the session, and shall contain the issues agreed for discussion by the SPT at the previous session, as well as issues proposed by the Secretariat.
2. The first item on the provisional agenda and draft order of business of any session shall be the amendment and adoption of the agenda and order of business.
3. The agenda and order of business may be revised by the SPT in the course of the session in the light of the emerging needs.

Rule 5
Transmission of documentation

The Secretariat shall transmit documents other than the draft agenda and draft order of business in the working languages of the SPT to the members of the SPT as early as possible in advance of the session. All working documents prepared or other documents received in advance of the session by the Secretariat shall be transmitted forthwith to the SPT (including in electronic form if available and appropriate, taking into account the requirements for confidentiality) in the original language of the document, and as soon as possible thereafter in translation in the other working languages of the SPT.

II. Members of the SPT

Rule 6
Election of members of the SPT

1. Members of the SPT shall be the twenty-five experts elected in accordance with article 5 of the Optional Protocol.
2. Members shall be eligible for re-election once if renominated.
3. Members of the SPT shall serve in their individual capacity and may not be represented by alternates.

Rule 7
Term of office

1. The term of office of the members of the SPT shall begin on 1 January of the year after the date of their election by the meeting of the States Parties. The term of office shall expire on 31 December four years later, except for those members chosen by lot to serve for two years, whose terms shall expire on 31 December two years after their election.
2. In accordance with article 8 of the Optional Protocol, the term of the member appointed to fill a casual vacancy begins on the date of her or his approval, and shall end on the date of expiration of the term of office of the member being replaced.

Rule 8
Casual vacancies

1. In accordance with article 8 of the Optional Protocol, if a member of the SPT dies or resigns or declares that for any other cause she or he can no longer perform her or his duties as a member of the SPT, the Secretariat shall immediately inform the State Party that nominated the member to nominate, within two months, another eligible candidate subject to the approval of the majority of the States Parties. Approval shall be considered given unless half or more of the States Parties respond negatively within six weeks of having been informed of the proposed nominee.
2. When a member of the SPT is consistently unable to carry out her or his duties for any cause other than absence of a temporary nature, the member shall resign. Such a resignation shall be notified to the SPT and to the Secretariat. The Secretariat shall inform the State Party who nominated that member so that action can be taken in accordance with article 8 of the Optional Protocol.
3. The Secretariat shall inform the States Parties of the name of the member of the SPT filling the casual vacancy as soon as possible after approval.
4. Where the approval of a replacement under the first paragraph of this rule is declined, the State Party that nominated the expert shall be invited to nominate another eligible candidate, meeting the requirements of article 5 of the Optional Protocol.

Rule 9
Solemn declaration

Before assuming her/his duties, each member of the SPT shall, at the first meeting of the SPT at which she or he is present after her of his election, make the following solemn declaration:

"I solemnly declare that I will perform my duties and exercise my powers as a member of the Subcommittee on Prevention of Torture and Other Cruel, Inhuman or Degrading Treatment or Punishment impartially, independently and efficiently."

III. Bureau of the SPT

Rule 10
Election of the Bureau

1. The SPT shall elect from among its members a Chairperson and four Vice-Chairpersons who shall constitute the Bureau of the SPT. The Bureau shall select one of its Vice-Chairpersons to act as Rapporteur. Three members of the Bureau shall constitute a quorum.
2. Members of the Bureau shall be elected for a term of two years and be eligible for re-election.
3. Where there is only one candidate for election of one of its officers, the SPT may decide to elect that person by consensus. Where there are two or more candidates for election as one of its officers, or where the SPT otherwise decides to proceed with a ballot, the person who obtains a simple majority of the votes cast shall be elected. If no single candidate receives a majority of the votes cast, the members of the SPT shall endeavour to reach a consensus before holding a further ballot. Elections shall be held by secret ballot.

Rule 11
Functions of the Bureau

1. The Bureau shall direct the work of the SPT and shall perform all other functions conferred upon it by these Rules of Procedure and by the SPT. In particular, when the SPT is not in session, the Bureau may make decisions on urgent or delegated matters on its behalf. Members shall be consulted on such decisions whenever time and circumstances permit and each such decision shall be communicated to all members as soon as possible, account being taken of the requirements for confidentiality. The Bureau shall report to the SPT at each session on any decisions or actions of an urgent or delegated nature which have been taken on behalf of the SPT since the previous session.
2. The Bureau shall meet as required during regular sessions and at special sessions as necessary to fulfil its obligations and the mandate of the SPT.

Rule 12
Powers of the Chairperson and Vice-Chairpersons

1. The Chairperson exercises her or his functions under the authority of the SPT.
2. In accordance with these Rules, the Chairperson shall ensure the orderly conduct of the proceedings of the SPT, including observance of these Rules.
3. The Chairperson shall represent the SPT at the United Nations and other meetings. If the Chairperson is unable to represent the SPT at such meetings, she or he may designate one of the Vice-Chairpersons. If no Vice-Chairperson is available, with the permission of the SPT, she or he may designate a member of the SPT, to attend on behalf of the SPT.

Rule 13
Acting Chairperson

1. If, during a session, the Chairperson is unable to be present at a meeting or any part thereof, she or he shall designate a Vice-Chairperson, to act in her or his place.
2. If the Chairperson and the Vice-Chairpersons are unable at the same time to carry out their duties or they have not been elected, the SPT shall entrust such duties to any member of the SPT until such time as the Chairperson or the Vice-Chairpersons take over or they are elected. If need be, the Secretariat may, in consultation with the SPT, call for a meeting of the SPT for that purpose.
3. Any member acting as Chairperson shall have the same powers and duties as the Chairperson.

IV. Secretariat of the SPT

Rule 14
Provision of the SPT Secretariat

In accordance with article 25, paragraph 2 of the Optional Protocol, the SPT shall be provided with a targeted Secretariat, including a Secretary to the SPT and a targeted team of staff able to engage in fieldwork with the SPT. The Secretariat provision shall include the necessary staff and facilities for the effective performance of the SPT's functions.

Rule 15
Functions of the SPT Secretariat

1. The Secretariat of the SPT shall be responsible for all necessary arrangements for sessions of the SPT.
2. The Secretariat shall attend all sessions of the SPT and may make oral or written statements at those sessions.
3. The Secretariat shall provide working documents in advance of the sessions to enable the SPT to address all the items on its draft agenda and to carry out its fieldwork effectively. The Secretariat shall provide the SPT during sessions with all information which the SPT considers necessary in order for the SPT to fulfil its mandate effectively.
4. The Secretariat of the SPT shall respond as early as possible to requests made by the Bureau for information, and shall provide draft correspondence and draft documents upon request as soon as possible.

Rule 16
Financial implications of proposals

1. The expenditure incurred by the SPT in the implementation of the Optional Protocol shall be borne by the United Nations.
2. Before any proposal, involving additional expenditure to that already approved by the General Assembly, is approved by the SPT, the Secretariat shall indicate to the SPT what

additional expenditure is involved and shall prepare and circulate to the members of the SPT as early as possible an estimate of the cost involved in the proposal. It shall be the duty of the Chairperson to draw the attention of members to this estimate prior to a decision being taken on the proposal.

V. Communications

Rule 17
Incoming and outgoing communications

1. The Secretariat shall bring to the SPT's attention all communications received containing information submitted for the SPT's consideration.
2. Communications received by the individual members of the SPT which relate to the SPT's mandate shall be forwarded to the Secretariat.
3. The Secretariat shall keep a record of all communications received and shall, where appropriate, send an acknowledgement of receipt to the authors of such communications.
4. All correspondence sent from the SPT or on behalf of the SPT shall be agreed in advance by the Bureau. The Secretariat shall provide the Bureau with copies of all such correspondence sent out with the date of transmission.
5. The Secretariat shall be responsible for informing the SPT of any questions that may be brought before them for consideration or of any other developments that may be of relevance to the SPT. The Secretariat shall transmit to the SPT information on all correspondence and other communications addressed to the SPT or relevant to its mandate.

Rule 18
Meetings with States Parties

The Secretariat shall be responsible for informing the SPT in advance of all meetings with States Parties at which the SPT is the subject of discussion, and shall consult with the SPT in advance as to any input about the SPT at such meetings, and ensure that the SPT has the opportunity to be represented at such meetings in person or by contributing to and agreeing information to be provided about the SPT.

VI. Languages

Rule 19
Official and working languages

1. Arabic, Chinese, English, French, Russian and Spanish shall be the official languages of the SPT. Statements made in an official language shall be interpreted into the other official languages.
2. English, Spanish and French shall be the working languages of the SPT. The working languages of the SPT may be changed by its decision. All formal decisions and official documents of the SPT shall be issued in the working languages.

VII. Confidentiality

Rule 20
In camera sessions

1. The meetings of the SPT shall be held in camera. Its deliberations shall remain confidential.
2. The SPT may hear any person whom it considers to be in a position to assist it in the performance of its functions under the Optional Protocol. Such persons shall attend by invitation of the SPT only, in consultation with the Secretariat, and shall be bound by strict confidentiality.
3. The SPT may decide on an ad hoc basis that the SPT meeting shall be public.

VIII. SPT documents

Rule 21
Confidentiality

The documentation and information of the SPT shall be kept strictly confidential, unless the SPT decides otherwise in relation to a particular document.

Rule 22
Summary reports

1. The Secretariat shall produce in a working language of the SPT a draft summary report of each session, including the main observations, issues addressed and decisions taken. The draft summary report shall be analytically structured in accordance with the items of the agenda, and shall be transmitted to the SPT for comments and amendments within one month of the session concerned. A revised version of the summary report incorporating amendments suggested by the SPT shall be circulated to the SPT at least three weeks prior to the next session in the working languages of the SPT.

Rule 23
List of decisions

A draft list of decisions taken by the SPT during each session shall be prepared by the Secretariat, in consultation with the Bureau, and adopted by the SPT.

Rule 24
Annual report

In accordance with article 16, paragraph 3, of the Optional Protocol, the SPT shall produce a public annual report on its activities. The SPT shall present its public annual report to CAT.

IX. Conduct of business

Rule 25
Quorum

Fourteen members of the SPT shall constitute a quorum.

Rule 26
Adoption of decisions

1. The SPT shall attempt to reach all of its decisions by consensus. If consensus cannot be reached, decisions of the SPT shall be put to a vote, and shall be made by a simple majority vote of the members present and voting.
2. Each member of the SPT shall have one vote.
3. The SPT may adopt decisions by e-mail in accordance with the established set of procedures.

Rule 27
Working groups and Rapporteurs

The SPT may appoint Rapporteurs and it may set up ad hoc working groups comprising a limited number of its members. The terms of reference of such rapporteurships and working groups shall be defined by the SPT.

Rule 28
Conflict of interest

No member of the SPT shall participate either in the conduct of a visit or in the consideration of the report on the visit to the State Party in respect of the nationality of which she or he was elected or of the State Party which nominated her or him. No member of the SPT shall participate in activities which may imply, or may be seen to imply, a conflict of interest with their capacity as independent and impartial SPT members.

X. Co-operation with United Nations organs and mechanisms and other international, regional and national institutions or organizations

Rule 29
Consultation with other bodies

1. The SPT may invite relevant bodies to submit, or receive, for consideration information, documentation and written statements on such matters dealt with in the Optional Protocol as fall within the scope of their activities.
2. In accordance with Article 31 of the Optional Protocol, the SPT may consult with bodies established under regional conventions with a view to co-operating with them and

avoiding duplication, in order to promote effectively the objectives of the Optional Protocol.

Part two
Rules concerning national preventive mechanisms

Rule 30
Relationship with national preventive mechanisms

1. The SPT shall advise and assist States Parties, when necessary, in the establishment of national preventive mechanisms. It shall maintain direct, and if necessary confidential, contact with them, which includes the right to receive information from them and meet with them, in accordance with articles 11 and 20 (f) of the Optional Protocol.
2. The SPT shall offer the national preventive mechanisms training and technical assistance with a view to strengthening their capacities.
3. The SPT shall advise and assist the national preventive mechanisms in the evaluation of their needs and the means necessary to strengthen the protection of persons deprived of their liberty against torture and other cruel, inhuman or degrading treatment or punishment.
4. The SPT shall make recommendations and observations to the States Parties with a view to strengthening the capacity and the mandate of the national preventive mechanisms for the prevention of persons deprived of their liberty against torture and other cruel, inhuman or degrading treatment or punishment.
5. In its relations with the national preventive mechanisms, the SPT shall give due consideration to the Principles relating the status of national institutions for the promotion and protection of human rights.
6. The SPT has adopted a separate set of guidelines on national preventive mechanisms.

Part three
Rule relating to interpretation

Rule 31
Interpretation

For the purpose of the interpretation of the present rules, the headings, which are inserted for reference purposes only, shall be disregarded.

Part four
Rules relating to suspension and amendments of these rules

Rule 32
Suspension

Any of the present rules may be suspended by a decision of the SPT, provided such suspension is not inconsistent with the provisions of the Optional Protocol.

Rule 33
Amendments

The present rules may be amended by a decision of the SPT, at least twenty-four (24) hours after the proposal for the amendments has been circulated, provided that the amendment is not inconsistent with the provisions of the Optional Protocol.

Rule 34
Additions

The SPT may decide to add to the present rules at any time; an additional rule may be adopted by a decision of the SPT, at least twenty-four (24) hours after the proposal for the additional rule has been circulated, provided that the additional rule is not inconsistent with the provisions of the Optional Protocol.

APPENDIX III

Guidelines of the Subcommittee on Prevention of Torture and Other Cruel, Inhuman or Degrading Treatment or Punishment in relation to Visits to States Parties

I. Procedure concerning visits

Guideline 1
Visits

1. In accordance with the mandate conferred on the Subcommittee on the Prevention of Torture and Other Cruel, Inhuman or Degrading Treatment or Punishment by the Optional Protocol to the Convention against Torture and Other Cruel, Inhuman or Degrading Treatment or Punishment, the Subcommittee shall organize visits to places of deprivation of liberty in States parties in order to prevent torture and other cruel, inhuman or degrading treatment or punishment and to strengthen the protection of persons deprived of their liberty against torture and other forms of ill-treatment.

Guideline 2
Periodic and follow-up visits

2. The Subcommittee shall carry out visits of a periodic nature to States parties. If the Subcommittee considers it appropriate, it may decide to carry out a short follow-up visit.

Guideline 3
Establishment of programme of visits

3. In accordance with article 13 of the Optional Protocol, the Subcommittee shall establish a programme of regular visits to the States parties. The Subcommittee may subsequently modify this programme, in the light of circumstances. At the end of a calendar year, the Bureau shall present to the Subcommittee its suggestion for the countries to be visited the following year, including the timing of the visits and the number of delegates (taking into account the size and complexity of the country and the composition of the delegation) and the Secretariat shall present its suggestions for the number of participating staff.
4. In drawing up this programme, the Subcommittee shall have regard to the provisions of articles 1, 11, paragraph 1 (c), and 31 of the Optional Protocol.
5. The Subcommittee shall, after consultation, notify the States parties of its programme in order that they may, without delay, make the necessary practical arrangements for the visits to be conducted. The Subcommittee shall inform each State party of the information (see guideline 6), the facilities, including the designation of (a) focal point(s) for

contact and cooperation with the Subcommittee, and the credentials required to enable the visiting delegation to carry out its tasks.

Guideline 4
Visiting delegations

6. The Subcommittee will designate, for each visit, and in accordance with article 13, paragraph 3, of the Optional Protocol, at least two of its members to conduct the visit, who shall report to the Subcommittee within a time limit which may be set thereby. Each delegation for a regular visit shall comprise at least one lawyer and one medical doctor, and it is intended that members from different forms of civilization and legal systems also be included. In the selection of members, consideration may be given to members' experience working with the country and language skills. Members of the delegation—apart from external experts with specific terms of reference—must be available for the entire visit. In such cases as fall under rule 11, paragraph 1, of the Subcommittee's rules of procedure, the Bureau shall designate the members of the delegation.
7. The members of the Subcommittee with responsibility for carrying out a visit shall act in the name of the Subcommittee. In consultation with the Bureau, the members of the delegation shall appoint a head of the delegation; if possible, a member who speaks the United Nations language to be used during official meetings.
8. The members designated by the Subcommittee for the visit shall devise their own methods of work in conformity with the provisions of the Optional Protocol, the Subcommittee's rules of procedure and the present guidelines, taking into account the specific focuses of the visit.
9. The Subcommittee may decide that a delegation conducting a visit shall be assisted by one or more experts if they have expertise that is essential for conducting the visit, provided that such expertise does not exist among available members of the Subcommittee. The Subcommittee shall select from the roster established in accordance with article 13, paragraph 3, any expert(s) who is (are) to accompany its delegation on a visit. A delegation shall not be assisted by an expert who is a national of the State party to be visited.
10. The Subcommittee shall be assisted by interpreters sufficient in number to ensure that all delegates can work efficiently with persons deprived of their liberty in the language of the latter.
11. At least one member of the Secretariat shall participate in each visit.

Guideline 5
Notification of visits

12. A programme for intended visits for the upcoming year shall be published by the Subcommittee by the end of each year and States parties to be visited shall be notified through their Permanent Mission in Geneva.
13. A second notification containing the dates of the visit and the names of the members of the visiting delegation shall be communicated to the State party together with requests for information (see guidelines 7 and 8) not later than two months prior to the visit.

14. The notification may indicate some of the places that the delegation intends to visit. This shall not prevent the visiting delegation from visiting other places of detention not indicated in the notification.

Guideline 6
Preparation of visits

15. For the planning and preparation of the visit, the Secretariat shall prepare a compilation and analysis of detailed information concerning the State party to receive the visit. The minimum information requested from the State party and available from other sources should include, but is not limited to:
   (a) Legal information: texts of each State party's current legislation and regulations in areas related to the mandate, including Constitution, Criminal Code, Code of Criminal Procedure, Penal Code, Law on Execution of Penalties and Police Regulations (or equivalents in the individual jurisdictions); these materials, in so far as they are available in the working languages of the Subcommittee, should be provided to the members in the language of their preference;
   (b) Lists of places of deprivation of liberty, official statistical information relating to average annual custodial populations and to the custodial estate, disaggregated by type of custody;
   (c) Information on the legal mandate, terms of reference, funding, appointment, organization and operation of national preventive mechanisms and the annual and other reports thereof;
   (d) Information from United Nations human rights mechanisms, including treaty bodies and special procedure mandate holders working in areas relevant to the Subcommittee's mandate;
   (e) Information from other institutional sources;
   (f) Information concerning the national human rights institutions and other bodies active in areas relevant to the Subcommittee's mandate;
   (g) Information from national human rights institutions concerning key areas falling within the Subcommittee's mandate, including reports of ill-treatment, and the annual report of those institutions from the calendar year prior to the visit of the Subcommittee;
   (h) Information concerning non-governmental organizations (NGOs) and other bodies active in areas relevant to the Subcommittee's mandate;
   (i) Information from NGOs concerning key areas falling within the Subcommittee's mandate, including reports of ill-treatment;
   (j) Communications received by the Subcommittee, including allegations of ill-treatment.
16. Where the key information is available, the head of delegation, in consultation with the Secretariat and other delegates may decide on the focus of the visit and draft a programme for the visit that is presented to the Subcommittee for approval. The programme including the meetings with various authorities and other actors may be subject to change as more information emerges.

Guideline 7
Cooperation and facilitation of visits

17. The Subcommittee and the State parties shall cooperate in the implementation of the Optional Protocol. Further to the requirements of article 12 of the Optional Protocol, the Subcommittee shall request the State party concerned, inter alia:
    (a) To inform the Subcommittee of the authority to which notifications of visits should be addressed and to designate (an) accredited representative(s) (focal point(s)) to meet with the members of the Subcommittee's delegation and facilitate their task;
    (b) To provide members of the visiting delegation with credentials for facilitating the conduct of the visit and the fulfilment of the mandate of the Subcommittee, in accordance with article 12 (a) of the Optional Protocol.

Guideline 8
Conduct of visits

18. In conducting the visit, members of the delegation act on behalf of the Subcommittee and not in their individual capacities.
19. The Subcommittee may decide that one or more members of the delegation should arrive to the country ahead of the remaining members to hold meetings with authorities and other actors. If so decided, that part of the visit is included in the programme of the whole visit and is subject to approval of the Subcommittee.
20. The visiting delegation works as a team under the leadership of the head of delegation or the head of a subgroup, if the delegation divides into such subgroups for the conduct of its work on a visit. Normally, the delegation shall hold meetings on a daily basis to debrief and consider adjustment of the programme in the light of information obtained.
21. If a member of the delegation contravenes the Subcommittee's rules and guidelines and the instructions of the head of delegation, the latter may, in extremely serious cases and in consultation with the Bureau, request the member to leave the delegation.
22. Visits to places of deprivation of liberty shall include discussions and private interviews with staff at various levels as well as with persons deprived of liberty, after having obtained the latter's express informed consent.
23. As a general rule, the Subcommittee considers that photo documentation from places of detention is unnecessary and does not use this modality. Only very exceptionally, when such documentation is regarded essential for the mission, photos may be taken of and in places of detention and only with the express acceptance of the head of delegation.
24. A visiting delegation or subgroup thereof may provide the head or senior management team of a large institution visited, other than a police station, with some preliminary feedback on its visit to that institution; the guiding principle should be to highlight generic and systemic issues rather than to discuss matters related to a specific individual or individuals, who could be identified from the information provided.
25. A visiting delegation may at the end of the visit communicate some of its observations and recommendations to the authorities of the State party concerned, particularly those concerning generic and systemic issues and those concerning urgent needs for protection of persons deprived of their liberty ('preliminary observations'). If relevant, the

preliminary observation may be communicated to the national preventive mechanism(s) and the delegation may consider suggesting to the State party that it invite the national preventive mechanism to the reading of the preliminary observations or to other relevant meetings. Normally, the Subcommittee shall submit an edited version of the preliminary observations to the State party shortly after the visit. The delegation may consider inviting NGOs to report to the Subcommittee any observed change in policy and practice in places of detention, particularly those visited by the delegation.

26. The delegation may, with the consent of the person(s) concerned and taking into account the risk of possible reprisals, address the State party about individual cases, if it deems it necessary in order that the State may intervene to avoid irreparable damage to the person(s) concerned.

27. If a delegation encounters obstacles to exercising its mandate, the focal point of the State party shall be contacted forthwith to solve the problem. If the intervention of the focal point does not solve the problem, the delegation may consider meeting with the relevant minister. Where the problem is considered to jeopardize the mission, the delegation may consider suspending the programme until a solution is found or ending the visit; such decisions must involve the Bureau.

28. The Subcommittee may adopt more detailed rules of procedure relating to the conduct of visits, and in particular in relation to follow-up visits, as well as with respect to visits to particular types of establishments, which are or may be used for deprivation of liberty.

II. Post-visit procedure

Guideline 9
Report of visits

29. After each visit, the members of the delegation assisted by the Secretariat shall draft a report for consideration by the Subcommittee's delegation, on the basis of written visit notes delivered by the members thereof and in the light of its observations and findings on the visit. The draft report shall include the facts found during the visit and the recommendations to the State party visited with a view to strengthening the protection of persons deprived of their liberty against torture and other cruel, inhuman or degrading treatment or punishment.

30. The Subcommittee's delegation shall take into account any comments and information that the State party concerned might submit to it before, during and after a visit. It may at its own initiative request additional information from the State party, the national preventive mechanism(s) and any other relevant bodies which the Subcommittee may choose to address.

31. The final draft of the Subcommittee delegation's visit report shall be agreed by the delegation through a process of consultation, before circulation to the Subcommittee for consideration. The Subcommittee shall adopt each visit report at a plenary session or by e-mail between sessions.

32. The reports on the visits of the Subcommittee are subject to United Nations editing procedures only at the request of the Subcommittee.

33. The adopted visit report shall be transmitted confidentially to the State party concerned under a letter of transmission from the Chairperson on behalf of the Subcommittee.

The State party shall be invited to inform the Subcommittee within a stated period of the action taken to implement its recommendations. The Subcommittee may also, if relevant, confidentially communicate its recommendations and observations or its report to the national preventive mechanism(s).

Guideline 10
Consultations

34. After transmission of the Subcommittee's report, the Subcommittee and the State party concerned may hold consultations with respect to the implementation of any recommendations set out in the report, in accordance with article 12 (d) of the Optional Protocol. Such consultations may also be held with the national preventive mechanism(s).

Guideline 11
Follow-up

35. The response of the State party shall be analysed by Subcommittee members who have participated in the visit and/or by the Bureau or other members appointed by the Bureau or the Subcommittee. The working group formed by those appointed shall draft a reply to the State party, which shall be considered by the Subcommittee. The Subcommittee may decide, on the basis of all information, to undertake a short follow-up visit with terms of reference that are decided by the Subcommittee, in order to continue the dialogue on prevention of torture and ill-treatment with authorities and to verify the state of implementation of some key recommendations.

Guideline 12
Publication of the report

36. The Subcommittee shall publish its report, together with any comments of the State party, whenever requested to do so by that State party. The Subcommittee may publish the report in whole or in part if the State party makes part of the report public, in accordance with article 16, paragraph 2, of the Optional Protocol, or if the State party makes a public statement summarizing the report or commenting upon its content.

Guideline 13
Public statements

37. If the State party refuses to cooperate with the Subcommittee according to articles 12 and 14 of the Optional Protocol, or to take steps to improve the situation in the light of the Subcommittee's recommendations, the Subcommittee may request the Committee against Torture to make a public statement on the matter or to publish the report of the Subcommittee, in accordance with article 16, paragraph 4, of the Optional Protocol. Before a decision to make such a statement is taken, the State party concerned shall be given an opportunity to make its views known.
38. The Subcommittee shall be released from the obligation of confidentiality when a public statement is made.

III. Confidentiality

Guideline 14
Confidentiality

39. Information gathered by the Subcommittee in relation to a visit, its report on that visit prior to the State party requesting publication, and its consultations with the State party concerned and with national preventive mechanisms shall be and shall remain confidential.

40. No personal data shall be published without the express consent of the person concerned.

41. Members of the Subcommittee, experts and other persons accompanying the Subcommittee are required, during and after their terms of office, to uphold the confidentiality of the facts or information of which they have become aware during the discharge of their duties.

APPENDIX IV

Preliminary Guidelines for the Ongoing Development of National Preventive Mechanisms

As contained in the First Annual Report of the Subcommittee on Prevention of Torture and Other Cruel, Inhuman or Degrading Treatment or Punishment, CAT/C/40/2, 14 May 2008.

In order to facilitate dialogue with national preventive mechanisms generally, the Subcommittee wishes to indicate some preliminary guidelines concerning the process of establishing those mechanisms, by the development of new or existing bodies, and concerning certain key features of them:

(a) The mandate and powers of the national preventive mechanism should be clearly and specifically established in national legislation as a constitutional or legislative text. The broad definition of places of deprivation of liberty, in accordance with the Optional Protocol, shall be reflected in that text;

(b) The national preventive mechanism should be established by a public, inclusive and transparent process, including civil society and other actors involved in the prevention of torture; where an existing body is considered for designation as the national preventive mechanism, the matter should be open for debate, involving civil society;

(c) The independence of the national preventive mechanism, both actual and perceived, should be fostered by a transparent process of selection and appointment of members who are independent and do not hold a position that could raise questions of conflict of interest;

(d) Selection of members should be based on stated criteria relating to the experience and expertise required to carry out national preventive mechanism work effectively and impartially;

(e) National preventive mechanism membership should be gender-balanced and have adequate representation of ethnic, minority and indigenous groups;

(f) The State shall take the necessary measures to ensure that the expert members of the national preventive mechanism have the required capabilities and professional knowledge. Training should be provided to national preventive mechanisms;

(g) Adequate resources should be provided for the specific work of national preventive mechanisms, in accordance with article 18, 3 of the Optional Protocol; these should be ring-fenced, in terms of both budget and human resources;

(h) The work programme of national preventive mechanisms should cover all potential and actual places of deprivation of liberty;

(i) The scheduling of national preventive mechanism visits should ensure effective monitoring of such places with regard to safeguards against ill-treatment;

(j) Working methods of national preventive mechanisms should be developed and reviewed with a view to effective identification of good practice and gaps in protection;

(k) States should encourage national preventive mechanisms to report on visits with feedback on good practice and gaps in protection to the institutions concerned, and address recommendations to the responsible authorities on improvements in practice, policy and law;

(l) National preventive mechanisms and the authorities should establish an ongoing dialogue based on the recommendations for changes arising from the visits and the action taken to respond to such recommendations, in accordance with article 22 of the Optional Protocol;

(m) The annual report of national preventive mechanisms shall be published in accordance with article 23 of the Optional Protocol;

(n) The development of national preventive mechanisms should be considered an ongoing obligation, with reinforcement of formal aspects and working methods refined and improved incrementally.

APPENDIX V

Guidelines on National Preventive Mechanisms

Introduction

1. The Optional Protocol to the Convention against Torture and Other Cruel, Inhuman or Degrading Treatment or Punishment (the "Optional Protocol") provides considerable, detailed guidance concerning the establishment of a National Preventive Mechanism ("NPM"), including its mandate and powers. The most relevant of these provisions are Article 3, 4, 17–23, 29 and 35, though other provisions of the Optional Protocol are also of importance for NPMs. It is axiomatic that all NPMs must be structured in a manner which fully reflects these provisions.
2. It is the responsibility of the State to ensure that it has in place an NPM which complies with the requirements of the Optional Protocol. For its part, the SPT works with those bodies which it has been informed have been designated by the State as its NPM. Whilst the SPT does not, nor does it intend to formally assess the extent to which NPMs conform to OPCAT requirements, it does consider it a vital part of its role to advise and assist States and NPMs fulfil their obligations under the Optional Protocol. To this end, the SPT has previously set out 'Preliminary Guidelines' concerning the on-going development of NPMs in its First Annual Report. It has had the occasion to further amplify its thinking in subsequent Annual Reports and also in a number recommendations set out in its visit Reports. In the light of the experience it has gained, the SPT believes it would be useful to issue a revised set of Guidelines on National Preventive Mechanisms which reflect and respond to some of the questions and issues which have arisen in practice.
3. These Guidelines do not seek to repeat what is set out in the text of the Optional Protocol but to add further clarity regarding the expectations of the SPT regarding the establishment and operation of NPMs. Section I sets out a number of 'Basic principles' which should inform all aspects of the work of an NPM. This is followed in Section II by guidelines addressed primarily to States and concerning a number of issues relating to the establishment of NPMs, and in Section III by guidelines to both the State and to the NPM itself concerning the practical functioning of an NPM.
4. As it gains further experience, the SPT will seek to add additional sections to these Guidelines, addressing particular aspects of the work of NPMs in greater detail.

I. Basic principles

5. The NPM should complement rather than replace existing systems of oversight and its establishment should not preclude the creation or operation of other such complementary systems.

6. The mandate and powers of the NPM should be in accordance with the provisions of the Optional Protocol.
7. The mandate and powers of the NPM should be clearly set out in a constitutional or legislative text.
8. The operational independence of the NPM should be guaranteed.
9. The relevant legislation should specify the period of office of the member/s of the NPM and any grounds for their dismissal. Periods of office, which may be renewable, should be sufficient to foster the independent functioning of the NPM.
10. The visiting mandate of the NPM should extend to all places of deprivation of liberty, as set out in Article 4 of the Optional Protocol.
11. The necessary resources should be provided to permit the effective operation of the NPM in accordance with the requirements of the Optional Protocol.
12. The NPM should enjoy complete financial and operational autonomy when carrying out its functions under the Optional Protocol.
13. The State authorities and the NPM should enter into a follow-up process with the NPM with a view to the implementation of any recommendations which the NPM may make.
14. Those who engage or with whom the NPM engages in the fulfilment of its functions under the Optional Protocol should not be subject to any form of sanction, reprisal or other disability as result of having done so.
15. The effective operation of the NPM is a continuing obligation. The effectiveness of the NPM should be subject to regular appraisal by both the State and the NPM itself, taking into account the views of the SPT, with a view to its being reinforced and strengthened as and when necessary.

II. Basic issues regarding the establishment of an NPM

A. The identification or creation of the NPM

16. The NPM should be identified by an open, transparent and inclusive process which involves a wide range of stakeholders, including civil society. This should also apply to the process for the selection and appointment of members of the NPM, which should be in accordance with published criteria.
17. Bearing in mind the requirements of Article 18 (1) and (2) of the Optional Protocol, members of the NPM should collectively have the expertise and experience necessary for its effective functioning.
18. The State should ensure the independence of the NPM by not appointing to it members who hold positions which could raise questions of conflicts of interest.
19. Members of NPMs should likewise ensure that they do not hold or acquire positions which raise questions of conflicts of interest.
20. Recalling the requirements of Articles 18 (1) and (2) of the Optional Protocol, the NPM should ensure that its staff have between them the diversity of background, capabilities and professional knowledge necessary to enable it to properly fulfil its NPM mandate. This should include, *inter alia*, relevant legal and health-care expertise.

B. Designation and notification

21. The NPM should be established within one year of the entry into force of the Optional Protocol for the State concerned, unless at the time of ratification a declaration has been made in accordance with Article 24 of the Optional Protocol.
22. The body designated as the NPM should be publicly promulgated as such at the national level.
23. The State should notify the SPT promptly of the body which has been designated as the NPM.

III. Basic issues regarding the operation of an NPM

A. Points for States

24. The State should allow the NPM to visit all, and any suspected, places of deprivation of liberty, as set out in Articles 4 and 29 of the Optional Protocol, which are within its jurisdiction. For these purposes, the jurisdiction of the State extends to all those places over which it exercises effective control.
25. The State should ensure that the NPM is able to carry out visits in the manner and with the frequency that the NPM itself decides. This includes the ability to conduct private interviews with those deprived of liberty and the right to carry out unannounced visits at all times to all places of deprivation of liberty, in accordance with the provisions of the Optional Protocol.
26. The State should ensure that both the members of the NPM and its staff enjoy such privileges and immunities as are necessary for the independent exercise of their functions.
27. The State should not order, apply, permit or tolerate any sanction, reprisal or other disability to be suffered by any person or organisation for having communicated with the NPM or for having provided the NPM with any information, irrespective of its accuracy, and no such person or organisation should be prejudiced in any way.
28. The State should inform the NPM of any draft legislation that may be under consideration which is relevant to its mandate and allow the NPM to make proposals or observations on any existing or draft policy or legislation. The State should take into consideration any proposals or observations on such legislation received from the NPM.
29. The State should publish and widely disseminate the Annual Reports of the NPM. It should also ensure that it is presented to, and discussed in, by the national legislative assembly, or Parliament. The Annual Reports of the NPM should also be transmitted to the SPT which will arrange for their publication on its website.

B. Points for NPMs

30. The NPM should carry out all aspects of its mandate in a manner which avoids actual or perceived conflicts of interest.

31. The NPM, its members and its staff should be required to regularly review their working methods and undertake training in order to enhance their ability to exercise their responsibilities under the Optional Protocol.
32. Where the body designated as the NPM performs other functions in addition to those under the Optional Protocol, its NPM functions should be located within a separate unit or department, with its own staff and budget.
33. The NPM should establish a work plan/programme which, over time, encompasses visits to all, or any, suspected, places of deprivation of liberty, as set out in Articles 4 and 29 of the Optional Protocol, which are within the jurisdiction of the State. For these purposes, the jurisdiction of the State extends to all those places over which it exercises effective control.
34. The NPM should plan its work and its use of resources in such a way as to ensure that places of deprivation of liberty are visited in a manner and with sufficient frequency to make an effective contribution to the prevention torture and other cruel, inhuman or degrading treatment or punishment.
35. The NPM should make proposals and observations to the relevant State authorities regarding existing and draft policy or legislation which it considers to be relevant to its mandate.
36. The NPM should produce Reports following their visits as well as produce an Annual Report and any other forms of Report which it deems necessary. When appropriate, Reports should contain recommendations addressed to the relevant authorities. The Recommendations of the NPM should take account of the relevant norms of the United Nations in the field of the prevention of torture and other ill-treatment, including the comments and recommendations of the SPT.
37. The NPM should ensure that any confidential information acquired in the course of its work is fully protected.
38. The NPM should ensure that it has the capacity to and does engage in a meaningful process of dialogue with the State concerning the implementation of its recommendations. It should also actively seek to follow-up on the implementation of any recommendations which the SPT has made in relation to the country in question, liaising with the SPT when doing so.
39. The NPM should seek to establish and maintain contacts with other NPMs with a view to sharing experience and reinforcing its effectiveness.
40. The NPM should seek to establish and maintain contact with the SPT, as provided for and for the purposes set out in the Optional Protocol.

APPENDIX VI

The approach of the Subcommittee on Prevention of Torture to the concept of prevention of torture and other cruel, inhuman or degrading treatment or punishment under the Optional Protocol to the Convention against Torture and Other Cruel, Inhuman or Degrading Treatment or Punishment

I. Introduction

1. It is beyond doubt that States Parties to the Optional Protocol to the Convention against Torture and Other Cruel, Inhuman or Degrading Treatment or Punishment ("the Optional Protocol") are under a legal obligation to "prevent" torture and other cruel, inhuman or degrading treatment or punishment. Article 2, paragraph 1, of the Convention, to which all States Parties to the Optional Protocol must also be parties, provides that "Each State Party shall take effective legislative, administrative, judicial or other measures to prevent acts of torture in any territory under its jurisdiction". Article 16, paragraph 1, of the Convention extends this obligation, providing that "each State Party shall undertake to prevent in any territory under its jurisdiction other acts of cruel, inhuman or degrading treatment of punishment which do not amount to torture . . . ". As explained by the Committee against Torture in its General Comment No 2, "article 2, paragraph 1, obliges each State party to take actions that will reinforce the prohibition against torture".[1] Whilst the obligation to prevent torture and ill-treatment buttresses the prohibition of torture, it also remains an obligation in its own right and a failure to take appropriate preventive measures which were within its power could engage the international responsibility of the State, should torture occur in circumstances where the State would not otherwise have been responsible.
2. Drawing attention to article 2 of the Convention, the International Court of Justice has observed that "the content of the duty to prevent varies from one instrument to another, according to the wording of the relevant provisions, and depending on the nature of the acts to be prevented".[2] The Committee has said that the duty to prevent is "wide-ranging"[3] and has indicated that the content of that duty is not static since "the Committee's understanding of and recommendations in respect of effective measures are

[1] CAT/C/GC/2, para. 2.
[2] *Application of the Convention on the Prevention and Punishment of the Crime of Genocide (Bosnia and Herzegovina v Serbia and Montenegro)*, Merits, Judgment of 26 February 2007, para. 429.
[3] CAT/C/GC/2, para. 3.

in a process of continual evolution"[4] and so are "not limited to those measures contained in the subsequent articles 3 to 16".[5]

3. The Subcommittee on Prevention of Torture is of the view that, as these comments suggest, it is not possible to devise a comprehensive statement of what the obligation to prevent torture and ill-treatment entails *in abstracto*. It is of course both possible and important to determine the extent to which a State has complied with its formal legal commitments as set out in international instruments and which have a preventive impact but whilst this is necessary it will rarely be sufficient to fulfil the preventive obligation: it is as much the practice as it is the content of a State's legislative, administrative, judicial or other measures which lies at the heart of the preventive endeavour. Moreover, there is more to the prevention of torture and ill-treatment than compliance with legal commitments. In this sense, the prevention of torture and ill-treatment embraces – or should embrace – as many as possible of those things which in a given situation can contribute towards the lessening of the likelihood or risk of torture or ill-treatment occurring. Such an approach requires not only that there be compliance with relevant international obligations and standards in both form and substance but that attention also be paid to the whole range of other factors relevant to the experience and treatment of persons deprived of their liberty and which by their very nature will be context specific.
4. It is for this reason that the Optional Protocol seeks to strengthen the protection of persons deprived of their liberty, not by setting out additional substantive preventive obligations but in contributing to the prevention of torture by establishing, at both the international and national levels, a preventive system of regular visits and the drawing up of reports and recommendations based thereon. The purpose of such reports and recommendations is not only to bring about compliance with international obligations and standards but to offer practical advice and suggestions as to how to reduce the likelihood or risk of torture or ill-treatment occurring and will be firmly based on, and informed by, the facts found and circumstances encountered during the visits undertaken. As a result, the Subcommittee is of the view that it is best able to contribute to prevention by expanding on its understanding of how best to fulfil its mandate under the Optional Protocol rather than by setting out its views on what prevention may or may not require either as an abstract concept or as a matter of legal obligation. Nevertheless, there are a number of key principles which guide the Subcommittee's approach to its preventive mandate and which it believes it would be useful to articulate.

II. Guiding principles

5. The guiding principles are the following:
   (a) The prevalence of torture and ill-treatment is influenced by a broad range of factors, including the general level of enjoyment of human rights and the rule of law, levels of poverty, social exclusion, corruption, discrimination, etc. Whilst a generally high level of respect for human rights and the rule of law within a society or community does not provide a guarantee against torture and ill-treatment occurring, it offers the best prospects for effective prevention. To that end, the Subcommittee is deeply

[4] Ibid, para 4. [5] Ibid, para 1.

interested in the general situation within a country concerning the enjoyment of human rights and how this affects the situation of persons deprived of their liberty.

(b) In its work the Subcommittee must engage with the broader regulatory and policy frameworks relevant to the treatment of persons deprived of their liberty and with those responsible for them. It must also be concerned with how these are translated into practice, through the various institutional arrangements which are established in order to do so, their governance and administration and how they function in practice. Thus a holistic approach to the situation must be taken, informed by, but not limited to, its experience gained through its visits to particular places of detention.

(c) Prevention will include ensuring that a wide variety of procedural safeguards for those deprived of their liberty are recognized and realized in practice. These will relate to all phases of detention, from initial apprehension to final release from custody. Since the purpose of such safeguards is to reduce the likelihood or rise of torture or ill-treatment occurring, they are of relevance irrespective of whether there is any evidence of torture or ill-treatment actually taking place.

(d) Detention conditions not only raise issues of cruel, inhuman or degrading treatment or punishment but in some circumstances can also be a means of torture, if used in a manner which accords with the provisions of article 1 of the Convention. Therefore, recommendations regarding conditions of detention play a critical role in effective prevention and will touch on a wide variety of issues, including matters relating to physical conditions, the reasons for, and levels of, occupancy and the provision of, and access to, a wide range of facilities and services.

(e) Visits to States parties and to particular places of detention should be carefully prepared in advance taking into account all relevant factors, including the general legal and administrative frameworks, substantive rights, procedural and due process guarantees pertaining to detention as well as the practical contexts in which they operate. The manner in which visits are conducted, their substantive focus and the recommendations which flow from them may vary according to such factors and in the light of the situations encountered in order to best achieve the overriding purpose of the visit, this being to maximize its preventive potential and impact.

(f) Reports and recommendations will be most effective if they are based on rigorous analysis and are factually well grounded. In its visit reports, the Subcommittee's recommendations should be tailored to the situations which they address in order to offer the greatest practical guidance possible. In formulating its recommendations, the Subcommittee is conscious that there is no logical limit to the range of issues that, if explored, might have a preventive impact. Nevertheless, it believes that it is appropriate to focus on those issues which, in the light both of its visit to the State party in question and its more general experience, appear to it to be most pressing, relevant and realizable.

(g) Effective domestic mechanisms of oversight, including complaints mechanisms, form an essential part of the apparatus of prevention. These mechanisms will take a variety of forms and operate at many levels. Some will be internal to the agencies involved, others will provide external scrutiny from within the apparatus of government, whilst others will provide wholly independent scrutiny, the latter to include the National Preventive Mechanism (NPM) to be established in accordance with the provisions of the Optional Protocol.

(h) Torture and ill-treatment are more easily prevented if the system of detention is open to scrutiny. NPMs, together with national human rights institutions and ombudsman's offices, play a key role in ensuring that such scrutiny takes place. This is supported and complemented by civil society, which also plays an important role in ensuring transparency and accountability by monitoring places of detention, examining the treatment of detainees and by providing services to meet their needs. Further complementary scrutiny is provided by judicial oversight. In combination, the NPM, civil society and the apparatus of judicial oversight provide essential and mutually reinforcing means of prevention.

(i) There should be no exclusivity in the preventive endeavour. Prevention is a multifaceted and interdisciplinary endeavour. It must be informed by the knowledge and experience of those from a wide range of backgrounds—eg legal, medical, educational, religious, political, policing and the detention system.

(j) Although all those in detention form a vulnerable group, some groups suffer particular vulnerability, such as women, juveniles, members of minority groups, foreign nationals, persons with disabilities, and persons with acute medical or psychological dependencies or conditions. Expertise in relation to all such vulnerabilities is needed in order to lessen the likelihood of ill-treatment.

APPENDIX VII

Members of the Subcommittee on Prevention of Torture (SPT) as at January 2011

Name of member	Country of nationality	Term of office
Ms Mari Amos	Estonia	31 December 2014
Mr Mario Luis Coriolano	Argentina	31 December 2012
Mr Arman Danielyan	Armenia	31 December 2014
Ms Marija Definis-Gojanovic	Croatia	31 December 2012
Mr Malcolm Evans	United Kingdom of Great Britain and Northern Ireland	31 December 2012
Mr Emilio Ginés Santidrián	Spain	31 December 2014
Ms Lowell Patria Goddard	New Zealand	31 December 2012
Mr Zdenek Hajek	Czech Republic	31 December 2012
Ms Suzanne Jabbour	Lebanon	31 December 2012
Mr Goran Klemencic	Slovenia	31 December 2012
Mr Paul Lam Shang Leen	Mauritius	31 December 2012
Mr Zbigniew Lasocik	Poland	31 December 2012
Mr Petros Michaelides	Cyprus	31 December 2014
Ms Aisha Shujune Muhammad	Maldives	31 December 2014
Mr Olivier Obrecht	France	31 December 2014
Mr Hans Draminsky Petersen	Denmark	31 December 2014
Ms Maria Margarida E Pressburger	Brazil	31 December 2012
Mr Christian Pross	Germany	31 December 2012
Mr Victor Manuel Rodriguez-Rescia	Costa Rica	31 December 2012
Ms Judith Salgado	Ecuador	31 December 2014
Mr Miguel Sarre Iguíniz	Mexico	31 December 2014
Ms Aneta Stancevska	The Former Yugoslav Republic of Macedonia	31 December 2014
Mr Wilder Tayler-Souto	Uruguay	31 December 2014
Mr Felipe Villavicencio Terreros	Peru	31 December 2014
Mr Fortuné Gaétan Zongo	Burkina Faso	31 December 2014

APPENDIX VIII

Chronology of States Visited by the SPT

Country visited	Date of first visit	Date of follow-up visit (if applicable)
Mauritius	8–18 October 2007	
Maldives	10–17 December 2007	
Sweden	10–14 March 2008	
Benin	17–26 May 2008	
Mexico	27 August–12 September 2008	
Paraguay	10–16 March 2009	13–15 September 2010
Honduras	13–22 September 2009	
Cambodia	2–11 December 2009	
Lebanon	24 May–2 June 2010	
Bolivia	30 August–8 September 2010	
Liberia	6–13 December 2010	

Bibliography

TREATIES

Hague Convention for the Suppression of Unlawful Seizure of Aircraft (860 UNTS 105), 1970

Montreal Convention for the Suppression of Unlawful Acts against the Safety of Civil Aviation (974 UNTS 177), 1971

New York Convention on the Prevention and Punishment of Crimes against Internationally Protected Persons (1035 UNTS 167), 1973

New York International Convention against the Taking of Hostages Convention (1316 UNTS 205), 1979

Convention against Torture and Other Cruel, Inhuman or Degrading Treatment or Punishment, GA Res A/RES/39/46, adopted 10 December 1984 (1465 UNTS 85)

European Charter on Regional or Minority Languages (CETS No 148, in force March 1998)

Optional Protocol to the Convention Against Torture and Other Cruel, Inhuman or Degrading Treatment or Punishment, A/RES/57/199, adopted on 18 December 2003

UN DECLARATIONS

Universal Declaration on Human Rights, GA Res 217A(III) adopted 10 December 1948

Declaration on the Protection of All Persons from Being Subjected to Torture and Other Cruel, Inhuman or Degrading Treatment or Punishment, GA Res 3452 (XXX), adopted 9 December 1975

UN DOCUMENTS FROM HUMAN RIGHTS TREATY AND CHARTER BODIES

Reports of the Subcommittee on Prevention of Torture (SPT)

Preliminary Guidelines for the On-Going Development of National Preventive Mechanisms (NPMs), <http://www2.ohchr.org/english/bodies/cat/opcat/mechanisms.htm>

First Annual Report of the Subcommittee on Prevention of Torture and Cruel, Inhuman or Degrading Treatment or Punishment, February 2007–March 2008, CAT/C/40/2, 14 May 2008

Report on the Visit of the Subcommittee on Prevention of Torture and Other Cruel, Inhuman and Degrading Treatment or Punishment to Sweden, CAT/OP/SWE/1, 10 September 2008

Report on the Visit of the Subcommittee on the Prevention of Torture and other Cruel, Inhuman and Degrading Treatment or Punishment to the Maldives, CAT/OP/MDV/1, 26 February 2009

Second Annual Report of the Subcommittee on Prevention of Torture and Cruel, Inhuman or Degrading Treatment or Punishment, February 2008–March 2009, CAT/C/42/2, 7 April 2009

Report on the Visit of the Subcommittee on Prevention of Torture and Other Cruel, Inhuman or Degrading Treatment or Punishment to Honduras, CAT/OP/HND/1, 10 February 2010

Third Annual Report of the Subcommittee on Prevention of Torture, Cruel, Inhuman or Degrading Treatment or Punishment, CAT/C/44/2, 25 March 2010

Report on the Visit of the Subcommittee on the Prevention of Torture and other Cruel, Inhuman and Degrading Treatment or Punishment to Mexico, CAT/OP/MEX/1, 31 May 2010

Report on the Visit of the Subcommittee on Prevention of Torture and Other Cruel, Inhuman or Degrading Treatment or Punishment to the Republic of Paraguay, CAT/OP/PRY/1, 7 June 2010

The Approach of the Subcommittee on Prevention of Torture to the Concept of Prevention of Torture and Other Cruel, Inhuman or Degrading Treatment or Punishment under the Optional Protocol to the Convention against Torture and Other Cruel, Inhuman or Degrading Treatment or Punishment, CAT/OP/12/6, 30 December 2010

Fourth Annual Report of the Subcommittee on Prevention of Torture and Other Cruel, Inhuman or Degrading Treatment or Punishment (April–December 2010), CAT/C/46/2, 7 January 2011

Guidelines of the Subcommittee on Prevention of Torture and Other Cruel, Inhuman or Degrading Treatment or Punishment in Relation to Visits to States Parties, CAT/OP/12/4, 18 January 2011

Committee Against Torture (CAT)

Annual Report A/56/44 (2001)

Annual Report A/57/44 (2002)

Concluding Observations on Saudi Arabia, UN Doc CAT/C/CR/28/5/, 2002

Rules of Procedure, Rule 114(4) (CAT/C/3/Rev.4, 9 August 2002)

Annual Report A/58/44 (2003)

Annual Report A/59/44 (2004)

Conclusions and Recommendations of the Committee Against Torture; United Kingdom of Great Britain and Northern Ireland, Crown Dependencies and Overseas Territories, UN Doc CAT/C/CR/33/3, 10 December 2004

Conclusions and Recommendations of the Committee Against Torture; United States of America, UN Doc CAT/C/USA/CO/2, 25 July 2006

General Comment No 2, Implementation of Article 2 by States Parties, CAT/C/GC/2, 24 January 2008

Report of the Committee against Torture (43rd and 44th Sessions), UN GA Doc A/65/44

Annual Report A/63/44 (2008)

Concluding Observations Benin, CAT/C/BEN/CO/2, 19 February 2008

Concluding Observations Sweden, CAT/C/SWE/CO/5, 4 June 2008

Committee on the Rights of the Child (CRC)

Committee on the Rights of the Child, General Comment No 2, The role of independent national human rights institutions in the promotion and protection of the rights of the child, CRC/GC/2002/2, 15 November 2002

Committee on the Rights of the Child, General Comment No 8, The Right of the Child to Protection from Corporal Punishment and other cruel and degrading forms of punishment, CRC/C/GC/8, 2 March 2007

Human Rights Committee

Human Rights Committee General Comment No 7, Torture or cruel, inhuman or degrading treatment or punishment (Art 7), 3 May 1982

Human Rights Committee, General Comment No 8, Right to liberty and security of persons (Art 9), 30 June 1982

Human Rights Committee, General Comment No 20, Replaces general comment 7concerning prohibition of torture and cruel treatment or punishment (Art 7), 10 March 1992

Human Rights Committee, General Comment No 21, Replaces general comment 9 concerning humane treatment of persons deprived of liberty (Art 10), 10 April 1992

Human Rights Committee, General Comment No 28, Equality of rights between men and women (Art 3), 29 March 2000, CCPR/C/21/Rev.1/Add.10

Concluding Observations of the Human Rights Committee: Israel, 21 August 2003, CCPR/Co/78/ISR

Human Rights Committee, General Comment 31, Nature of the General Legal Obligations Imposed on States parties to the Covenant, 26 May 2004, CCPR/C/21/Rev.1/Add.13

Human Rights Committee Rules of Procedure, Rule 101, concerning follow-up to individual communications, 22 September 2005, CCPR/C/3/Rev.8

Special Rapporteur on Torture

Resolution 1995/41, 'Human rights and the administration of justice, in particular of children and juveniles in detention', Report to the fifty-second session of the Commission on Human Rights, the Special Rapporteur considered the issue of torture and children, E/CN.4/1996/35

Interim report of the Special Rapporteur of the Commission on Human Rights on the question of torture and other cruel, inhuman or degrading treatment or punishment, A/55/290, 11 August 2000

Special Rapporteur on Torture, Report of the Special Rapporteur on the question of torture and other cruel, inhuman or degrading treatment or punishment, in accordance with Assembly Resolution 57/200 of 18 December 2002, A/58/120, 3 July 2003

Special Rapporteur on Terrorism and Human Rights, Visit to South Africa, 2007, A/HRC/6/17

Interim report of the Special Rapporteur on torture and other cruel, inhuman or degrading treatment or punishment, A/63/175, 28 July 2008

Special Rapporteur on Terrorism and Human Rights, Mission to Spain, 2008, A/HRC/10/3/Add.2

Report of the Special Rapporteur on Torture and Other Cruel, Inhuman or Degrading Treatment or Punishment, Manfred Nowak, Mission to the Republic of Moldova, A/HRC/10/44/Add.3, 12 February 2009

Report of the Special Rapporteur on Torture and Other Cruel, Inhuman or Degrading Treatment or Punishment, Manfred Nowak, Mission to Denmark, A/HRC/10/44/Add.2, 18 February 2009

Joint study on global practices in relation to secret detention in the context of countering terrorism of the Special Rapporteur on the promotion and protection of human rights and fundamental freedoms while countering terrorism, the Special Rapporteur on torture and other cruel, inhuman or degrading treatment or punishment, the Working Group on Arbitrary Detention and the Working Group on Enforced or Involuntary Disappearances, A/HRC/13/42, 26 January 2010

Other UN Special Procedures

Working Group on Arbitrary Detentions, Annual Report 2009, A/HRC/10/21, para 48

Other UN documents

UN Commission on Human Rights Resolution 1986/56 on Torture and Other Cruel, Inhuman or Degrading Treatment or Punishment, 13 March 1986, E/CN.4/RES/1986/56

UN Commission on Human Rights Resolution 1989/104 on Postponement of Consideration of a Draft Optional Protocol to the Convention Against Torture and Other Cruel, Inhuman or Degrading Treatment or Punishment, 6 March 1989, E/CN.4/RES/1989/104

UN General Assembly Resolution 48/134 on National Institutions for the Promotion and Protection of Human Rights, A/RES/48/134, adopted 20 December 1993

Strengthening the United Nations: An Agenda for Change, A/57/387, 9 September 2002

UN document E/CN.4/1991/66, reproduced in the 10th Annual report of the Working Group to the UN Commission on Human Rights, E/CN.4/2002/78, Annex II

Conclusions of the International Roundtable on the Role of National Human Rights Institutions and Treaty Bodies, Berlin, 23–24 November 2006, UN Doc. HRI/MC/2007/3

Press Release, Committee Against Torture and Subcommittee on Prevention of Torture held first meeting in Geneva, 20 November 2007, <http://www.unhchr.ch/huricane/huricane.nsf/view01/1EC7F431C8341C09C125739A0036955C?opendocument>

Decision Paper on the Review of ICC Accreditation Procedures for National Human Rights Institutions (NHRI) of March 2008, <http://nhri.net/2008/DecisionPaper-NHRI-March2008.DOC>

Guidelines for Accreditation and Re-Accreditation of National Human Rights Institutions to the International Coordinating Committee of National Human Rights Institutions, Version 3, April 2008

ICC Sub-Committee on Accreditation, General Observations, Geneva, April 2008, <http://nrhi.net/2008/General_Observations_En.pdf>

UN Human Rights Council Resolution 8/8 on Torture and Other Cruel, Inhuman or Degrading Treatment or Punishment, adopted 18 June 2008

Rules of Procedure of the Committee on the Rights of Persons with Disabilities, 13 August 2010, CRPD/C/4/2; available at: <http://www.ohchr.org/EN/HRBodies/CRPD/Pages/CRPDIndex.aspx>

Human Rights Council, First Session, Czech Republic, A/HRC/8/33

Human Rights Council, First Session Ecuador, A/HRC/8/20; First Session Netherlands, A/HRC/8/31

Charter of the Status of National Institutions Accredited by the International Coordinating Committee of National Institutions for the Promotion and Protection of Human Rights, <http://www.nhri.net>

DOCUMENTS FROM OTHER INTERNATIONAL ORGANIZATIONS

Council of Europe, Parliamentary Assembly Recommendation 909 (1981) on the International Convention against Torture, adopted 26 January 1981

Berrier Report, Council of Europe Doc AS/Jur (33) 18 of 9 September 1981

Council of Europe, Parliamentary Assembly Recommendation 971 (1983) of 28 September 1983

1st General Report on the CPT's activities covering the period November 1989 to December 1990; CPT/Inf(91) 3 [EN]

Meier Report, Council of Europe Doc AS/Jur (32) 22 of 8th December 1990

Report of the Special Rapporteur on Prisons and Conditions of Detention to the 21st Session of the African Commission on Human and Peoples' Rights, Tenth Activity Report 1996–1997, Annex VII

Mali: Prisons in Mali: Report of the Special Rapporteur on Prisons and Conditions of Detention, Report on a Visit 20–30 August 1997, Professor E V O Dankwa, Series IV, No 2

Mali Prisons Revisited: Report of the Special Rapporteur on Prisons and Conditions of Detention in Africa, Report of a Visit 27 November to 8 December 1998, Series IV, No 4

African Commission on Human and Peoples' Rights, Resolution on the Guidelines and Measures for the Prohibition and Prevention of Torture, Cruel, Inhuman or Degrading Treatment or Punishment in Africa (Robben Island Guidelines), 32nd session, Banjul, The Gambia, October 2002, <http://www.achpr.org>

European Committee for the Prevention of Torture, 13th General Report on the CPT's Activities, covering the period 1 January 2002 to 31 July 2003, CPT/CPT.Inf (2003) 35

Report to the Swedish Government on the visit to Sweden carried out by the European Committee for the Prevention of Torture and Inhuman or Degrading Treatment or Punishment (CPT) from 27 January to 5 February 2003, CPT/Inf (2004) 32

Implementation of the EU Guidelines on Torture and other Cruel, Inhuman and Degrading Treatment or Punishment—Stock Taking and New Implementation Measures, 8407/1/08, Rev.1, PESC 417

European Committee for the Prevention of Torture, *20 Years of Combating Torture'*, pp 7–12, 19th General Report of the CPT (CPT/Inf (2009) 27)

Letter from ICJ to the Clerk of the Parliamentary Assembly in Council of Europe Doc AS/Jur (24) 2

UNHCR, Revised Guidelines on Applicable Criteria and Standards Relating to the Detention of Asylum Seekers, February 1999, IOM/22/99/Rev.1-FOM/22/99/Rev.1

Inter-American Commission on Human Rights, Principles and Best Practice on the Protection of Persons Deprived of Liberty in the Americas, OAS Doc OEA/Ser/L/II.131 doc.26

ACADEMIC REFERENCES

Bizjak, I, (1999) 'European Ombudsman and the Rights of People Deprived of their Liberty' in *The International Ombudsman Yearbook* Vol 3 (1999), pp 89–107

Burgers, J and Danelius, H, *The United Nations Convention against Torture: A Handbook on the Convention against Torture and Other Cruel, Inhuman or Degrading Treatment or Punishment* (The Hague: Martinus Nijhoff, 1988)

Campbell, A I L, 'Positive Obligations under the ECHR: Deprivation of Liberty by Private Actors' (2006) *Edinburgh Law Review* 399

Carver R, 'A New Answer to an Old Question: National Human Rights Institutions and the Domestication of International Law' (2010) 10(1) *HRLR* 1–32

Casale, S, 'A System of Preventive Oversight' (2009) 6(1) *Essex Human Rights Review* 9

Cassese, A, 'A New Approach to Human Rights: the European Convention for the Prevention of Torture' (1989) 83 *AJIL* 130

Clapham, A, *Human Rights in the Private Sphere* (Oxford: Oxford University Press, 1993)

Day, P and Klein, R, *Accountabilities. Five Public Services* (London: Tavistock Publications, 1987)

De Beco, G, 'Le Protocole Facultatif a la Convention Contre la Torture et Autres Peines ou Traitements Cruels, Inhumains ou Dégradants du 18 Décembre 2002: L'instauration de mécanismes de visites des lieux de détention au niveau national et international' (2007) 2 *Revue Belge de Droit International*

De Beco, G, 'Networks of National Human Rights Institutions' (2008) 14(6) *European Law Journal* 860–877

Decau, E, 'La Convention européene pour la prévention de la torture et peines ou traitments inhumains ou dégradants' (1988) 34 *Annuaire français de droit international* 618

Dennis, 'Human Rights in 2002; The Annual Session of the UN Commission on Human Rights and the Economic and Social Council' (2003) 97 *AJIL* 364

Dodson, M, 'The Human Rights Ombudsman in Central America: Honduras and El Salvador Case Studies' (2006) 3(1) *Essex Human Rights Review* 29–45. Also available at <http://projects.essex.ac.uk/ehrr/archive/pdf/Dodsonfinal.pdf>

Edwards, A, 'The Optional Protocol to the UN Convention Against Torture and Refugees' (2008) 57(4) *ICLQ* 789–825, at 798.

Evans, M D, 'The Place of the Optional Protocol in the Scheme of International Approaches to Torture and Torture Prevention and Resulting Issues' in H C Scheu and S Hybnerova (eds), *International and National Mechanisms against Torture* (University Karlova (Prague) Law School Publication, 2004)

Evans, M D, 'The OPCAT at 50', in G Gilbert, F Hampson, and C Sandoval (eds), *The Delivery of Human Rights: Essays in Honour of Professor Sir Nigel Rodley* (Routledge, 2011), pp 85–113

Evans, M and Haenni-Dale, C, 'Preventing Torture? The Development of the Optional Protocol to the UN Convention against Torture' (2004) 4 *HRLR* 19

Evans, M and Morgan, R, *Preventing Torture: A Study of the European Convention for the Prevention of Torture and Inhuman or Degrading Treatment or Punishment* (Oxford: Oxford University Press, 1998)

Foley, C, *Combating Torture. A Manual for Judges and Prosecutors* (Human Rights Centre, University of Essex Publication, 2003). Also available at <http://www.essex.ac.uk/combatingtorturehandbook/english/combating_torture.pdf>

Giffard, C, *The Torture Reporting Handbook* (Human Rights Centre, University of Essex Publication, 2000). Also available at <http://www.essex.ac.uk/torturehandbook/handbook(english).pdf>

Gomez, M, *National Human Rights Commissions and Internally Displaced Persons. Illustrated by the Sri Lankan Experience*. An Occasional Paper of the Brookings-SAIS Project on Internal Displacement (July 2002). Also available at <http://www.brookings.edu/fp/projects/idp/articles/gomez2002.pdf>

Greer, S, 'Should Police Threats to Torture Suspects Always be Severely Punished? Reflections on the *Gafgen* Case' (2011) 11 *HRLR* 67

Haenni, C, *20 Ans Consacrés à la realisation d'une idée* (Geneva: Association for the Prevention of Torture, 1997)

Hallo de Wolf, A, 'Visits to Less Traditional Places of Detention' (2009) 6(1) *Essex Human Rights Review* 103–137

Ingelese, C, *The UN Committee against Torture: An Assessment* (The Hague: Kluwer Law International, 2001)

Kessing, P V, 'New Optional Protocol to the UN Torture Convention' (2003) 72 *Nordic Journal of International Law* 571–592

Kissane, J, Optional Protocol to the United Nations Convention Against Torture. Presented during the Seminar of the Implementation in Latvia and other Baltic States, Riga, Latvia, 27–28 May, 2006

Livingstone, S and Murray, R, 'The Effectiveness of National Human Rights Institutions', in S Halliday and P Schmidt (eds), *Human Rights Brought Home: Socio-legal Perspectives on Human Rights in the National Context* (Oxford; Portland OR: Hart, 2004), pp 139–164

McDermott, N, 'How to Enforce the Torture Convention' in ICJ/SCAT, *How to Make the International Convention Effective* (Geneva: ICJ/SCAT, 1979)

MacDonald, R St John, 'The European Convention for the Prevention of Torture and Inhuman or Degrading Treatment or Punishment' in E Bello and B Abjibola (eds), *Essays in Honour of Judge Taslim Olawale Elias* (Dordrecht: Martinus Nijhoff, 1992)

Mischler (ed), *Jean-Jacques Gautier et la Prévention de la Torture: de l'Idée à l'Action: Recueil des Textes* (Geneva: Association for the Prevention of Torture/Institut Europe, Université de Genève, 2003)

Moore, L, Protecting the rights of people in detention: the role of the Northern Ireland Human Rights Commission. Presented during the Seminar of the Implementation in Latvia and other Baltic States, Riga, Latvia, 27–28 May, 2006

Murdoch, J, *The Treatment of Prisoners: European Standards* (Strasbourg: Council of Europe Publishing, 2006)

Murray, R, 'The Relationship between Parliaments and National Human Rights Institutions', in J Morison, K McEvoy, and G Anthony, *Judges, Transition and Human Rights*, (Oxford: Oxford University Press, 2007), pp 357–376

Murray, R, 'Special Rapporteurs', in M D Evans and R Murray, *The African Charter on Human and Peoples' Rights*, 2nd edn (Cambridge: Cambridge University Press, 2008)

Murray, R, 'National Preventive Mechanisms under the Optional Protocol to the Torture Convention: One Size Does Not Fit All' (2008) 26(4) *Netherlands Quarterly of Human Rights* 485–516

Nagan, W P and Atkins, L, 'The International Law on Torture: From Universal Proscription to Effective Application and Enforcement' (2001) 14 *Harv Hum Rts J* (Spring). Also available at <http://www.law.harvard.edu/students/orgs/hrj/iss14/nagan.shtml>

Niyizurugero, J-B and Lessène, G P, 'The Robben Island Guidelines: An essential tool for torture prevention in Africa' (2010) 6(2) *Essex Human Rights Review* 91

Nollkaemper, A, 'Concurrence between Individual Responsibility and State Responsibility in International Law' (2003) 52 *ICLQ* (July) 615–640. Also available at <http://iclq.oxfordjournals.org/cgi/reprint/52/3/615>

Nowak, M and McArthur E, *The United Nations Convention Against Torture* (Oxford: Oxford University Press, 2008)

'Note. Beyond Independent Directors: A Functional Approach to Board Independence' (2006) 119(5) *Harv L Rev* 1553–1575

O'Brien, N, 'Human Rights and Accountability in the UK: Deliberative Democracy and the Role of the Ombudsman' (2010) 5 *EHRLR* 504–512

O'Flaherty, M, 'Reform of the UN Human Rights Treaty Body System: Locating the Dublin Statement' (2010) 10(2) *HRLR* 319–335

Okafor, O C and Agbakwa, S C, 'On Legalism, Popular Agency and "Voices of Suffering": The Nigerian National Human Rights Commission in Context' (2002) 24(3) *Hum Rts Q* 662–720

Peel, M, Lubell, N, and Beynon, J, *Medical Investigation and Documentation of Torture. A Handbook for Health Professionals* (Human Rights Centre, University of Essex Publication, 2005).

Pirjola, J, 'The Parliamentary Ombudsman of Finland as a National Preventive Mechanism under the Optional Protocol to the United Nations Convention against Torture and Other Cruel, Inhuman or Degrading Treatment or Punishment' (2008) *Nordic Journal of International Law* 77

Pollard, A and Court, J, *How Civil Society Organisations Use Evidence to Influence Policy Processes: A literature review.* Overseas Development Institute; Working Paper 249 (2005). Also available at <http://www.globalpolicy.org/ngos/intro/general/2005/07evidence.pdf>

Pringle, M, 'The Importance of the Ratification of the Optional Protocol to the United Nations Convention Against Torture for the Worldwide Prevention of Torture' in H C Scheu and S Hybnerova (eds), *International and National Mechanisms against Torture* (University Karlova (Prague) Law School Publication, Prague, 2004)

Quinn, G, 'Resisting the "Temptation of Elegance": Can the Convention on the Rights of Persons with Disabilities Socialise States to Right Behaviour?', in O M Arnardottir and G Quinn (eds), *The UN Convention on the Rights of Persons with Disabilities: European and Scandinavian Perspectives* (Leiden: Martinus Nijhoff, 2009), pp 39–40

Reif, L C, 'Building Democratic Institutions: The Role of National Human Rights Institutions in Good Governance and Human Rights Protection' (2000) 13 *Harvard Human Rights Journal.* Also available at <http://www.law.harvard.edu/students/orgs/hrj/iss13/reif.shtml>

Reydams, L, 'The Rise and Fall of Universal Jurisdiction' in W Schabas and N Bernaz (eds), *Handbook of International Criminal Law* (London: Routledge, 2010)

Rodley, N S, 'The Evolution of United Nations' Charter-Based Machinery for the Protection of Human Rights' (1997) 1 *EHRLR* 1–40

Rodley, N, 'The Definition(s) of Torture under International Law' (2005) *CLP* 467

Rodley, N, with Pollard, M, *The Treatment of Prisoners under International Law*, 3rd edn (Oxford: Oxford University Press, 2009)

Steinerte, E and Murray, R, 'Same but Different: National Human Rights Commissions and Ombudsman Institutions as National Preventive Mechanisms under the Optional Protocol to the UN Convention against Torture' (2009) 6(1) *Essex Human Rights Review* 54–72

Svanidze, E, The Role of Prosecutors in Monitoring Places of Detention. Presented during the Seminar of the Implementation in Latvia and other Baltic States, Riga, Latvia, 27–28 May 2006

de Vargas, F, 'History of a Campaign' in International Commission of Jurists and the Swiss Committee against Torture, *Torture: How to Make the International Convention Effective* (Geneva: ICJ/SCAT, 1979)

Vigny, D, 'La Convention européene de 1987 pour la prévention de la torture et peines ou traitments inhumains ou dégradants' (1987) 43 *Annuaire Suisse de droit international* 62

van Zyl Smit, D and Snacken, S, *Principles of European Prison Law and Policy* (Oxford: Oxford University Press, 2009)

REPORTS AND DOCUMENTS FROM NPMS

Children's Commissioner of New Zealand, Annual Report 2008, presented to the House of Representatives pursuant to section 28 of the Children's Commissioner Act 2003 and Section 150(3) of the Crown Entities Act 2004, 2008

Human Rights Commission, Monitoring Places of Detention. Annual Report of Activities under the Optional Protocol to the UN Convention Against Torture (OPCAT), 1 July 2008 to 30 June 2009, December 2009, <http://www.hrc.co.nz>

HMIP, Report on an unannounced full follow-up inspection of Campsfield House Immigration Removal Centre, 12–16 May 2008 by HM Chief Inspector of Prisons, HMIP, 2008

HMIP, *Detainees under escort at Manchester Detention Centre, Manchester Airport.* Report on one unannounced and one announced escort inspection, 3–4 September 2007, 2008, by HM Chief Inspector of Prisons, 2008

HMIP, Report on a Full Announced Inspection of the Military Corrective Training Centre, 14–18 June 2004, by HM Chief Inspector of Prisons, 2004

The Independent Monitoring Board HMP Bristol, Annual Report 1 August 2009–31 July 2010, <http://www.imb.gov.uk/reports/Bristol_2009–2010.pdf>

Mental Health Act Commission, *Women Detained in Hospital.* A Report by the Mental Health Act Commission, March 2009

Report of the Human Rights Ombudsman of the Republic of Slovenia on the Implementation of the tasks of the National Preventive Mechanism under the Optional Protocol to the UN Convention Against Torture and other Cruel, Inhuman or Degrading Treatment or Punishment for the year 2008, Ljublijana, June 2009, <http://www.varuh-rs.sl>

Chancellor of Justice of Estonia, 2009 Overview of the Chancellor of Justice. Activities for the prevention of torture and other cruel, inhuman or degrading treatment or punishment, statistics of proceedings, Tallinn, 2010, <http://www.oiguskantsler.ee>

2008 Annual Report of the People's Advocate Activity of the People's Advocate on the Role of the National Mechanism on Prevention of Torture

UK Care Quality Commission, Inspection Report 2009/2010, Linden House

OTHER DOCUMENTS AND PAPERS

APT, *Visits under Public International Law; Theory and Practice:* Proceedings of an APT Workshop, Geneva, September 1999 (Geneva: APT, 2001)

APT, *Added Value of the Optional Protocol for States Parties to the European Convention for the Prevention of Torture*, Position Paper on the Optional Protocol to the UN Convention Against Torture, 3 March 2003 (Geneva: APT 2003)

APT, Inter-American Institute for Human Rights, *Optional Protocol to the UN Convention Against Torture and Other Cruel, Inhuman or Degrading Treatment or Punishment: A Manual for Prevention* (Geneva: APT/IIHR, 2005)

APT, *The International Subcommittee on Prevention of Torture under the Optional Protocol to the Convention Against Torture* (Geneva: APT, May 2006)

APT, Guide, *Establishment and Designation of National Preventive Mechanisms*, (Geneva: APT, May 2006)

APT, Comprehensive NPM Assessment Checklist (Geneva, APT, 2007)

APT, *Torture in International Law. A Guide to Jurisprudence*, (Geneva: APT, CEJIL, 2008)

APT, *National Human Rights Commissions and Ombudsmans Offices: Ombudsmen as NPMs* (Geneva: APT 2008)

APT, *Civil Society and National Preventive Mechanisms under the Optional Protocol to the UN Convention Against Torture* (Geneva: APT, June 2008) <http://www.apt.ch>

APT, *Visiting Places of Detention. Lessons Learned and Practices of Selected Domestic Institutions, Report on an Expert Seminar* (Geneva: APT, July 2008)

APT, *The Optional Protocol to the United Nations Convention Against Torture: An Opportunity for Refugee and Migrant Rights Protection* (Geneva: APT, May 2009)

APT, *Optional Protocol to the UN Convention Against Torture. Implementation Manual*, Revised Edition, (Geneva: APT, 2010)

APT, *Preventing Torture. An Operational Guide for National Human Rights Institutions*, (Geneva: APT, Asia Pacific Forum, OHCHR, May 2010)

Ayete Nyampong, Lilian, *Challenges facing the OPCAT in the Implementation of the OPCAT in the African Region*, Visiting places of detention-Methods, presentation to the OPCAT in the African Region: Challenges of Implementation, Cape Town, South Africa, 3–4 April 2008, p 6, see <http://www.bristol.ac.uk/law/research/centres-themes/opcat/docs.html#OPCATAfricanConference2008>

Black Sash, A Tilley, 'Process Problems May Haunt the HRC', *Democracy in Action* (1995)

Bristol OPCAT team, 'Comments on the SPT's Preliminary Guidelines for NPMs', 16 May 2008, <http://www.bristol.ac.uk/law/research/centres-themes/opcat/opcatdocs/bristol-commentsonsptnpmguidelines.pdf>

Bristol OPCAT team, 'The Relationship between Accreditation by the International Coordinating Committee of National Human Rights Institutions and the Optional Protocol to the UN Convention Against Torture', November 2008, see <http://www.bristol.ac.uk/law/research/centres-themes/hric/index.html>

Bristol OPCAT team, 'The Optional Protocol to the UN Torture Convention and the UN Convention on the Rights of People with Disabilities: some common issues' 15 December 2009, <http://www.bristol.ac.uk/law/research/centres-themes/opcat/opcatdocs/opcatcrpd.pdf>

Bristol OPCAT team, 'The Inter-American Commission on Human Rights' Principles and Best Practices on the Protection of Persons Deprived of Liberty in the Americas and the Optional Protocol to the Convention Against Torture', August 2009, <http://www.bristol.ac.uk/law/research/centres-themes/opcat/opcatdocs/iacmhrprinciples.pdf>

Commonwealth Secretariat, National Human Rights Institutions Best Practice, Commonwealth Secretariat, 2001

'The Dublin Statement on the Process of Strengthening of the UN Human Rights Treaty Body System', see <http://www.nottingham.ac.uk/hrlc/documents/specialevents/dublinstatement.pdf>, see also 2010 *Netherlands Quarterly of Human Rights*, 116

Dublin Statement on the Process of Strengthening the United Nations Human Rights Treaty Body System: Response by non-governmental organisations, November 2010

Inter-American Institute of Human Rights, Association for the Prevention of Torture, *Optional Protocol to the UN Convention Against Torture and Other Cruel, Inhuman and Degrading Treatment or Punishment. A Manual for Prevention*, 2005

Irish Human Rights Commission, *'Extraordinary Rendition'. A View of Ireland's Human Rights Obligations*, Irish Human Rights Commission, Dublin, 2007, <http://www.ihrc.ie/download/pdf/ihrc_rendition_report_final.pdf>

Joint Committee on Human Rights, *The UN Convention Against Torture (UNCAT), Nineteenth Report of the Session 2005–2006*, HL Paper 185-I; HC 701-I

Joint Committee on Human Rights, Fourteenth Report. Work of the Northern Ireland Human Rights Commission, 15 July 2003, HL 142, HC 132

Law School, University of Bristol, *The Optional Protocol to the UNCAT*. Conference Report, Report on the First Annual Conference on the Implementation of the Optional Protocol to the UN Convention Against Torture (OPCAT), University of Bristol, 19–20 April 2007

Human Rights Implementation Centre, Letter of 14 September 2010, <http://www.bristol.ac.uk/law/research/centres-themes/hric/docs.html#expertadv> See Database of UK NPM, <http://www.bristol.ac.uk/law/research/centres-themes/hric/hricnpmukdatabase/hmic.pdf>

Livingstone, S and Murray, R, *Evaluating the Effectiveness of National Human Rights Institutions. The Northern Ireland Human Rights Commission with comparisons from South Africa*, on file with author, February 2005

Long, D, *Commentary on the Optional Protocol to the UN Convention against Torture* in *Optional Protocol to the United Nations Convention against Torture and Other Cruel, Inhuman or Degrading Treatment or Punishment. A Manual for Prevention* (2005) Publication of the IIHR and APT

Mental Disability Advocacy Centre (MDAC), *Inspect! Inspectorates of Mental Health and Social Care Institutions in the European Union 2006*, <http://www.mdac.info/documents/122_Inspect.pdf>

Ministerial Council Decision No 12/2005 on Upholding Human Rights and the Rule of Law in Criminal Justice Systems of 6 December 2005

Northern Ireland Human Rights Commission, *Our Hidden Borders. The UK Border Agency's Powers of Detention*, NIHRC, April 2009

Office of the High Commissioner for Human Rights, Survey on National Human Rights Institutions. Report on the Findings and Recommendations of a Questionnaire addressed to NHRIs worldwide, Geneva, July 2009, <http://www.nhri.net>

OPCAT in the African Region: Challenges of Implementation, Summary and recommendations from Conference held 3–4 April 2008, Cape Town South Africa, <http://www.bris.ac.uk/law/research/centres-themes/opcat/opcatdocs/africaconference2008report.pdf>

Pollard, M, *Implementation of the Optional Protocol to the Convention against Torture and other Cruel, Inhuman or Degrading Treatment or Punishment (OPCAT) in Federal and other Decentralized States*, Discussion Paper for the Seminar 'The Optional Protocol to the UN Convention against Torture: Implementation in Federal States and Decentralized States' Sao Paulo, Brazil (22–24 June 2005), <http://www.apt.ch/component/option,com_docman/task,cat_view/gid,46/Itemid,99999999/lang,en/>

The Poznan Statement on the Reforms of the UN Human Rights Treaty Body System, Poznan, 28–29 September 2010

Question of the Human Rights of All Persons Subjected to Any Form of Detention or Imprisonment, in Particular Question of a Draft Optional Protocol to the Convention against Torture and Other Cruel, Inhuman or Degrading Treatment or Punishment, written statement submitted by a coalition of NGOs, 4 February 1992, E/CN.4/1992/NGO/27

Suntinger, W, 'National Visiting Mechanisms – Categories and Assessment', Background Paper, APT, Visiting Places of Detention. Lessons Learned and Practices of Selected Domestic Institutions, Report on an Expert Seminar, Geneva, July 2003, Annex II

'Alternative preliminary draft optional protocol to the Convention against Torture and Other Cruel, Inhuman or Degrading Treatment or Punishment submitted by the delegation of Mexico with the support of the Latin American Group (GRULAC)'.

This can be found in the 9th Report of the Working Group, E/CN.4/2001/67, at Annex I and in the 10th Report of the Working Group, E/CN.4/2002/78, at Annex II C

'Proposal of new and revised articles to be included in the original draft optional protocol to the Convention against Torture and Other Cruel, Inhuman or Degrading Treatment or Punishment submitted by the delegation of Sweden on behalf of the European Union', E/CN.4/2001/WG.11/CRP.2

Summary of the Thematic Meeting on the Implementation of the Optional Protocol to the Convention Against Torture and other Cruel, Inhuman or Degrading Treatment or Punishment before the Inter-American Commission on Human Rights requested by the APT, 7 March 2007, available at <http://www.apt.ch/region/americas/MemoCELS.pdf>

Index

References are to page numbers and their footnotes, indicated by *n*, e.g 147*n*

ad hoc visits
  European Convention for the Prevention of Torture 19, 20, 21
  OPCAT drafting process 34, 50, 51
Afghanistan 79, 80
Africa: Robben Island Guidelines 12*n*, 149–51
African Charter on Human Rights 149
Albania 116, 147*n*
American Declaration of the Rights and Duties of Man 151
Amnesty International 23*n*, 25*n*, 43*n*
Antilles 78
Arab Charter on Human Rights 166
Aruba 78
Association for the Prevention of Torture (APT) 7*n*, 43*n*, 176, 177
Association of South East Asian Nations (ASEAN) 166
asylum and immigration centres 74, 83, 84, 138
Australia 79, 167
aut dedere aut judicare 2, 4–5

Benin 106, 116, 121, 142, 166
Berrier Report 11, 15
best practice 121, 173
Bolivia 100, 106
budgetary provision 91, 101, 112–13, 123–4, 178–9

Cambodia 107
Canadian Charter 80
care homes 70, 72, 76–7, 84
Channel Islands 78
children *see* young people
Chile 171
civil society organizations *see* NGOs
Commission on Human Rights 7, 22, 23
Committee Against Torture (CAT) 5, 27, 53, 160
  General Comment No 2 60, 61, 117
Committee for the Prevention of Torture (CPT) 10, 18–21, 31*n*, 44*n*, 160
  consistent application of legal norms 156, 179
  CPT Standards 64–6
  effect on ratification of OPCAT 164–5, 167
  engagement with the SPT 139–42, 146–8
  jurisdiction 78
confidentiality 41, 155, 160
consistency 87–9, 156–9, 179–80
Convention Against Torture *see* UN Convention Against Torture (UNCAT)
Convention on the Rights of Persons with Disabilities (CRPD) 180–2
coordination 85–7, 159–61
corporal punishment 72
Costa Rica 171
Costa Rica Draft (1980) 8–9, 10, 13, 22, 29
Costa Rica Draft (1991) 22–3, 26, 27, 28*n*, 29, 30*n*, 31, 40, 44, 63*n*
Council of Europe 148, 164
criminalization of torture 2, 3
cruel, inhuman, or degrading treatment or punishment 58–9, 62, 72
cultural contexts 88
Cyprus 79

Denmark 119*n*, 147*n*, 167, 168
deprivation of liberty 46, 69–70
detention centres 70*n*, 71, 74–5, 83, 84–5, 119, 138
domestic law 4, 70

enforced disappearances 73
Estonia 104
EU proposals 25, 26, 43–5
European Convention for the Prevention of Torture (ECPT) 10, 146–7, 148
  data collection 13–14
  drafting process 10–17
  emphasis on prevention 15–16
  preventive visiting mechanism 18–21
  experts 13–14, 16–17
  Explanatory Report 16, 17, 19, 20
  nature and scope 14–17
  need for a regional convention 12–13
  scope and jurisdiction 78
  signatories who are also party to OPCAT 164
European Convention on Human Rights (ECHR) 15
European Court of Human Rights 71, 77, 160
European NPM Project 148–9, 173
European Prison Rules 88
expertise 83–5, 92–3, 134–6, 176–7
extra-territoriality 79–81
extradition 2, 4
extraordinary rendition 75

financial resources 91, 101, 112–13, 123–4, 178
follow-up visits
  European Convention for the Prevention of Torture 19, 21
  OPCAT drafting process 50, 51
  SPT 101, 106–8
foster homes 76–7
funding 91, 101, 112–13, 123–4, 178

Gautier, Jean-Jacques 7, 8, 10, 11
Ghana 76
Group of Latin American and Caribbean States (GRULAC) 25, 40

Honduras 99, 107, 121, 165
hospitals 70, 72, 74, 75–6, 84
  see also mental health institutions
Human Rights Committee 69, 70*n*, 143
Human Rights Council 144
human rights instruments 1, 4, 63–4, 80
Human Rights Watch 25*n*, 43*n*

ICJ *see* International Court of Justice
ICRC *see* International Committee of the Red Cross
ill-treatment 59, 62
immigration detention centres 74–5, 83, 84, 138
inquiry procedure 5–6
Inter-American Commission on Human Rights 100, 152, 158
Inter-American Convention on Human Rights 151–2
Inter-American Principles 157, 158
inter-state procedure 5*n*
International Association of Penal Law (IAPL) 2*n*, 7
international bodies 5, 10
  regional and other bodies 146–55, 160–1
  UN bodies 143–6
International Committee of the Red Cross (ICRC) 7, 153
International Court of Justice (ICJ) 11, 13, 14, 22, 80
international law 1, 170
  international human rights law 80
  international humanitarian law 80
international mechanisms 40–3, 46
international standards 63–4
Iraq 79
Israel 80

juveniles *see* young people
jurisdiction 3, 70, 77–81

Kazakhstan 118*n*, 142*n*, 174*n*

Lebanon 106
legal norms 63–7
  consistency 87–9, 156–7, 179–80
Liberia 106

Maldives 98, 101, 106, 167
Mali 171
Mauritius 98, 101, 106, 107, 171
medical expertise 84, 135
Meier Report 10–11, 14
mental health institutions 74, 75–6, 83, 84, 102–3, 119, 134, 135, 138
Mexican Draft 25, 26, 40–3, 46, 53, 57
Mexico
  appointment of NPM 171
  visited by SPT 99, 102, 103, 106, 152
    publication of report 165
military detention facilities 75, 79, 82, 84–5, 88, 135
Moldova 135, 148
monitoring bodies 5, 10
Montenegro 174*n*

National Human Rights Institutions (NHRIs) 43, 55, 82, 115, 116, 119, 121, 134, 173
  accreditation by the International Coordinating Committee (ICC) 129–30, 145
  Africa 151, 166
  monitoring and implementation of Convention on the Rights of Persons with
    Disabilities 180–2
National Institutions Unit (NI Unit) 145
national mechanisms: Mexican Draft 40–3, 46
National Preventive Mechanisms (NPMs) 25, 31*n*, 45, 47, 48, 53–7, 115–17
  accountability 128–32
  Annual Reports 55
  avoiding duplication 159, 177
  broader mandates 138, 146
  clarity of role 136
  consistent application of legal norms 87–9, 156, 179–80
  contact with the SPT 56, 86, 108–11, 114, 128–32, 177
  consistency of approach 157–9
  SPT as adviser to the NPMs 111–12
  coordination 85–7
  different approaches and requirements 82–3
  effectiveness 136–7
  engagement with other UN bodies 143–4, 146
  engagement with regional and other bodies 147–9, 151, 154, 161
  ensuring State compliance with UNCAT 132–3
  European NPM Project 148–9, 173
  expectations of 136, 138, 177
  expertise of members 134–6
  expertise of visiting teams 83–5
  extension of the European CPT 133–4

forerunner to SPT visits 133
guidelines on NPMs 214–17
independence 119–20
appointment of members of the framework 120–3
factors within the control of the NPM itself 124–8
factors within the control of the State 120–4
financial autonomy 123–4
in engaging with others 125–7
in fulfilling its remit 124–5
integrity of institution's members 127–8
jurisdiction 70
minimum powers 68
National Human Rights Institutions (NHRIs) 82
preliminary guidelines for the ongoing development of NPMs 212–13
relevant norms 63–4
representativity in the membership of the NPM 127–8
significance 183
SPT members barred from visits to home States 94–5
trends in choices of institutions 170–2, 178
visiting powers and mandate 117–19
nationality 3
Nauru 79
Netherlands 78, 160
New Zealand 85, 87
NGOs (Non-Governmental Organizations) 23, 25, 40*n*, 43*n*, 121, 122, 126, 176–7
involvement in ratification of OPCAT 163
monitoring and implementation of Convention on the Rights of Persons with
Disabilities 180–2
see also National Human Rights Institutions (NHRIs)
Nigeria 171
non-state actors 70, 71
Northern Ireland Human Rights Commission 123*n*
NPMs *see* National Preventive Mechanisms

Office of the High Commissioner for Human Rights (OHCHR) 145, 154
older persons 76–7
ombudsmen 115, 116, 119, 134, 136*n*, 138, 170
OPCAT Contact Group 62*n*, 129, 176, 177, 181
Optional Protocol to the UN Convention Against Torture (OPCAT)
concept of prevention 57–8
approach of the SPT 69, 218–21
cruel, inhuman, or degrading treatment or punishment 58–9
omissions 59
prevention versus protection 62*n*
scope of the preventive obligation 60–3
connections with the Convention Against Torture 1*n*
differing language versions 46*n*, 47*n*, 77
drafting process
aftermath of a visit or mission 36–7, 52–3
Committee for the Prevention of Torture (CPT) 10, 18–21
compromise text 45–8
Costa Rica Draft (1980) 8–9, 10, 13, 22, 29
Costa Rica Draft (1991) 22–3, 26, 27, 28*n*, 29, 30*n*, 31, 40, 44, 63*n*
deadlock 38
establishment of the SPT *see* Subcommittee on Prevention of Torture (SPT)
EU proposals 25, 26, 43–5
first reading 24, 30*n*, 32
Mexican Draft 25, 26, 40–3, 46, 53, 57
ninth session of the Working Group (2001) 39–45
principal points in dispute prior to the 2001 session 31–7
principal points of agreement prior to the 2001 session 27–31
proposed visiting programme 32–4, 49–51
reservations 37, 48*n*
restrictions on access to persons in, or to places of, detention 35–6, 51–2
second reading 24, 32, 33
two-pillar system 26
USA Draft 26, 45
free-standing instrument 1*n*
interaction between the CAT and SPT 139–42
interaction with other mechanisms 180–3
NPMs *see* National Preventive Mechanisms (NPMs)
opt out provision 46–7
origins 6–10
ratification 145, 148, 162
added value of being a party 169–70
number of States Parties 163–6, 175
postponement of obligations 174
reasons for and against 162–7, 173
relationship with the European Convention for the Prevention of Torture (ECPT) 10
relationship with the ICRC 153
scope 68–9
'any place/all places of detention' 73–7
'... are or may be deprived' 73
Article 14(2) objection to a visit by the SPT 81–2
definition of deprivation of liberty 46, 69–70

Optional Protocol to the UN Convention Against Torture (OPCAT) (*cont.*)
different approaches and requirements 82–3
expertise of visiting teams 83–5
extra-territoriality 79–81
'installation and facilities' 73
nationally 78–9
public and private 70–3
'. . . under its jurisdiction or control' 77–81
SPT *see* Subcommittee on Prevention of Torture (SPT)
standard-setting 63–7
text in full 184–94
see also UN Convention Against Torture (UNCAT)
Organization for Security and Cooperation in Europe (OSCE) 154
orphanages 72

Paraguay
NPM process model of good practice 99, 121, 171–2, 173
visited by SPT 100, 101, 106, 107, 152
publication of report 165
paramilitary groups 70, 71
Paris Principles (1991) 41, 115, 121, 123*n*, 126, 129–30, 151
passive personality 3
periodic visits: European Convention for the Prevention of Torture 19, 20, 21
police cells 73, 74, 82, 110, 118, 119
pre-trial facilities 73
prevention
concept 57–8
approach of the SPT 69, 218–21
cruel, inhuman, or degrading treatment or punishment 58–9
omissions 59
prevention versus protection 62*n*
scope of the obligation 60–3
standard-setting 63–7
preventive visiting mechanism 6, 7, 8, 9
European Convention for the Prevention of Torture 15–16, 18–21
points in dispute in the OPCAT drafting process 48
aftermath of a visit or mission 36–7, 52–3
restrictions on access to persons in, or to places of, detention 35–6, 51–2
visiting programme 32–4, 49–51
see also Subcommittee on Prevention of Torture (SPT)
prisons 70*n*, 72, 73–4, 83, 110, 119, 134
European Prison Rules 88
Standard Minimum Rules for the Treatment of Prisoners 63, 64*n*
private institutions 70, 71, 72
psychiatric hospitals 74, 75–6, 83, 84, 102–3, 119, 134, 135, 138
public authorities 70–1
punishment 58–9, 62, 72

redress 59
refugee, asylum, and immigration centres 74, 83, 84, 138
regional bodies 146–55, 160–1
regular visits
OPCAT drafting process 34, 49–50
SPT 101
reservations 37, 48*n*
Robben Island Guidelines 12*n*, 149–51
Romania 174*n*

schools 72, 76
secure accommodation 70, 76, 134
Senegal 171
Slovenia 116*n*, 135
social care institutions 70, 72, 76–7, 84
South Africa 171
Spain 121
Special Rapporteur on Torture 22, 53*n*, 72*n*, 75*n*, 100, 143, 144*n*, 160
SPT *see* Subcommittee on Prevention of Torture
Standard Minimum Rules for the Treatment of Prisoners 63, 64*n*
standard-setting 63–7
consistency 87–9, 156–7, 179–80
State authorities 71
State reporting 5, 9*n*
State sovereignty 31, 32, 41, 43, 115
Subcommittee on Prevention of Torture (SPT)
Annual Reports 96–7, 112–13
avoiding duplication 159, 178
broad approach to prevention 69, 218–21
budgetary provision 91, 101, 112–13, 178
collaboration and cooperation 159, 160
confidentiality 155, 160
consistent application of legal norms 88–9, 156, 172–3, 179–80
contact with the NPMs 56, 86, 108–11, 114, 128–32, 177
consistency of approach 157–9
SPT as adviser to the NPMs 111–12
credibility 160, 176–7
engagement with other UN bodies 112, 143, 145, 159
engagement with regional and other bodies 112, 146–7, 149, 151, 152–3, 154, 155, 160–1
expectations of 177
impact of the CPT Standards 65–6
interaction with the CAT 139–42
interpretation of its own mandate and rules of procedure 95–7, 113–14
main duties 90
membership 91, 92–5

as at January 2011 222
expansion 174, 175
expertise 83–4, 92–3, 176–7
gender balance 94
geographical balance 93, 94, 95
NPM members barred from visits to home States 94–5
objection to a visit 81–2
OPCAT drafting process 27–31, 35–6, 42, 44, 47–8
relevant norms 63–4
rules of procedure 195–204
scope of OPCAT 68, 70
scope of the preventive obligation 62
visiting mandate 48, 97
aftermath of a visit 36–7, 52–3
choosing places of deprivation of liberty to be visited 102–3
chronology of States visited 223
content of the visit 102–3
frequency 101–2
guidelines in relation to visits 205–11
ongoing dialogue and follow-up 105–8
outcomes of a visit 105–8
preventive approach and visits 103–5
restrictions on access to persons in, or to places of, detention 35–6, 51–2
selection of countries 97–100
types of visits 100–1
visiting programme 32–4, 49–51
working languages 95, 179
Sweden
appointment of NPM 110–11, 142, 170, 172
funding of NPM 123*n*
visited by SPT 98, 103, 106, 107, 148*n*
publication of report 164–5
Swiss Committee Against Torture (SCAT) 7, 11, 13, 14, 22

territoriality 3
torture
criminalization 2, 3
definition in UNCAT 3
inadmissibility of statements made as a result of 59
prohibition under international law 1

Ukraine 164*n*, 165
UN Charter 63
UN Commission on Human Rights 7, 22, 23
UN Committee against Torture (CAT) 5, 27, 53, 160
General Comment No 2 60, 61, 117
UN Committee on the Rights of the Child 146
UN Convention against Torture (UNCAT)
connections with OPCAT 1*n*
definition of torture 3
drafting process 2, 7
ensuring State compliance 132–3
inquiry procedure 5–6
interaction between the CAT and SPT 139–42
jurisdiction 3, 77
obligations created and domestic law 4
specific obligations 58–61
State reporting 5, 9*n*
Swedish Draft 2*n*, 7, 11
UN Declaration against Torture 2
UN Human Rights Committee 69, 70*n*, 143
UN Human Rights Council 144
UN Special Rapporteur on Torture 22, 53*n*, 72*n*, 75*n*, 100, 143, 144*n*, 160
unannounced visits *see ad hoc* visits
UNHCR (United Nations High Commissioner for Refugees) 70, 75, 154–5, 160
United Kingdom
Crown dependencies 78–9
funding of the NPM 123*n*
institutions forming the NPM 83, 85, 116, 118, 134
military establishments 83, 153
Universal Periodic Review (UPR) 145
Uruguay 171
USA Draft 26, 45

Vienna Convention on the Law of Treaties 78
visits to place of detention *see* preventive visiting mechanism

witch camps 76
Working Group on Arbitrary Detention 143
working languages 95, 179

young people 70, 72, 76–7, 84, 119, 134, 138
UN Committee on the Rights of the Child 146